The Bank of Japan, the OECD, and Beyond

Kumiharu Shigehara

The Bank of Japan, the OECD, and Beyond

Reflections from a lifetime's work

palgrave macmillan

Kumiharu Shigehara
International Economic Policy
Studies Association (IEPSA)
Neuilly-sur-Seine, France

ISBN 978-981-97-5306-2 ISBN 978-981-97-5307-9 (eBook)
https://doi.org/10.1007/978-981-97-5307-9

This Palgrave Macmillan imprint is published by the registered company Springer Nature Singapore Pte Ltd.
The registered company address is: 152 Beach Road, #21-01/04 Gateway East, Singapore 189721, Singapore

This book is dedicated to Seizaburo, Rutsu, and Akiko Shigehara.

Acknowledgements

This book would not have been written were it not for the active encouragement and support that I received from many of my friends abroad. In addition to those whose names are noted specifically in Chapter 1 "Introduction", I would like to express my special thanks for the contributions from the following friends of mine.

I must first note that Chapter 2 "Prologue" which briefly describes my family situation in the early years of my life and my education would not have been added to this book without strong encouragements from Charles Goodhart and Thomas Andersson.

My special thanks are due to Paul Atkinson who devoted a lot of his time and energy to reading the entire manuscript, checking factual descriptions, and offering valuable suggestions. Charles Goodhart, Robert Price, and Niels Thygesen read a substantial portion of the manuscript relating to monetary policy and some other issues, and provided useful comments for improving the texts. James Boughton, Graham Hacche, and Paula Simonin read and improved the draft of Chapter 7 "My Work at the OECD Monetary Division in the early 1970s". Stephen Potter, Andrew Dean, and Nicholas Vanston made helpful comments on some chapters dealing with OECD surveillance activities from the 1970s onwards. Edwin Truman read the chapters and sections on Japan's international balance of payments adjustment and exchange rate policy issues, as well as United States monetary policy management. His comments saved me from mistakes of fact and judgement in a number of places.

John Taylor read and commented on some sections in Chapters 12 and 14 relating to Japan's international economic policy issues. Peter Jarrett read and commented on the draft chapter dealing with the bursting of Japan's bubble and external shocks in the 1990s. André Icard read a portion of the manuscript dealing with the process of European monetary integration and offered useful comments. Nicholas Bray read Chapter 18 "The Role and Limits of Multilateral Surveillance" and made valuable suggestions and comments. John Martin read sections dealing with the impacts of globalisation on employment and income distribution in OECD countries and made valuable suggestions. Richard Carey read sections concerning OECD relationships with newly industrialising economies as well as its core development assistance work and provided helpful perspectives.

It is a great pity that I could not have benefited from comments on the entire manuscript from Philip Turner, one of my closest former colleagues at the OECD Economics Department. In May 2023, he offered very useful comments on the draft of Chapter 1 and asked me to send him the drafts of all other chapters as they were prepared. But his health problems prevented him from reading and commenting on them. Sadly, he passed away in early January 2024. I would have liked to give him a copy of this book as a token of my appreciation for our long-standing friendship. I would also have liked to do the same for the late Tommaso Padoa-Schippa who, as described in Chapter 1, first advised me to write my memoirs back in 2001, and for the late Donald Johnston who, at the time of the publication of the Japanese edition of my memoirs in December 2019, sent me a letter in which he wrote "(Y)our new book is very important for the OECD where there is little living institutional memory".

Tokyo
April 2024

Kumiharu Shigehara

Contents

1 **Introduction** 1

Importance of International Mindedness 1

Japan's Turn 5

Advice from Foreign Central Bankers and Former OECD Officials 8

Writing My Memoirs in Japanese or English? 10

2 **Prologue** 15

Family Situation in the Early Years of My Life 15

Education 18

The Beginning of My Professional Career at the Bank of Japan 23

Part I Internal and External Equilibrium under the Bretton Woods System

3 **Japan's Economic Policy Management under the Bretton Woods System** 33

OECD Report on Japan in 1969 and Its Monetary Policy Management 34

Price Stability and Monetary/Fiscal/Foreign Exchange Rate Policy Management in Japan under the Bretton Woods System 37

4 **The Internal versus External Dilemma: West German and Japanese Episodes** 43

5 **Discipline in Reserve Currency Countries: The United Kingdom and the United States** 55

6 **Frameworks for International Monetary and Economic Co-Operation under the Bretton Woods System** 71
International Co-operation Starting within Western European Countries 73
Creation of the OECD and the Roles of its Economic Policy Committee and its Working Parties 75
Japan Invited to Join the OECD as its First Member Country from Asia 80

7 **My Work at the OECD Monetary Division in the Early 1970s** 85
The "Nixon Shock" and its Aftermath 86
Proposal of OECD Monetary Policy Studies 88
Beginning of OECD Monetary Policy Studies 90
Report on Japanese Monetary Policy 92
Completing OECD Reports on Monetary Policy Studies in their Entirety 95

Part II Japan's Economic Policy Management and Balance of Payments Adjustment under the Floating Exchange Rate System

8 **Japan's Economic Policy and Foreign Exchange Market Management in the Second Half of the 1970s** 107
Monetary Policy Planning at the Bank of Japan 107
Start of International Economic Diplomacy at the Summit Level 110
The So-Called "Locomotive Theory" 113
Criticisms of Japan at September 1977 International Meetings in Washington 114
Carter Bonds and Intervention Currencies for Supporting the US Dollar 116
Medium-Term Economic Growth Scenarios by the OECD and the IMF 117

OECD's "Concerted Action Programme" 120
The 4th G7 Summit in Bonn in July 1978 121
Reinforcing US Dollar Defence Measures 122
Views Exchanged Between IMF Managing Director de Larosière and BOJ Governor Morinaga 124
IMF/World Bank Annual Meetings in Belgrade, September 1979 126
Multilateral Co-Operation for the Defence of the Yen 128
Accompanying Mayekawa on His Overseas Trips as Bank of Japan Governor 131

9 **High US Interest Rates and Fiscal and Monetary Policy Mix in Three Largest Economies in the Early 1980s** 137
US Economic Policy Management in the Early 1980s 139
Growing Criticism of High US Interest Rates 141
Discussion on Money Supply Targeting Policies 142
Fiscal and Monetary Policy Mix in the United States, Japan, and West Germany 145
OECD's "Differentiated Approach" versus the US Administration's Views 151
Saving–Investment Balance and Balance of Payments Adjustment 157
Kit McMahon and Stephen Marris 158

10 **The Plaza and Louvre Accords and Japan's Balance of Payments Adjustment** 163
Bank of Japan Institute for Monetary and Economic Studies 163
OECD EPC Discussion on the US Economy 168
The Plaza Accord and the Louvre Accord 169
Japan's Balance of Payment Adjustment under Price Stability 173

11 **Black Monday, 19 October 1987, and its Aftermath** 179
Black Monday—19 October 1987 180
Asset Price Hikes and the Yen Depreciation 182

12 **Dealing with Domestic and International Economic Policy Issues as Bank of Japan Chief Economist** 187
Domestic and International Policy Requirements for Price Stability 188

Revival of "Elasticity Pessimism" and the "Saving–Investment Balance" Approach 190
Assessment of the Japanese Economic Situation after the Bubble Burst 192
Supplementary Note on "Japan Bashing" 195

13 Coping with the Bursting of Japan's Bubble and External Shocks 205
Dealing with the Aftermath of the Bursting of Japan's Bubble 206
Yen Overshooting 212
Foreign Exchange Market Intervention and Monetary Policy 214
Banking Problems and the Introduction of Public Funds 219
The East Asian Financial Crisis 222
Volatile Movements in the Yen Exchange Rate 225
Disposal of Non-performing Assets and Introduction of Public Funds 227

14 Japan's Economic Policy Management since the Beginning of the Twenty-First Century 233
Japan's Economic Policy Management after the Bursting of the "Dot-Com" Bubble 235
A Flaw in the IMF World Economic Outlook 237
Measures to Cope with the Global Economic Slowdown 239
Beggar-Thy-Neighbour Policy? 242
Fiscal Policy Management under the Koizumi Administration 245
Breaking the Vicious Circle of Deflation and a Strong Yen 247
Responding to the Global Financial and Economic Crisis 253
Abenomics and the Bank of Japan's Failure in Achieving its 2 Per Cent Inflation Target 262

Part III Domestic and International Frameworks for Economic Policy Management

15 Frameworks and Conduct of Monetary Policy in Europe 271
Strategies for Lowering Inflation 271
The 1992–1993 ERM Crisis 273
Wider Bands in the ERM 277
Introduction of the European Single Currency 278

Annex 1 281
Kumiharu Shigehara's Introductory Statement at the Working Party No. 3 Meeting on 9 September 1992 281
Annex 2 283
Kumiharu Shigehara's Introductory Statement at the Working Party No. 3 Meeting on 3 December 1992 283
Annex 3 286
Kumiharu Shigehara's Statement at the Press Conference on 17 December 1992 to Introduce Economic Outlook 52 (Excerpt) 286
Annex 4 287
Kumiharu Shigehara's Statement at the Working Party No. 3 Meeting on 5 March 1993 287
Annex 5 290
Kumiharu Shigehara's Statement at the Economic Policy Committee Meeting on 10 November 1993 (Excerpt) 290

16 Inflation Targeting and Alternative Monetary Policy Approaches 295
Adoption of Numerical Inflation Targets 295
The Optimal Rate of Inflation and Two Per Cent as an Inflation Target 299
Errors in Forecasting and Analysis of Root Causes of Financial and Economic Shocks 301
Central Bank Independence 303
The Role of Central Banks in Globalised Financial Markets 308

17 Macroeconomic and Prudential Controls on International Financial Markets 315
Oil Money in the Eurodollar Market 315
Bank of Japan Guidance on Commercial Banks' International Financial Market Operations 317
Establishment of the BIS Committee on Banking Regulation and Supervision 318
Growth of International Bank Credit and the Recycling of Oil Money 320
Basel Capital Accord 322

Policy Implications of Globalised and Deregulated Financial Markets 323
Causes and Implications of the East Asian Financial Crisis 325
Causes of East Asian Financial Crisis 326
Lessons from the Crisis 329
The Role of Capital Controls 332

18 The Role and Limits of Multilateral Surveillance 339
The Role of Multilateral Surveillance 339
Lessons from the Global Financial and Economic Crisis 341
Lessons from the Euro-Area Crisis 344
The Role of Inter-Governmental Institutions in Public Opinion Formation 351

Part IV New Challenges for the Global Economy

19 Regionalisation, Globalisation, and Social Cohesion 365
External Dimension of Europe 1992 365
Policy Implications of Trade and Currency Zones 367
Globalisation, Employment, and Social Cohesion 370
Setbacks in Multilateral Negotiations on International Investment and Trade 377
Supplementary Note 1: New Technology, Innovation, and Employment 380
The Costs and Benefits of Technological Change 380
Policies to Establish a Proper Framework for Innovation 383
Adapting to a More Innovative Society 384
Supplementary Note 2: A View of the Global Economy in the Twenty-First Century 386

20 OECD Co-operation with Non-members 391
Co-operation with China 392
Co-operation with the Russian Federation 395
Co-operation with the Baltic States 399

21 Welfare, Global Order, Environment, and Climate Change 405
How to Deal with Population Ageing? 406
New Policy Proposals 408
New Order for Global Economic Governance 411

Peace and Economic Prosperity in East Asia 415
Regional Economic Integration In East Asia 416
Seeking A New Security Framework For East Asia 418
Economic Growth, Environmental Protection, and Climate Change 420

22 Epilogue—Looking for Models in Pursuit of Economic Prosperity 427

Index 435

List of Figures

Photo 1.1	The main building of the OECD (Le Château de la Muette) in Paris (© Kumiharu Shigehara)	2
Photo 1.2	The head office of the Bank of Japan around the time Kumiharu Shigehara joined it in 1962 (© Bank of Japan; *Source* The Bank of Japan, "One Hundred Year History of the Bank of Japan", Vol. 5)	3

Photo 1.3 At a lunch held at the dining room of the Bank of Japan on the occasion of the OECD WP3 meeting in May 1974 (© Kumiharu Shigehara; Masaru Hayami [Director-General of the Bank of Japan Foreign Department, later its Executive Director and subsequently Governor]; Haruo Mayekawa [former Executive Director and just before appointed Deputy Governor of the Bank of Japan, subsequently Governor]; John Fay [Deputy Head of OECD Economics and Statistics Department]; Henry Wallich [Member of the US Federal Reserve Board]; Stephen Marris [Director of the General Economics Branch of OECD Economics and Statistics Department, subsequently Economic Advisor to the OECD Secretary-General]; Shijuro Ogata [Head of the General Management Division of the Bank of Japan Foreign Department, later Executive Director of the Bank of Japan]; and Kumiharu Shigehara [Head of Monetary Division, OECD Economics and Statistics Department]) 4

Photo 1.4 At a dinner hosted by the OECD Secretary-General at his dining room (© OECD-OCDE; From left to right: Jean-Claude Paye [OECD Secretary-General], Tommaso Padoa-Schioppa [Deputy Governor of the Bank of Italy], Kumiharu Shigehara [OECD Chief Economist], Mario Graf von Matuschka (German ambassador to the OECD), Jean-Claude Trichet [Directeur Général du Trésor at the French Ministry of Economy and Finance], and Hans Tietmeyer [Vice-President of German Bundesbank]) 6

Photo 2.1 A picture of the members of the Shigehara family taken in May 1958 soon after Kumiharu Shigehara entered the University of Tokyo (© Kumiharu Shigehara; Left side of front row: Rutsu [Kumiharu's mother]; centre: Iye [his grandmother]; right side: Kumiharu; Back row: Itaru [his younger brother]) 21

Photo 2.2 Kumiharu Shigehara with Mr Warner at the Peace Memorial Park in Hiroshima (© Kumiharu Shigehara) 25

Photo 9.1 Kumiharu and Akiko Shigehara, Stephen and Margaret Marris, at the Peace Memorial Park in Nagasaki (© Kumiharu Shigehara) 160

Photo 10.1 The head office of the Bank of Japan taken around the time of its centenary celebrations in 1982 (*Source* The Bank of Japan, "One Hundred Year History of the Bank of Japan", Vol. 6. © Bank of Japan) 164

Photo 10.2 The head office of the Bank of Japan taken around 1910 (*Source* The Bank of Japan, "One Hundred Year History of the Bank of Japan", Vol. 2. © Bank of Japan) 165

Photo 12.1 Akiko Shigehara, Rhoda and Stanley Fischer, Kumiharu Shigehara, and Allan Meltzer at a reception on the occasion of the 5th international conference of the Bank of Japan Institute for Monetary and Economic Studies in October 1991 (from left to right) (© Kumiharu Shigehara) 189

Photo 13.1 Participants of OECD Working Party No. 3 meeting: (from left to right) Laurence Summers (US Treasury Under Secretary), Edwin Truman (Director of Fed International Finance Division), William White (Deputy Governor of the Bank of Canada), Scott Clark (Associate Deputy Minister of Finance of Canada), Jürgen Stark (State Secretary of the German ministry of finance), Jean-Claude Paye (OECD Secretary-General), Hans Tietmeyer (OECD Working Party No. 3 Chairman, Deputy President of the German Bundesbank), and Kumiharu Shigehara (OECD Chief Economist and Head of Economics Department) (the positions mentioned in parentheses are those held at the time the photo was taken in 1993) (© OECD-OCDE) 207

Photo 14.1 Kumiharu Shigehara's former colleagues at the OECD Economics Department: (from left to right) Andrew Dean, Nicholas Vanston, Robert Price, the author, Jeffrey Shafer and Paul Atkinson (© Kumiharu Shigehara) 234

Photo 19.1 Participants of OECD Ministerial Council meeting of June 1997: (from left to right) Renato Ruggiero (Director-General of the World Trade Organisation), Erik Asbrink (Swedish Minister of Finance), Leif Pafgrotsky (Swedish Minister of Trade) and Kumiharu Shigehara (Deputy Secretary-General) (© OECD-OCDE) 378

Photo 20.1	Kumiharu Shigehara as OECD Deputy Secretary-General shaking hands with Anatoly Chubais, First Deputy Prime and Minister of Finance of the Russian Federation at the Kremlin Palace in Moscow in October 1997. At the centre is Donald Johnston, OECD Secretary-General (© OECD-OCDE)	397
Photo 21.1	Honorary Doctor of Economics award ceremony at the University of Liège in November 1998, Belgium: (from left to right) Akiko Shigehara, the author, Bernard Jurion (Doyen de la Faculté d'Économie, de Gestion et de Sciences sociales at the University of Liège) and Guy Quaden (then Executive Director, later Governor of the National Bank of Belgium) (© TIL/LLG-DR)	410
Photo 22.1	Kumiharu Shigehara, recent photo (© Kumiharu Shigehara)	432

List of Tables

Table 8.1	OECD medium-term economic growth scenarios	118
Table 8.2	OECD Economic Outlook (three largest economies)	121
Table 9.1	OECD Economic Outlook (three largest economies)	148
Table 11.1	Outlook for short-term money market interest rates in Japan	182
Table 11.2	Outlook for short-term money market interest rates in Japan	183
Table 13.1	Effects of a 10 per cent depreciation in the effective exchange rate of the Japanese yen	216
Table 13.2	Effects of a 10 per cent appreciation in the effective exchange rate of the Japanese yen	223
Table 13.3	OECD Projections on Japanese Economic Growth (per annum, per cent)	224
Table 14.1	OECD Economic Outlook on Japan	236
Table 14.2	OECD Economic Outlook on Japan	248
Table 14.3	OECD Economic Outlook on Japan	254

CHAPTER 1

Introduction

Importance of International Mindedness

"Forget about Japan and the Bank of Japan" were the words Haruo Mayekawa used to give me his personal advice as I was moving from Tokyo to Paris to be seconded, at his suggestion, to the Organisation for Economic Co-operation and Development (OECD) from the Bank of Japan (BOJ) in early 1970 (Photos 1.1, 1.2, and 1.3). At that time, he was member of the Executive Board of BOJ and oversaw its international affairs. As such, he represented the BOJ on behalf of its Governor at important meetings of international institutions concerned with monetary, financial, and economic matters.

I took it that by these words, Mayekawa meant that, while I was on secondment to an international organisation, I should work first and foremost as an international civil servant from a global perspective, freed from a rather narrow framework of thinking and working as a Japanese central bank official. This open-mindedness was also to help me see afresh Japan's monetary and economic policy challenges.

I finished my first service at the OECD as Head of the Monetary Division of the Department of Economics and Statistics (ESD) in late 1974, and returned to Tokyo and worked in the areas of domestic monetary policy planning and international finance at the BOJ for two years, after which I became Associate Advisor on International Affairs and Personal

K. Shigehara, *The Bank of Japan, the OECD, and Beyond*,
https://doi.org/10.1007/978-981-97-5307-9_1

Photo 1.1 The main building of the OECD (Le Château de la Muette) in Paris (© Kumiharu Shigehara)

Photo 1.2 The head office of the Bank of Japan around the time Kumiharu Shigehara joined it in 1962 (© Bank of Japan; *Source* The Bank of Japan, "One Hundred Year History of the Bank of Japan", Vol. 5)

Assistant to Teiichiro Morinaga, BOJ Governor for the latter half of his term of office (December 1974–December 1979).

On Haruo Mayekawa's appointment as BOJ Governor succeeding Morinaga, I worked directly for him until the start of my second service at the OECD in September 1980, this time as Deputy Director of the General Economics Branch of the ESD for some two years.

Right after the announcement of my third service at the OECD, this time as Director of the General Economics Branch of the ESD in September 1987, Asahi Shimbun, a leading Japanese newspaper,

Photo 1.3 At a lunch held at the dining room of the Bank of Japan on the occasion of the OECD WP3 meeting in May 1974 (© Kumiharu Shigehara; Masaru Hayami [Director-General of the Bank of Japan Foreign Department, later its Executive Director and subsequently Governor]; Haruo Mayekawa [former Executive Director and just before appointed Deputy Governor of the Bank of Japan, subsequently Governor]; John Fay [Deputy Head of OECD Economics and Statistics Department]; Henry Wallich [Member of the US Federal Reserve Board]; Stephen Marris [Director of the General Economics Branch of OECD Economics and Statistics Department, subsequently Economic Advisor to the OECD Secretary-General]; Shijuro Ogata [Head of the General Management Division of the Bank of Japan Foreign Department, later Executive Director of the Bank of Japan]; and Kumiharu Shigehara [Head of Monetary Division, OECD Economics and Statistics Department])

described my profile in a column "This Person" with a large picture of me. The article was based partly on my remarks made at a press interview in which I told the reporter that it was my practice to convey the personal advice I had received from Mayekawa to younger staff members of the BOJ on their secondment to international organisations. This episode was later described also in Osamu Namikawa's book[1] on the achievements of Haruo Mayekawa as a distinguished Japanese central banker (written in

Japanese and published in 2008) as an example of his outstanding international mindedness even though he had no experience of working in international organisations.

Japan's Turn

A rather sarcastic view of Japan's role in international organisations was expressed in the Financial Times of 22 January 1992. The article was entitled "Japan's turn", and it said: "Japan has been better at donating money, rather than its brightest civil servants, to international organisations. So, Kumiharu Shigehara's career as the OECD's next Chief Economist will be watched with more than usual interest". It added: "the 52-year-old Bank of Japan official takes over from David Henderson, who has been doing the job since 1984. Until now, heads of economics at the Paris-based group have been either British, like Henderson, or North Americans".

As to my profile, the article wrote as follows: "A tall, donnish man, he is noted abroad for espousing a tough, autonomous and not excessively pro-American monetary policy at the Bank of Japan. He has frequently advocated greater deregulation for the Japanese economy and insists that he will not change his tune in his new post even on the sensitive issue of liberalising the rice market. Fluent in English, he is said to be typical of the new breed of assertive and international-minded Japanese who are not afraid to speak their mind. In which case, his appointment will be welcome".

Could I live up to the billing? To tell the truth, I initially declined a personal invitation from Jean-Claude Paye, then Secretary-General of the OECD, who sent his chief of staff to my office in Tokyo in autumn 1991 to ask me to consider running for the post of OECD Chief Economist and Head of the Economics Department.[2] I had heard rumblings of dissatisfaction from the finance ministry and central bank officials from major OECD countries, particularly about how two key bodies—the Economic Policy Committee (EPC) and the enigmatic-sounding Working Party No 3 (WP3)—were being run. Moreover, I had already worked at the OECD on three previous occasions, including as a director in the Economics Department (ECO), so I was well aware that the task of reviving these bodies would be daunting. Besides, the personal costs of curtailing my career as Chief Economist at the BOJ and going back to Paris would be high. But I decided to take up the challenge "when some months later the OECD Secretary-General himself rang me to persuade me to put my name forward" (Photo 1.4).

The announcement of my return to the OECD generated some interesting reactions. Mervyn King (then Executive Director, later Deputy Governor and subsequently Governor, of the Bank of England) sent me a letter of congratulations and strong encouragement. A more nuanced letter came from Stephen Axilrod, who was the most powerful Staff Director at the US Federal Reserve Board (FRB) and the right-hand man of Paul Volcker, chairman of the Board. While he thought it good for Japan to have someone of my ability in a key international position, he felt it might be even better for Japan if I remained at home. Whatever one makes of this message, at least I realised that all eyes would be on my performance at the OECD.

Photo 1.4 At a dinner hosted by the OECD Secretary-General at his dining room (© OECD-OCDE; From left to right: Jean-Claude Paye [OECD Secretary-General], Tommaso Padoa-Schioppa [Deputy Governor of the Bank of Italy], Kumiharu Shigehara [OECD Chief Economist], Mario Graf von Matuschka (German ambassador to the OECD), Jean-Claude Trichet [Directeur Général du Trésor at the French Ministry of Economy and Finance], and Hans Tietmeyer [Vice-President of German Bundesbank])

This impression was confirmed several months after my return to the OECD, when the Financial Times reported on my reform efforts at the Organisation with the headline "Think-tank operator seeks a refill of ideas". Even the main picture was of me.[3]

Refill and reform I did with positive results. In February 1994, Secretary-General Paye passed on very favourable comments on the OECD Economics Department's recent work from senior officials of the UK treasury who had been most critical of its past performance. The OECD Economic Policy Committee's work had been "dramatically transformed" and "very satisfactory". They even went as far as to describe the WP3 as "the best-prepared international meeting".[4]

Outsiders may be able to hazard a guess at what the Economic Policy Committee does: as its name suggests, it monitors and reviews the economic and financial situation and policies of OECD member countries, in line with the organisation's objectives. But it is much harder to understand the value of work done at the highly confidential WP3. Yet as a body that watches over policy impacts on international balance of payments, not only does it have global influence, but it also attracts top international financial and monetary policy officials. To be effective, those people need to know each other, speak candidly off the record, and express their own opinions on monetary, fiscal, and foreign exchange rate policies in major OECD member countries. Restoring that sense of personal contact at WP3 was a goal I set. The late Andrew Crockett, who was the General Manager of the Bank for International Settlements (BIS), wrote in 2011: "(I)n the end, what one remembers of a two-decade hitch with WP3 is not so much the policy issues (after all, these discussions were going on in multiple other fora as well). It is the individuals, and the sense of camaraderie that builds up as economists responsible for policy issues put their trade at the service of public policy".[5]

Right after his appointment as OECD Secretary-General to succeed Jean-Claude Paye in 1996, Donald Johnston, former minister of justice in the Trudeau government in Canada, asked me to join his management team as a Deputy Secretary-General. As my frail elderly mother wanted me to return to Japan around that time, I had some hesitation to lengthen my fourth term of office at the OECD for some 2 more years after 5 years' work as OECD Chief Economist. But, in the end, I decided to accept Johnston's request.

On my appointment as a Deputy Secretary-General in May 1997, Henderson, my predecessor as OECD Chief Economist, sent me a personal letter of 12 June 1997 in which he wrote "My warmest congratulations—though in fact, I think it is the OECD, and Mr Johnston, to which and to whom congratulations are mainly due. It is very good news that you are staying on in the Secretariat, and that the group of Deputy Secretaries-General will now include someone who combines economic expertise with first-hand experience of the operational side, and who has the confidence of the Economics Department and the Secretariat generally". Henderson's letter was preceded by a letter dated 8 May 1997 from Jeffrey Shafer, who had worked as Deputy Director of the Policy Studies Branch of OECD Economics Department when I was its Director, in which he wrote "it Mis more the Membership that should be congratulated than you, but congratulations anyway. Best of luck in your new role at a difficult time for the OECD".

With this new phase of my career as an international civil servant which proved to be worthwhile, the total length of my service at the OECD amounted to 18 years, almost equal to that at the BOJ. In the history of the OECD, there has been no member of its management team (composed of the Secretary-General, a few Deputy Secretaries-General, and/or Assistant Secretaries-General, all of whom are to be appointed by its Council) other than me who had working experience at senior posts within its Secretariat before her/his appointment as such a member.

Advice from Foreign Central Bankers and Former OECD Officials

My experience of working on four different occasions each at both the BOJ and the OECD over four decades gave me a unique insight into what lay behind economic policy controversies of those turbulent years. Among my former colleagues at foreign central banks, it was the late Tommaso Padoa-Schippa who first advised me to write my memoirs. His view was that my career paths both as a central bank economist and practitioner and as an international civil servant at the OECD are unique. The insights I had gleaned should be documented in the form of my memoirs. His advice was made on my visit to the headquarters of the European Central Bank (ECB) in Frankfurt in October 2001 to give a seminar on my views about the management of the world economy which had been weakening significantly with the severe correction in the high-technology sector since the autumn of 2000.

My association with Padoa-Schioppa dated back to the early 1970s when the OECD Secretariat initiated a series of studies on monetary policy in major OECD countries at the request of the Economic Policy Committee and WP3. All of the draft reports prepared by the Monetary Division where I worked first as an economist, subsequently as a senior economist, and finally as Head of the Division, were discussed at OECD's ad hoc meetings of national monetary experts. As an economist at the Research Department of the Bank of Italy, Padoa-Schippa accompanied Antonio Fazio, Head of the Department (who later became Governor). Two decades later, when I assumed the responsibility for running the Economic Policy Committee and WP3 as OECD Chief Economist and Head of Economics Department, Padoa-Schippa was Deputy Governor of the Bank of Italy and represented it at WP3 (Photo 3). On the establishment of ECB in 1998, he moved from Rome to Frankfurt as member of its Executive Board of ECB and as such he regularly attended WP3 meetings. He was Italy's Minister of Economy and Finance from May 2006 until May 2008. Born in 1940, just a year later than I, he unfortunately passed away in December 2010, aged 70, after suffering a fatal heart attack, which was quite a blow to me.

While I highly appreciated Padoa-Schippa's advice about writing my memoirs which I understood was based on our long-standing genuine friendship, I did not follow it immediately. The basic reason was that soon after I received his advice in October 2001, I was informed that Junichiro Koizumi, then Japanese prime minister, and Yasuo Fukuda, his cabinet minister, were considering me as one of the short-listed candidates for succeeding Masuru Hayami whose term of office as Governor of the Bank of Japan was to terminate in March 2003. As I myself was not seeking the post, I thought I should avoid writing my memoirs, which would include records and some self-assessment of my past work at the BOJ and the OECD, and might be wrongly seen as if it were intended for my self-promotion and office-hunting.

Prime Minister Koizumi's decision to appoint Toshihiko Fukui as the next Governor despite an earlier report that the cabinet minister had suggested that the successor to Hayami should be someone respected in the international financial circle as the late Mrs. Sadako Ogata was as the United Nations High Commissioner for Refugees, provoked some critical comments in the foreign press. Following some Japanese press comments that Koizumi's decision announced on 24 February 2003 was made under pressure from Japan's domestically oriented conservative establishment which desired the status quo, in an editorial column entitled "Koizumi's Timidity", the Financial Times of 25 February 2003 wrote that it showed a lack of courage from the prime minister. While I respected Fukui who, in contrast to me with careers both at the BOJ and the OECD as an economist, had followed a brilliant straightforward career path up to the post of a Deputy Governor at the BOJ, the Financial Times noted that the news about the next governor was "disappointing", noting that Fukui was "the candidate renowned for the weakest punch" against continuing falling prices in Japan since the burst of the bubble economy at the beginning of the 1990s.[6] A similar remark was published in the 27 February 2003 edition of The Economist, a respectable UK weekly economic magazine.[7]

It was in the wake of such foreign media reactions that Mervyn King, then Deputy Governor of the Bank of EnglandBOE), came to Tokyo. At his suggestion, our private tête-à-tête meeting at the UK ambassador's residence was organised outside his official schedules in late March 2003, where he told me that I should write my memoirs as a free man in the new situation.

I had met King for the first time in London soon after his appointment as the BOE's Chief Economist in 1991; I was then the BOJ's Chief Economist. Our association became even closer after my appointment as OECD Chief Economist as he represented the BOE at OECD EPC meetings and later succeeded Andrew Crockett as the BOE's representative at WP3, following the latter's appointment as General Manager of the BIS.

I considered King's advice as seriously as the one Padoa-Schippa had previously given me. But, I did not follow it for the same reason: I did not wish to engage in writing activities that could be regarded as self-promotion and office-hunting in a situation where the view existed in some circles that, recruited by the BOJ 4 years later than Fukui under its conventional seniority-based personal management system, I should better succeed him after his terms of office of 5 years as its Governor.

Writing My Memoirs in Japanese or English?

Time passed on while I continued to avoid writing on those topics which I thought should better be dealt with more naturally in my memoirs. However, things developed in a rather unexpected way in the late 2010s as I was approaching eighty.

At a lunch meeting with Donald Johnston in Paris in 2017, he told me that he was working on his own memoirs[8] and then said to me: "Kumi… keep the memories flowing". Moreover, in the context of e-mail exchanges that some of my former OECD colleagues and I had about the lack of a proper history of WP3 at the OECD in early February 2008, Stephen Potter, former Director of Country Studies Branch of the Economics Department, sent me a note in which he wrote: "There is obviously a very good case for you to write your memoirs: you have had rich experiences, you have an excellent memory (and apparently very good personal archives), and you have been encouraged to do so by eminent persons. You would be best advised to devote your material and energies to your memoirs".

On the day after I received Potter's e-mail, I visited the BOJ to have a tête-à-tête meeting with Haruhiko Kuroda, then its Governor, and to ask for his personal view on the advice I had received from former foreign central bankers and high officials of the OECD about writing my memoirs. Based on his past work at international fora including his association with OECD WP3 as Vice Minister of Finance for International Affairs, he supported the advice given to me by those foreign friends of mine and instructed Shigenori Shiratsuka, then Director of the Bank's Institute for Monetary and Economic Studies to assist me in launching my new work.

A few days later, Shiratsuka paved the way for my contact with Professor Kazuhiko Yago of Waseda University who had earlier published an article "A Crisis Manager for the International Monetary and Financial Systems? The Rise and Fall of the OECD Working Party, 1961–1980".[9] He was then planning a follow-up study to cover more recent activities of OECD WP3, and was in that context considering to ask me about the possibility of interviewing me on my past work at the OECD as well as the BOJ. Following my agreement with his request, he meticulously prepared a long and detailed list of questions for his interviews with me. The interviews were held on 15–16 March 2018 at my home in Tokyo and covered a wide range of topics, not just my professional life at the BOJ and the OECD but also my education as well as my family background and childhood including the sad experiences I had as a small boy during World War II and in its aftermath.

All of my verbal responses to Professor Yago's questions were recorded and the transcription of this recording was then used as a basic material for drafting the main body of the memoirs in Japanese. However, in this drafting process, I also added fairly detailed descriptions to respond to the questions that several of my former colleagues at the BOJ asked me to answer.

Having been informed that I was writing my memoirs, they asked me to add my remarks on the working environment as an economist at the OECD in comparison with that at the BOJ. More specifically, they hoped that I would explain how an annual job evaluation and merit-based promotion system functioned when I worked at the OECD and how I was treated under a conventional seniority-based personal management system during my services at the BOJ. Some of them also asked me to explain how I, a Japanese economist, acquired the capacity required for the management of many professional and auxiliary staff members of various nationalities in its Economic Department and for the running of OECD meetings where the two languages are used interchangeably. As a matter of fact, I was not just the first OECD Chief Economist chosen from the non-English-speaking area but was also the first holder of the post who used both English and French at OECD meetings as well as at my press conferences for introducing the OECD Economic Outlook—a twice-yearly flagship publication—and television and radio interviews as OECD Chief Economist.

These and other topics, which I would consider to be matters of interest mostly for Japanese readers, are not dealt with in this book written in English. Nor does it represent accurate English translations of the Japanese texts after deleting sections dealing with those topics. The facts and statistical materials provided, as well as my views expressed, herein, are the same as in the Japanese version of my memoirs published in December 2019. It remains my contribution to economic policy debates and controversies—many of which are still highly relevant today. These perspectives are presented in a more succinct manner, with more emphasis on economic policy issues of wider international interest.

This book is therefore a stand-alone piece of work in English, partly in response to the observation shared by Donald Johnston in the letter he sent me in English and its Japanese translation both shown at the beginning of my memoirs published in Japanese: "your new book is very important for the OECD where there is so little institutional memory" as well as the comments of some of my former colleagues at the OECD Economics Department who expressed hope for the publication of my memoirs in English.

But, it is also my long-overdue, however imperfect it may be, response, to the advice from the late Tommaso Padoa-Schippa: while my memory is still clear, I should write down the insights gained from my working experience as a Japanese central bank economist and practitioner which started several years before the demise of the Bretton Woods system of fixed exchange rates as well as those as an international civil servant at the OECD on four different occasions over the three decades from the beginning of 1970.

Nobody would, I think, consider that this piece, written at the age I have reached (85), was intended for my office-hunting, though some might still consider that it was published at least in part for self-promotion—not just for the purpose of transmitting some selections of my memories of the past as an economist and practitioner at the BOJ and an economist (and, for a while, a political appointee of Deputy Secretary-General) at the OECD as well as a free man after leaving these institutions to the younger and future students of economics and economic history more generally. Many of them will doubtless detect parallels with difficult issues central banks, national governments, and international institutions are grappling with today.

In the main part of this book, I delve into a selective account of my professional life, alternating between roles at the BOJ and the OECD. This narrative aims to offer glimpses into the inner workings of these esteemed institutions without attempting a comprehensive history of either organisation or the nations they represent. Rather than a comprehensive chronicle, it presents a curated collection of pivotal moments, strategic insights, and professional reflections garnered during my tenure. It seeks to highlight the nuanced intersections of policy, finance, and global dynamics within the scope of my experiences. They are not meant to be a comprehensive description, and still less a general appraisal, of domestic and international economic policies of the time. The focus here is on specific events and observations that contributed significantly to my understanding of the economic landscapes within which these institutions and global economies operate. It is an attempt to distil the essence of my professional journey, offering a perspective on the issues involved, rooted in the practicalities and challenges faced within these esteemed spheres.

Notes

1. Osamu Namikawa, "Haruo Mayekawa—*Dogan no Tetsugaku*" (in Japanese), Tôyôkeizaishimpôsya, 2008, pp. 143–144.
2. Just before my return to the OECD in 1992, the name of the Department was changed from the Economics and Statistics Department (ESD) to the Economics Department (ECO).
3. David Marsh, "Think-tank operator seeks a refill of ideas", The Financial Times, 5 March 1993.
4. *The Secretary-General asked about the EPC—whether it works satisfactorily, whether its documents are appropriate. Mr. Budd said that he and Mr. King, who had been rather dissatisfied, as new arrivals, by the meeting, considered that the meeting was now "much better—even dramatically transformed". EPC had become "almost a monument to demand management policies". But at the last meeting it discussed monetary policy, yet "the heavens did not fall in". Mr. Sedqwick said that WP3 is functioning well. The two papers for the forthcoming meeting, which are short, and "very good", and make it "the best-prepared international meeting that I attend".* (OECD, internal memorandum, February 1994).
5. Andrew Crockett, "WP3: High-level policy making in a stimulating forum", in "The OECD at 50", OECD, 2011.
6. Comment, "Koizumi's timidity", The Financial Times, 25 February 2003.
7. Leaders, "Muddleheart Koizumi", The Economist, 27 February 2003.
8. Donald Johnston, "Missing the Tide ~ Global governments in retreat", McGill-Queen's University Press, 2017.
9. Kazuhiko Yago, "A Crisis Manager for the International Monetary and Financial Systems? The Rise and Fall of the OECD Working Party, 1961–1980" in Matthieu Leimgruber and Matthias Schmeizer (eds.) "The OECD and the International Economy Since 1948", Palgrave Macmillan, 2017.

CHAPTER 2

Prologue

Before describing my recollections about my work at the Bank of Japan, the OECD, and beyond, as well as my reflections on related matters in the following chapters, I thought I should write briefly about my family situation in the early years of my life and my education which I think have had some significant influences on my professional life. It could perhaps help readers, if only a little, if I explained how the path was paved for the beginning of my professional career at the Bank of Japan (BOJ), and how I was trained as a young central bank official before becoming an economist at the BOJ Research Department.

Family Situation in the Early Years of My Life

My childhood memories are filled with dark and painful personal events associated with the Second World War. Born in February 1939, as the eldest son of Seizaburo Shigehara, a primary school teacher, I had no way of knowing that World War II broke out in Europe with Nazi Germany's invasion of Poland in September that year. Nor did I remember what I did on 8 December 1941 when the war in the Pacific began with the Japanese attack on Pearl Harbour. However, the scene of the day in 1944, when I was five years old and my father, the vice-principal of the most prestigious public primary school in Maebashi City, was drafted and left home to enlist in the army, remains firmly in my mind. My father was

K. Shigehara, *The Bank of Japan, the OECD, and Beyond*,
https://doi.org/10.1007/978-981-97-5307-9_2

32 years old at the time of his departure for the war. He was too old to be trained as a soldier. However, common sense did not prevail in the Japanese Army, which was dominated by madness at a time when the war was deeply tinged with the defeat of Japan. My father graduated from Gunma Normal School with the highest distinction and was one of the most successful of his classmates. Although he could have become headmaster of a rural primary school when he was just in his 30s, he chose to become vice-principal of the best primary school in Maebashi City of his own volition. My father's classmates believed that if he had chosen the path of a school headmaster, he would not have been called up for military service. Perhaps because of his profession, he did not take part in actual combat on the battlefields of Okinawa, but was tasked with document management at the military headquarters. However, the 32nd Okinawa Defence Force, his main unit, was forced by the onslaught of the US Army to leave Shuri, the central city of the main island of Okinawa, for the coastal area at the southern tip of the island, where he was killed in action four days before the Japanese Army's surrender on 23 June 1945.

After the air raid by American B-29 bombers that reduced downtown Tokyo to ashes, killing about 95 thousand civilians on the late night of 9th and the early morning of 10 March 1945, American military aircraft began to fly over my native city, Maebashi, the capital of Gunma Prefecture, about 100 kilometres north of Tokyo. As a kindergarten pupil at the time, I had the experience of rushing home from kindergarten when the air-raid siren sounded, wearing an air-raid hood that all the children had brought with them to kindergarten. On 5 August that year, the day before the atomic bomb was dropped on Hiroshima, Maebashi City was attacked at night by 92 US B-29 bombers, and according to an official record, around 55 per cent of the approximately 21 thousand buildings in the city centre burned down, about 7 hundred people were burned to death and 6 hundred injured. My family's main house and storehouse and air-raid shelter in the garden were all destroyed, but all members of my family, my grandparents, my mother, my younger brother, and myself, who lived in the same house, fortunately managed to escape on foot to the suburbs after an air-raid warning and survived. On my way to the suburbs, I was injured by shards of glass from a bombed-out building, but was able to receive first aid.

The Pacific War ended on 15 August 1945, but confusion ensued. My father's whereabouts remained unknown for a long time. In October 1946, more than a year after Japan's defeat, we were officially informed of my father's death in the war, and later received a white wooden box from the authorities, containing only Okinawan pebbles and sand. My father had cut off part of his hair and fingernails and left them, along with his will, to my maternal grandfather before his departure to Okinawa. Instead of his remains, my father's hair and nails were placed in an urn together with Okinawan soil and sand, and a burial ceremony was held at a nearby Japanese Buddhist temple. On that day, my mother wrote in her diary: "Kumiharu is seven years old and Itaru is two. From now on I alone must work hard until they come of age". My younger brother, Itaru, was born one month before my father's departure to Okinawa, so he has no memory of his father. The grief of my mother and grandparents was painfully felt even by me as a seven-year-old boy. I still remember almost every night after dinner, in a dark living room of a shabby wooden house hastily constructed on the site of the main house that had burned down and not yet equipped with electric light, my grandparents sobbing as they listened to my mother sitting by the candlelight reading out the letters my father had sent us from Okinawa before his death.

I was told that there were soldiers who returned home after the official announcement of their death in battle and after the funerals had been held. Many times, when I myself was walking through the streets of Maebashi, I thought that a man with glasses coming from a distance might have been my father. However, when I got closer, I found that in each case I had mistaken someone else for him. My father did not come back after all. And his remains have not returned home to this day. On his departure for war, my father left a memoir titled "Notes to my beloved child" addressed to me. This memoir, which ended with a four-page note he wrote just after waking up at 4.30 am on the day of his departure for war, contained words of instruction for me as a shy and timid child.

My mother (neé Rustu Tanabe), who was widowed at the age of 28 following my father's death in the war, refused offers of remarriage and chose the arduous path of raising two children on her own. Her first name "Rustu" was given after "Ruth" described in the Book of Ruth in the Old Testament, according to which Ruth was a Moabite immigrant to Judea who accepted the God of the Israelites as her God and the Israelite people as her own, and struggled to adjust to the culture.

My paternal grandfather, Kiyosaku Shigehara, was a small farmland owner, but lost his cash income when the farmland was liberated after the war. So, to support our livelihood, my mother decided to work in an elderly care facility run by her own father, Kumazo Tanabe, who was a Christian, and one of the pioneers of elderly care facilities in pre-war Japan. Thus, during the daytime hours when my mother assisted her father in running his facility, it was my paternal grandmother, Iye Shigehara, who looked after my brother, who was a baby less than two years old when my mother started to work outside our home. My maternal grandmother, Sato Tanabe, was also a Christian, originally a mathematics teacher, and joined her husband in running the care facility after their marriage. Their work was supported by employees during the daytime, but at night my grandparents were on their own, making rounds to see how the old people were doing in their bedrooms in the facility. My maternal grandmother ended her life in tragedy, dying of a heart attack in the middle of a tour of duty on a cold night. I thus spent my childhood watching my maternal grandparents live a modest way of life, devoting most of their time and energy to collecting money from donors and working for the good of old people hit by ill fortune.

My mother's younger brother, Makoto Tanabe, also grew up in this kind of family environment and later became a politician. He was influenced by his own father to go into the field of social welfare work and eventually became the 11th Chairman of the Japan Socialist Party in the early 1990s. It was on Makoto's advice that I decided not to take the national senior civil service examinations which were held immediately after I had been offered a job at the Bank of Japan. He told me that bad luck could occur in the upper echelons of the government bureaucracy, which inevitably mingles with politicians of all kinds.

Education

Throughout my primary and junior high school years, although my father was no longer with me, I was proud to see his former school colleagues, seniors, and students visiting our home and talking to my mother about their memories of him. Several teachers whom my father had taught at the Gunma Normal School told me about my father's love of philosophy and his skill at playing the piano, performing Mozart's piano sonatas at the Normal School concert, and beautifully singing Italian canzones with his baritone voice. And the words of my father written in his "Notes to my beloved child" that he had left behind became my spiritual support. At some point, I vaguely thought that if I could, I would like to follow in my father's footsteps and become a teacher. I was also brought up in an environment where I could closely observe my maternal grandparents living for the common good rather than for personal gain, and this seems to have influenced my decisions on the way I should follow in my professional life.

When I became a student at Maebashi High School, the best school in Gunma prefecture, my homeroom teacher recommended that I take the entrance examination for the University of Tokyo, the most difficult of all national universities to enter, and I spent virtually all my time preparing for it. English was my strongest subject, and I had been ranked top not only in Maebashi High School but also in the national mock examinations for Tokyo University entrance examinations since my second year of senior high school. However, when it was almost time to take the entrance examination, I was suddenly summoned to the headmaster's office and informed of a system for studying at an American university for four years under the programme of the Grew Foundation, which I was advised to apply for. This Foundation was established by Joseph Grew who was US Ambassador to Japan until the start of the Pacific War (from 1932 to 1941), with the money given to him by Emperor Showa after the war as a token of gratitude for Grew's efforts during the war to discourage the US government and military from bombing Kyoto and other Japanese cities with rich cultural heritages. Under this system, one Japanese student was to be selected each year from among high school students from all over the country who were of "academic excellence, good conduct and physical fitness". The scholarship from the Grew Foundation was not a loan, but a grant with no obligation to repay, which would help me and my family in financial difficulty.

Following the headmaster's advice, I travelled to Tokyo without any special preparation. The final day of the three-day examination was on English conversation skills, with one American and one Japanese examiner. After the test, the examiners asked me how I had learnt to speak English so well in Maebashi, my hometown without English-speaking residents. When I told them that I had learned it only by listening to

NHK's Radio English conversation programme, they looked at me in disbelief. Sometime later, I was summoned by the headmaster once again to be told that the Grew Foundation decided to send me to an American university. However, some weeks later, to apply for a visa for a long-term stay in the United States, I was asked to undergo a medical examination at a designated hospital in Tokyo where they discovered a slight shadow on my chest x-ray. To take precautions, the Grew Foundation decided to send the second successful applicant to an American university in my place.

While reading the Nihon Keizai Shimbun a while ago, I came across a column written by Makoto Utsumi, who had held important positions in the Japanese Ministry of Finance, including the post of Vice Minister of Finance for International Affairs. In it, he recalled an episode in his senior high school days when he passed the Grew Foundation's examination for studying at an American university, but was rejected at the physical examination, as was my case. In his column, he noted that he would not have entered the Ministry of Finance if he had studied in the United States under Grew Foundation's programme. In my case, if I had obtained a degree from an American university, I would not have been qualified to sit for the senior civil service examinations of the Japanese government, nor would I have been recruited by the Bank of Japan. The Bank's policy of only employing students who had graduated with excellent achievements from top universities in Japan remained the same as when Utsumi graduated from the University of Tokyo. The personal letter I received from the Grew Foundation's secretary-general ended with encouraging words, "Please do not let this decision we have regrettably had to take discourage you from going forward. We eagerly hope you will have an opportunity to study in the United States after your graduation from the University of Tokyo".

When I entered the University of Tokyo in April 1958 (Photo 2.1), all students were enrolled in the Faculty of Liberal Arts for the first two years before entering specialised faculties. There, we received education in a wide range of social and natural sciences, and it was obligatory to learn at least one foreign language in addition to English. I chose French as my second and German as my third foreign language. In retrospect, this choice paid off very well: years later I was assigned to work at the OECD, where French and English are official languages.

While studying at the faculty of liberal arts, a new discipline that caught my interest was the philosophy of science. I thus visited the office

Photo 2.1 A picture of the members of the Shigehara family taken in May 1958 soon after Kumiharu Shigehara entered the University of Tokyo (© Kumiharu Shigehara; Left side of front row: Rutsu [Kumiharu's mother]; centre: Iye [his grandmother]; right side: Kumiharu; Back row: Itaru [his younger brother])

of Professor Shozo Omori to discuss the possibility of choosing this discipline for my higher education. He appreciated my passion for the discipline, but told me that there was little prospect of a large increase in the number of teaching posts in the philosophy of science at Japanese universities, so the risk of choosing this path would be great. He advised me to go on to the faculty of law, the most difficult and prestigious to enter among various faculties around social science at the University of Tokyo, as he knew that I had the highest achievement among all the students who entered the university in the same year. I followed Professor Omori's advice and filled in my application form, stating that my first choice was the faculty of law, which was readily accepted.

Although I became a student of law at the University of Tokyo, I could also attend classes at its faculty of economics. For monetary theory, I eagerly attended the lectures of Professor Ryuichiro Tachi who had just returned from the United States. I learned international finance from Kunio Horie, a special lecturer at the faculty of economics, and president of the Bank of Tokyo, the only Japanese bank specialised in foreign exchange business at the time. At the faculty of liberal arts, Professor Takeyasu Kimura had taught me about general economic theory. These three professors provided me with basic knowledge useful for my self-study on modern monetary economics which I began immediately after starting to work at the Bank of Japan.

The law faculty of the University of Tokyo had an academic foundation established in honour of Nobushige Hozumi and his son, Shigetou Hozumi, both of whom contributed greatly to the modernisation of Japanese jurisprudence. Immediately after I entered the law faculty in April 1960, I was selected as the recipient of its scholarship which was to be given to the best law school student among those who joined the faculty in the same year. Originally, Hozumi scholarship students were expected to contribute to the legal profession after graduation from the law faculty, but this was no longer an absolute obligation by the time I was chosen and I thought a government civil servant would be a good choice for me. Just before the government official recruitment examinations began on 1 September 1961, however, the Director and Deputy Director as well as the Head of Personnel Division at the Personnel Department of the Bank of Japan (BOJ) came to a classroom of the law faculty of the University of Tokyo to explain the important role of the

BOJ and the significance of central bank officials. Right after their presentations, Susumu Nakamura, Head of Personnel Division, came over to my seat and said to me, "I was told that it would be the Bank of Japan's loss if it failed to recruit you. Please, come to join us at the Bank", and walked away. I later found out that he had worked under Haruo Maekawa, then Director-General of the Foreign Department, later member of the Board of Executive Directors, Deputy Governor, and Governor of the BOJ. Nakamura eventually rose to the position of Executive Director of the BOJ. His invitation for me to work at the Bank of Japan was made probably because he was informed that I was the Hozumi scholarship student of the year 1960.

The Beginning of My Professional Career at the Bank of Japan

The year 1962 was a time when the internationalisation and liberalisation of the Japanese economy had advanced. It was also an exceptional year for the BOJ's personnel management in that six outstanding graduates from the law faculty of the University of Tokyo joined the BOJ. In the same year, one brilliant student who studied Keynesian economics at the faculty of economics of the University of Tokyo also joined the BOJ, as did two graduates with the highest distinctions each from the faculties of economics at Hitotsubashi University and Kyoto University. At the time, it was generally the case that students who went on to work at the Ministry of Finance of the Japanese government and the BOJ immediately after finishing four-year university courses had better academic achievements than those who remained at universities to advance to master's and doctoral studies.

Thus, I joined the Bank in April 1962. My first task at the BOJ's head office in Tokyo was an apprenticeship in its cashier's department. It involved scrutinising Bank notes collected from commercial banks and replacing soiled or damaged notes with new ones so that they could circulate in the market again. It was better to learn the basics of central banking operations at the BOJ's local branches than in the head office, where specialised activities are divided into different departments. So, half a year later, 21 university graduates who joined the BOJ in April 1962 were transferred en masse in November that year to branches scattered around the nation from Hokkaido in the north to Kyushu in the south. I was assigned to the Hiroshima Branch where I learned how to handle the central government treasury funds, and how to follow the cash management operations of the head offices of local banks and the Hiroshima branches of city banks with nation-wide branch networks. Eventually, I was also engaged in research work on the local economy.

Outside my official working time, I began some preparatory work for studying economics at a postgraduate course in the United States under the Fulbright programme. While working at the head office, I read John Maynard Keynes' *A Treatise on Money,* a copy of which I bought from a second-hand bookshop in Tokyo. After my transfer to the Hiroshima Branch, I read Paul Samuelson's influential textbook, *Economics,* and George Stigler's *Theory of Prices,* among others. When the Personnel Department at the head office in Tokyo circulated a notice to local branches, inviting young staff who had completed a certain amount of basic central banking training to apply for the Fulbright programme, I immediately applied for it, but was told to hold off on it. My path to study at an American university was thus again closed following an abortive attempt at the end of my high school years.

The following year, I was told that the BOJ was considering sending me to France, where I would have the opportunity to master French in addition to English before starting to engage in the international activities of the Bank. This policy of the BOJ seemed to me to be related to an unexpected event in Hiroshima. At the time of a visit to Hiroshima City by Mr Warner, an American who had been teaching English conversation to the then BOJ Governor Masamichi Yamagiwa, I was asked to accompany him on a tour of the city (Photo 2.2) and had the opportunity to speak in English with him all day. On his return to Tokyo, he reported his assessment about my English language skills as "the Bank's best English-speaking employee" to the Governor who immediately shared it with the Personnel Department as well as the Hiroshima Branch Manager. The Personnel Department was already aware that I had been the top scorer in the Grew Foundation's examinations for sending a Japanese senior high school graduate to an American university, and the Warner assessment became more evidence of my English language skills. It was probably considered for my appointment in later years as a Personal Assistant to BOJ Governor Teiichiro Morinaga for his meetings with foreign central governors and other foreign visitors in which English was used as the language of their oral communication, as noted in Chapter 8.

In September 1964, the IMF and the World Bank held their joint annual meetings in Tokyo. Around that time, momentum for the BOJ's international co-operation with the central banks of major countries built up, and in this context, the BOJ considered establishing a new training programme in co-operation with the Banque de France under which the two central banks would exchange staff members of their respective Foreign Departments into their own workplaces. I was then told that I would be transferred from the Hiroshima branch to the head office to stand by for going to France under this new programme.

In April 1965, I married Akiko Yoshizawa. She had studied at a British college while her father was Chief Representative of the BOJ in London, and returned to Tokyo when Takeshi Yoshizawa, her father, was appointed Director-General of the BOJ's Foreign Department (later its

Photo 2.2 Kumiharu Shigehara with Mr Warner at the Peace Memorial Park in Hiroshima (© Kumiharu Shigehara)

Executive Director). She was a postgraduate student at Sophia University and worked as an assistant in the office of the IMF delegation to the IMF/World Bank annual meetings in Tokyo in the autumn of 1964. At our wedding dinner held in Tokyo, Tadashi Sasaki, then Deputy Governor (later Governor) of the BOJ, gave a table speech in which he said "the life of the bride of a Bank of Japan official will be with no major upheavals and no cause for concern for the groom, the guardian of his home". In retrospect, however, the burden on Akiko proved to be far greater than not just Sasaki but we, as the bride and groom, had anticipated. It turned out that in later years, we moved back and forth between Japan and France with two distinct cultures and languages as well as divergent social norms and values, as I worked not only at the Bank of Japan but also at the OECD where I served as an international civil servant four times for a total of 17 years.

On returning to the head office from the Hiroshima Branch. I was assigned to the Research Department rather than the Foreign Department, even though I was awaiting the start of my stay at the Banque de France under the new programme which was essentially designed for the exchange of staff members of the two central banks' respective Foreign Departments. It was not appropriate from a personnel policy perspective for me to be assigned to the Bank's Foreign Department, which was then headed by my father-in-law. During my four months' stay in the Research Department, I worked as an assistant economist at the French desk of the Europe and America Division, while preparing myself for departure to France.

The year-long programme prepared by the Banque de France started in March 1966 after a month's study at the Alliance Française de Paris. The first part of the programme consisted of my stay at La Société Générale, then one of the big four nationalised French banks. I went down to the South of France and commuted to its Marseille Branch for about two months to study its commercial banking operations such as export and import finance, after which I stayed at the Foreign Department at its head office in the centre of Paris for two months to learn how foreign exchange business operations with bank clients and interbank foreign exchange dealings were conducted. I was also allowed to visit Paris money market dealers.

During the French summer holiday season of July and August, my wife and I attended courses on the French language at a branch of the University of Poitiers in Tours, some 240 kilometres south-west of Paris. Among the Japanese who followed the advanced courses, including a young diplomat from the Japanese Ministry of Foreign Affairs, I was the only one who passed the examination to obtain the diplôme des études françaises (diplôme of French studies).

Under the latter half of the programme which started in September 1966, the Banque de France was generous enough to provide me with a private office in the large building of its head office where I was allowed to read the Bank's internal documents on their foreign exchange operations and the French exchange control system. In those days, interbank foreign exchange buying and selling operations in Paris were conducted not just on the telephone market but for some fixed hours of the day but also carried out directly among cambists who gathered in a dealing room at La Bourse de Paris, and I accompanied the Bank's chief foreign exchange dealer to watch them dealing there.

As I was a member of the BOJ's Research Department, I was also allowed to read the internal documents of the Banque de France on its domestic monetary policy operations and the French banking and financial system. At the time, under President Charles de Gaulle, who had a strong sense of rivalry with the United States and the United Kingdom, various reforms were in the process of being implemented with the aim of developing the Paris money and capital market to become on a par with the London and New York markets. In the light of this development, during the latter part of my stay at the Bank of France, I prepared a report on the results of my year-long study in France and on return to Tokyo in February 1967, I presented it to Akira Oka, head of the Europe and America Division of the Research Department (later the BOJ's Executive Director). He immediately decided to have it printed in a booklet titled "The Paris Money Market and the Operations of the Bank of France" (BOJ Research Department Working Paper, February 1967) and its copies were distributed within the Bank and shared with the Ministry of Finance and the National Diet Library.

To my surprise, I was then assigned to work as an economist monitoring the UK economy in the Europe and America Research Division.

It turned out to be a stroke of luck. The papers I wrote about the UK economy at its turbulent time were eventually used to demonstrate my capacity as an economist in the summer of 1969 at the OECD recruitment examinations for an economist post in its Economics and Statistics Department which Haruo Mayekawa, then the Bank's Executive Director for International Affairs, directly ordered me to take.

The first piece I completed on the UK economy was an article entitled "Measures to improve the UK banking structure", published in the July 1967 issue of the BOJ Research Department's Monthly Bulletin. This was followed by a paper entitled "The evolution of British incomes policy and its effects", published in the September 1967 issue of the BOJ Monthly Bulletin (referred to also in Chapter 5 of this book). At the time, I was aware that Japanese academics such as Professor Ryuichiro Tachi, who had taught me at the economics faculty of the University of Tokyo, argued about causes of inflation in Europe and the United States in terms of "cost-push" and "demand-pull" factors, and at the OECD, a study was being undertaken on the problem of inflation, though I was not informed about its internal work. Against this background, I decided to conduct my own research into the question of how British incomes policy aimed at price stability was implemented, and how effective it was. While I was dealing with relevant statistical data from this perspective, an interesting idea came to my mind: why not try a regression analysis, rather than just a chart analysis? I tried various ideas as to variables to be explained, equation forms to be used relating them with explanatory variables, and time lag structures for explanatory variables. In the end, I obtained statistically significant and theoretically interesting results, with help for my computer work from a member of the Bank's Statistics Department. The conclusion of my paper was that the British government's policy of trying to control inflation by focusing on incomes policy, on the assumption that inflation in the United Kingdom resulted mainly from cost-push factors, was wrong; this policy alone would not stop inflation in the United Kingdom; and an appropriate combination of demand management policies and measures to enhance labour market mobility would be indispensable. Oka, head of the Europe and America Research Division, was interested in this work of mine, and he and his colleagues in the Research Department decided to publish it as a major article in the Research Department Monthly Report. When I took the OECD recruitment examinations, a résumé in which I summarised the main points of this paper in English and my paper on the devaluation of the British pound (which I will discuss in Chapter 5) were submitted as documents to demonstrate my competence as an economist.

PART I

Internal and External Equilibrium under the Bretton Woods System

CHAPTER 3

Japan's Economic Policy Management under the Bretton Woods System

In April 1964, Japan accepted the obligations of Article VIII of the IMF Articles of Agreement under which Japan is required to take appropriate steps to liberalise its legal framework and administrative practices in the area of foreign exchange regulation, abandoning the earlier regime under its Article XIV which allowed it to maintain restrictions on the free convertibility of its currency for payments and transfers for current international transactions.

In the same month, Japan joined the OECD as its 21st member of the organisation and the first Asian member country. Earlier, in the midst of the Cold War, the US President Dwight Eisenhower had proposed to transform the Organisation for European Economic Co-operation (OEEC) into a new more global organisation, the Organisation for Economic Co-operation and Development (OECD) by opening up the possibilities for full memberships for itself, Canada and Japan. But, faced with opposition from several European countries, the US administration had agreed not to push for the full Japanese membership of the OECD immediately after its creation in 1961.[1]

K. Shigehara, *The Bank of Japan, the OECD, and Beyond*,
https://doi.org/10.1007/978-981-97-5307-9_3

OECD Report on Japan in 1969 and Its Monetary Policy Management

Some five years after Japan's accession to the OECD, it was observed in its Economic Survey of Japan for 1969[2] that:

> (T)he radical change of Japan's external position sets a promising new frame for future developments, but will also pose new problems. Relieved for the foreseeable future from the necessity to protect the country's low level of (external) reserves and to submit the economy every two or three years to a 'recession' or cooling-off period, the problem of maintaining cost and price stability over time and of avoiding the building up of excess capacity may require greater attention than hitherto. In the likely absence of important balance of payments constraints, the enforcement of quick policy adjustments may become more difficult and the reaction of business slower. Moreover, with the attainment of a more adequate level of external reserves, Japan is, for the first time in her history, experiencing the problems of surplus countries trying to avoid undue strains on international liquidity.
>
> From the point of view of international equilibrium, it seems desirable in present circumstances to sustain a high rate of growth of the economy and to continue efforts to discourage borrowing from abroad. But, given the recent strength of domestic demand, the maintenance, up to now, of cautious demand management policies seems justified. Although there are no signs of domestic overheating, at present or for the immediate future, the authorities attach particular importance to the possible effects of the recent acceleration of wage increases. But they also intend to keep policy flexible. Indeed, if the official export forecasts were to materialize (implying a change from a 30 per cent annual rate of growth to an almost flat trend of exports between mid-1969 and early 1970) the change might well have a depressive effect particularly on the private investment boom, which is entering its fourth consecutive year. If such a situation were to arise later on, it would probably call for a reconsideration of demand management policy. It should, in any case, be noted that the growth potential of the Japanese economy has been persistently underestimated in recent years. The progressive acceleration of growth of GNP from 10 per cent (in volume) in 1966 to 14.4 per cent in 1968 was associated with a decline of the GNP price deflator from 4.5 per cent to 3.7 per cent. It is also interesting to note that the rise of consumer prices in 1968 (5.5 per cent) was smaller than that registered during the 'recession year' 1965 (6.6 per cent) and that by April 1969, the year-over-year advance was down to 4.7 per cent. Furthermore, the recent faster increase of wholesale prices (by 1.8

> per cent between May 1968 and 1969) is almost fully attributable to price rises of food products, iron and steel and non-ferrous metals; the two latter components were heavily influenced by developments in overseas markets.
>
> Nevertheless, the price problem has emerged as a principal policy issue since the balance of payments difficulties have been removed. The behaviour of main price indicators during the last three business cycles suggests that factors other than excessive demand have played the more important role in the persistent upward movement of prices. Among such factors are government policies in respect of agriculture and public services. The price rise in private services can largely be explained by the tendency for wage increases in industry to spread to the service sector. Prices of manufactured goods have, on the whole, shown a high degree of stability in recent years, thanks to the rapid increase in productivity which has largely kept pace with the progress of wages. It would appear, therefore, that the price problem is, to a large extent, of a structural nature which can best be coped with by policies designed to raise the level of productivity in low-productivity sectors and to stimulate labour mobility, thereby keeping the economy growing at an optimum rate.
>
> The Japanese authorities are seeking progressively to fulfil their commitments for the adoption of more liberal policies concerning imports, current invisible transactions and capital exports. Since, if present trends continue, a large surplus on Japan's balance of payments may remain even though fast growth in the economy is maintained, further progress in liberalising current external transactions and capital exports is highly desirable from the international point of view. A more liberal import policy would also help to dampen price pressures and speed up the shift of labour from low to high productivity sectors a shift necessary to close the important gap in living standards which still exists between Japan and other advanced industrialised nations. The present strong domestic expansion should make it easier for the Japanese authorities to overcome the social problems that have to be taken into account when accelerating the movement towards the removal of the remaining restrictions on imports. (pp. 41–42)

This report was published on 1 September 1969, the very day when the Bank of Japan (BOJ) raised its official discount rate from 5.84% to 6.25%. In *Nihon Kinyuu Nenpyou* (Japanese Financial Chronology) which was compiled and published by the Bank of Japan Institute for Monetary and Economic Studies, this action was noted as "the first monetary policy tightening the Bank undertook at a time when Japan's balance of payments was in surplus". As such it was foreseen that, in his press interviews immediately after the public announcement of its monetary policy measure, Makoto Usami, then BOJ governor, would be asked by journalists to comment on the policy recommendations about the management of Japan's monetary policy included in the OECD report.

It was in this situation that I, as a staff economist in the Money and Finance Section of the Domestic Research Division of the BOJ's Research Department, was requested by Kastumi Sôma, Head of the Section, to draft a note to be sent to the Co-ordination Department prior to the public announcement of the BOJ's policy change. The latter department was in charge of preparing briefing materials for the Governor's use, in which Sôma, considered that arguments should be set forth to justify the BOJ's policy action, providing a rebuttal to the OECD's view on the desirable orientation of Japanese monetary policy in the face of rising inflation pressure.

While I had not had access to the full text of the final version of the 1969 OECD Survey of Japan before its publication on September 1, I was aware of the main gist of its policy proposals and broadly in agreement with its view about the importance of import liberalisation which should help ease pressure on domestic prices. In the OECD's published report, there was no explicit argument about the role of exchange rate policy in Japan's domestic demand management and inflation control as well as in its balance of payment adjustment. But, in my view which will be explained below, some yen upvaluation would be more desirable than domestic monetary policy tightening in the face of rising inflation pressure at home coupled with detectable changes in Japan's current balance of payments position towards underlying surplus. Thus, I could not obey my superior's instruction. Instead, a colleague of mine in the same section prepared a note to be sent to the BOJ's Policy Co-ordination Department, the text of which I did not have a chance to see.

Sometime later, Sôma, privately expressed his concern about my future at the BOJ. He told me that my capacities and work performances were highly appreciated among the BOJ's senior members and they generally considered me to be one of most promising young officials, but that a somewhat more flexible attitude on my part would help shape my successful career within the BOJ. By the time he gave me this helpful advice with genuine kindness, however, I was about to begin my new professional life by joining the OECD as an economist of the Monetary Division of its Economics and Statistics Department, see Chapter 7.

Price Stability and Monetary/Fiscal/ Foreign Exchange Rate Policy Management in Japan under the Bretton Woods System

As noted in the above-mentioned 1969 OECD Survey of Japan, divergent patterns of price measures had emerged in the then ongoing period of high productivity growth in the manufacturing sector: virtual stability over time in the wholesale price index (WPI) which contains prices of manufactured products as a main component and sustained rises in the consumer price index (CPI) which includes prices of agricultural products and services as its major components (Box).

The cumulative rise in Japan's consumer price index (CPI) over the 15-year period from 1953 to 1968 amounted to 78.6% (4.0% on average per year). The comparable figure for the United States was 30.0% (1.8% on average per year) and 36.4% (2.1% per year) for West Germany. It was 60.9% (3.2% per year) in the United Kingdom, a country which experienced a currency devaluation against the US dollar during this period, and 77.3% (3.9% per year) in France which also devalued its currency against the US dollar.

On the other hand, Japan's price performance was outstanding in terms of wholesale price index (WPI). It rose by 7.5% only (0.5% on average per year) over the same 15-year period. The comparable figures were 15.6% (1.0% per year) in West Germany, 17.3% (1.1% per year) in the United States, 39.6% (2.3% per year) in the United Kingdom, and 49.6% (2.7% per year) in France. Particularly notable was Japan's wholesale prices for industrial products, which fell by 1.9% over the period. Therefore, measured in terms of wholesale and export prices, the international price competitiveness of Japan, which maintained a fixed parity of 360 yen per US dollar throughout this period, strengthened considerably.

In the 1960 Report on the Bank of Japan System prepared by the Financial System Research Board for the Japanese government, it was stated that "the Bank of Japan shall be governed by the principle of stable currency value for the sound development of the national economy" but the definition of "stable currency value" was not made clear.

Under the Bretton Woods fixed gold-dollar standard system then in force, the maintenance of the stability of the external value of national currencies (stability of their US dollar exchange rates) was an international responsibility for all member countries of the IMF including Japan. However, it was not clear what the maintenance of the yen's internal value (domestic price stability) meant precisely.

Under these circumstances, debates developed among Japanese economists on the choice of price measures to be used for the definition of price stability. Osamu Shimomura, who played a key role in formulating the Hayato Ikeda government's National Income Doubling Plan in the first half of the 1960s, regarded economic growth as the top priority and argued that, to this end, a certain degree of consumer price inflation was unavoidable to achieve this. On the other hand, Toshihiko Yoshino, the most influential economist in the BOJ's Research Department (later, its Executive Director), insisted that consumer price stability should be the most important objective of the BOJ.

In this setting, a meeting was organised for several young staff officials selected from the BOJ's policy-related departments to discuss various aspects of Japan's price problems and the gist of their discussions was published in the May 1969 issue of the BOJ's in-house magazine *Nichigin* (an abbreviation of "Bank of Japan " in Japanese). Its printed copies were distributed not only to all current members of the BOJ but also to members of its Old Friends Association.

Working as an economist at the International Economic Research Division of the Research Department at the time, I observed that:

- given large differences in productivity performance between manufacturing and services sectors in Japan, the stabilization of consumer prices rather than wholesale prices would be associated with persistent declines in wholesale and export prices, which would significantly strengthen Japan's international price competitiveness and result in growing current account surpluses;
- in the current setting, the policy of achieving domestic price stability in terms of consumer prices rather than wholesale prices in Japan would need to be supported by a shift from the prevailing rigid fixed exchange rate system to a more flexible regime such as a crawling-peg.[3]

These remarks took my colleagues by surprise. To my knowledge, no other Japanese economists expressed such a view at that time.

After Japan's official discount rate was raised on 1 September 1969, an article entitled "Various issues surrounding recent price increases" was published in the November 1969 issue of the BOJ's Research Department Monthly Report. It explained that the Bank's monetary tightening measures were implemented in response to the recent sharp rise in prices, bullish business sentiment, and the rapid increase in the money supply. It then stated that there would be limits to attempting to stabilise prices through monetary tightening alone, and recommended careful management of fiscal policy, rationalisation of low-productivity sectors, increased labour mobility, strengthening of competitive conditions and, in particular, the promotion of import liberalisation. It was also pointed out in the article that, while domestic supply and demand conditions were the main factors behind the sharp rise in wholesale prices at the time, there were also overseas factors, such as the rising prices of imported goods included in wholesale prices and Japan's strong export performance which was further tightening domestic supply and demand conditions. However, no mention was made of the revaluation of the yen as a policy option which would have the effect of preventing these overseas factors from accelerating domestic inflation.

In the 22nd White Paper of Trade published in June 1970, the Ministry of Industry and Trade of the Japanese government stated: "(S)ince business fixed investment is a demand factor as well as a supply factor, careful consideration should be given to the management of monetary policy so that its tightening will not deter productivity growth and hinder stable economic expansion in the near future". A month later, the Economic Planning Agency published its 1970 Economic White Paper and stated that it would be necessary to consider alternative ways for conducting domestic economic adjustment policy at a time when the balance of payments is in surplus, referring to the BOJ's official discount rate increase on 1 September of the previous year. It argued that "one way should be a tightening of fiscal policy to restrain economic expansion".[4] In this connection, the results of simulations with the short-term economic model developed by the Economic Research Institute of the Economic Planning Agency were reported in the White Paper, according to which a 0.1 per cent increase in the Bank of Japan's official discount rate would have the same effect of restraining aggregate demand as a ¥27 billion cut in government investment, or a 0.53 per cent point increase in corporate tax and a ¥68.1 billion increase in personal income tax. It was then argued that "if domestic demand restraint is exercised from the fiscal side also, monetary tightening can be relatively moderate, and accordingly increases in foreign capital inflows and foreign exchange reserves can be contained". However, it did not show the magnitude of the impact on Japan's balance of payments resulting from tighter fiscal policy.

Be that as it may, neither the aforementioned article in the November 1969 issue of the BOJ's Research Department Monthly Report nor the Economic Planning Agency's 1970 White Paper discussed the yen's upvaluation as a policy option for moderating domestic inflation in Japan. In this connection, it is interesting that a table titled "Examples of different patterns in domestic and external balances", attached to the White Paper as reference material, showed that West Germany had implemented a revaluation of its currency and border tax adjustment measures in a situation where the balance of payments was in surplus and the domestic economy was overheating. In my view, the implication of this West German episode for Japan's exchange rate policy management should have been discussed in the White Paper.

A year later, more precisely on 30 July 1971, just before US President Richard Nixon's announcement of a series of measures including the unilateral cancellation of the direct international convertibility of US dollars to gold (the so-called "Nixon shock") surprised the world, the Economic Planning Agency published the 1971 White Paper titled "The Road to Internal and External Balances". In a section "Policy issues under balance of payments surplus" (pp. 79–81), it argued that "(T)he basic task for Japan is to actively reduce the balance of payments surplus to a smaller level with the aim of achieving domestic and foreign balance", but it only advocated a "change in the economic structure" as a measure to deal with this, without discussing any specific measures to achieve this. In the section "Future international economic policy", it simply stated that "export promotion measures have made a significant contribution to economic policy over 25 years since the end of the war. However, even if the system was necessary in the past, its role must be fundamentally reviewed in the context of major changes in the economic structure to achieve domestic and foreign balance. Furthermore, as part of external economic policy, liberalisation of capital and foreign exchange transactions should be promoted while preventing disruptive capital movements" and "in light of the current situation where the global inflationary trend remains strong, it is necessary to examine ways to prevent the balance of payments surplus from increasing prices through domestic monetary expansion". However, no mention was made of yen revaluation as a possible measure to achieve better internal and external balance.

Policy options such as changes in parity would require a high degree of political judgement and need to be treated with caution even when discussed within the monetary authorities. Discussing the pros and cons of such a change in the BOJ's Research Department Monthly Report or in Japanese Government publications on economic policy management could have caused unforeseen confusion in the foreign exchange market, and the authorities may have considered it wise to refrain from open discussion on foreign exchange rate policy options. In fact, the turmoil of the Tokyo foreign exchange market caused by the Nixon shock of August 1971 occurred even with the "world-class exchange controls" in place in Japan at the time, indicating the need for careful consideration when the monetary authorities make statements on the international monetary system and foreign exchange rate policy matters.

Be that as it may, Japan's response to rising inflationary pressure was to tighten monetary policy without using parity revaluation as a measure to stabilise domestic prices at a time when the current balance of payments was in surplus as was the case in West Germany. In contrast, with its central bank independent from the government and ensured as the guardian of price stability, West Germany revalued its currency against the US dollar in order to control inflation pressure associated with import from abroad, as reviewed in somewhat more in detail in the next chapter.

Japan was eventually forced to make a major upward currency adjustment in the wake of the Nixon shock, and the monetary easing implemented in response to concerns about falling exports and domestic deflation caused by the yen revaluation went too far, creating excess domestic liquidity in 1972–1973 which resulted in the bitter experience of accelerating inflation in 1973–1974.[5]

Notes

1. Peter Carroll and William Hynes, "Japan and the OECD: How the sun rose on a global era", OECD Observer, No. 298, Q1 2014, pp. 8–9.
2. The OECD's 1969 Survey of Japan was based on the study prepared by the OECD Economics and Statistics Department for the annual review of Japan by the Economic and Development Review Committee on 26th June of that year. Final approval of the Survey

was given by the Committee after revisions in the light of discussions during the review.

3. Bank of Japan, "*Nichigin*" (an abbreviation of "Bank of Japan" in Japanese), May 1967 issue, p. 14.
4. Section "Domestic and External Balance" (pp. 62–64) in the Economic Planning Agency's 1970 Economic White Paper, published in July 1970, was subtitled "New Dimensions of the Japanese Economy", whereas the 1969 Economic White Paper for 1969, published in July 1969, was focused on Japan's domestic economic prosperity and had a subtitle "The Challenge of Prosperity". In Part 2 "The Japanese Economy in a New Stage" of the latter White Paper, it was pointed out that "even though the Japanese economy has become the world's second largest in terms of overall economic size, its per capita national income at $1110 in 1968 (about 400,000 yen), is still at around 20th place" (pp. 100–101). It then noted that "the Japanese economy has a great deal of potential and "the next challenge for the Japanese economy is to increase the productivity of the economy as a whole and furthermore to resolve the economic and social imbalance" (p. 111).
5. Consumer price inflation in Japan rose from 4.5 per cent in 1972 to 11.7 per cent in 1973 and 24.5 per cent in 1974 whereas that in Germany rose from 5.5 per cent to 6.9 per cent and 7.0 per cent respectively. The international commodity price boom and the first oil shock were two significant inflationary factors common to the two countries and Japan's far worse price performance was essentially a result of the mismanagement of Japan's monetary and foreign exchange rate policy.

CHAPTER 4

The Internal versus External Dilemma: West German and Japanese Episodes

The global economy in the post-Second World War world was, until the early 1970s, governed by the Bretton Woods system of fixed, but adjustable, exchange rates with the US dollar as a predominant reserve currency. During most of this period, international capital transactions were extensively subjected to exchange controls while international trade was only gradually liberalised under the GATT regime.

This system had two asymmetries.

First, countries with current account deficits, in particular those with financing problems, were subjected to multilateral surveillance on their policies, but surplus countries were not. This tended to retard upward adjustment of currencies of surplus countries and ran a risk of undermining the international competitiveness of the United States and weakening its external account unless US inflation is kept below those of its trade partners.

Second, given the role of the US dollar as the key reserve currency, the macroeconomic policy management of the United States was not constrained by the limitation of foreign exchange reserves as in the case of non-reserve currency countries running external deficits.

Nevertheless, the system functioned fairly well in promoting macroeconomic stability and economic growth in the particular environment prevailing in the 1950s and the early part of the 1960s, when US inflation was kept fairly low.

K. Shigehara, *The Bank of Japan, the OECD, and Beyond*,
https://doi.org/10.1007/978-981-97-5307-9_4

That said, inflation divergences among European countries led to significant balance of payments imbalances. They were followed by the succession of devaluations and revaluations of important European currencies in 1967 and 1969.[1]

In an essay published in 1970, Otmar Emminger noted:

> *One of major lessons arising from these events is that countries tend to resist, for various reasons, such parity changes for too long. The consequences are severe speculative crises and, in the end, the need to alter exchange rates in a more massive and disruptive way than would have been required with timely adjustment. Moreover, in the interval, the structure of production may have become gravely distorted – e.g. too export-oriented (Germany) or too concentrated on the home market (Great Britain) – or domestic equilibrium may have become seriously disturbed, as Germany's was, by inflation which imported from abroad through an undervalued currency; in these circumstances, even after parity adjustment, it will take considerable time before external and internal equilibrium can be regained. Such delays will often be criticised as a "failure" of the respective adjustment measures, though in reality they are simply the result of undue hesitation before adopting the appropriate measures.*[2]

Emminger wrote this essay when he was the chairman of Working Party No. 3 (WP3) of the OECD Economic Policy Committee, which played an important role as a consultative forum for balance of payments adjustment in its major member countries.

In West Germany, established as a member country of the liberal camp in the post–war division of Germany into two countries with the other joining the Soviet Bloc, the concept of a "social market economy",[3] which combined social welfare and free competition, was developed under the leadership of Ludwig Erhard, who became Minister of Economics and Deputy Prime Minister under Chancellor Konrad Adenauer of the Christian Democratic Union (CDU) and later succeeded him as Chancellor. Under his leadership, West Germany revived its economic strength over that of the victorious World War II countries in Europe, the United Kingdom and France, and became a balance of payments surplus country.

Emminger as a member of the board of the Deutsche Bundesbank first publicly addressed the problem of imported inflation in Germany during a speech at the IFO Institute for Economic Research in Munich on 6 July 1956. His statement that "we are importing inflation from other countries through trade surpluses from exports and inflows of foreign money" was reported by a leading South German newspaper the following day.[4] Later in the same month, Willhelm Roepke, professor of economics and social critic, published an article titled "Dilemma of Imported Inflation" in a leading Swiss newspaper which was followed by another article to the same effect published in the 7 October 1956 issue of the same newspaper.[5]

In July 1956, in advance of the OEEC Ministerial Council meeting, Erhard sent a letter to Harold Macmillan, then UK Chancellor of the Exchequer, to inform its intention to maintain the West German mark (Deutsche mark, DM) parity and proposed a devaluation of UK pound as the currency of a balance of payments deficit country, or a widening of its exchange rate fluctuation band to 5 per cent above and below parity. Subsequently, at the OEEC Ministerial Council meeting, Macmillan responded by saying that Germany should tolerate higher domestic inflation for reducing its external surpluses, and added that Germany could eventually upvalue DM.[6]

Emminger prepared an internal document titled "External position and exchange rate policy" in which he argued for DM upvaluation (upward adjustment of the DM exchange rate) to deal with the internal and external dilemma of the West German economy. It was discussed at a meeting of the board of the Bundesbank in December 1956. Emminger's proposal was rejected by Wilhelm Vocke,[7] its President and other members of the Board. Emminger recalled that Vocke could not understand the concept of the internal vs external dilemma under the fixed exchange rate system.[8] At that meeting, it was decided that the discussion which took place at the Bundesbank board on that day should remain secret and Emminger's document should not be disclosed. Furthermore, while Emminger himself believed that DM revaluation should be tackled as soon as possible, but refrained from making any public statements on this policy option.

Outside the Bundesbank, however, Roepke's article published in 1956 was followed by a call for DM revaluation by Herbert Giersch of Kiel Institute for World Economic Research (IfW) in 1957.

West Germany upvalued DM parity in March 1961, but only by a modest 5 per cent. According to James Harold,[9] Per Jacobsson, then Managing Director of the IMF, was against the DM revaluation, as he believed that any parity change would be interpreted as a signal, not that the right rate had been arrived at, but that further changes might be undertaken, and that it would destroy part of the credibility associated with a fixed exchange rate system, and set off yet more intense speculative onslaught on exchange parities. However, in his memoirs,[10] Emile van Lennep, the first chairman of OECD WP 3, who later succeeded Thorkill Kristensen as the second Secretary–General of the OECD, recalled that most experts, including the IMF staff, agreed that an upvaluation of DM by 10–15 per cent was desirable. Inside West Germany, industry and agricultural organisations opposed DM upvaluation. Both Erhard and Emminger argued for its revaluation by 7.7 per cent, while Karl Blessing, then its President opposed it. In the end, DM upvaluation was limited to 5 per cent at the behest of Adenauer, who expected industry support in the 1961 federal election.

Even after the March 1961 DM revaluation, significant payments imbalances persisted among member countries of the European Payments Union, an organisation created by the OEEC and in existence from July 1950 to December 1959 when it was replaced by the European Monetary Agreement. Inside West Germany, from 1965 onwards, an academic body, the German Council of Economic Experts (the so–called "Five Wise Men") recommended DM revaluation in their annual reports to the Federal government which rejected it.

Flaws in the Bretton Woods system became more visible towards the end of the 1960s when the US inflation rate continued to rise above those in Germany and some smaller European countries such as the Netherlands and Switzerland as well as Japan. By that time, the international spillover of US inflation into these European countries became a matter of particular concern.

It was true that international surveillance was not carried out as effectively for balance of payments surplus countries as it was for deficit countries. However, countries that wished to prevent foreign inflationary impulses from undermining their domestic price stability could, on their own initiative, make upward adjustment of parities. In their book "Changing Fortunes: The World's Money and the Threat to American Leadership",[11] Paul Volcker and Toyo Gyoten wrote that the Bundesbank was beginning to feel that the control of German domestic money supply was becoming less effective with the inflow of dollars and that Germany was in danger of being exposed to inflation pressure, probably brought in from the United States. This concern put West Germany in the camp of those countries willing to reform their international currencies, especially towards a more resilient foreign exchange rate system.

On 29 September 1969, West Germany moved to a floating of DM and then returned to a fixed rate system with a revaluation of DM by 9.29 per cent on 24 October. Japan did not follow the German move to my disappointment. As already reviewed briefly in Chapter 3, on 1 October 1969 when the OECD published the Economic Survey of Japan in which it argued that Japan's current account balance had shifted into a persistent surplus position, the BOJ raised its official rate to ward off inflation. It was also noted in Chapter 3 that, I as an economist at the BOJ's Research Department, had argued that Japan should revalue the yen exchange rate first rather than tightening monetary policy. In my view, the mistake of hesitation in making timely foreign exchange rate adjustment in several European countries, which Emminger indicated in his essay of 1970, was committed also by Japan.

At the time of the Smithsonian agreement of parity changes in December 1971, Japan was forced to accept a yen revaluation of 16.88 per 308 yen cent against the US dollar (from 360 to to the dollar). Despite multilateral adjustments to currencies, including the revaluation of the yen at that time, the balance of payments imbalances among the major countries remained conspicuously large, and international currency instability continued. The Smithsonian agreement collapsed within a year and two months. The British pound shifted to a floating exchange rate in June 1972; Italy moved to a dual exchange rate system in late January 1973; Switzerland switched to a floating exchange rate system which triggered large-scale currency speculation in February; and major countries closed their foreign exchange markets in early March. Japan moved to a floating exchange rate system in mid-March. It was followed by the joint floating of the currencies of the six EC countries (West Germany, France, the Netherlands, Belgium, Luxembourg, and Denmark) with the rate fluctuation band of 2.25 per cent between the currencies in the region), announced later in the same month, and the revaluation of DM against the SDR.

In such a situation, the BOJ, controllable by the finance minister under the archaic central bank law introduced during war time following the German Reichsbank law of 1937 under the Nazis regime and still in force in post-war Japan, was forced to adopt excessively expansionary monetary policy. The result in Japan was huge increases in money supply and credit leading to real estate and stock price bubbles and accelerated general price inflation in 1973 and 1974. In contrast, West Germany with an independent central bank did not experience such a disaster in the aftermath of the Smithsonian agreement. International spillovers of US inflation into West Germany were more effectively offset by more prudent domestic monetary policy and greater readiness to adjust DM upward if not at a sufficiently early timing and by a sufficiently large amount.

As mentioned in Chapter 3, the OECD's 1969 Economic Survey of Japan observed that Japan's balance of payments, when viewed on a trend basis after eliminating fluctuations associated with economic cycles, began to show a surplus from around 1964, with its current account surplus increasing exponentially. At that time, the Japanese authorities considered that there was no strong need to be concerned about a huge shift of funds from the dollar to the yen in the event of domestic monetary tightening, since strict exchange controls were in place in Japan. However, domestic monetary tightening in Japan worked in the direction of increasing its trade and current account surpluses, as imports fell due to a decline in domestic demand and export drives strengthened. It was important for Japan as well as for West Germany to prevent the balance of payments surplus from increasing, and in order to simultaneously achieve this external requirement and the internal objective of domestic price stability, it was preferable to revalue the yen parity against the US dollar rather than tightening its monetary policy. It should have helped to defend the Bretton Woods system.

According to a later account by Yusuke Kashiwagi who was Vice Minister of Finance for International Affairs from June 1968 to June 1971, Daizo Hayashi in his capacity as Deputy Director-General of the Research Department at the Ministry (Director-General of the International Finance Bureau from June 1972 to June 1973) led a secret study of the international monetary system called "Alpha work" towards the end of 1969. In the internal document prepared under his leadership, it was noted that it would be appropriate to revalue the yen.[12] Kashiwagi testified that he had discussed this proposal with Hayashi, together with the Vice Minister of Finance and the Director of the International Finance Bureau, but that all three including Kashiwagi himself were opposed to Hayashi's proposal. The first reason for their opposition was that, from the perspective of an emphasis on domestic economic growth, they believed that it was justified for Japan to promote Japan's exports and discourage imports until the international balance of payments constraints, which had been a bottleneck to domestic economic growth in Japan, were eliminated. Another reason was that they believed that import liberalisation and deregulation in other areas were priorities for Japan, and a sudden upward adjustment of the yen rate should be avoided.[13]

In 1967, Japan's trade balance deteriorated considerably due to increased domestic demand and a slowdown in overseas economies, which led to monetary policy tightening and negotiations with the IMF on a borrowing arrangement. These negotiations were terminated in 1968 due to a turnaround in foreign exchange reserves resulting from an increase in exports and inflows of foreign capital. But the Japanese monetary authorities were still strongly conscious of the need to raise "the ceiling on the balance of payments" as late as in 1969. As of March 1969, Japan's foreign exchange reserves amounted to $3.1 billion, less than half of West Germany's ($7.6 billion).

An interesting episode before the Nixon Shock was that when BOJ Governor Tadashi Sasaki attended a meeting of central bank governors at the Bank for International Settlements in Basel in May 1971, Masaru Hayami, then the Bank's chief representative in London (later its Executive Director, and subsequently its Governor), told to Sasaki that he hoped Japan's foreign reserves would soon amount to $10 billion. Hayami's remark at the time is said to have been based on a simple idea that if the reserves reached that level, the yen would attract attention from foreign countries and Japan's status in the international financial circles would be strengthened.[14] At the time, Japan's foreign exchange reserves stood at $6 billion, double their level in March 1969.

In the book "The yen and the Bank of Japan" written by Shijuro Ogata,[15] who succeeded Hayami as the Bank of Japan Executive Director in charge of international affairs, it is noted that young Bank of Japan staff members were gathered under Governor Sasaki to discuss the pros and cons of yen revaluation, its floating, and other options in 1970. But he wrote nothing more detailed than that. As I had moved to Paris to work at the OECD Secretariat in January 1970, it is not clear to me what exactly was discussed at that meeting and what concrete conclusions were reached.

Outside the Japanese monetary authorities, Kazutaka Kigawada, Chairman of Japan Association of Corporate Executives *(Keizai Doyukai)* in the spring of 1971 announced that "the need to make a proactive decision on revaluation was becoming a reality". In July 1971, a group of 36 academic experts including Ryutaro Komiya, professor of economics at the University of Tokyo, proposed a series of minor upward adjustments in the yen exchange rate. However, such views never saw the light of day because they were overwhelmed by public opinions and arguments within the Japanese government circles where emphasis was on the importance of maintaining the fixed exchange rate of 360 yen to the US dollar.

After all, it was only after the revaluation to 308 yen to the US dollar as part of the multilateral adjustment of the major currencies at the Smithsonian Institution in Washington in December 1971 that the Government's Economic White Paper in its 1972 edition (published on 1 August 1972) first acknowledged that the undervalued yen was a factor in Japan's growing international balance of payments surplus. It was stated in the document that:

- Japan had not been well prepared to deal with the surplus in its international balance of payments;
- this situation resulted partly from the United States' benign neglect of its responsibility as the predominant reserve currency country, and partly from Japan's delay in revising its fixed view that Japan's balance of payments deficits imposed a severe constraint on its economic growth and its failure to address international frictions caused by external imbalances;
- the currency adjustment taught Japan that both the United States and Japan must mutually share the responsibility for maintaining external balance of payments equilibrium (p. 136);
- the currency adjustments have amply demonstrated that Japan's economic development would not be possible without harmony with the world economy (p. 217), and
- the government must make use of exchange rate policies in accordance with the direction of future reform of the international monetary system, while coping with the fluid international economic situation (p. 56).

Moreover, the Economic White Paper in its 1992 edition also argued that exchange rate policy was "also a powerful instrument for price stability". It was noted that the policy of reducing Japan's balance of payments surpluses by raising domestic prices is unacceptable, and efforts should be made to co-operate internationally in order to prevent the acceleration of world inflation. The use of exchange rate policy should also be considered where necessary (p. 217).

In the 1973 edition of the Economic White Paper (released on 10 August 1973), it was noted that the Japanese government reaffirms that price stability is its top policy priority. It was then argued that "in retrospect, it could be said that the transition to a floating exchange rate system was needed also for domestic equilibrium" (p. 56).

Comparison of this statement with the argument for the use of exchange rate policy as an instrument for price stability made in the Economic White Paper published in August of the previous year suggests that Japan did not actively promote the transition to a floating exchange rate system. Nor did the Japanese government take a leading role in international discussions on the reform of the international monetary system at that time.

From the beginning of 1970, I worked as an economist in the Monetary Division of the OECD Economics and Statistics Department. As such, I was in charge of preparing discussion papers on monetary and exchange policy issues to be submitted to OECD Working Party 3 (WP3) then under the chairmanship of Emminger and attended its meetings as a member of the secretariat. In these meetings, I never saw a Japanese representative leading WP3 discussions on issues relating to the balance of payments or the international monetary system issues.

According to the testimony of Yusuke Kashiwagi, who was Vice Minister of Finance for International Affairs, senior officials from the Ministry of Finance and the Bank of Japan discussed Japan's international policy response around the end of 1972.

He there recalled that a suggestion was made that the revaluation of the yen against the dollar at the Smithsonian Institution was insufficient and yen should be upvalued further. However, this suggestion was not adopted in the end, partly because of concern about the adverse effects on Japan's domestic economic growth and partly because of concern about igniting the further negative reaction of the public who had strongly opposed to the appreciation of the yen that had already taken place.[16]

In my view, the fundamental problem in Japan's economic policy-making towards the end of the Bretton Woods system was that neither Japanese economic policy-makers nor external economic experts in Japan had properly appreciated that, at a time of accelerating inflation in the United States and other trading partners, a sustained increase in productivity in the Japanese manufacturing sector was resulting in a significant strengthening of its international price competitiveness, affecting both its underlying balance of payments position and the distribution of international liquidity. Under these circumstances, it was unsurprising that the Japanese public continued to be preoccupied with the fear of dollar shortages and the need for foreign borrowing they had experienced in the immediate post-war period.

Notes

1. The UK Pound, then the second most important reserve currency, was devalued by 14.3 per cent from 2.80 dollars to 2.40 dollars per pound in November 1967.
2. Otmar Emminger, "Practical difficulties of balance of payments adjustment" in "Essays in honour of Thorkil Kristensen" (page 5), OECD, 1970.
3. Otmar Emminger, "The Social Market Economy and Monetary Stability", London, 1999.
4. Süddeutsche Zeitung, 7 July 1956.
5. Neuer Zurcher Zeitung, 28 July, and 7 October 1956.
6. Volker Hentschel, "Ludwig Erhard. Ein Politikerleben", Olzog-Verlag, München, 1996.
7. Wilhelm Vocke, "Gesundes Geld. Gesammelte Reden und Aufsätze zur Währungspolitik. Mit einer Einleitung von Volkmar Muthesius. Schriftenreihe zur Geld- und Finanzpolitik", Band 1. Frankfurt am Main, 1956; "Um die Stabilität der Währung". Köln 1957.
8. Otmar Emminger, "D-Mark, Dollar, *Währungskrisen*", Stuttgart, 1986, pp. 75–76. Wilhelm Vocke, "Gesundes Geld. Gesammelte Reden und Aufsätze zur Währungspolitik. Mit einer Einleitung von Volkmar Muthesius. Schriftenreihe zur Geld- und Finanzpolitik", Band 1. Frankfurt am Main, 1956; "Um die Stabilität der Währung". Köln 1957.
9. Harold James, "International Monetary Cooperation Since Bretton Woods", Oxford University Press, 1996.
10. Emile van Lennep, "Working for the World Economy", Nederlands Instituut voor het Banken Effectenbedrijf, Amsterdam, 1998, p. 90.
11. Paul Volker and Toyoo Gyoten, "Changing Fortunes: The World's Money and the Threat to American Leadership", Times Books, 1992, p. 43.

12. Daizô Hayashi, "'*Alfa—En Kiriage—Sagyou' Tenmatsuki*" (Compte rendu of 'Alpha—yen revaluation-Work'), Kinyuu-Zaisei-Jijô, 24 June 1974 and 1 July 1974.
13. Keikichi Honda and Tadao Hata, "*Kashiwagi Yuusuke no Shôgen: Sengo-Nihon no Kokusai-Kinyuu-shi*" (Testimonies of Yuusuke Kashiwagi: The history of international finance in the post-war Japan)", Toyo-Keizai-Shimpôsha, Tokyo, 1982, p. 48.
14. Masaru Hayami, "*Kaizu Naki Koukai*" (Voyage in the unchaeted sea), Yuuhikaku, Tokyo,1998, p. 48.
15. Shijuro Ogata, "*En to Nihonginkô*" (The Yen and the Bank of Japan), Chukô Shinsho, p. 12.
16. Keikichi Honda and Tadao Hata, ditto, p. 6.

CHAPTER 5

Discipline in Reserve Currency Countries: The United Kingdom and the United States

Japan's response to the OECD's policy recommendations in its Economic Survey of Japan in 1969, when its balance of payments was turning into a surplus, is an example of how limited the effectiveness of multilateral surveillance under the Bretton Woods system was with regard to surplus countries. Unlike Japan, West Germany which had emerged as a balance of payments surplus country earlier than Japan did implement a revaluation of DM parity in 1961 and another one in 1969 in the face of continuing external surpluses. As pointed out in Emminger's essay reviewed in the previous chapter, however, these relatively modest revaluations were undertaken with noticeable delays in the timing of their implementation. Rather than actively planned from the perspective of international co-operation to support the international monetary system with the US dollar as the predominant reserve currency, the West German currency revaluations were conducted essentially as defensive measures with domestic price stability as a top policy priority in the face of higher inflation in the United States and some of West European trade partner countries.

That said, the delay and hesitation in revaluing parities by sufficiently large magnitude in countries with balance of payments surpluses such as West Germany and Japan under the Bretton Woods system alone would not have caused its collapse. Reserve currency countries were also accountable.

K. Shigehara, *The Bank of Japan, the OECD, and Beyond*, https://doi.org/10.1007/978-981-97-5307-9_5

During 1966, important progress was made at Working Party No.3 (WP3) of the OECD Economic Policy Committee (see Chapter 6 on its establishment) towards developing a greater international consensus on policies best suited for adjusting external payments imbalances. Its report titled "The Balance of Payments Adjustment Process", prepared by representatives of the ten major industrial countries participating in WP3, carefully explored the nature of the adjustment process and pointed to various possibilities for improving it.

WP3 recommended various ways of strengthening national policy instruments and outlined a set of informal guidelines regarding appropriate adjustment policies. In addition, it suggested a number of steps to improve adjustment procedures through greater international co-operation, including collective reviews of countries' balance of payments aims; the setting up of an "early warning" system for prompter identification and better diagnosis of payments imbalances; and the strengthening of international consultations with respect to the sharing of responsibilities for adjustment.

These suggestions stemmed from the report's major conclusions, which included the following[1]:

> First, countries need to formulate their balance of payments aims more clearly and base their individual and joint policies on aims that are mutually consistent as well as desirable from the viewpoint of a healthy world economy.
>
> Second, responsibility for adjustment must fall on both surplus and deficit countries.
>
> Third, countries need to have available and make use of a wider range of policy instruments—both general and selective—and to tailor such instruments more finely to the requirements of different circumstances and multiple policy goals. There is particular need in many cases to place greater reliance on fiscal policies, and less on monetary policies, in achieving internal economic balance, because of the important international ramifications of changes in monetary policy.
>
> Fourth, the proper combination of policy instruments depends on the situations encountered and the particular characteristics of the country concerned. No single policy prescription is appropriate in all cases.
>
> Fifth, countries must take continuous account of the impact of their actions on other countries. A special need for international consultation exists in the field of monetary policy to avoid inappropriate levels of interest rates.

In this chapter, with these recommendations in mind, we will first look back at the case of the United Kingdom (UK), which was the second important reserve currency country after the United States (US) under the Bretton Woods system.

The United Kingdom had established a trading bloc (customs bloc) linked by a preferential tariff regime through the Ottawa Agreement of 1932 and, to complement it, a currency area (sterling area) in which bloc member countries held British pound-denominated assets in London as their external reserves. However, the United Kingdom could not escape constraints arising from its balance of payments deficits with non-sterling area countries such as the United States. The United Kingdom maintained the fixed parity of 4.03 US dollars to the pound set at the time of the establishment of the Bretton Woods system, but in the post-war economic crisis, it was forced to drastically devalue the pound by 30.5 per cent (to 2.80 dollars to the pound) in 1949. At that time, however, Ireland, Australia, New Zealand, India, South Africa, Denmark, Norway, Egypt, and Israel followed suit with follow-on devaluations, so the United Kingdom's international price competitiveness was not enhanced in relation to these countries. In other words, the United Kingdom's role as a reserve currency country remained in some respects a burden at the time.

Thus, despite the apparently very large devaluation of the pound in 1949, the UK balance of payments did not show any noticeable improvement and its pound-denominated external debt remained at a high level. The share of the United Kingdom's pound-denominated external debt in the foreign exchange reserves held by the world as a whole fell from a high of 87 per cent in 1947, just after the end of the Second World War, to nearly 60 per cent in the early 1950s, but was still about twice the share of reserves held in US dollars. Subsequently, the share of the world's foreign exchange reserves held in the UK pound fell to around 30 per cent in the early 1960s, while the share in reserves held in US dollars rose to nearly 70 per cent. However, the external reserves (gold and US dollar assets) held by the United Kingdom were paltry compared to the reserve assets held by foreign countries in the UK pound (the United Kingdom's external liabilities). And once the pound unrest occurred, the United Kingdom's foreign exchange reserve provision was strained.

The OECD Working Party No.3 meeting, held just before the British general election in October 1964, was the last occasion for Professor Suard Postuma, Dutch central banker, to attend before his retirement. According to the recollections of van Lennep, who chaired the meeting,

Postuma suggested at the meeting that the UK balance of payments situation was extremely serious and that the British pound was overvalued, a view that many participants shared.[2]

However, under the Bretton Woods system, parity adjustments could only be made as a last resort with the IMF approval, when there was a state of "fundamental disequilibrium" where all other means of balance of payments adjustment had been tried to no avail. Moreover, it was not clear how "fundamental disequilibrium" was to be defined.

Before the 1949 devaluation, the British pound suffered another devaluation in 1931, both during Labour governments. Thus, when the Labour Party returned to power in place of the Conservatives at the October 1964 general election, there were rumours of a new devaluation of the British pound. In this setting, the Harold Wilson government sought to maintain the external value of the pound in order to wipe out the stigma of the former Labour governments. Unfortunately for this government, the Conservative government's pre-election expansionary fiscal policy management in a bid to gain public popularity in the hope of winning the election resulted in a significant deterioration in the UK current account in the face of growing domestic demand shortly after the Wilson Government started. In response, the Bank of England raised the official rate by 0.5 per cent to 5 per cent in February, then raised it to a critical level of 7 per cent in November and introduced an import surcharge. Furthermore, to extend rescue loans to the United Kingdom, the IMF decided to invoke the General Agreement to Borrow (GAB) for the first time and borrowed funds amounting to $450 million from eight countries including Japan, followed by an emergency loan of $ 3 billion with the central banks of 11 industrialised countries including the Bank of Japan, the Bank for International Settlements (BIS) and the US Export–Import Bank.

With such international supports, the Wilson Government succeeded in overcoming the first major pound crisis, and the Bank of England was able to reduce the official exchange rate from a critical level of 7 per cent to 6 per cent in June 1965. However, about a year later, with an outbreak of shipping strikes, another major pound crisis occurred amidst the declaration of a state of emergency on 23 May 1966. In response, in July that year, the Bank of England again returned the official exchange rate to the critical level of 7 per cent to defend the pound, and in October, the Labour Government invoked executive powers to freeze wages and prices for six months. Following these emergency measures, the United

Kingdom's overall balance of payments returned to surplus in the fourth quarter of 1966, and the Bank of England was able to cut the official discount rate by 0.5 per cent each in January and March 1967.

However, from the summer of 1967 onwards, the United Kingdom was again hit by major crises, both internally and externally. First, the third Middle East crisis erupted in June, followed by the port strikes in September. In response to the resulting selling pressure on the pound in the foreign exchange market, the Bank of England raised the official rate by 0.5 per cent in mid-October. But the attack on the pound did not abate and in November the Bank was forced to raise the official rate by 0.5 per cent again. The two increases in the official rate were followed on Tuesday 14 November by the announcement of the establishment of new loans to the United Kingdom by the central banks of major countries including the Bank of Japan through the BIS. However, the situation did not stop there, and a few days later, the British Government decided to implement a 14.6 per cent devaluation of sterling from 2.80 to 2.40 US dollars per pound.

As noted above, at the OECD WP3 meeting held just before the UK general election in October 1964, Postuma suggested that the British pound was overvalued, but the Bank of England including its "pound-first" Governor, Rowland Stanley Baring, 3rd Earl of Cromer, was opposed to its devaluation. And among economists, Roy Harrod and Joan Robinson, both highly respected Keynesians, had long argued against the pound devaluation. These two economists were so-called "elasticity pessimists", who argued that even if the devaluation of the pound caused a fall in the dollar value of UK exports, it would not bring about a significant increase in UK export volumes and a rise in the total value of exports in US dollar terms.[3] Roy Harrod argued in an article he contributed to The Times in August 1966 that the rise in import prices resulting from the devaluation of the pound would lead to spiral rises in wages and prices, which would weaken British price competitiveness. This scepticism about the effectiveness of the UK pound devaluation was shared by many British economists across the political spectrum. For example, John Hicks, Lionel Robbins, and Ralph Hawtrey were also of this opinion.

As an economist monitoring the UK economy in the Bank of Japan's Research Department, I closely followed the rapidly evolving economic and financial situation in the United Kingdom and debates among British economists over this period, and my reading in early autumn 1967 was that the devaluation of the British pound was inevitable and imminent.

As shown in a Box in Chapter 3, the cumulative decline of the domestic value of the British pound was enormous over the 15-year period from 1953 to 1968, with its loss measured in terms of consumer prices amounting to 61 per cent. A 40 per cent loss of its value in terms of wholesale prices was of the same magnitude as for the French franc. Unlike the French currency which was devalued by 17.5 per cent in the context of the 1958 monetary reform plan designed by Antoine Pinay and Jacque Rueff under the presidency of Charles de Gaulle (see below), the par value of the British pound remained unchanged since 1949 when it was devalued by 30.5 per cent to 2.80 dollars per pound.

In a paper entitled "The evolution of British incomes policy and its effects", published in the September 1967 issue of the Monthly Bulletin (referred to also in Chapter 2 of this book), I argued that the United Kingdom's poor price and economic performance was basically a result of policy mistakes with the priority of fiscal policy attached to economic growth and to running the UK economy at the limit of its capacity, assigning monetary policy basically to the defence of the pound exchange rate, not as a tool of domestic demand management and inflation control, and using incomes policy to contain upward pressure on nominal wages and prices. This argument was supported by my rather simple econometric analysis of the relationship between the UK unemployment rate and pay drift, the difference between average earnings growth and basic pay settlements in a situation where the National Board for Prices and Incomes, created by the Wilson government in 1965, was used as a main body to influence wage formation in the United Kingdom.

As the Bank of Japan, together with the central banks of some Western countries, was extending lines of credit to the Bank of England to help maintain the par value of the UK pound, some top BOJ officials were informed about the November 1967 Pound devaluation prior to the public release of Chancellor James Callaghan's statement scheduled at 9.30 pm on Saturday 18 November (*Greenwich* Mean *Time*), which was 6.30 am on Sunday 19 by Japan Standard Time. I received a telephone call from Kunikazu Takahashi, head of Europe Section of the Europe and America Division of the BOJ Research Department, at around 8 pm on Saturday at my home. He asked me to prepare a commentary note on the British pound devaluation to be sent immediately to the residence of Makoto Usami, then BOJ Governor.

Given my reading of the situation in the United Kingdom, I had brought analytical and statistical material on the UK economy back home from my office at the Bank to ensure that if there were any significant policy changes in the United Kingdom, and was ready to produce my commentary note on them quickly at home. My handwritten note, prepared overnight, was seen by my superiors at the BOJ and its original copy without any amendment was then handed to Toshihiko Yoshino, Director of Research Department, who immediately brought it to the Governor's residence before Chancellor Callaghan's statement was delivered in London.

In my note, I offered a short summary of my analysis of the fundamental causes for the weakening of UK international price competitiveness—as discussed in my aforementioned article published in the September 1967 Monthly Report of the Research Department—as well as burdens associated with UK military expenditure abroad and the intrinsic instability in British pound balances of the sterling area countries.

Soon afterwards, I worked out a publishable version of my commentary paper, to which Kazuhiko Isohata, Head of America Section added a short note on the implications of the British pound devaluation for the future of the US dollar and the Bretton Woods system. This revised version was published as a top article in the December 1967 issue of the Research Department Monthly Report.

The UK Treasury had not been as pessimistic as Harrod and other "elasticity pessimists" about the effect of the pound devaluation. According to an internal document dated 15 October 1964, the date of the UK general election, the Treasury measured that the price elasticity for UK exports was unlikely to fall below 2. However, on the assumption that the devaluation of the British pound would reduce UK export prices in US dollar terms by 10 per cent, it was judged that about half of the improvement in the UK trade balance resulting from this would be lost because of higher wages due to higher demand pressure arising from increases in UK exports as well as cost-push factors such as higher import prices resulting from the pound devaluation.[4] I was not aware of the internal document of the UK Treasury at the time of preparing my article, but argued for fiscal tightening in the United Kingdom to facilitate expenditure switching from domestic spending to exports for improving UK trade balance.

Roy Jenkins, who succeeded James Callaghan as Chancellor of the Exchequer after the failed defence of the pound and his resignation in

November 1967, was initially hesitant to raise taxes and cut spending. In the follow-up notes I published in the Monthly Reports of the Research Department in the early months of 1968, I continued to argue about the importance of further fiscal tightening in the United Kingdom. Eventually, Jenkins had to put forward further austerity measures in his budget proposals for the new financial year beginning in April 1968. Partly due to these fiscal measures, the growth rate of UK gross domestic demand fell slightly to 2.5 per cent in 1968 from 3.2 per cent in the previous year. With the J-curve effect after the pound devaluation, the UK current account deficit was reduced only modestly to $800 million in 1968 from some $1 billion in the previous year. The current account surplus (of about $1 billion) was finally achieved in 1969 when the growth of domestic demand fell to near zero. Real GDP growth in that year was about 2 per cent due essentially to an increase in UK exports. Thus, the United Kingdom finally achieved an adjustment in its balance of payments through expenditure switching.

In the process of external adjustment process in the United Kingdom with a status of the second important reserve currency country we have reviewed above, it is noteworthy that the Labour government put its prestige on the defence of the pound parity backed up with massive financial supports from other industrial countries. The Wilson government's last-minute attempt to avoid implementing drastic fiscal stringency, after succeeding the Conservative governments which had placed emphasis on maintaining high employment levels by expansionary policies, see Dow,[5] may be seen by outsiders as its "naivety" as a reserve currency country. Moreover, it should be noted that in November 1968, one year after the pound devaluation, the United Kingdom introduced, without prior notice to its trading partners, an import deposit system that required imports, excluding raw fuel, ships, and food, to deposit 50 per cent of import values for six months in order to deal with UK balance of payments difficulties. This can be seen as another example of the United Kingdom's "naivety" based on its status as the second most important reserve currency country.

* * *

Compared with the unsatisfactory economic policy management of the successive UK governments established by its Conservative Party, the conduct of economic policy in France, a non-reserve currency country, is noteworthy at least under the presidency of Charles de Gaulle. In 1958, Finance Minister Pinay succeeded in strengthening the French domestic economy and restoring the balance of payments position in a short time through a comprehensive economic restructuring plan as reviewed briefly immediately below.

France had devalued the franc six times since 1944 and had long been referred to as the "sick man of Europe". The successive devaluations of the French franc had been no more than passive measures to deal with past profligacy and were not effective in correcting the underlying weakness of the French economy. In contrast, the Pinay plan was based on a set of recommendations for economic reform made by the group of experts presided over by Jacques Rueff, an economist and advisor to the French government. It was composed of (i) a significant 14.93 per cent devaluation of the French franc, (ii) a change in the currency unit (a change in denomination with one-hundredth of the previous franc currency as a unit of the new franc currency), (iii) the government statement of its determination to maintain the par value of the new currency, (iv) fiscal austerity, and (v) the liberalisation of trade and foreign exchange transactions at a rapid pace with the restoration of the convertibility of the French franc in 1959.[6]

In his memoirs, James Callaghan recalled that balance of payments adjustment measures were undertaken by the United Kingdom under multilateral surveillance, mainly by the OECD WP3.[7] In contrast, the reform measures in France were designed and implemented at its own initiative.

Charles de Gaulle, under whose presidency the reform was pursued, is said to have criticised the reserve currency countries' ability to settle their balance of payments deficits by their currencies as an "exorbitant privilege". In fact, the term was used by *Valéry Giscard d'Estaing, who was appointed French minister of economy and finance in a reshuffle of Michel Debré's cabinet.*[8]

* * *

In an article "The devaluation of the British pound and its effects" which was published in the December 1967 issue of the BOJ Research Department Monthly Report, it is stated that "(T)he burden on the US dollar as practically the only reserve currency is likely to increase further. This will make an improvement in the US balance of payments more urgent and will call for greater international cooperation among the industrial countries to strengthen the stability of the international monetary system".

In the United States, Treasury Secretary Henry Fowler, at the request of President Lyndon Johnson himself, had made last-minute plans to avert a devaluation of the pound by means of a large loan to the United Kingdom. However, the British Labour government could not follow a policy of maintaining the pound parity at the expense of undergoing domestic deflation in exchange for obtaining loans from the United States.

Following the British pound devaluation of 17 November 1967, the US Federal Reserve (Fed) announced an increase in its official discount rate from 4.0 per cent to 4.5 per cent on Monday 20 November. On Wednesday 22 November, however, a big gold rush occurred in the London and Paris gold bullion markets. The central banks of eight Western countries, including the United States, the United Kingdom, West Germany, France, and Italy, had formed the London Gold Pool[9] in 1961 and co-ordinated concerted methods of gold sales to balance spikes in the market price of gold as determined by the London morning gold fixing while buying gold on price weaknesses so that the price of gold on the London bullion market did not deviate significantly from the USD 35/oz level. The Bank of France withdrew from the Gold Pool in July 1967, and the governors of the remaining seven central banks met in Frankfurt on Sunday 26 November to issue a statement on maintaining the gold value of the dollar and stabilising exchange rates. However, its effect was short-lived. By mid-December, the gold rush had resumed in the London and Paris gold markets. As a result, the United States, which had a 50 per cent share in the Gold Pool, had to sell about $1 billion worth of gold between the devaluation of the Pound and the end of 1967, and its gold holdings at the end of the year fell below 12 billion dollars for the first time since 1937.

On 1 January 1968, US President Lindon Johnson issued a special statement on strengthening the defence of the dollar, which included restrictions on direct investment and bank lending abroad and cuts in Federal government spending outside the United States. Despite this, there was another gold rush in the London and Paris gold markets in late February, and on 10 March a statement on maintaining the current price of gold was issued after a meeting of central bank governors in Basel, Switzerland, with no notable effect. Eventually, on 14 March, the

United States passed a law on the removal of statutory gold reserves (25 per cent gold reserve removal), which led to the closure of the London gold market on 15 March at the request of the United States. This was followed on 17 March by a meeting in Washington of the central bank governors of the seven countries participating in the Gold Pool, who decided to adopt a dual pricing system for gold. Thus, the market for gold traded by the private sector at a free price was separated from the market for gold traded between monetary authorities at the official price of 35 US dollars an ounce. This meant a partial cessation of the US dollar's convertibility with gold.

Prior to the adoption of the dual pricing system for gold, on 14 March, the Fed held a meeting of the Federal Open Market Committee (commonly known as the FOMC) to discuss a proposal from Charles Coombs, a senior vice-president of the Federal Reserve Bank of New York and special manager of the Open Market Committee of the entire Federal Reserve System, to expand the swap network between major central banks, including the BOJ, and the Bank for International Settlements. According to the minutes of the meeting,[10] which were subsequently made public, Governor Mitchell stated that the world was moving towards a fundamental imbalance and stated that the rules of the 1960s were no longer applicable in a situation where the demonetarisation of gold had begun to take shape. He then argued that the situation in the United States was different in some respects from that in the United Kingdom, but that the United States should not play second fiddle to the United Kingdom, which had sacrificed so much to defend the Pound.

In July 1968, shortly after the introduction of the gold dual price system, one of strong monetarists in the United States, Darryl Francis, President of the Federal Bank of St Louis, warned that the gold dual price system would cease to function if the free market price of gold deviated significantly from the official price of 35 dollars per ounce. He also argued that gold, the supply of which could fluctuate unpredictably due to factors such as the discovery of new gold mines, should be demonetised and that the Special Drawing Rights (SDRs), which the IMF Executive had decided to create in 1967, should be placed on the axis of the international monetary system alongside the US dollar. He suggested that if European monetary authorities and others did not wish to hold the US dollar as a reserve currency, the SDR should absorb the US dollars held by European monetary authorities. Furthermore, Francis criticised the capital outflow restrictions announced by President Johnson on 1 January that year to defend the dollar, arguing that the main way to restore confidence in the dollar was to control inflation and improve US trade balance by tightening fiscal and monetary policy.

Francis' emphasis on economic stability through tighter domestic demand management policies was in line with the view he expressed at the May 1967 meeting of the FOMC where he had argued that monetary policy should be tightened, but his views had been rejected.

The Fed raised the official discount rate from 4.5 per cent to 5.0 per cent on 22 March 1968, following the adoption of the dual price system, and from 5 per cent to 5.5 per cent on 19 April 1968. These modest monetary tightening measures were not driven by international considerations at the expense of domestic economic management. The accelerated monetary expansion that had begun in early 1967 was to reach 7 per cent by the end of 1968. This was considerably higher than the average annual growth rate of 2.6 per cent over the previous decade. Looking at domestic price developments, wholesale price inflation rose from an annual rate of 2 per cent in the second half of 1968 to 7.1 per cent in the first quarter of 1969. Consumer price inflation also increased from an annual rate of 4.7 per cent in the second half of 1968 to a sharp 6.3 per cent at an annual rate in the first quarter of 1969.

The Fed chairman at the time was William McChesney Martin, appointed in 1951 during the Truman presidency. He held the chairmanship for a long time, through the Eisenhower, Kennedy, and Johnson presidencies, until the end of January 1970, just after Nixon became president. Immediately after the official discount rate increase in December 1965, President Johnson called Martin to his ranch and asked him to keep interest rates low. Their discussions are said to have ended in a parallel line.[11] Martin replied to the President that if that was the case, someone else should be appointed Chairman of the Fed. He was also known to have said in a speech on 19 October 1955 that it is the job of the Fed to "take away the punch bowl just when the party gets going".[12]

In his book "Inside the Fed", Stephen Axilrod,[13] who joined the Fed as an economist during Martin's time as chairman and worked for successive chairmen up to Volcker and was his right-hand man in monetary policy planning during Volcker's time, commented on Martin as follows:

> I at first viewed Martin as little as more than a pleasant man with reasonable administrative skills, but without a strong understanding of the economics behind policy. Later, ... I came to view him as something of an artist in

policy, a man with an intuitive sense, and a man perceived, at least from my perspective, by his colleagues as fundamentally fair—all of which helped make him a very effective leader in the decision-making process.[14]

Judging from the portrait of Martin that emerges from Axilrod's description, the failure of US monetary policy to respond to inflation pressure adequately in the final period of his Fed chairmanship was the result of the Fed's group think, rather than Martin's personal policy initiative. I have already noted that St Louis Fed President Francis preached tighter monetary policy at the May 1967 FOMC meeting, but he was a heretic on that committee. Strong monetarists such as Milton Friedman criticised the Fed under Chairman Martin for its "capricious" decisions to manipulate interest rates and manage the money supply.

Arthur Burns, who succeeded Martin, was the first Fed chairman I met in person. In contrast to Martin, he had a distinguished career as an economist before becoming chairman of the Fed in 1970. After serving as chairman of the President's Council of Economic Advisers (CEA) during the Eisenhower administration, Burns taught at Columbia University and served as director of the National Bureau of Economic Research (NBER). When Burns visited Japan in April 1978, shortly after his resignation as Fed chairman, he had a *tête-à-tête* lunch meeting with BOJ Governor Teiichiro Morinaga. There he repeatedly used the phrase "as an economist, I think ..." in expressing his views. As Personal Assistant to Governor Morinaga, I attended their meeting and acted as interpreter for their conversation, as Morinaga used Japanese.[15]

Despite Burn's high reputation as an economist, the Fed's performance under his command was unsatisfactory as the guardian of currency value, far different from the German Bundesbank whose independence from the government was well ensured. Limiting my comment on his performance as Fed chairman during the period under review in this Chapter, I would simply note that while he opposed President Nixon's decision to close the "gold window", he "assured the President that I would support his new program fully", notwithstanding his reservations about the suspension of US dollar convertibility to gold.[16]

After his retirement, Burns delivered the 1979 Per Jacobson lecture with the title "The Anguish of Central Banking"[17] on the occasion of the IMF/World Bank Annual Meetings in Belgrade, Yugoslavia in September 1979. In his lecture, he explained a lot of reasons for the failure to control inflation in the United States during his time at the Fed, and stated: "(M)y conclusion that it is illusory to expect central banks to put an end to the inflation that now afflicts the industrial democracies does not mean that central banks are incapable of stabilizing actions; it simply means that their practical capacity for curbing an inflation that is continually driven by political forces is very limited". Commenting on this part of Burn's lecture, Axilrod wrote[18]: "Quite possibly true, certainly to a degree, but his statement was also perhaps either a recognition that he had not risen to the occasion or a rationalization for not having done so".

Notes

1. This summary is taken from an article "Balance of Payments Adjustment Policies" published by the Federal Reserve Bank of St. Louis in 1967.
2. Emile van Lennep, "Working for the World Economy", Nederlands Instituut voor het Bank-en Effectenbedrijf, Amsterdam, 1998, p. 149.
3. A. P. Thirlwall, "Balance of Payments Theory and the United Kingdom Experience", 3rd ed. Basingtoke, Macmillan, 1986, p. 156.
4. TNA: PRO T171/758/2(xlix), papers on exchange rate policy, 15 October 1964.
5. Christopher Dow, "The Management of the British Economy, 1945–1960", Cambridge University Press, 1964; "Major Recessions: Britain and the World, 1920–1995", Oxford University Press, 1998.
6. Michel-Pierre Chélini, "Le plan de stabilization Pinay-Rueff, 1958", Revue d'Histoire Moderne et Contemporaine, 2001/4, pp. 102–123.
7. James Callaghan, "Time and Chance", London, 1987, p. 171.
8. Michel-Pierre Chélini, ditto.
9. The contribution of the United States to the gold pool amounted to 120 tonnes, or 50 per cent of the total. The share of contributions from European countries were 11 per cent for West Germany, 9 per cent each for the United Kingdom, France, and Italy, and 4 per cent each for Belgium, the Netherlands, and Switzerland.
10. Federal Reserve Open Market Committee, Memorandum of discussion, 14 March 1968.

11. The Economist, "William Martin", 6 August 1998; Melody Petersen, "William McChesney Martin Die 91; Defined Fed's Role", New York Times, 29 July 1998.
12. Martin's quote is generally regarded as "take away the punch bowl just when the party gets going". His actual remarks were as follows: "The Federal Reserve, as one writer put it, is in the position of the chaperone who has ordered the punch bowl removed just when the party was really warming up". See William McChesney Martin,, Jr., "Address before the New York Group of the Investment Bankers Association of America", 19 October 1955.
13. Stephen Axilrod, "Inside the Fed: Monetary Policy and its Management, Martin through Greenspan to Bernanke", the MIT Press, Revised Edition, 2011, p. 26.
14. Axilrod and I became acquainted in 1970 when he was Deputy Director of the Research Division of the Federal Reserve Board and the author was an economist at the OECD Monetary Division, working on the OECD special project "Monetary Policy Studies", see Chapter 7. See also Chapter 1 of this book about his comment on my appointment as OECD Chief Economist in 1992.
15. Kumiharu Shigehara, Bank of Japan internal memorandum, 'Summary of Governor Morinaga's meeting with former Federal Reserve Chairman Burns', 10 April 1978, p. 7.
16. Doug French, "Burns Diary Exposes the Myth of Fed Independence", Mises Institute, 27 December 2012.
17. Arthur Burns, "The Anguish of Central Banking", the 1979 Per Jacobsson Lecture, Belgrade, Yugoslavia, 30 September 1979, The Per Jacobsson Foundation.
18. Axilrod, ditto, p. 64.

CHAPTER 6

Frameworks for International Monetary and Economic Co-Operation under the Bretton Woods System

This chapter relies rather extensively on Emile van Lennep's memoirs "Working for the World Economy".[1] *See* Chapter 22 *of this book on the Emile van Lennep Memorial Conference on a "Global Order for Sustainable Economic Growth".*

Let us now look at how the OECD came to be deeply involved in the UK balance of payments adjustment in the runup to the British pound devaluation of 1967 and thereafter (see Chapter 5).

James Callaghan, UK Chancellor of Exchequer at the time of the 1967 devaluation of the pound (later Prime Minister), wrote in his memoirs that shortly after taking office in October 1964, he had a meeting with van Lennep, Chairman of OECD Working Party No. 3 (WP3) who explained him about the need to devalue the UK pound but was unsure whether other countries would agree not to follow suit with its devaluation with parallel moves. Callaghan wrote that he himself at the time also thought such an agreement with other countries would be unlikely.[2]

On 4 November 1967, two weeks before the announcement of the pound devaluation, Denis Rickett, who was the UK representative at the OECD WP3, telephoned van Lennep to say that Callaghan wanted to meet him to follow up the discussion he had with van Lennep some three years ago.[3] In Callaghan's memoirs, it is stated that he had come to the conclusion that a pound devaluation was inevitable just before Rickett called van Lennep.

K. Shigehara, *The Bank of Japan, the OECD, and Beyond*,
https://doi.org/10.1007/978-981-97-5307-9_6

Van Lennep met Callaghan in London on 8 November. Callaghan's main concern was whether the six original members of the EEC, then known as the Inner Six,[4] would follow the devaluation of the British pound. In response, van Lennep, who was Chairman of the EEC Monetary Committee as well as Chairman of OECD WP3, said that he was not in a position to speak for the Inner Six, but that he would do his best to persuade its members not to follow through if the pound devaluation was not too large. Van Lennep also told Callaghan that according to IMF calculations, a pound devaluation of more than 15 per cent would likely be seen as a competitive devaluation.[5]

Van Lennep returned to Paris and immediately contacted his colleagues in the Inner Six. Germany, Belgium, Luxembourg, and Italy readily agreed, as did the Netherlands, namely they would not follow suit unless the devaluation of the British pound exceeded 15 per cent. In France, however, Finance Minister Michel Debré, who had served as Prime Minister under President de Gaulle, was uncomfortable that UK Chancellor of Exchequer had spoken about the pound devaluation through van Lennep rather than directly to him. While van Lennep was negotiating behind the scenes on the occasion of OECD Economic Policy Committee meeting at its Paris headquarters on 15 November, European Commission Vice-President Raymond Barre (later French Prime Minister under President Giscard d'Estaing) lobbied member countries, without consulting van Lennep as Chairman of the EEC Monetary Committee, for jointly acting to persuade the UK government not to devalue the pound in return for EEC's large-scale financial assistance. In van Lennep's eyes, this appeared to originate from a mercantilist motive—to prevent the pound devaluation from weakening France's international price competitiveness.

Eventually, at the last-minute meeting of the EEC Monetary Committee on Saturday 18 November, when the pound devaluation was announced, France reluctantly agreed that it would take co-ordinated action within the "Inner Six", i.e., not act alone in following the pound devaluation. This agreement was reported by van Lennep, in his capacity of Chairman of the EEC Monetary Committee, at a meeting of EEC finance ministers on 19 November, chaired by French Finance Minister Debré.

Immediately after the pound devaluation, Callaghan stated in a briefing to the UK House of Commons that he had a meeting with US Treasury Undersecretary Robert (Bob) Rosa shortly after his meeting with

OECD WP3 Chairman van Lennep. According to Callaghan's statement, Rosa was strongly opposed to a devaluation of the pound, arguing that international currency adjustment would be "impracticable" and that a devaluation of the pound would have a profoundly adverse impact on the stability of the international monetary system.

Van Lennep, who had read Callaghan's memoirs, later wrote in his own memoirs that while it was true that at the OECD WP3 meeting held just before the UK general election in October 1964, Postuma, Director of the Netherlands Bank, suggested that the British pound was overvalued and the representatives of other countries agreed on his observation, Callaghan's description that van Lennep told him about the need for a devaluation of the UK pound at their meeting was not accurate. In any event, Callaghan's version of their meeting was passed on by the Governor of the Bank of England to the central bank governors of other major countries and van Lennep became the target of their criticism.

International Co-operation Starting within Western European Countries

Let us now look back at the main events leading to the creation of OECD WP3.

After the end of the Second World War, the main foreign policy concern of the administration led by US President Truman was to rebuild the Western European countries, whose productive facilities had been severely damaged in the war, into a force capable of competing with the Soviet Union countries and their Eastern European allies in the Cold War. At the time, however, the US current account balance was in surplus and Western European countries were in a state of "dollar shortage" rather than "dollar excess" and dollar funds needed for them to import the materials necessary for their economic reconstruction were not readily available.

Against this backdrop, in July 1947, George Marshall, Secretary of State of the Truman administration, announced the European Economic Recovery Aid Plan (the so-called "Marshall Plan") in a commemorative speech at Harvard University. In 1948, the Organisation for European Economic Co-operation (OEEC) was created to allocate and distribute Marshall Plan aid and to plan for and effect a European Recovery Programme (ERP) for Western European countries and territories. The OEEC had 18 members: Austria, Belgium, Denmark, Greece, Ireland,

Iceland, Italy, Luxembourg, the Netherlands, Norway, Portugal, Sweden, Switzerland, Turkey, the United Kingdom, plus Western Germany (originally represented by Bizonia and the French occupation one). The US–UK jurisdiction of the Trieste Free Zone (later returned to Italy) was also a member of the OEEC for a period. Its first Secretary-General was elected, Paul-Henri Spaak, Prime Minister and Minister of Foreign Affairs of Belgium, and the OEEC, with its headquarters in Paris, was tasked with assisting members in formulating aid programmes and, subject to US approval, distributing aid funds to member countries.

Eventually, there was a growing realisation within Western European countries of the need for economic integration between them, both to expand and improve the efficiency of the market economy and to avoid future wars between European countries. Thus, in 1957, six countries—Belgium, France, Italy, Luxembourg, the Netherlands, and West Germany—signed the Treaty of Rome, establishing the European Economic Community (EEC).

Article 104 of the Treaty of Rome stated that each member shall pursue the economic policies necessary to achieve a high level of employment and price stability, as well as to maintain balance of payments and confidence in the currency and Article 107 states that each member shall treat exchange rate policies as a matter of common interest. The EEC member countries were responsible for co-ordination of their policies to ensure that balance of payments difficulties do not arise as a result of uneven management of economic and monetary policies. For this purpose, the Monetary Committee was created, which was also responsible for the management of the European Payments Union (EPU) within the OEEC.[6]

In the process of selecting the chairman of the EEC Monetary Committee, Marius Hiltrop, then Governor of the Netherland Central Bank, recommended the Bank's director and economist, Professor Suard Postuma (see above), to finance minister Henk Hostra. The reasoning was that central bankers had more independence than government bureaucrats and were therefore better suited to chair the Monetary Committee, which was to discuss the policies of the governments of EEC member countries. On the other hand, government sources in the other participating countries considered that bureaucrats involved in government policy-making would be preferable as chairpersons of this committee, and in this context, van Lennep, who had the backing of the Dutch deputy prime minister, Enst van der Bürger, became the first chairman of the Monetary Commission.[7] To balance the Dutch man's accession to the chairmanship, Emminger, a member of the board of the Deutsche Bundesbank, and Pierre Calvet, deputy governor of the Banque de France, were appointed vice-chairmen.

According to the first report of the Monetary Committee's activities published in February 1959,[8] six meetings were held during all of 1958. The first meeting was held in June of the same year, which indicates that they met frequently, once a month.

In this way, international economic policy co-operation among Western European countries was conducted within two frameworks: the EEC and the OEEC, whose members included the United Kingdom and other countries that did not participate in the EEC.

Creation of the OECD and the Roles of its Economic Policy Committee and its Working Parties

When Western Europe achieved economic recovery, the OEEC was dissolved and the Organisation for Economic Co-operation and Development (OECD) was established in 1961, with the 18 European member states of the OEEC, the United States and Canada as equal partners, and the 20 industrialised countries as original members.[9] As noted in Chapter 3, the initial plan of US administration under President Eisenhower was to invite Japan as an original member, but in the face of objection from some European countries, the US administration had agreed not to pursue it.

John Fitzgerald Kennedy, who became the 35th US President in January 1961, tried to make active use of the OECD from its beginning.

The Economic Policy Committee (EPC), which deals with economic policy issues in the OECD, held its first meeting at its Paris headquarters as early as April that year, even before the OECD was officially established on 30 September 1961. The day before, the US delegation requested a confidential meeting with Van Lennep, chairman of the EEC Monetary Committee. At that time, the US delegation consisted of Walter Heller, Chairman of the Council of Economic Advisors for the President (CEA), and Robert Rosa, Undersecretary of the Treasury, both of whom had just been appointed by President Kennedy.

Before they flew out of Washington for Paris, they were summoned by President Kennedy and were ordered to submit the US proposal to the Economic Policy Committee that:

- two working groups would be created under the EPC;
- one of which would specialise in the issue of economic growth and be called Working Party 2 (WP2)[10];
- the other one would specialise in the issue of balance of payments adjustment and be called Working Party 3 (WP3);
- given the nature of the issues to be dealt with at WP3, it would not, like WP2, involve all OECD member countries, but would be a forum for top officials of finance ministries and central banks from a limited number of countries with important roles in international finance;
- these officials who are currently working on policy issues such as monetary, fiscal, and exchange rate policies in their capitals, would gather at the Paris headquarters of the OECD; and
- van Lennep should be the first chair of OECD WP3.

The US proposal had been developed after a thorough study of the activities of the EEC Monetary Committee of which the chairman was van Lennep.

At the US delegation's meeting with van Lennep, it became clear that President Kennedy's main concern was the promotion of US economic growth. To realise this objective, the United States wanted the OECD Secretariat to conduct a study on economic growth, which would then be examined by WP2, while policy issues necessary to adjust balance of payments imbalances that might arise in the process of promoting economic growth would be dealt with by WP3 at its meetings which would need to be kept confidential. It was also made clear that the US government was very concerned that the US dollar's status as the key reserve currency country might be threatened by the instability of the British pound, and wanted WP3 to conduct surveillance with special attention to developments in UK balance of payments.

After preliminary, informal groundwork had been done with Van Lennep, the US delegation presented its proposal at a meeting of the EPC. It met with some opposition from smaller countries, but an agreement was eventually reached that the ten participating member countries would be the same as the EPU's Managing Board: the United States, Canada, the United Kingdom, France, West Germany, Italy, Belgium, Luxembourg, the Netherlands, and Switzerland. The first meeting of WP3 was held at the Paris headquarters of the OECD on 18–19 May 1961. The United States was represented by Rosa, Under Secretary of the Treasury, Ralph Young, Director of Research and Statistics the Federal Reserve System, well known for a book "The Federal Reserve System: objectives and functions" he compiled, and James Tobin, member of CEA who later won the Nobel Prize for economics. Canada was represented by Louis Razminski (later Governor of the Bank of Canada), and from the European side as well, there was a strong line-up of competent finance ministry officials and central bankers including Rickett of the UK treasury and Emminger of the Deutsche Bundesbank.

In his memoirs, van Lennep also wrote about the relationship between the OECD and the IMF at his time as chairman of WP3: "The US Treasury believed that the OECD had far more influence over the management of the UK economy than the IMF".

During his first official visit to Washington in October 1969 after becoming Secretary-General of the OECD, van Lennep was invited to a welcome dinner in his honour by Paul Schweitzer who was IMF Managing Director from 1963 to 1973. Schweitzer there stated that the OECD had done the job that should have been done by the IMF.[11]

An important background to this fact is that, amidst the liberalisation of capital flows between OECD countries, reserve currency countries such as the United Kingdom were experiencing international payments difficulties arising not only from current account deficits but also from large capital outflows, and the IMF's regular resources were not sufficient for its assistance to the United Kingdom. In response, in January 1962, the IMF established the "General Agreements to Borrow" (GAB) from the Group of Ten (G10) whose members were the United States, Japan, Canada, West Germany, France, Italy, Netherlands, Belgium, and Sweden as well as the United Kingdom, allowing the IMF to borrow funds from the central banks of these advanced countries and lend them countries experiencing economic distress such as the United Kingdom.

The IMF received stand-by funding ($ 6 billion at inception) under the GAB from the United States, the United Kingdom, West Germany, France, Italy, Japan, Canada, the Netherlands, Belgium, and Sweden. A similar arrangement was concluded with Switzerland, which was not a member of the IMF. Of the 11 countries, including Switzerland, all but

Japan were original participants in OECD WP3. The group's meetings at the level of finance ministers and central bank governors used to be held twice a year at the margin of the IMF-related ministerial meetings while the meetings of their deputies chaired by Emminger, Member of the Board of the German Bundesbank, were held more frequently with the support of a small secretariat comprising staff from the IMF, OECD, and BIS. (The GAB was phased out at the end of 2018 after member countries agreed its usefulness was "diminished and limited".)

Van Lennep also wrote in his memoirs about the relationship between the OECD and the IMF at the time, describing the following episode: "The US Treasury believed that the OECD had far greater influence over the management of the UK economy than the IMF".

The policy conditions for IMF extending lending to the United Kingdom with the funds to be obtained through the GAB were discussed in advance at a meeting of the OECD WP3 chaired by van Lennep which, with the support of the OECD Economics and Statistics Department, monitored the economic situation and policy developments in the United Kingdom. Immediately afterwards, the same participants held a meeting of G10 deputies under the chairmanship of Emminger to discuss the procedural aspects of invoking the GAB. Following this, the IMF Board of Executive Directors meeting in Washington, chaired by Managing Director Paul Schweitzer, decided on the provision of GAB funds to the United Kingdom. This was how the system worked.

WP3 met four times a year on average, with each meeting usually a day and a half in length and English and French, the official languages of the OECD, were used for the Secretariat documentation as well as for discussion.

As with the Economic Policy Committee, which usually met twice a year, discussion at WP3 was based on notes prepared by the OECD Economics Department, covering the analysis of national and international economic and financial developments, economic and balance of payments forecasts, analysis of economic and monetary policy issues and policy recommendations. The papers for WP3 discussion prepared by the OECD Secretariat were sent directly to the regular representatives of WP3 who were requested to treat them as confidential documents.

The regular representatives from the United States were limited to one each from the Treasury, Fed, and CEA, and one each from the finance ministry and the central bank for the other countries.

In order to allow sufficient time for discussion between national representatives, participation in WP3 discussions from the OECD Secretariat side was limited to the Head of the Economics Department who was also asked to make opening remarks on each of the topics suggested for discussion, while the Secretary-General used to make opening remarks at the luncheon he hosted for main representatives on the first day of the meeting. Main delegates were invited to the Chairman's dinner on the evening of the first day where he took initiative for discussion on topics of his choice.

For each country, about three staff members were allowed to sit behind the main representatives sitting at a round table. A limited number of members of OECD staff economists wearing special badges were also allowed to follow discussion inside the meeting room.

At the end of each WP3 meeting, the Chairman orally summarised the discussions, and later a note from OECD Head of Economics Department covering a confidential letter written and signed by the Chairman with his summary of discussions was sent directly to each of the main national delegates who attended the meeting. There were no specific rules as to how this letter was to be handled within the participating countries, e.g., whether it was to be circulated to finance ministers, central bank governors, etc., and it was left to the discretion of the national delegates. However, it was strictly forbidden for either the participants or the Secretariat to divulge the contents of the meeting to the media.

Paul Volcker became one of the regular participants of WP3 after his appointment as Undersecretary of the Treasury in 1969. But he had earlier attended WP3 meetings from time to time at a staff level. In his book written with Toyoo Gyooten "Changing Fortunes: The World's Money and the Threat to American Leadership" he recalled that on those occasions, he had felt a firm sense of solidarity and camaraderie among the regular participants.[12] In it, he praised van Lennep as a typical example of a distinguished official of the Dutch monetary authorities who had been sent to international organisations, adding that this showed the sincerity of the Dutch attitude towards international organisations.[13]

In an article titled "WP3: High-level policy making in a stimulating forum", Andrew Crockett, who was a regular member of WP3 as executive director of the Bank of England and appointed its Chairman in 1993 before his service as General Manager of BIS starting in the following year, wrote that "a WP3 discussion was a rewarding intellectual, as well as policy-making, experience".[14]

Japan Invited to Join the OECD as its First Member Country from Asia

The Japanese monetary authorities had sought a way to join WP3 before Japan's formal accession to the OECD was achieved. After Japan joined the IMF in May 1952, shortly after West Germany joined it in February 1952, it concluded GAB as a member of G10 to supplement the IMF resources, as mentioned above. Japan took this opportunity to emphasise the important role it had come to play in international finance, and wished to join the OECD's EPC and WP3, and then, using this as a breakthrough, to become a member of other OECD committees and working parties, leading to full membership of the OECD.

With this plan, Japan lobbied the United States and approached representatives from European countries participating in the WP3 meeting held in November 1962 (the first meeting was held in May the previous year, see above). However, WP3 chairman van Lennep expressed concern that making Japan a member of WP3 at the stage before it joins the OECD would create difficult problems over the treatment of small European countries that were dissatisfied with their inability to participate in WP3. Subsequently, Japan held negotiations in the capitals of major Western countries towards participation in WP3, but eventually came to consider that it would be more sensible to realise its participation in WP3 through OECD membership rather than aiming to join WP3 before joining the OECD.

In his article "Japan and the OECD: How the sun rose on global era", Peter Carroll and William Hynes wrote that on the domestic front, only the Japanese Socialist Party opposed Japan's accession to the OECD, arguing that it was an anti-communist move that would alienate the Soviet Union and China, but there was no significant public opposition against Japan joining the OECD.[15] However, in the context of bilateral negotiations, UK Chancellor of the Exchequer Dereck Heathcoat Amory noted that the problem of Japan was "a bit awkward" and would complicate trade issues if it was brought into a "European organization". German Economics Minister Ludwig Erhard also noted that European countries could not agree on how to treat Japan regarding trade and membership issues.[16]

A solution to prepare Japan's entry into the OECD was found in the shape of its participation in the Development Assistance Group (DAG), established in January 1960 to promote official assistance to less developed countries. This group with a membership limited to the major aid donors associated with the OEEC had no difficulty in accepting the US proposal for Japan's joining it.[17] The DAG became the OECD's Development Assistance Committee (DAC) on the OECD's establishment in 1961.

In the above-mentioned book, Peter Carroll and William Hynes wrote: "Japan's entry transformed the OECD into a more inclusive organisation, and as the first Asian economy to achieve rapid and major economic development, for 50 years Japan has brought an Asian-Pacific perspective to a predominantly Atlantic organisation".

President Kennedy played an important role in promoting Japan's entry into the OECD, following the move initiated by the Eisenhower administration. He lived to see Japan sign an official invitation to join the OECD in 1963, but was assassinated in November of that year.

Immediately after Japan's accession to the OECD on 28 April 1964, at the EPC meeting held in June of the same year, it was decided that Japan would also become a member of WP3 along with the EPC. The first WP3 meeting in which Japan's representative participated was held in July of the same year. It was attended by Makoto Watanabe, Director-General of the International Finance Bureau of the Ministry of Finance, and Haruo Maekawa, Executive Director (later Deputy Governor and then Governor) from the Bank of Japan.

Notes

1. Emile van Lennep, "Working for the World Economy", Nederlands Instituut voor het Bank-en Effectenbedrijf, Amsterdam, 1998.
2. James Callaghan, "Time and Chance", London, 1987, p. 171.
3. Emile van Lennep, ditto, pp. 153–160.
4. The seven original members of the European Free Trade Association (EFTA), established in 1959—the United Kingdom, Denmark, Norway, Sweden, Switzerland, Austria, and Portugal—were known as the "Outer Seven".
5. Jacques Pollack, who, like van Lennep, was Dutch and an IMF Economic Adviser, had told van Lennep during the IMF Rio de Janeiro Annual Meeting in September 1967 that according to his staff's calculations the UK pound was overvalued by about 15 per cent (Emile van Lennep, ditto, p. 153).

6. This payment alliance was established in 1950 to enable countries receiving US aid funds under the Marshall Plan to diversify the settlement of funds between them in their own currencies rather than in scarce dollar funds.
7. Emile van Lennep, ditto, p. 90.
8. Communauté Economique Europeénne, "Premier Rapport d'Activité du Comité Monétaire", Bruxelles, février 1959.
9. Matthieu Leimguber and Matthias Schmelzer (eds), "The OECD and the International Political Economy since 1948", Palgrave Macmillan, 2017.
10. In addition to Working Party 2, which specialised in economic growth issues, Working Party 4 (abbreviated as WP4), which specialised in inflation problems, was established in a later year. Furthermore, in 1980, these two working parties were merged and renamed Working Party 1 (WP1 for short) on Macroeconomic and Structural Policies.
11. Emile van Lennep, ditto, p. 213.
12. Paul Volker and Toyo Gyoten, "Changing Fortunes: The World's Money and the Threat to American Leadership", Times Books, 1992, p. 30. Volcker was appointed Assistant Secretary of the Treasury for Currency by President John Fitzgerald Kennedy in 1963 and was appointed Under Secretary of the Treasury for Monetary Affairs by President Richard Nixon in 1969.
13. Volcker, ditto, p. 31 and p. 49. He did not identify any other names as typical examples of the Netherlands providing competent officials to international organisations when he made this point.

    In fact, there were many other Dutchmen besides Emile van Lennep who made important contributions to international organisations in the area of monetary and financial matters. Here, I would mention Marius Holtrop, who, as Governor of the Netherlands Central Bank, made constructive contributions to the reform of the international monetary system and was also President of the Bank for International Settlements (BIS), known as the "central bank of central banks".

    Jelle Zijlstra, who succeeded Holtrop as Governor of the Netherlands Central Bank after a short period in the post of Prime Minister of the Netherlands, was also President of the BIS. Johan Witteveen was Managing Director of the IMF in the 1970s, and more recently Willem Frederik Duisenberg was the first President

of the European Central Bank after his service as Governor of the Netherlands Central Bank.
14. Andrew Crockett, "WP3: High-level policy making in a stimulating forum" in "The OECD a 50: Better Policies for Better Lives", OECD, 2011.
15. Peter Carroll and William Hynes, "Japan and the OECD: How the sun rose on a global era", OECD Observer, No. 298, Q1 2014, pp. 8–9.
16. United States Department of State, "Memorandum of Conversation, Bonn, 11 December 1959", Item 85 in *Foreign relations of the United States, 1958–1960, Western European integration and security, Canada, (1958–1960)*, Volume VII, 1959; United States Department of State, "Memorandum of Conversation, 11 January 1960", Item 96 in *Foreign relations of the United States, 1958–1960, Western European integration and security, Canada, (1958–1960)*, Volume VII, 1960.
17. The Foreign Affairs Oral History Collections for Diplomatic Studies and Training, "Interview with C. Douglas Dillon", 1987.

CHAPTER 7

My Work at the OECD Monetary Division in the Early 1970s

My first assignment at the OECD Economics and Statistics Department (ESD) began in January 1970. The ESD consisted of two research wings: the General Economics Branch and the Country Studies Branch, in both of which a director and a deputy director managed several divisions specialised in specific fields. It also had the statistics division under the direct control of ESD Head who was also called OECD Chief Economist. The total number of staff in ESD was around 120 when I joined it. In the early 1990s, when I was appointed OECD Chief Economist, the Statistics Division had been separated from the Department whose name was changed to the Economics Department (ECO) and I was called Head of ECO and OECD Chief Economist. By that time, the total number of staff at ECO had increased to about 180.

At the time I joined ESD, its Head and OECD Chief Economist was Christopher Dow. His contribution to the OECD is well documented in Andrew Britton, "John Christopher Roderick Dow 1916–1998",[1] in which he wrote: "he (Dow) believed that economic policy was about the management of demand, using fiscal or monetary measures as appropriate. He did at one time consider that a monetary target could be a means to that end, but he never accepted the theory underlying monetarism". Dow's view was naturally reflected in the title of the OECD report "The Role of Monetary Policy in Demand Management: The experience of six major countries"

K. Shigehara, *The Bank of Japan, the OECD, and Beyond*,
https://doi.org/10.1007/978-981-97-5307-9_7

(1975), which I as Head of OECD Monetary Division co-authored with Niels Thygesen, see below.

While running ESD, Dow was also a member of the OECD management team as Assistant Secretary-General, the post below the Secretary-General and Deputy Secretary-General. At the time, British economists had key managerial posts in ESD, with John Fay as Dow's Deputy and Stephen Marris as Director of the General Economics Branch, which was composed of Balance of Payments Division, Monetary Division, Growth Studies Division, and Price Studies Division. The Head of Monetary Division was Robert Sammons, who was seconded from the US Federal Reserve (Fed)'s International Finance Division where he was Associate Director. He was succeeded by Niels Thygesen, Professor of Economics at the University of Copenhagen, and eventually I succeeded Thygesen as Head of Monetary Division.

The "Nixon Shock" and its Aftermath

One important task of the Monetary Division at the time was the preparation of background papers for monetary policy discussion at the Economic Policy Committee (EPC), which met twice a year in spring and autumn, and its Working Party No. 3 (WP3), which met about four times a year. In analysing the monetary and financial situation in major OECD countries, close attention was paid to developments in short- and longer-term interest rates, money supply as a quantitative monetary indicator and its sources, such as bank credit to the private and public sectors and the balance on non-monetary transactions under the Bretton Woods system of fixed exchange rates. The analyses submitted to these meetings were then updated and published in the OECD "Economic Outlook" (EO), which was published twice a year, in principle in June and December.

My recollection is that it was Netherlands Treasurer General Coen Oort who first stated at the May 1971 meeting of WP3 that the US economy was in a state of "fundamental disequilibrium". However, this is not mentioned in van Lennep's memoirs, and my memory may be wrong. Be that as it may, Yusuke Kashiwagi, then an influential bureaucrat at the Japanese Finance Ministry recalled: "I spoke to some people in Europe about the practical implications of the 'Nixon shock'. We in Japan had initially concentrated on the issue of what would happen to the yen-dollar exchange rate. But it turned out that the scale of the problem was much larger than that, and that a multilateral currency adjustment involving all major currencies was on the agenda. This point was most clearly explained to me by OECD Secretary-General Emile van Lennep whom I met in Paris immediately after the Nixon announcement on the night of 15 August 1971, US time (16 August, Japan Standard Time). Van Lennep said to me that the question was not just how to adjust the exchange rates of the US dollar against major non-US currencies but also about how the exchange rates among non-US currencies should be adjusted, and that such a large-scale multilateral currency adjustment would be a difficult task. He expected that it would be around Christmas time that we would be able to finalise our negotiations about it". Kashiwagi then observed: "It was a brilliant analysis and even recalling it later, van Lennep's conclusion was spot on".

Some aspects of negotiations at the levels of finance ministers and central bank governors and their deputies leading to the Smithsonian Agreement in December 1971 are described in van Lennep's memoirs (pp. 244–247). He there wrote that "(I)t proved possible to convene a meeting of ministers of the G10 countries at short notice. The Secretariats of the OECD and the IMF were asked to prepare estimates of the balance of payments adjustments which would be needed to attain lasting equilibrium, so as to provide a basis for negotiations on the required exchange rate adjustments. The reports from the OECD and the IMF, which were, incidentally almost identical, were discussed within the Working Party 3. Although the national delegates were usually tireless in arguing that the Secretariats' estimates of national balance of payments positions are much too pessimistic, on this occasion the very opposite was in evidence".[2]

I would add that since shortly after the devaluation of sterling in 1967, ESD had been analysing the sustainability of current account imbalances and the effects of multilateral currency adjustment on the international price competitiveness of major countries and their trade and current account balances. In this context, measures of nominal effective exchange rates were first published in the July 1972 issue of EO (p. 109), shortly after the United Kingdom's transition to a floating rate system in June that year. After I returned to the Bank of Japan, ESD worked on real effective rate measures of the international competitiveness of OECD member countries which take into account not only nominal exchange rate movements but also relative changes in domestic prices and export prices, as well as the cost competitiveness index based on total costs per unit of output in the manufacturing sector. Trends in the real effective exchange rates using export prices were first published in the December 1976 issue of OECD Economic Outlook (p. 62) and trends in the real effective exchange rates using export prices, consumer prices, and unit labour costs in the manufacturing sector were first published in its July 1977 issue (p. 71).

Proposal of OECD Monetary Policy Studies

In June 1969, *ESD* submitted a note "Proposed Studies of the Effects of Monetary Policy" to the EPC.[3] It was spelled out in this note that "(T)he papers which have hitherto been presented to the Committee have taken the form of notes on recent trends in major countries. Various reasons suggest that it would be desirable to undertake more detailed analysis of monetary developments than was made in the previous studies:

a. Increased use has in the recent period been made of monetary policy, and in more countries than previously, as a means of controlling demand, and as a consequence more evidence is becoming available as to the nature of its impacts. It would be useful to examine this evidence on an international basis, and to compare the effects on demand of monetary policy in different countries.
b. The volatility of capital movements appears to have increased; and the increased use of monetary policy has meant that national monetary policies have had larger effects on international capital flows. … Since the effects depend on the relative posture of monetary policies in different countries, they can clearly best be evaluated in the context of studies of different monetary policies in at least the major financial countries".

In this context, *ESD* proposed that "more detailed studies should be made of both (a) the effects of monetary policy on internal demand and (b) the external effects on capital flows and balance of payments" and the results when available should be presented to EPC and to WP3.

In retrospect, one might find it striking that *ESD* at the time did not propose more detailed studies on the effects of monetary policy on inflation in addition to (a) and (b) above. In this connection, I would recall that the report of the OECD Secretary-General, entitled "Inflation - The Present Problem",[4] published at the end of 1970, shortly after the start of the OECD monetary policy studies, stated that "(A)lthough there has been much debate in recent years as to whether fiscal or monetary policy is more important, the OECD's own practical experience on economic stabilisation issues indicates that fiscal and monetary policy both have important roles and should operate in close coordination. They should not be used in a one-sided way". It went on to say that "(I)n terms of monetary policy, the growing impact of international capital flows raises the question of whether new policy instruments need to be used in the light of recent experience".[5]

ESD proposed that monetary policy studies would be carried out by the Monetary Division within it, which would however need to be strengthened by the employment of short period consultants, and that a set of its studies of the effects on monetary policy would represent an undertaking comparable in scale with the study on the use of fiscal policy—proposals for which were approved by the Committee as long ago as 1964.

In that year, in order to deepen the understanding of the role of demand management policy, which was considered to be an important policy instrument not only for running the domestic economy but also for facilitating the adjustment of the balance of payments, the OECD had commissioned a special group of experts, chaired by Walter Heller, a professor at the University of Minnesota who was chairman of the US President's Council of Economic Advisers, to produce a report on the use of fiscal policy. Professor Bent Hansen of Uppsala University, the oldest university in Scandinavia, played a central role in the work of this group. Professor Ryutaro Komiya from Japan also participated in the group. The results of their work were published by the OECD in 1968 as "Fiscal Policy for a Balanced Economy: Experience, Problems and Prospects" by Walter Heller and others, and Professor Bent Hansen's book "Fiscal Policy in Seven Countries" published in January 1969.

In its note sent to EPC, *ESD* stated that the methods of work proposed for detailed studies on monetary policy would be "very different" from these reports on fiscal policy. It stated that "(T)he need appears to be not for a discussion of the use of monetary policy, but study of its effects; and this can best be undertaken as a Secretariat Study not an independent report". It stressed that the Secretariat Study would have the limited aim of factual assessment of the operations and effects of monetary policies, and that discussion of the appropriateness of monetary policies, in the light of their domestic and international effects, would remain the business of WP3 and EPC.

Beginning of OECD Monetary Policy Studies

The OECD Monetary Division's work on monetary policy studies along the line proposed by the ESD management was a pioneering task and a difficult undertaking. Even when it came to the instruments of monetary policy in the major countries, at that time, in addition to the traditional instruments of central bank lending policy, securities dealing operations, and reserve ratio changes, there were various forms of quantitative regulation of bank credit flows and market interest rates, as well as foreign exchange controls on international capital transactions, not merely for external purposes but for domestic liquidity management. The question was how these instruments of monetary policy were used, how domestic financial conditions changed because of their use, how the total volume of domestic credit, short-term money market interest rates, bank lending rates and yields on longer-term financial and capital market investment instruments changed, and how the real economy changed as a result of these changes in the financial sector of the economy. What was the impact on the real GDP growth rate, the output gap and the inflation rate as a result, and what was the impact on international capital flows and current balance of payments under the fixed parity system of the time?

The plan was to produce a syntheses report after the completion of individual country reports dealing with these issues. It was the time when the central bank literature on monetary policy was on presenting the instruments and their impact on operational targets with very little on the further process of its transmission, and ESD stated in its note submitted to EPC that "(T)aking account of the convenience of undertaking the studies in succession, and the difficulties of finding appropriate experts rapidly, the studies would best be envisaged as requiring a number of years to complete".

It was my involvement in this project that led to my appointment to the OECD Monetary Division. The work actually started in early 1970. Peter Till, an English economist, had started a study on Germany by the time I arrived at the OECD. It was being followed by a study on Italy by Isaac Menashe, a Greek-American from the Federal Reserve Bank of New York.

On learning that my wife Akiko was due to give birth to our second child at the end of the year 1969, Robert Sammons, then Head of Monetary Division, kindly had told me that the timing of my arrival at the OECD should be postponed until sometime after that. This gave me six months after my passing the OECD examinations, and I was able to work at the two key sections in the Domestic Research Division of BOJ's Research Department: the Industry and Trade Section and the Monetary and Fiscal Section, which proved to be useful for my later work on the OECD study on the working and effects of Japanese monetary policy. (I actually started my work at the OECD in January 1970, and in March of that year, Akiko joined me in Paris from Tokyo with our son Hiroaki, who had just turned two, and our daughter Fuyumi, who was only three months old.)

While Till and Menashe were working on the two countries, my main task was to prepare background notes on recent financial developments and monetary policy trends for discussion at each WP3 meeting.

When the EPC approved ESD's proposal for its studies on the working and effects of monetary policy in major OECD countries, it was agreed that once draft reports were prepared, meetings of high-level experts of these countries were to be convened to seek their comments. It was envisaged that six countries would be covered and the chief representatives from these countries had their first meeting at the Paris headquarters of the OECD just before my arrival at the OECD in late January 1970. They were: Robert Solomon, Adviser to the Board and Director of the Division of International Finance, and Stephen Axilrod, Associate Director of the Division of Research and Statistics (later Director of the Monetary Policy Division), both at Fed, Sadao Ishida, Advisor of the Research Department at BOJ, Horst Bockelmann, Bundesbankdirektor at Deutsche Bundesbank (later Head of its Research Department, after which Economic Adviser of the BIS), Pierre Berger, Directeur Général des Etudes at the Banque de France, Leslie Dicks-Mireaux, Advisor of the Bank of England, and Antonio Fazio, Head of the Economics Department of the Banca d'Italia (later its Governor).

The studies on Germany and Italy proved to be very difficult, and the draft reports on Germany, rewritten three times, were rejected at the experts' meetings. One of the problems was that the Bundesbank itself did not have a clear view of the issues addressed in the draft reports, and the verbal explanations made by its representatives at the meetings themselves could not convince the monetary experts of the other countries nor the OECD Secretariat. Similar problems arose in the draft report on Italian monetary policy.

Report on Japanese Monetary Policy

When I started to work on the OECD report on Japanese monetary policy as the third project in 1971, I was fortunate to have the chance to discuss the conduct of BOJ's money market operations with Shinichiro Shirai (later Chairman of a big money market dealing house in Japan), who had worked at its Market Operations Department (*Eigyou-kyoku)* before coming to Paris as a member of the BOJ's representative office there. On the basis of his verbal explanations about the way the Department conducted its money market operations at times of monetary policy tightening, I from an economist's point of view, developed my own conception of how to explain the mechanism through which the impacts of BOJ's monetary policy instruments were transmitted to the financial and real sectors of the economy to affect its ultimate objective. In doing so, I paid attention to an analytical framework for monetary policy management which was being developed by US academics at the time: the "three-stage approach" in which the financial variables that the central bank could closely control were called its "operating targets" while such variables as monetary and credit aggregates and yields on longer-term financial and capital market investment instruments were considered as its "intermediate targets", and such variables as real economic growth, the rate of inflation or external balance of payments adjustment that the central bank wished to achieve were called its "final targets".

In Japan under the fixed parity system, when the domestic economy heated up, the current balance of payments deteriorated and monetary policy tightening became necessary, BOJ used to raise its official interest rate and impose quantitative controls on major banks' credit to the non-bank private sector through the so-called "window guidance", but it did not impose quantitative credit controls on other financial institutions. However, its operations to adjust the availability of funds in the short-term money market and resultant changes in market interest rates affected the lending attitude of those banks not subjected to its "window guidance". My tentative proposition using the framework of the three-stage approach to monetary policy management was that BOJ had de facto adopted two operating targets concomitantly: (a) major banks' credit to the non-bank sector, subjected to quantitative credit controls, and (b) short-term money market interest rates, as a means to influence credit to the non-bank sector by the financial institutions not subjected to BOJ's "window guidance". At the same time, BOJ relied on exchange controls to restrain the availability of external funds to the Japanese non-bank sector. In this setting, the development of broad measures of money supply was largely in line with domestic bank credit, and both could be called BOJ's "intermediate targets" to achieve its "final target" which was Japan's current account adjustment under the fixed exchange rate system. This proposition was supported by my econometric work on the effects of changes in short-term money market interest rates on domestic bank credit to the non-bank private sector.

With regard to the effects of monetary policy on the real economy, I conducted an econometric analysis on the impacts of Japanese commercial bank lending rates on business inventory investment, private capital formation, private housing construction, and private consumption, with help from Akira Yajima who was head of the Econometric Unit in ESD. The results of our joint work were quite convincing in showing the effectiveness of Japanese monetary policy as an economic stabilisation measure along the line of my proposition about its transmission mechanism.

By the time my first draft on the main analytical part of the draft report was completed, Niels Thygesen replaced Sammons as the Head of Monetary Division and he drafted succinct concluding remarks for the draft report. We then travelled to Japan to hold discussions with senior officials of BOJ on the draft report. The Market Operations Department was represented by Takashi Tamaki, then Head of the General Affairs Division (later Executive Director in charge of domestic monetary policy, after which President of Chiba Bank, the second largest local bank in Japan), who accepted my proposition for explaining the transmission mechanism of Japanese monetary policy within the financial sector, although BOJ did not officially admit the use of the three-stage approach to monetary policy management.

My analysis of the effects of Japanese monetary policy on the real economy was discussed at our meeting with Bunji Kure, then Deputy Director of the Bank's Research Department. My reading of longer-run trends in various macroeconomic indicators suggested that one could make a more positive assessment of the role of Japanese monetary policy as an instrument of demand management than the BOJ's official view shown in its publications. At the end of our discussion, Kure came to agree on the monetary policy implications of my reading of these economic indicators.

The draft report on Japanese monetary policy was therefore sent to a meeting of OECD monetary experts without any major revision. It was fortunately well received by them, in particular by Axilrod from the Fed. The final report, thus completed in less than a year after the start of my work, was submitted first to WP3 in May 1972 and then to the EPC, which agreed to its publication as the first volume of the OECD Monetary Studies Series. However, at this time, Secretary-General van Lennep was unable to agree on a proposal from Dow and other senior officials in ESD that I should be named as the author of the report. In the end, the report's "preface" stated that the publication was under the full responsibility of the OECD Secretary-General. When the report was published in December 1972, "The Economist" in the United Kingdom ran a two-page article on it, and Dow sent me a note stating: "I am very sorry that we were unable to include your name in the published report. I am very pleased that 'The Economist' has presented your research in such detail and with such care. I hope that this recognition of your work will be some reward for your diligence".

In an article on the great achievements of Christopher Dow as an economist, Andrew Britton (see above) added a comment: "Christopher had been seen as a rather difficult person to work for, not least because of his close attention to details. ... it was aesthetic as well as intellectual. He would pay close attention to the design of publications, and consult widely about the colour to use on the covers". But, for the OECD publication of "Japanese Monetary Policy" as the first in the OECD Monetary Policy Studies Series, Dow let me alone decide the colour of its cover. I chose dull pale green mixed with blue, and the same colour was used for all the other volumes in the Series.

By the way, Dow's appointment as an Executive Director responsible for economic research at the Bank of England in 1973 was a big surprise to many in the central bank circle and to me as well. One day before his departure from the OECD, he came to my office without prior notice. He said to me "money matters" and then smiled. Sometime earlier, he had asked me to write a think piece on the importance of money. Marris proposed my piece to be published in the forthcoming EO, but Dow did not agree to it for some unknown reasons. I was unsure if Dow had this episode in his mind when he came to see me on that day, but I guessed that what he meant by "money matters" was that the salary and fringe benefits he would earn as an Executive Director of the Bank of England and its Chief Economist compared favourably with the money he received as OECD Assistant Secretary-General and Chief Economist.

Many years later, in early 1992, immediately after reading the Financial Times report on my appointment as OECD Chief Economist, Dow sent me a handwritten letter of congratulations at the BOJ Institute of Monetary and Economic Studies I then headed. In return, I wrote to him that I still treasured the comforting letter he had sent me about the "The Economist" article on the OECD Report on Japanese Monetary Policy, enclosing a copy. He wrote back to me, saying: "I had forgotten all about that, but I didn't realise how much you cared about it ... In fact, my wife also still remembers your wife. She suggests that we should have dinner together next time you both come to London". Eventually, when I visited London as OECD Chief Economist and saw Mervyn King, then Executive Director of Research at the Bank of England (later Deputy Governor and then Governor) in his office, Dow was present by his arrangement, and I had the opportunity to meet my former boss at the OECD again after almost 30 years.

Completing OECD Reports on Monetary Policy Studies in their Entirety

In the summer of 1972, when the OECD report on Japanese monetary policy was submitted to the EPC, Dow asked Masaru Hayami, then BOJ's Chief Representative in London (later the Bank Governor of 1998–2003) whether BOJ could agree to my promotion to Head of the OECD Monetary Division and the extension of my original three-year fixed term contract for one year until early 1974. Earlier, Marris had asked me to become a permanent member of ESD, which I declined. BOJ agreed to Dow's proposal and in September 1972, I was promoted to Head of Monetary Division to succeed Thygesen. Before the end of my extended term of office, the ESD management team established a list of both internal and external candidates to succeed me as Head of Monetary Division, but it found none of them satisfactory and asked BOJ to extend my term of office for the second time. Thus, I had to remain in the post until the OECD Monetary Policy Studies were completed in their entirety.

One of the difficult problems with the Italian monetary policy study, which had started as the second in the series of country report, was that Fazio insisted that the monetary base was the Banca d'Italia's operating target. However, the Bank's economic model which included the monetary base as an explanatory viable was an annual model, and did not clarify causality by carefully incorporating the lag structures for explanatory variables used in the model. In addition, the concept of the monetary base in Italy was peculiar and included postal savings as a component. In my view, which was reflected in our revised draft OECD report, the adoption of the monetary base as a key financial variable in Italian monetary policy operation helped the Banca d'Italia to deal with relatively longer-term policy issues, but the question of whether any separate monetary variable had ever been used as the Banca d'Italia's short-term operating target remained unanswered in its model. In the end, this observation was accepted by the Banca d'Italia, and our version of the OECD report on Italian monetary policy went on to be published in May 1973 as the second in the OECD Monetary Policy Studies Series.

One of the reasons for the difficulty in finalising the OECD report on German monetary policy, which started as the first in the series of country studies, was that the Bundesbank, following the view of Helmut Schlesinger, then Head of Economic Research Department (later Vice-President and President), had positioned the level of "bank liquidity" and its ratio to bank deposits as its operating targets. However, the issue I raised as to whether they were indeed optimal operating targets was not convincingly addressed by Horst Bockelmann who represented the Bundesbank at the OECD monetary experts' meetings.

After the resignation of Till who started the OECD study on German monetary policy, Hermann Dudler, who had been in charge of the German economy at the Country Studies Branch, joined me to continue our work on the German country report. Eventually, the Bundesbank agreed to our proposition that interbank money market rates, for which information was available at any time, were more important as the Bank's short-term operating target than "bank liquidity" and its ratio to bank deposits for which data were available on a monthly basis only. The Bank thus accepted a version of the German country report Dudler and I produced. It was published in December 1973 as the third in the OECD Monetary Policy Studies Series. Subsequently, in March 1974, the Bundesbank abandoned the traditional analysis of bank liquidity by sources and uses.

With regard to the report on French monetary policy, I was at ease in supervising Jean-Claude Chouraqui's work on it because, during my stay at the Banque de France in 1966, I had studied the working of key instruments of monetary policy and the mechanism of short-term money market operations by the Banque de France as well as the main features of the French financial system and the mechanism of extensive foreign exchange controls. The structure of the draft report on France was similar in many respects to the OECD report on Japan which had been already published. Jean-Claude and I visited the Banque de France to discuss the first draft report written in French, one of the two official languages of the OECD together with English. Naturally, in our meeting to discuss the draft report with the senior officials of the Banque de France, I used French, which apparently made them comfortable and our consultation with them went very smoothly. We fairly quickly sent a revised version to a meeting of monetary experts and completed the final report which was published in 1974.

In the early 1970s, research on US monetary policy by US academics ranged from the theoretical to the practical, and debates on the question of what financial variables should be considered as the optimal targets of monetary policy had become active among them. Pioneering work was undertaken by senior Federal Reserve economists such as William Poole (later President of the Federal Reserve Bank of St Louis). Moreover, beyond various attempts that were made to measure relatively simple monetary multiplier functions, Fed economists and US academics worked on building large-scale econometric models that included financial variables within a Keynesian framework. However, the results of these research efforts were not widely shared among US policymakers nor elsewhere. Furthermore, no systematic empirical analysis had been conducted on the question of how the operation of monetary policy instruments affected the balance of payments through its spillover channels.

Because there was no ESD staff economist appropriate for preparing the US country report, Dow decided to hire David C. Rowan, Professor of Economics at the University of Southampton, as a consultant to prepare a report on US monetary policy. However, it was not easy for him to digest a considerable amount of published literature on US monetary policy and prepare a reasonably well-written analytical report. Dow hired two other academics, Gordon Fisher and David Sheppard, as consultants for reviewing and assessing the results of the extensive econometric research done in the United States, concerning the impacts of financial variables on real economic activity. But, unlike the OECD report on Japanese monetary policy for which I initiated some independent econometric analysis of the effects of monetary policy on both the financial and real sectors of the Japanese economy, these consultants did not make any new contributions in this area. Their review work "Effects of Monetary Policy on the United States Economy – A Survey of Econometric Evidence" was published separately in the OECD Economic Outlook Occasional Studies in December 1972.

James Pierce at the Fed research wing, who attended the OECD monetary experts' meetings together with Axilrod also at the Fed, provided the OECD Secretariat with the results of monetary policy simulations with the Fed-MIT-Penn large-scale econometric model.[6] But views differed between the two US representatives at the OECD monetary experts' group about the role of such economic model exercises in Fed's policy-making in which Axilrod was deeply involved. In the end, for finalising the OECD report on US monetary policy, we relied on the help of Niels Thygesen who had returned to his professorship at the University of Copenhagen. Like the OECD report on France, the report on the United States was published in 1974.

UK monetary policy was undergoing a period of major change through "competition and credit control" over a period of about three years from autumn 1971, and the UK monetary authorities did not wish the OECD to launch its study on UK monetary policy. But, they did not object to its inclusion in the comparative report on monetary policy in the six major countries.

Dow hired an outside monetary expert Victor Argy, who was Chief of the Financial Studies at the IMF, to prepare the first draft of the comparative report, but his product was not considered to be satisfactory. In the end, Thygesen as Professor of Economics at the University of Copenhagen and I as Head of the OECD Monetary Division co-authored the report titled "The Role of Monetary Policy in Demand Management: The Experience of Six Major Countries". We were well aware that there were limits to what we could do for synthesising the five country reports covered in the OECD Monetary Policy Studies and outside researchers' work on the effects of UK monetary policy into a summary report on the six countries in an internationally comparable manner. Nevertheless, the OECD monetary experts considered our draft summary report to be a useful addition to the Studies Series. It was only in this report completed by Thygesen and me in September 1974 that Secretary-General van Lennep agreed to identify the names of the authors in its "preface". The report was published in mid-1975 and had an annex "A Note on Criteria for Selecting an Optimal Target for Monetary Policy", where we drew on Argy's work "An Evaluation of Financial

Targets in Six Countries" produced at the time when he was a consultant at the OECD Monetary Division. This piece was not published in the OECD Monetary Studies Series, but in the March 1974 issue of Banca Nazionale del Lavoro Quarterly Review.

The main conclusion which emerged from the Studies on the working and the effects of monetary policies in the six countries covering the period 1960–1971 (or 72) was that they had been able to influence private-sector demand to an important degree. The case was clearest for the two largest OECD economies, the United States and Japan. These two countries provided the clearest documentation of the effects of monetary policy. This was interesting because they were two extremes among the six countries in terms of the set-up of the financial system and the choice of monetary policy instruments. The United States was featured with the most flexible financial system, and the working of monetary policy relied heavily on the interest rate mechanism. In contrast, the Japanese financial system was characterised by the division of work among different types of financial institutions and the less developed long-term securities market than in the United States. In this financial set-up, a notable feature of monetary policy tightening in periods of balance of payments difficulties in Japan was BOJ's reliance on quantitative control to restrain the total amount of Japanese bank lending to the non-bank private sector. That said, the OECD Secretariat's own econometric analysis conducted in its study on the working on Japanese monetary policy demonstrated the importance of the interest rate mechanism based on BOJ's short-term money market operations in influencing the total amount of credit to the non-bank private sector by Japanese financial institutions not subjected to BOJ's direct quantitative credit control.

During the period covered in the studies, the financial system was still rigidly managed not only in Japan but also in the United Kingdom, France, and Italy. A framework had not yet been well established to regulate overall domestic financial conditions and aggregate demand through flexible adjustment of money market interest rates by the central banks. And in the United Kingdom, the second most important reserve currency country under the Bretton Woods system of fixed exchange rates, interest rate policy was largely directed at adjusting the difference between domestic and foreign interest rates, which was important for international movements of short-term capital, and to adjust pressure on exchange rates. Above all, it was a time when monetary policy was not generally considered and used as the primary means for controlling inflation. Although there was some acceleration of inflation towards the end of the period, it would not be much of an exaggeration to say that the main internal task of monetary policy during the period was seen as one of stabilising real demand at around a level commensurate with current output capacity (see Chapter 16).

In late October 1974, just before my first departure from the OECD, the Banca d'Italia organised an international conference "Econometric Research in European Central Banks" at Perugia where Thygesen and I presented a paper "The Effects and Design of Monetary Policy" in which we specified the names of our colleagues who contributed to the OECD Monetary Policy Studies.[7] The opening address given by Guido Carli, then Governor of the Banca d'Italia, and the opening lecture delivered by Nobel laureate John Hicks added to the significance of the event. In the concluding section of the conference volume, published by the Banca d'Italia in1975, Francesco Masera wrote: "the international co-operation that we all desire will be achieved through a dialogue, in a common language, aimed at finding a solution to the problem which ~~we~~ confronts us".

At my farewell party at the ESD held near the end of October 1974, a card with an English poem written by Paula Simonin, my private secretary, was given to me as her gift.

KUMI
An Appreciation by his Secretary

There was a young man, known as Shige-ha-ra,
Who decided that life was a bit ra-pla-pla.
So he sat down and wrote an 'etude' on Japan,
With the rest of his time, the Division he ran.

But this work on the yen,
Well, it didn't take ages,
It was only a book of some hundred odd pages.

So he thought he would tackle the land of the dollar.
Even though such a feat would daunt many a scholar.

Like the other, this study upon the U.S.
Was published and proved to be quite a success.

For a while then our Kumi just sat and reflected,
Was his time really filled by the work he directed?
This ridiculous thought was quite promptly rejected.

"What I wrote on those other two countries was fun,
But this time I must do something more than just one."

So he started to write, not on one, but on SIX,
And he wrote and he wrote till he ran out of Bics.

At the end, his employers said,
"Kumi can go",
"We are sure he has told us all there is to know"
"And we're sending him back to The Bank, Tokyo."

So all that is left now to say is "Cheerio".

I was touched by her thoughtfulness. My wife and I maintain a very friendly relationship with Paula and Gerard, her husband.

After my departure from the OECD, the post of Head of Monetary Division remained vacant for a while. In the end, the ESD management decided on the internal promotion of Dudler to the post.

I would add that my unexpectedly deep involvement with the OECD Monetary Division's work on country studies on monetary policies of the six major countries provided me with precious chances of association with high-level monetary experts of these countries and greatly helped my work at both the Bank of Japan and the OECD in later years, in particular when I returned to the OECD as Deputy Director of the General Economics Branch and assisted Sylvia Ostry, then Head of ESD, chairing monetary experts' meetings, and when I myself chaired their meetings in my capacity as Director of the General Economics Branch from 1987 to 1989, and Head of ECO from 1992 to 1997 (see Box).

*****

My Associations with Western Monetary Economists in the First Half of the 1970s

In the Western academic community around the time when I joined the OECD Monetary Division in 1970, there were a growing number of studies on the significant effects of monetary policy on domestic aggregate demand and thereby on the level of employment and the rate of inflation on the one hand and the external effects of monetary policies on the other. In the United Kingdom, the Money Study Group was formed in 1969. Its members were all monetary economists working in universities, banks, research institutes, and government departments. The Group's purpose was to bring them together in seminars and conferences to discuss developments in British monetary economics. The Chairman was Harry Johnson, a Canadian-born expert in international economics and Professor of Economics at the London School of Economics and at the University of Chicago.[8] He, together with A. R. Nobay, organised a large conference in Bournemouth, England in January 1972, where the Group's members as well as economists at the Bank of England and the OECD were invited to participate. I attended it with Niels Thygesen, then Head of the OECD Monetary Division, and became acquainted with bright British monetary economists, such as Michael Parkin and David Laidler. At the conference, Johnson called our attention to "global monetarism" which, as I will discuss in some of the following chapters, became an important issue for international policy discussion as international capital markets expanded and the significance of international financial linkages propagating domestic economic and financial disturbances across countries increased over time.

Around the same time in continental Europe, Karl Brunner, a Swiss-born strong monetarist, organised annual seminars in the German town of Konstanz, which borders Switzerland, and I regularly attended his seminars where monetary economists not only from Germany and Switzerland, but also with those from North America as well as the German Bundesbank and the OECD were invited to participate. Alan Meltzer, known for his critical comments on the monetary policy management of the US Federal Reserve System, together with Brunner on the "Shadow Open Market Committee", led discussions at these seminars and criticised the Bundesbank's monetary policy management from a monetarist's point of view. Rudiger Dornbusch and Manfred Neumann, protégées of Brunner and Melzer, actively participated in the discussions. In the United States, Harry Johnson and Robert Aliber, both at the University of Chicago , organised a large international finance conference in Racine, a suburb of

Chicago in 1972. It was attended by North American academics and Fed officials as well as economists from the Bank of England and the OECD from Europe, which I attended. There, I met Koichi Hamada who was at Yale.

Somewhat later, Franco Modigliani, MIT Professor, together with his Finnish student, Pentti Kouri, organised a large international finance conference, "The Conference on Monetary Mechanism in Open Economies" under the sponsorship of the central bank of Finland, at a magnificent resort hotel in the suburbs of Helsinki in the summer of 1975.[9] In this conference, economists with monetarist orientation including Harry Johnson and Karl Brunner as well as Edmund Phelps, who would eventually be awarded the Nobel Prize in Economics in 2006, participated together with Keynesian economists. I recall the names of Stanley Fisher, Michael Mussa, Jacob Frenkel, Benjamin Friedman, Robert Shiller, Stanley Black, and Alexandre Lamfalussy, who would eventually become chief economist and later General Manager of the BIS. Mauno Henrik Koivisto, then Governor of the central bank of Finland, a politician who had been Prime Minister twice before and after that, and President of Finland for many years, was a keen participant in the discussions at the conference.

I was fortunate to have had opportunities to associate myself with those economists. I renewed associations with many of them later when I became responsible for organising international monetary conferences at the Institute for Monetary and Economic Studies of the Bank of Japan, and eventually the Director-General of the Institute and the Bank's Chief Economist.

****

Notes

1. Andrew Britton, "John Christopher Roderick Dow 1916–1998", Proceedings of the British Academy, 105, pp. 397–413, The British Academy, 2000, https://www.thebritishacademy.ac.uk/documents/1440/105p397.pdf. See also Christopher Dow, edited by Graham Hacche and Christopher Taylor, "Inside the Bank of England: Memoirs of Christopher Dow, Chief Economist 1973–84 (Palgrave Studies in Economic History)", Palgrave Macmillan, 2012.

2. The process has been described in the book written by three of my former OECD colleagues about international economic analysis and policy, where they take the Smithsonian episode as a case study in international co-ordination: John Llewellyn, Stephen Potter and Lee Samuelson, "Economic Forecasting and Policy—The International Dimension", Routledge and Kegan Paul, 1985.
3. OECD, Note by the Secretariat for the Economic Policy Committee, "Proposed Studies of the Effects of Monetary Policy", CPE (69)8, June 13, 1969.
4. OECD, Report by the Secretary-General, "Inflation—The Present Problem", December 1970, p. 11 and p. 36.
5. Dow hired William H. Branson and R. D. Jr. Hill as consultants for an empirical study "Capital Movements in OECD Countries", which was published in OECD Economic Outlook Occasional Studies, in December 1971.
6. Antonella Rancan, "Empirical Macroeconomics in a Policy Context: The Fed-MIT-Penn Model Versus the St. Louis Model, 1965–1975", History of Political Economy, 2019, 51 (3): 449–470.
7. Kumiharu Shigehara and Niels Thygesen, "The Effects and Design of Monetary Policy" in a conference volume "Econometric Research in European Central Banks", Banca d'Italia, 1975. It was written in the footnote of this article that "(T)he authors are grateful to former colleagues in the OECD (notably, V. Argy, J. Boughton, J.-C. Chouraqui, H. Dudler, I. Menashe, F. Meyer-zu-Schlochtern, D.D. Rowan, R. Sammons and P. Till) for close co-operation in the study surveyed in the present article".
8. H. G. Johnson and associates, "Reading in British Monetary Economics", Oxford University Press, 1972.
9. Niels Thygesen recalls that the Helsinki conference in 1975 where a paper summarising the OECD monetary policy study reports was presented was highly appreciated by both European central banks and international monetary economist, and that it was a fore-runner of the Jackson Hole symposiums organised by the Federal Reserve Bank of Kansas City (see the Supplementary Note on "Japan Bashing" in Chapter 12 of this book) and, much later, of the Sintra conferences of the European Central Banks, started by Mario Draghi, a student of Modigliani and a close friend of Kouri.

PART II

Japan's Economic Policy Management and Balance of Payments Adjustment under the Floating Exchange Rate System

CHAPTER 8

Japan's Economic Policy and Foreign Exchange Market Management in the Second Half of the 1970s

During the first half of the 1970s when I served the OECD, the Bank of Japan struggled with foreign exchange market turbulences in the aftermath of the Nixon shock and the deflationary effects of successive huge appreciations of the Japanese yen following the Smithsonian agreement and thereafter. Subsequently, the Japanese economy was hit by the first oil shock which was followed by the worst recession in Japan since the early 1950s. The contractionary phase lasted five quarters up to the first quarter of 1975, and during this period, output fell by 2.2 per cent. The subsequent recovery of the Japanese economy marked a clear departure from earlier medium-term growth trends. In the five years to 1979, the average rate of economic growth did not exceed 5.25 per cent, half the rate experienced in the previous period of high growth.

Monetary Policy Planning at the Bank of Japan

It was around this turning point of the Japanese economy that I returned to the Bank of Japan (BOJ) and was assigned to work as Counsellor in the Policy Co-ordination Department. Co-ordination Department (*Sômubu*). The Department had two divisions: the General Affairs Division, which functioned as the Bank's legal department, and the Planning Division, which was responsible for the planning of domestic monetary policy management. At that time, the Department was headed

K. Shigehara, *The Bank of Japan, the OECD, and Beyond*,
https://doi.org/10.1007/978-981-97-5307-9_8

by Yasushi Mieno (later Executive Director, Deputy Governor, and Governor of the BOJ). The Planning Division was headed by Akira Aoki (later, Executive Director in charge of domestic monetary policy), with Michio Fukai (later succeeded Aoki as Executive Director in charge of domestic monetary policy, and subsequently Deputy Governor of the Export–Import Bank of Japan) as first Associate Advisor, Toshihiko Fukui (later succeeded Fukai as Executive Director in charge of domestic monetary policy, and subsequently Deputy Governor and Governor of the BOJ) as second Associate Advisor, and myself as Counsellor, along with several staff members who were all young talents with a promising future. The Executive Director in charge of domestic monetary policy at the time was Takatomo Watanabe, who had been Deputy Director of the Personnel Department when I was recruited by the BOJ. He later became Governor of the Development Bank of Japan.

One of my tasks in the Planning Division was to prepare documents to be presented to the Board of Executive Directors on monthly plans for the BOJ's money market operations. The exercise was carried out in co-operation with the Market Operations Department (*Eigyou-kyoku*) which was in charge of daily money market management. The Planning Division was also in charge of providing papers for the Executive Board's periodic discussion on the assessment of the Japanese economic situation and monetary policy orientation. I was asked to prepare the first drafts of such papers with my staff. I also participated in the preparation of notional questions and answers when BOJ Governor was called as a witness to Parliament, as well as notional questions and answers for his periodic press conferences.

Occasionally, to address some underlying problems related to the framework of monetary policy management, the Planning Division submitted "think pieces" to the Executive Director in charge of domestic monetary policy, and eventually to all members of the Executive Board. In this context, in early 1975 Aoki asked me to prepare a short note on the adoption of the money supply as the BOJ's monetary policy target. My own view was that the BOJ should not set a numerical target for the money supply. One reason was that, although Japan's money demand function appeared to be more stable than those of Western countries that had set numerical money supply growth targets for conducting monetary policy, ongoing financial market liberalisation in Japan would likely destabilise the money demand function significantly and strict money supply targeting would disrupt domestic financial and foreign exchange markets and real economic activity and inflation performance. Another important matter of concern was that failure to achieve targets, even if only due to vagaries of the demand for money, might distort market expectations about the BOJ's future course of action and undermine the credibility of policy, see Shigehara, "Japan's Experience with Use of Monetary Policy and the Process of Liberalization".[1]

My paper was circulated within the Policy Co-ordination Department just before the time when the BOJ's Research Department sent us the near final version of a major article entitled "On the Importance of the Money Supply in Japan" with the aim of publishing its final version in the July 1975 issue of the Monthly Research Report. The languages which could be read as if Research Department were advocating the adoption of monetary targeting were modified in the final version in the light of the Policy Co-ordination Department's cautious view.

In July 1978, the BOJ started to publish forecasts on broad money supply developments. The announcements were made on a quarterly basis and in terms of a range of year-on-year growth rates of broad money supply (M2). By announcing the projected course of broad money and commenting on its possible implications for the BOJ's ultimate objectives with due caution about the possibility of a short-run instability in the relationship between money on the one hand and real income and prices on the other, the BOJ hoped that it could obtain valuable assistance in expediting anti-inflationary monetary policy.

In a review paper published in 1985, Koichi Hamada and Fumio Hayashi, Japanese academics, observed that an important feature of the conduct of monetary policy in Japan during the period they examined—the 1970s and early 1980s—was that the BOJ aimed at not immediate but medium-run control of broad money without paying too much attention to narrow money which often exhibits erratic movements. They noted that "the Bank pays sufficient attention to other indicators than a single monetary aggregate. The Bank watches levels of interest rates, price indices, liquidity conditions of firms, the retail-sales index, the general business outlook, and the yen exchange rate. Monetary policy in Japan has been successful because the perspective of the Bank is multi-scoped rather than single-scoped on a single aggregate".[2] In contrast to the period they reviewed, however, the BOJ made several serious mistakes in the conduct of monetary policy for various reasons in the second half of the 1980s onwards, as I will describe later in this book.

Start of International Economic Diplomacy at the Summit Level

Around the mid-1970s, while the exchange rates of the UK pound, the French franc and the Italian lira fell sharply against the US dollar, the West German mark (Deutsche mark, DM) and Swiss franc rose sharply against it. By the spring of 1975, the latter two's appreciation against the US dollar amounted to more than 70 per cent compared with their levels some ten years earlier.

Against this backdrop, international economic diplomacy at the summit level gained momentum. In November 1975, the first meeting of the so-called Summit of six major industrialised countries (France, West Germany, Italy, Japan, the United Kingdom, and the United States) was held in the Paris suburb of Rambouillet. Before this Summit, the Group of Five (G5) without Italy had held secret meetings at the level of finance ministers and central bank governors. G5 continued to hold secret meetings thereafter, and I was involved in its activities as personal assistant to BOJ Governor Morinaga in later years. Unlike these G5 meetings, the G6 Summit at Rambouillet attracted a great deal of media attention and was followed in June 1976 by the second Summit in San Juan, Puerto Rico. That time, it was the G7 Summit including Canada.

Between 1975 and 1976, the Japanese yen maintained a relatively stable exchange rate against the US dollar, and the international price competitiveness of Japanese manufacturing industries measured in terms of real effective exchange rates strengthened rapidly. I expressed my concern about this development to Sadaichi Motoya, chief dealer of the BOJ's foreign exchange market operation, noting that such a shift in the Japanese yen's real effective exchange rate movement might eventually cause problems for the international economy. However, the concept of real effective exchange rates did not ring a bell to the senior officials of the BOJ's Foreign Department at the time. They focused on the Japanese yen–US dollar exchange rate in nominal terms and to my knowledge, there was no one other than myself within the BOJ who paid attention to the yen's external value in terms of real effective measures. Incidentally, the BOJ started to publish data on the nominal and real effective rates as late as the July 1995 issue of its quarterly review on the Japanese economic situation. At that time, I was OECD Chief Economist.

OECD economic forecasts presented to the WP3 meeting held in July 1976 showed that the current account surplus of oil-producing countries would rise again due to a slowdown in their imports of industrial products, and a large swing into current account deficit was projected for the United States. Against this background, Japan's current account balance was projected to turn from deficit to surplus, with a surplus of $3 3/4 billion that year, the largest among OECD countries, while West Germany's current account surplus was projected to fall by almost half to $2.0 billion. Reiichi Shimamoto, Advisor to the Governor on international affairs, who represented the BOJ at the WP3 meeting, pointed out that temporary factors such as the build-up of overseas inventories of Japanese products contributed to the rapid increase in Japan's exports in the first half of 1976, but the OECD Secretariat countered that its projection of Japan's annual trade surplus had been lowered to its fullest by forecasting low exports and very high imports in the second half of the year.

Edwin Yeo, then Under Secretary of US Treasury, who had been critical of the weak yen, held a meeting with Michiya Matsukawa, Vice Minister of Finance for International Affairs, on 18 July 1976, the day before the WP3 meeting in Paris. He subsequently visited Japan in August to meet Japanese Finance Minister Masayoshi Ohira as well as Takeo Fukuda, Deputy Prime Minister and Director-General of the Economic Planning Agency, and Teiichiro Morinaga, the BOJ Governor. A leading Japanese newspaper, Nihon Keizai Shimbun (14 August 1976), reported that Yeo had met with the BOJ Governor and Japanese business leaders to stress Japan's responsibility as an external surplus country and to urge them to adjust the Japanese yen exchange rate upward. The same newspaper (25 August 1976) also reported that in view of the growing criticism in the United States and Europe of Japan's trade surplus, the Japanese Ministry of Finance decided to send Matsukawa on a ten-day trip from 31 August to Western countries to discuss the yen issue with the heads of the monetary authorities in these countries. Following his discussions with Matsukawa on 2 September, Yeo reportedly said that domestic economic stabilisation in the United States and exchange rate movements resulting from exchange market operations should be combined to produce a stable balance of payments. It was also reported in the same newspaper (3 September 1976) that the two sides had agreed that external surplus countries should be prepared to provide transitional loans to support appropriate adjustment policies on the part of external deficit countries, and that surplus countries should accept to make upward exchange rate adjustment as they could not afford to adopt inflationary policies.

Meanwhile, Masao Fujioka, then Director-General of the International Finance Bureau of the Ministry of Finance (later President of the Asian Development Bank), pointed out in the September 1976 issue of a Japanese periodical (*Finance*) that Japan's foreign exchange reserves were $16.3 billion as of the end of August 1976, only half the size of West Germany's, whereas both the Japanese and West German economies were of the same size.

Around the time that Fujioka's article was published, Nihon Keizai Shimbun (4 September 1976) reported that, although the Ministry of Finance had opposed the revaluation of the yen, it was obliged to agree in principle with the US government argument that external surplus countries should review their exchange rates. The same newspaper also reported that the Japanese Ministry of Finance did its best to deflect the US criticism by explaining that Japan's surplus was temporary rather than structural.

Later, after returning from a visit to four European countries and the United States on 10 September 1976, Matsukawa reportedly stated at a press conference that if the yen exchange rate problem were linked to the trade problem as a result of rapid increases in exports to the United States, it would become more complicated, and that the Japanese government would need to solve the currency issue quickly to avoid the Japan–US trade problem (Nihon Keizai Shimbun, 11 September 1976). On the following day, the same newspaper reported that the Ministry of Finance, which at the time had taken the US criticism towards Japan in its stride, took the surge in exports to the United States more seriously than the Ministry of Industry and Trade and the Ministry of Foreign Affairs (Nihon Keizai Shimbun, "From criticism of the weak yen to criticism of trade", 12 September 1976). It was said at the time that, partly due to the efforts by the Ministry of Finance, criticism of the weak yen had disappeared around the time of the IMF and World Bank annual meetings in Manila at the beginning of October 1976, which I attended just after my appointment as personal assistant to BOJ Governor Morinaga.

The So-Called "Locomotive Theory"

In January 1977, a new administration was formed in the United States with Jimmy Carter, a Democrat, as US President. At the time, the pace of recovery of the world economy as a whole after the first oil crisis was slow. While the United States, Japan, and West Germany were in relatively good shape in terms of economic growth and balance of payments taken together, another group of OECD countries including the United Kingdom, France, and Italy were in less good shape. Against this background, a group of international economists in the United States developed the so-called "locomotive theory": Japan and West Germany, together with the United States, should act as "locomotives" to overcome the global economic stagnation.

Early in his administration, President Carter sent Vice-President Walter Mondale to Japan and requested that the Japanese government's economic forecast for Fiscal Year 1977 ending in March 1978 be achieved with a real economic growth rate of 6.7 per cent. In response to this request from the new US government, the Japanese government agreed to assume the role of a "locomotive" at the US–Japan Summit in March 1977. On this basis, at the third summit of the industrialised countries held in May at the UK prime minister's official residence in London, Takeo Fukuda as prime minister of Japan stated that Japan would achieve an economic growth rate of 6.7 per cent in Fiscal Year 1977. However, no specific figures for the economic growth rates of G7 countries were included in the communiqué. West Germany did not agree to the "locomotive theory", fearing a recurrence of inflation which rapid stimulus measures might cause.

During this period, the foreign exchange market saw upward pressure on the yen, triggered by a report that Lawrence Klein, professor of economics at the University of Pennsylvania and a Nobel laureate in economics in 1980, argued for a 10 per cent upvaluation of the Japan yen and West German mark. In June, Assistant Secretary of US Treasury Fred Bergsten said at a meeting of US–Japan business leaders that the Japanese authorities should refrain from intervening in the foreign exchange market and let the market prevail, as the yen's appreciation had been slow despite Japan's current account surplus.

Furthermore, on 24 June 1977, in his speech to the OECD Council of Ministers on growth strategies in OECD countries, US Treasury Secretary Michael Blumenthal reportedly said that according to the OECD

Economic Outlook, neither West Germany nor Japan were likely to achieve their announced growth targets with their current policies; he was particularly concerned that too much of Japan's output was directed to exports, but that he had faith in Chancellor Helmut Schmidt's and Prime Minister Fukuda's commitment to take further steps, if necessary, to achieve their economic growth targets and reduce the current account surpluses.[3] It was also reported that at the OECD meeting to review the Japanese economy, held immediately after the OECD Ministerial Council meeting, there were arguments for a sharp revaluation of the yen, and Nihon Keizai Shimbun published an article that such a currency adjustment would adversely affect Japan's industrial base.

The OECD Secretariat's forecast presented to the July 1977 meeting of WP3 was for Japan's current account balance to increase from a surplus of \$3.7 billion in 1976 to a surplus of \$6 billion in 1977. It considered this to be "the change, arguably the over-adjustment", pointing out that, in addition to Japan's export-oriented industrial structure, the yen's real effective exchange rate in terms of export prices fell by 5.5 per cent between 1974 and 1976, strengthening Japan's international price competitiveness. In response, Reiichi Shimamoto, Advisor to the Governor of the Bank of Japan, argued that the yen was at a significantly high level in 1973 and that it was problematic to measure Japan's international price competitiveness using this as a reference year. In concluding the meeting, however, WP3 Chairman Emminger commented that there appeared to be a consensus at the WP3 that "Japan's problem was a hard-core issue for the OECD policy coordination process", and he hoped that "a solution could be found in the right direction in the future".

Criticisms of Japan at September 1977 International Meetings in Washington

One important international event during the period when I was responsible for accompanying BOJ Governor Teiichiro Morinaga on his overseas trips was the IMF/World Bank Annual Meetings in Washington in September 1977. The Japanese delegation was headed by minister of finance Hideo Bô who was assisted by Matsukawa, while BOJ Governor Morinaga was assisted by Genso Fujimoto Executive Director, Shimamoto, and me as personal assistant to the Governor.

On 3 September, before the IMF/World Bank Annual Meetings in Washington, the Japanese Government had announced a "comprehensive economic stimulus package" totaling 2 trillion yen, mainly to boost public works, and on the same day the Bank of Japan also lowered its official discount rate from 5.0 per cent to 4.25 per cent, in an effort to show its commitment to expanding domestic demand. But this did not receive sufficient recognition in Washington meetings. At the general meeting of the IMF Board of Governors, Minister Bô gave a speech in Japanese in which he outlined the new package, emphasising Japan's awareness of its responsibility for the management of the global economy. But its English translation was not well received by the Western media which accused him of being an "inscrutable Japanese". My memory of this happening is very clear as I found its antonym in an article about my profile written by David Marsh, a well-known reporter of the Financial Times, about a year after my appointment as OECD Chief Economist in 1992, in which he reported that Charles Goodhart, a senior Bank of England official, described me as a "scrutable, highly approachable, personable" Japanese.[4]

At the WP3 meeting which was held alongside the IMF/World Bank Annual Meetings in Washington, Japan came under even more intense criticism than at the general assembly of the IMF Board of Governors. Stephen Marris, Economic Adviser to OECD Secretary-General van Lennep, criticised Japan, and argued that "the locomotive called Japan is moving backwards". The OECD Secretariat's discussion paper distributed locally prior to the WP3 meeting included a recommendation that Japan should expand domestic demand and increase imports by reducing personal income tax rather than increasing public works investment. My memory at the time was that there was no significant difference in the import-inducement coefficient between public works investment and private consumption in Japan. Having read the OECD paper the day before the WP3 meeting, I gave a telephone call from our hotel in Washington late at night US Eastern Time to the Statistics Department at the BOJ head office in Tokyo to obtain relevant data based on Japan's Input–Output Table. My memory about the statistical data proved to be correct. I then handwrote a draft rebuttal statement in English and handed it to Shimamoto. After his oral intervention at the WP 3 meeting made on the basis of my note, the OECD Secretariat staff approached us to get the data Shimamoto used, about which they had not been aware. My own view was that fiscal expansion focused on public works investment with its favourable supply-side effects over the medium term would be better than personal income tax cuts, and that it should be accompanied by structural policy measures such as further import liberalisation.

Finance Minister Bô returned to Japan before the series of meetings in Washington were all over. On his return to Tokyo, he did not mention that Japan had been criticised at his press conference there. BOJ Governor Morinaga, who remained in Washington, was to give his press conference immediately after the closing of all the scheduled international meetings. Shimamoto and I thought that he should make a candid statement on what happened in the Washington meetings to let the Japanese people know about the serious international situation surrounding Japan. We jointly prepared the Governor's opening statement and a set of possible questions and answers to be used at his press conference.

Making direct use of the material we prepared for him, Morinaga made his press remarks about the criticism the Japanese delegation had received at the Washington meetings, and they were soon reported in the Japanese newspapers.

Carter Bonds and Intervention Currencies for Supporting the US Dollar

In mid-January 1978, Fritz Leutwiler, President of the Swiss National Bank visited Tokyo and had a meeting with BOJ Governor Morinaga and Deputy Governor Mayekawa which I attended as personal assistant to the Governor. The main topic of their discussion concerned the US dollar issue. Leutwiler informed us that Fed chairman Arthur Burns had told Leutwiler privately that he and Treasury Secretary Michael Blumenthal had reached an agreement on the issues of US Treasury securities denominated in foreign currencies to raise the funds needed for foreign exchange market intervention to support the US dollar (later called "Carter bonds"). Mayekawa immediately said: "the intervention currency to be used by the US authorities should not be limited to the DM. If the yen were not concomitantly used as an intervention currency to support the US dollar in the foreign exchange market, speculation against the US dollar would concentrate on the yen, and it would eventually spread to the dollar's relationships with other currencies. I am concerned about this scenario".[5]

The January 1978 meeting held in Tokyo was followed by an unsatisfactory meeting held in Mexico City between Morinaga and G. William Miller who succeeded Burns as Fed Chairman in March that year. The Mexico City meeting was held immediately before the April 1978 meeting of the IMF Interim Committee in Mexico. Just prior to these meetings, the Bundesbank and the Federal Reserve had concluded an arrangement for co-ordinated intervention to support the US dollar. Around that time, the dollar declined below the 220-yen level from 240 yen at the beginning of the year. To our great disappointment, Miller told us that Fed was not willing to intervene directly in the yen-dollar market, adding that the use of DM to support the dollar should have a "moonlight effect" on other currencies, including the yen. What Miller meant by that was unclear to us.

Medium-Term Economic Growth Scenarios by the OECD and the IMF

An important issue for discussion at the IMF Interim Committee in Mexico City was world economic growth for which the IMF Research Department presented the medium-term growth scenarios. This work was carried out in the context of the IMF surveillance of member countries' economic policy management which was strengthened by the amendment of the IMF Articles of Agreement that came into force in 1978.[6]

Prior to the IMF exercise, at the OECD, in the year leading up to the June 1976 Ministerial Council meeting, Working Party No. 2 of the Economic Policy Committee considered economic growth scenarios for OECD countries in the medium term up to 1980. The Working Party was composed of experts from OECD member countries on issues related to economic growth and resource allocation, and the final draft document based on their discussions was entitled "A Growth Scenario to 1980", which was subsequently published in the OECD Economic Outlook of July 1976 (pp. 126–152). According to the basic scenario, real economic growth rate for Japan was set to average 7.0 per cent per year between 1975 and 1980, and 5.75 per cent for the United States. Based on a set of assumed economic growth rates and other factors for Japan, the United States and other countries, the projected ratios of current account balances to GDP, calculated at 1975 prices, were a surplus of 1.5 per cent (0.1 per cent in 1975) for Japan and a surplus of 1 per cent (1.3 per cent in 1975) for the United States. It should be noted that Japan's international commitment, as promised by Prime Minister Fukuda at the Third G7 Summit held in London in July 1977, was to achieve an economic growth rate of 6.7 per cent in Fiscal Year 1977 ending in March 1978 and that the actual rate achieved was only 5.3 per cent (Table 8.1).

Table 8.1 OECD medium-term economic growth scenarios

	Real GDP growth rates (annual average, per cent)				
	1975/1974	*1980/1975*		*1975/1974*	*1980/1975*
Japan	2.2	7.0	France	−2.4	6.0
US	−2.0	5.75	Italy	−3.7	4.5
W. Germany	−3.4	5.0	UK	−1.6	3.5

Source OECD Economic Outlook, July 1976, p. 133

According to the OECD Economic Outlook published at the end of 1977, Japan's real GDP growth rate was projected to decline from 6.3 per cent in 1976 to 6 per cent in 1977 and 5 per cent in 1978, and the current account surplus to increase from $3.7 billion in 1976 to $10 billion both in 1977 and 1978. At the WP3 meeting in November of the same year, observing that Japan's imports were growing at a sluggish pace while exports continued to increase as its international price competitiveness recovered, Marris argued that an 8–9 per cent annual growth in Japan's gross domestic demand was desirable, along with an increase in the value of the yen.

The IMF Research Department also worked on the medium-term economic growth scenarios, and a meeting was held at its European Office to discuss the department staff draft report on them with experts from major countries. In this report, the IMF used its world trade model together with the model of real effective exchange rates. A peculiar feature of the Japanese export function developed by the IMF was that Japan's output gap was used as a significant explanatory variable. This meant that in Japan, when the capacity utilisation rate of the manufacturing sector fell, a non-price factor worked to accelerate export growth even if there was no profit margin in exporting. It was thus argued that in order to put the brakes on Japan's exports, it would be necessary to strengthen the yen and at the same time narrow the output gap by realising higher-than-potential growth centred on domestic demand in Japan. The IMF staff argued that with Japan's potential growth rate per annum set at 5 per cent, economic growth at 7.5 per cent per annum from 1979 to 1980 and around 7 per cent should be maintained over the medium term in Japan.

Heinrich Mattes, a former OECD colleague of mine as head of the German desk at the ESD, represented the Bundesbank, together with me as the BOJ representative at this meeting. He and I argued that it would not be appropriate to present the IMF staff's draft paper as it stood as a document for discussion to the IMF Interim Committee, because there were some serious technical problems relating to the measurement of existing output gaps and uncertainty about the impact of huge oil price increases on the future performance of manufacturing industries with heavy use of oil and hence on the potential growth rates for the overall economies in Japan, West Germany, and elsewhere over the medium term. At the time, I expressed my concern about the risk of inflationary consequences of demand expansion along the lines of the IMF economic growth scenarios which were prepared basically in a closed-economy framework. My memory is that the risk of joint demand expansion in OECD countries with its roundabout effect leading to increases in international commodity prices was not considered at the meeting. Had the IMF world economic model incorporating the endogeneity of oil and other international commodity prices been available, our discussion at the meeting would have been more concrete and precise about the global economic risks of the IMF medium-term economic growth scenarios. In fact, international commodity prices were assumed as exogenous factor in the IMF economic growth scenarios. In concluding the meeting, Charles Schwartz, Deputy Director of the IMF Research Department stated that the final version of the IMF staff paper would not be submitted to the Interim Committee for discussion at its meeting in Mexico.

For Johannes Witteveen, this was his last IMF Interim Committee meeting before his term of office as IMF Managing Director came to an end in June 1978. To my surprise, at his last press conference held immediately after the Committee meeting, copies of the IMF's confidential document on its medium-term growth scenarios were distributed to the press. IMF Research Department officials later explained to me that this resulted from the decision made by Witteveen himself, despite the understanding reached earlier at the national experts' meeting at the IMF European Office. In Japan, the Asahi Shimbun was the first to report that the IMF called for a high economic growth target in Japan, giving momentum to Japanese parliamentarians who had been advocating for the adoption of further expansionary fiscal policy measures in the country.

OECD's "Concerted Action Programme"

OECD Secretary-General van Lennep visited BOJ Governor Morinaga in Tokyo on 23 May 1978. For me, it was the first time to meet van Lennep since my return to the BOJ in late 1974. As a matter of fact, within a year after my departure from the OECD, he approached BOJ Deputy Governor Mayekawa to recruit me again to the OECD, this time as his adviser and not as a member of the ESD. Mayekawa declined van Lennep's request immediately.

The meeting lasted about an hour. The duration of their conversation was effectively about half an hour, as I helped them with my consecutive translation, van Lennep using English and Morinaga Japanese, rather than relying on a professional interpreter. The meeting was attended also by Hayami, then Executive Director (later BOJ Governor), and Shimamoto, then Director-General of the Research Department (later Executive Director of BOJ, and Deputy Governor of the Japan Export–Import Bank). The main points of van Lennep's remarks were as follows.

First, according to a report by OECD experts who recently visited Japan for the preparation of OECD annual economic review of Japan, the Japanese economy was likely to run out of steam in the first half of 1978, if current expansionary policies alone were in place. Secondly, while the lull in the foreign exchange market had somewhat brightened the economic outlook, no one could say for sure that the turmoil in the foreign exchange market would not occur again. Thirdly, it would not be desirable for both economic growth and the exchange rate to go through ups and downs, rising at one time and falling at the next, and to avoid this, forward-looking policy management would be needed to be conducted with a view to the year 1979. Fourthly, with regard to Governor Morinaga's remark that "both the average growth rate of 7.5 per cent for Japan from 1979 to 1980, which was considered desirable in the IMF's medium-term scenario, and 7.5 per cent growth rate for the first half of 1979 suggested in the OECD's 'Concerted Action Programme' were a little too high, and that a growth rate of 6 per cent plus α would be appropriate for Japan in the medium term", it would be important to clear up a misconception about the OECD "Concerted Action Programme".

According to van Lennep's explanation, the OECD's recommendation that "Japan's growth rate in the first half of 1979 should be raised by 3 percentage points from 4.5 to 7.5 per cent" referred to the "end result" of concerted actions by Japan and other countries put together, and the only

Table 8.2 OECD Economic Outlook (three largest economies)

	Per cent per annum					
	1976	*1977*	*1978*	*78/1st H*	*78/2nd H*	*79/1st H*
Real GNP growth						
US	6	5	3.75	2.5	4.5	3
Japan	6	5	5.5	6.5	5.5	4.5
W. Germany	5.75	2.5	2.5	2.25	3.5	2.75
Domestic final demand						
US	5	5.25	3.75	3.25	3.5	2.75
Japan	4	3.75	5.75	6.25	6.25	5.25
W. Germany	3.75	2.5	2.75	2.25	4.25	3.5
Current balance ($bn)						
US	−1.4	−20.2	−25.0			
Japan	3.7	11.0	17.5			
W. Germany	3.8	3.8	5.0			
CPI inflation (%)						
US	5.25	5.5	7			
Japan	8.5	7.5	5			
W. Germany	4.5	4	3			

Source OECD Economic Outlook, July 1978, pp. VI–VII

effort Japan should make on its own would be to raise its growth rate by a little less than half of the three percentage points; the remaining increase in Japan's growth rate would be a roundabout result of the concerted efforts of other countries to raise their growth rates (Table 8.2).[7]

The 4th G7 Summit in Bonn in July 1978

The fourth Summit was held in Bonn, West Germany between 16 and 17 July 1978.[8] At this Summit, the Japanese Prime Minister Takeo Fukuda made an international commitment to achieve an economic growth rate of 7 per cent for FY 1978 ending in March 1979. This figure was the same as the one shown for Japan in the IMF medium-term economic growth scenario and the one published in the July 1976 issue of the OECD Economic Outlook. The Japanese government prepared a large budget for fiscal year 1978, giving priority to boosting the economy by expanding public works.[9]

Regardless of pressures from the US government for Japan to accelerate economic growth, there were domestic political reasons for Prime

Minister Fukuda, former finance ministry bureaucrat, to shift the stance of Japanese fiscal policy towards expansion. His power base was weak, and not so popular among voters as Takeo Miki, his political rival and predecessor as Japanese prime minister. He was thus obliged to adopt a fiscal policy that would gain popularity among the electorate. The actual economic growth rate for Fiscal Year 1978 ending in March 1979 remained at 5.2 per cent and, as in the previous year, Japan's growth target was not achieved. However, Fukuda's failure did not give rise to increased tensions with the US administration, as the outbreak of the second oil crisis in 1979 turned Japan's current account balance into a huge deficit.

Compared with the Japanese prime minister, West German Chancellor Helmut Schmidt seemed to me at the time to be more cautious in making West Germany's commitment to a numerical economic growth target. It was revealed later that relations between the United States and West Germany had been so strained that in February 1978 it had even been hinted that the United States would boycott the Bonn Summit.[10] In the end, West Germany accepted an additional economic stimulus package equivalent to 1 per cent of GNP in exchange for a concession from the United States in terms of a change in its energy policy. Schmidt only made an international commitment on specific economic measures, whereas Fukuda made a pledge on Japan's economic growth for the 1978 fiscal year ending in March 1979 in numerical terms. In fact, most Japanese economists had expected that Fukuda's international commitment would not be achieved.

Reinforcing US Dollar Defence Measures

The year 1978 was a difficult year for the US dollar. In a lecture entitled "The Political Economy of the Dollar", delivered at the Fred Hirsch Memorial Lecture at the University of Warwick, United Kingdom on 9 November 1978, Paul Volcker, then President of the Federal Reserve Bank of New York, described the anguish of the process that led to the Smithsonian Agreement and then to the floating exchange rate system. He recalled that there was a judgement that it was politically and economically untenable for the United States to assume the role of the so-called "N-th" country in the international monetary system which ultimately coordinates the balance of payments of other countries.[11] More specifically, it was unacceptable for the United States to restore dollar convertibility without the prospect of maintaining a balance of payments position strong enough to meet its gold convertibility obligations. This suggested the need for a fundamental overhaul of the international monetary system that reflected the new balance of global economic powers.

This speech was delivered nine months before the man, who as Under Secretary of US Treasury, had attended OECD WP3 and other international monetary meetings and negotiated with European and Japanese monetary officials in the runup to and in the aftermath of the breakdown of the Bretton Woods system, replaced G. William Miller as Fed chairman.

In the early autumn of 1978, the dollar began to weaken across the board and by the end of October, compared with the level at the end of September 1977, the US currency's fall amounted to 59 per cent against the Swiss franc, 51 per cent against the Japanese yen, 34 per cent against DM, 22 per cent against the French franc, and 19 per cent against the UK pound.

In the face of this situation, on 1 November 1978, President Carter issued a statement to the effect that it had become necessary to correct the recent excessive depreciation of the dollar as an important measure to combat inflation. At the same time, Treasury Secretary Blumenthal and Fed Chairman Miller issued a joint statement in which the United States launched full-scale dollar defence measures, such as tightening monetary policy, together with concerted intervention to support the US dollar by expanding swap facilities with the central banks of Japan, West Germany, and Switzerland and the issuance of the Carter Bonds (US Treasury securities denominated in foreign currencies, namely DM and the Swiss franc). This was quite a departure from the position Fed Chairman Miller had taken at his meeting with BOJ Governor Morinaga in Mexico City in April 1978 where he did not show interest in the idea of using the Japanese yen in the Fed's foreign exchange market intervention to support the US dollar.

The change in the US Administration's primary interest from faster global economic growth to domestic price stability and the defence of the US dollar was discussed in a tripartite discussion between Masuru Hayami (then Executive Director), Shijuro Ogata (then Advisor to the Governor) and me in the December 1978 issue of the Bank's in-house magazine *Nichigin*. I commented that among US monetary policy tightening measures, the increase in the reserve ratio should be taken as a symbolic message from the Fed about its determination to defend the US dollar.

Views Exchanged Between IMF Managing Director de Larosière and BOJ Governor Morinaga

In December 1978 Masayoshi Ohira was nominated as head of the Japanese government to replace Fukuda. Around that time, a drop in oil production in the wake of the Iranian Revolution and the decision of the OPEC General Assembly to raise oil prices in stages during 1979 led to the second oil crisis. It triggered an intensifying outflow of capital from Japan, and the yen continued to fall from its peak at the end of October 1978, just before the announcement of the US dollar defence measures, while BOJ's intervention in the foreign exchange market to support the yen led to a rapid decline in Japan's foreign exchange reserves.

Under these circumstances, in March 1979, Governor Morinaga took the opportunity of attending an IMF Interim Committee meeting in Washington, D.C., to meet for the first time with Jacques de Larosière, who had succeeded Witteveen as IMF Managing Director. The meeting was attended by William Dale, Deputy Managing Director, and John Woodley, Deputy Director of the Asian Department of the IMF, as well as by Hayami and myself from BOJ.

Following a detailed presentation Governor Morinaga and Hayami of the Japanese domestic economic and balance of payments situation, *de Larosière* stated that the Japanese authorities' forecast of 6.0 to 6.3 per cent economic growth for Fiscal Year 1979 was impossible to achieve, assuming current policies, and that Japan should bring forward the execution of the initial budget and compile a supplementary budget to achieve the growth rate of around 5 per cent at least. He also stated that he did not fully understand the true meaning of Morinaga's statement at the IMF Interim Committee that he did not agree with the IMF's medium-term scenario, and that the 7 per cent average annual growth rate for 1980–1981 proposed by the IMF for Japan was feasible without rekindling inflation. He then asked Morinaga what growth figure he would prefer if the IMF's figure was not appropriate, adding that while Japan's fiscal deficit situation was unique, Japan's external payments situation was also unique.

Governor Morinaga refuted this, stating that the medium-term potential growth rate in Japan was no longer as high as generally believed, as underlying conditions had changed since the end of its high growth period. He also explained in detail sector by sector that while the GDP gap was estimated to be approximately 15 per cent based on the actual capacity utilisation rate of the manufacturing sector, capital stocks in many industries could no longer be readily useable because of fundamental structural changes in response to the successive oil price shocks. He expressed concern that aggerate demand at a faster pace would create bottlenecks and throw the economy out of balance. On the political economy issue associated with fiscal policy expansion advocated by *de Larosière*, Morinaga looked back to the time immediately after he joined the Ministry of Finance and spoke passionately about his experience of inflation following the aggressive fiscal policy promoted under Finance Minister Korekiyo Takahashi who was assassinated by right-wing military officials in a coup d'état before the start of the Pacific War.

The two did not budge, with a promise to meet again. The meeting started at 4 pm and lasted for two hours and 20 minutes, with my consecutive translation as was the case with the meeting of Morinaga and van Lennep noted above. Morinaga was aware that, in my translation into English of his talk, I added more than what he said. Both he and Hayami fully understood my English translation and were not unhappy about what I did as Morinaga's personal assistant. While I felt exhausted from interpreting and taking notes at the meeting,[12] Morinaga returned to the Watergate hotel in Washington with a refreshed look on his face, saying he had said everything he needed to say.

Some months later when Woodley came to BOJ to meet Governor Morinaga for the preparation of the IMF annual consultation with Japan, he smiled at me and said "I am here to listen to what Governor Shigehara has to say". As a further aside, when Governor Morinaga spoke at the Foreign Correspondents' Club in Tokyo, during the question-and-answer session, a very sensitive question was raised about the possibility of his reappointment as BOJ Governor, and I tried my hand at translation of his answer in Japanese into English. Morinaga told me on our way back to BOJ in his official car that "the English words that Shigehara-kun used will be the correct text". This was my way of interpreting as personal assistant to Morinaga, and I remained as such throughout his term of office as BOJ Governor.

Following the tense March meeting in Washington, *de Larosière* visited Japan in May 1979 for his second meeting with BOJ Governor. Morinaga expressed concern about the rise in wholesale prices, the excessive depreciation of the yen and the state of Japanese government bond issues, and explained that the official interest rate hike (by 0.75 per cent) in April was in part a response to capital outflows caused by domestic and foreign interest rate differentials. In response, *de Larosière* expressed some understanding of the increase in the official interest rate, but requested him not to overreact to the rise in wholesale prices, which had been significantly affected by the surge in international commodity prices and the depreciation of the yen. *De Larosière* also stated that the stability of the yen at a sufficiently strong level would be in the interest of Japan as well as other countries, and that it was necessary to ensure that an excessively weak yen would not lead to a sharp increase in Japan's current account surplus later in the 1980s. He agreed to the BOJ's intervention in the foreign exchange market to support the yen and requested further easing of restrictions on short-term capital inflows. He also pointed out that he had doubts as to whether the timing of the introduction of a general consumption tax was appropriate. In response, Morinaga stated that he personally believed that the timing of the introduction of the general consumption tax should be carefully considered, and replied that it was, however, absolutely necessary to improve Japan's fiscal position over time.[13] This second meeting lasted approximately 45 minutes, during which time *de Larosière* did not make any stout statements such as "I have faith in the opinions of my staff", as he had done at the first meeting in Washington in March 1979. The impression I had at that time was that he, a former French bureaucrat, had not flexibly adjusted his policy views on the management of the world economy quickly enough in the face of the rapid rises in oil prices and turbulences in the foreign exchange market.

IMF/World Bank Annual Meetings in Belgrade, September 1979

Following the decision at the OPEC meeting at the end of June 1979 to further increase its oil prices, a gradual process of raising the Fed's official discount rate began in late July. In August, Volcker became Fed chairman, while Miller was appointed Treasury Secretary, and the US delegation went to the joint IMF/World Bank annual meetings in Belgrade, the capital of Yugoslavia with this new line-up. However, on 27 September, the gold price in the New York market rose to $400 an ounce, and Volcker left the meeting early and returned to Washington in a hurry. On 6 October, the Fed announced tightening measures through a new operating procedure designed to more closely control money growth. Specifically, the Fed switched its monetary policy operating target from the Federal Funds rate to non-borrowed reserves (the funds which commercial banks hold in cash at the central bank—that are their own, and not money on loan from the central bank) and turned to stricter money supply management. Under this monetary control scheme, which was considered a major monetarist experiment, short-term market interest rates in the United States fluctuated wildly at high levels, and at the same time the money supply, which was supposed to become more stable, became more volatile, until the Fed began to withdraw from this approach in the summer of 1982.

As I will discuss in more detail later, the new US monetary adjustment scheme was discussed at WP3 meetings and a good deal of the OECD Secretariat work on it was carried out during my second service at the OECD which started in September 1980.

At the Belgrade meetings, Governor Morinaga explained that domestic demand had grown by a high 8.1 per cent in real terms during 1978 and that the objective of eliminating the current account surplus had also been achieved as a combined result of the strong yen and rapid domestic demand expansion.

The biggest incident in Belgrade occurred during Governor Morinaga's last press conference. Morinaga had the strong confidence of Masayoshi Ohira, who was, like Morinaga, a former bureaucrat at the Ministry of Finance and was appointed Japan's prime minister in December 1978, and it had been generally expected that Morinaga would be reappointed after his first term of office of five year, which was coming to end in December 1979. In concluding his press conference, however, he said that he would not want to be reappointed, to our great surprise.

My duties as personal assistant to Morinaga continued until late November 1979, when Woodley as Deputy Director of the IMF Asian Department visited him in BOJ Governor's office in the context of IMF mission for the Executive Board annual review with Japan. The main topic at that time was the weak yen. Morinaga expressed concern that the yen had fallen too far to which Woodley replied that he was not confident that further increases in Japan's interest rates or official foreign currency borrowing would be effective in reversing the yen's decline, and the meeting ended without any strong opinions being expressed.[14]

Multilateral Co-Operation for the Defence of the Yen

At the end of December 1977, an agreement of the Japanese Ministry of Finance and the Bank of Japan with the Federal Reserve Bank of New York (hereafter New York Fed) was reached for the New York Fed to intervene in the New York foreign exchange market on behalf of the Japanese Foreign Exchange Account run by the Bank of Japan as an agent of the Japanese government. Under this agreement, the New York Fed's intervention to support the yen started in January 1978. It did not involve the foreign exchange risk of the New York Fed as it acted only on behalf of the Japanese Foreign Exchange Account.

With the change in the BOJ governorship in December 1979, my work as an interpreter ceased, except when Mayekawa in person asked me to act as such. This happened—for example at his foreign press conferences, where he deemed it necessary to be discreet. On the other hand, I began to receive direct phone calls from him to write the manuscripts of speeches he intended to deliver in English, as described briefly in Chapter 10.

The yen enjoyed a lull early in 1980, but yen selling increased again in February. As noted above, Woodley of the IMF Asian Department expressed concern about the yen's weakness in his visit of Morinaga, but at the same time he was not confident about how effective an increase in Japanese interest rates would be in reversing the yen. Indeed, selling pressure on the yen continued even after the BOJ's official discount rate hike in mid-February 1980.

It had been the understanding of the Japanese finance ministry and the Bank of Japan that the US Treasury was reluctant to agree to the Fed's intervention to defend the yen on its account. However, before noon on Saturday 1 March 1980 Japan Standard Time, Takashi Kato, Director-General of the International Finance Bureau at the Ministry of Finance, informed BOJ Executive Director Hayami that US Treasury sources had suggested that Governor Mayekawa should call Chairman Volcker on the same day to discuss the Fed's yen buying operation in the New York foreign exchange market.

In order to prevent any leakage of information about our action in this regard, Hayami, and I secretly gathered in the Governor's office on Saturday afternoon and started to arrange a telephone call to Chairman Volcker. Given the time difference between Tokyo and American East Coast of 13 hours, we had to wait until Saturday evening to call him.

Governor Maekawa, Hayami, and I remained in the Governor's office with all the shutters down on the windows of his office, so that no one from outside could see us working in the office on the Saturday evening.

Hayami gave a ring to Henry Wallich, his counterpart at the Fed, to obtain Volcker's private telephone number by which Mayekawa could talk directly to Volcker. He was told that Volcker was in the habit of returning from Washington to his home in New York to join his ailing wife over weekends. Using the telephone number given by Wallich and sitting next to Mayekawa at his office desk, I gave a ring on his behalf to Volcker's New York home on Saturday morning New York time. Mrs. Volcker answered my phone call to say that her husband was staying at his flat in Washington for this weekend as an exception. I told her that Mayekawa wished to talk directly with her husband, and she kindly let me have the phone number of Volcker's private flat in Washington. I immediately used this telephone number and was relieved to hear Volker himself respond in his New Yorker-accented English. I handed the receiver to Mayekawa and intercepted their telephone conversation at his side. Volcker agreed to the Fed's intervention in the New York market to support the yen against the dollar, but asked Mayekawa to make it as a multilateral arrangement involving the West German Bundesbank and the Swiss National Bank as well under which the four central banks would issue a joint press statement to announce their readiness to intervene in the foreign exchange markets in Tokyo, New York, Frankfurt, and Zurich in co-ordination to support the yen.

We had to wait until early afternoon on Sunday 2 March Tokyo time—early on the morning of the same day in Frankfurt/Zurich time—to speak with Bundesbank President Karl Otto Pöhl (Poehl) and Swiss National Bank President Fritz Leutwiler on the telephone. I was able to get through to Leutwiler in one shot and he immediately agreed to co-operate with us. On the other hand, Pöhl, who had only recently succeeded Emminger as Bundesbank President, was more circumspect in his reply than Leutwiler. He said that he could not make an immediate commitment on his own, as the decision to intervene in a co-ordinated manner using the yen was a Board matter. But he agreed to include a statement about his Bank's co-operative stance. Taking into account Pöhl's reaction, I prepared the draft statement in English, and Governor Mayekawa discussed it with Chairman Volcker by telephone. It was agreed that the text agreed in English would be published by the Fed and that the text in Japanese by the Japanese finance ministry and the BOJ before the Tokyo foreign exchange market opened on Monday morning.

This new scheme was announced on Sunday evening Japan time. We worked in the Governor's office from the afternoon of Saturday March 1st to the afternoon of Sunday March 2nd without going home over the weekend. The main reason for this was that two items of bad news were scheduled to be published during the coming week. We hoped that the announcement by the four central banks before the opening of the Tokyo market on Monday morning that they were ready to intervene in the foreign exchange markets to support the yen would calm the market. One item was that the wholesale price index for February, due to be released on Tuesday, would show a sharp rise as a combined result of higher dollar-denominated oil prices and a weaker yen. The second was a large increase in electricity prices, scheduled to be announced later in the week. Under the agreed multilateral scheme, the Fed New York would intervene in the New York foreign exchange market to support the yen *on its own account*. This meant that the Fed New York would run the foreign exchange risk of holding yen balances, and the West German and Swiss central banks would also co-operate in concerted action in the Frankfurt and Zurich foreign exchange markets. It was also noted in the announcement that the use of non-residents' free yen accounts at Japanese banks would be made more flexible in order to promote capital inflows to Japan.

This extremely quick establishment of a multilateral framework for co-ordinated intervention involving the four central banks was made possible because of strong personal ties that Governor Mayekawa had built up with Volcker and other top central bankers. He had developed close ties with his counterparts in major Western countries since the days he was Director-General of the BOJ Foreign Department. His successors in the post, Genso Fujimoto and Hayami also formed close working relationships in the so-called "Group of Four", including Henry Wallich, member of the US Federal Reserve Board, Leon Gleske, member of the Board of the West German Bundesbank, and Pierre Languetin, member of the Board of the Swiss National Bank. The Group met regularly on the occasions of BIS monthly meetings of G10 central banks in Basel, Switzerland.

Accompanying Mayekawa on His Overseas Trips as Bank of Japan Governor

Mayekawa's first overseas trip as BOJ Governor was primarily to attend the BIS Monthly Governors' Meeting in March 1980. At this Governors' meeting, there was an exchange of information on financial and economic developments in G10 countries and a short report on Eurocurrency market regulatory issues. Prior to this meeting, Mayekawa also met separately with Chairman Volcker, Bundesbank President Pöhl (Poehl) and Swiss National Bank President Leutwiler, and expressed his gratitude for their co-operation in the defence of the yen measures announced on 2 March. Mayekawa of course did not need my help for communication in English in these bilateral meetings and I was present only for notetaking.

During his meeting with Volcker, Mayekawa said that, with regard to the conduct of BOJ's monetary policy, he would enter into discussions about further monetary policy action with the Japanese government after his return to Tokyo, as it was necessary to break the effects of the sharp rise in wholesale prices in February and the electricity price hike on inflationary sentiment, and that he was personally inclined to take interest rate measures. Volcker did not express any opinion on this issue. Regarding the situation in the United States, he explained that in view of strong inflationary expectations among the general public and strong consumer spending as well as large increases in the money supply, the Fed was trying to control the increase in bank reserves. At the same time, he was keenly aware of the risk of a major recession if consumer confidence changed, and said that the United States was currently in a dangerous situation.[15]

In Mayekawa's meeting with Pöhl, the latter expressed strong concern that if the Unites States continued to tighten monetary policy strongly, there would be a risk of a debacle in savings banks and the housing finance market leading to a collapse of the financial system as a whole. Pöhl added that he felt that Volcker was "confused" about what to do to fight inflation in the United States.[16]

During Mayekawa's meeting with Leutwiler, the latter also told us that he was under the impression that Volcker was not sure what should be done about US interest rates. Leutwiler then proposed to increase the swap facility between the BOJ and the Swiss National Bank to an amount equivalent to $1 billion.[17]

Governor Mayekawa also held a meeting with Al Quraishi, Governor of the Saudi Arabian Monetary Authority (SAMA), who informed us that he was keeping a close eye on the development of the yen, that he had received a visit from an official of the Japanese Ministry of Finance ten days earlier and that a basic agreement had been reached to double the purchase of yen-denominated Japanese government bonds. He then proposed to strengthen the SAMA's communication with the BOJ.[18]

I also accompanied Mayekawa when he attended the Hamburg meeting of the IMF Interim Committee in the spring of 1980. The main topics of discussion were the balance of payments deficits of non-oil-producing countries and the strengthening of IMF financial resources. Japan was no longer a particular topic of discussion at the IMF Interim Committee.

Governor Mayekawa also attended the BIS Governors' Meeting in July, which occasioned my last visit to Basel as a BOJ official before starting my second service at the OECD. As an aside, the BOJ officials' usual hotel accommodation in Basel was the Euler, but when I travelled to Basel from the OECD, I used the Hilton Hotel, partly to show that l was an international civil servant at the OECD and no longer an official of BOJ.

During his stay in Basel on the occasion of the July 1980 BIS Governors' meeting, Mayekawa also had a bilateral meeting with Volcker to follow up their March meeting at the same place. Mayekawa informed Volcker that the increase in the BOJ's official discount rate to 9 per cent on 19 March was perceived by Japanese financial institutions and industry as an emergency measure, and that there were expectations for a reduction in the official discount rate, based on the view that the worst was over for the price situation, but that he would like to wait and see how the situation would develop further. Volcker stated that there would be no problem if the yen remained between 200 and 220 yen per US dollar, while Anthony Solomon, then president of the Fed New York, who was also present at the meeting, remarked that 215 yen per US dollar would not be a bad level. In response, Mayekawa commented that from the Japanese central bank's perspective, a slightly stronger yen would be desirable.[19]

The OECD Secretariat's paper submitted to the WP3 meeting, which was held just prior to the July monthly BIS Governors' meeting, Japan's current account deficit was estimated to be approximately $10 billion for the first half of 1981. It was pointed out in the paper that a deficit of this magnitude would not be seen as inappropriate, as its current account was certain to improve from mid-1981 onwards.

At the margin of the WP3 meeting, Henry Wallich had suggested to Hayami, both of whom attended it, that he personally had no problem with what the BOJ was doing, including its interest rate and exchange rate policies, and that since Volcker and Solomon would be attending the monthly BIS Governors' meeting in July, it would be good if Mayekawa would take his time to discuss the BOJ's policy management with both of them.

Notes

1. Kumiharu Shigehara, "Japan's Experience with Use of Monetary Policy and the Process of Liberalization", Bank of Japan Monetary and Economic Studies, Vol. 9, No. 1, March 1991. https://www.imes.boj.or.jp/research/papers/english/me9-1-1.pdf.
2. Koichi Hamada and Fumio Hayashi, "Monetary Policy in Postwar Japan", A. Ando et al. eds., "Monetary Policy in Our Times" (the Proceedings of the First International Conference by the Institute for Monetary and Economic Studies, the Bank of Japan), MIT Press, 1985.
3. US Embassy Office of Public Information and Culture, Wireless Bulletin, "Blumenthal Discusses Growth Strategies in OECD Countries", Paris, 24 June 1977.
4. David Marsh, "Think-Tank Operator Seeks a Refill of Ideas", The Financial Times, 5 March 1993.
5. Kumiharu Shigehara, memorandum, "Summary of Governor Morinaga's Meeting with Leutwiler, President of Swiss National Bank", 17 January 1978, p. 4.
6. The Articles of Agreement, as amended in 1978, provide that members can adopt the exchange arrangements of their choice. This provision is supplemented by a prescription that firm surveillance over exchange rate policies will be exercised by the IMF under specific principles adopted for the guidance of all members. The responsibilities of the IMF changed from those of a guardian of member countries' observance of exchange rate rules to those of an overseer of individual country exchange rate policy.
7. Kumiharu Shigehara, memorandum, "Summary of Governor Morinaga's Meeting with van Lennep, OECD Secretary-General", 23 May 1978, pp. 3–4.

8. According to three economists who worked at the OECD around that time, the role played by the OECD secretariat in the preparation of this Summit was more intense than for other summits either before or since. See John Llewellyn, Stephen Potter and Lee Samuelson, "Economic Forecasting and Policy—the International Dimension", Routledge and Kegan Paul, 1985, pp. 244–249.
9. For critical comments on the Bonn Summit by Masataka Okura, Vice Minister of Finance at the time, see Ministry of Finance, History of Showa Finance: FY1974-1979, Vol. 7: "International Finance, External Relations Matters and Customs Administration", Part 1, "International Finance and External Relations Matters" (in Japanese), p. 60.
10. From Henry Owen to the Vice President, WHCF CO-26, 2 February 1978, Carter Library.
11. In a world of *n* independent countries, only *n*-1 external policies such as exchange rate target can be independently determined. If each of *n* countries tries to pursue its external policy independently, the most likely result is inconsistency. One solution to this problem calls for one country (the "*n*" th country) to abandon its external policy.
12. Kumiharu Shigehara, memorandum, "Summary of Governor Morinaga's Meeting with de Larosière, IMF Managing Director", 8 March 1979, pp. 1–17.
13. Kumiharu Shigehara, memorandum, "Summary of Governor Morinaga's Meeting with de Larosière, IMF Managing Director", 9 May 1979, pp. 1–7.
14. Kumiharu Shigehara, memorandum, "Summary of Governor Morinaga's Meeting with Woodley , Deputy Director of IMF Asian Department", 26 Nov 1979, p. 3.
15. Kumiharu Shigehara, memorandum, "Summary of Governor Maekawa's Meeting with Volcker, FRB Chairman", 10 Mar 1980.
16. Kumiharu Shigehara, memorandum, "Summary of Governor Mayekawa with Pöhl, German Bundesbank President", 10 Mar 1980.
17. Kumiharu Shigehara, memorandum, "Summary of Governor Mayekawa's Meeting with Leutwiler, President of Swiss National Bank", 10 Mar 1980.

18. Kumiharu Shigehara, memorandum, "Summary of Governor Mayekawa's Meeting Al Quraishi, Governor of Saudi Arabian Monetary Authority (SAMA)", 10 Mar 1980.
19. Kumiharu Shigehara, memorandum, "Summary of Governor Mayekawa's Meeting with Volcker, FRB Chairman", 7 July 1980.

CHAPTER 9

High US Interest Rates and Fiscal and Monetary Policy Mix in Three Largest Economies in the Early 1980s

Japan succeeded in containing inflation pressure in the aftermath of the second oil shock at the beginning of the 1980s without output contraction as experienced by many OECD countries such as the United States and West Germany. However, a sustained period of Japan's strong macroeconomic performance in the 1980s was followed by its unsatisfactory economic growth performance in the 1990s when the annual growth rate of per capita real GDP averaged about 1 1/2 per cent, less than a half of the average for 1980. Over the same period, real per capita GDP in the United States grew at an annual average rate of slightly more than 2 1 /4 per cent, somewhat faster than in the l980s. Thus, in 2000, per capita real GDP in Japan stood at 74 per cent of the US level in terms of purchasing power parity, whereas it was 82 per cent of the US level in 1990.

Per capita GDP growth performance in several high-income countries in Europe such as West Germany, France, Sweden, and Switzerland worsened in the 1990s in comparison with the 1980s also, and their per capita GDP levels declined relative not only to the United States but also to Japan. For example, Germany's per capita real GDP level, which was 78 per cent of the US level in 1990, declined to 70 per cent of the US level in 2000; the comparable numbers for France were 75 per cent and 64 per cent. On the other hand, far better growth performance was observed in a number of countries which was still in the catch-up process in terms of economic development in the 1990s such as South Korea (hereafter Korea) which became the second

K. Shigehara, *The Bank of Japan, the OECD, and Beyond*,
https://doi.org/10.1007/978-981-97-5307-9_9

Asian OECD member country in 1996, but also high-income countries such as Australia, the Netherlands, and Norway.

With this sketchy note on the economic growth performance of OECD countries in the 1980s and the 1990s in mind, in this chapter I will review the OECD Secretariat work and discussions which took place at OECD meetings about major international economic policy issues involving Japan as well as the United States and some other major OECD countries in the early 1980s when I worked as Deputy Director of the General Economic Branch of the OECD Economics and Statistics Department. My recollections and reflections either as an official of the Bank of Japan or an international civil servant at the OECD about the international balance of payments adjustment process of two major external surplus countries—Japan and West Germany—as well as the United States with persistent external deficits and some other economic issues in the latter part of the 1980s and the1990s will be described in the following chapters.

In September 1980, I started the second period of my service at the OECD, this time replacing Stephen Potter as Deputy Director of the General Economic Branch of the Economics and Statistics Department (ESD) headed by Silvia Ostry, who was formally Chair of the Economic Council of Canada and a close friend of Pierre Trudeau, Canada's Prime Minister from March 1980 to June 1984. In the spring of 1980, she wrote a letter to Mayekawa, Bank of Japan (BOJ) Governor, asking the Bank to release me to work for her while Potter would work at the Bank of England (BOE) on secondment from the OECD for two years. Mayekawa accepted her request as my second term of office for not longer than two years at the OECD was not considered within the BOJ to do harm to my career at the Bank even though it was then under a rigid seniority personnel management system.

On my return to the General Economic Branch of ESD, the division of responsibilities was established with its work for WP3 being entrusted to me, while Yves Ulmo, its Director, supervised its work for WP2 and WP4 (the two eventually merged to become WP1) which dealt with structural issues such as economic growth and employment issues.

As monetary policy issues were not Ostry's forte, I often flew alone from Paris to London to meet with WP3 Chairman, Christopher ("Kit") McMahon, Deputy Governor of the BOE, to decide on topics for discussion at WP3 meetings and the time management of each meeting. He was a friendly character originally from Australia who usually treated me to a cup of English tea from the teapot which he kept in his office.

WP3 discussions immediately after the start of the second period of my service at the OECD covered issues relating to the recycling of surplus funds of OPEC countries after the outbreak of the second oil crisis which I will review in Chapter 17 of this book,[1] the disturbingly high level of US interest rates after the introduction of its new monetary control scheme, the effects of the monetary policy management and relaxation of restrictions on inward capital inflows in Japan, West Germany, and Switzerland, and the situation of balance of payments deficit countries in Europe.

At the WP3 meeting on 10 and 11 December 1980, asked by Chairman McMahon, Marris as Economic Adviser to the OECD Secretary-General expressed concern about the appreciation of the dollar and the depreciation of the Japanese yen and the West German mark induced by higher US interest rates which had resulted from the monetary tightening implemented in the United States to reduce inflationary pressures. He suggested that a policy mix of fiscal tightening and monetary easing in the United States should be combined with fiscal expansion and monetary tightening in Japan and West Germany. Ostry was unable to stop Marris from presenting his own views, which were not reflected in the Secretariat notes for the WP3 prepared under my supervision with Ostry's agreement. Marris' personal views were expressed orally and spontaneously at the WP3 meeting. The divergence of his views from those of the ESD became even clearer in the course of the OECD Secretariat work for the preparation of its policy recommendations to be put forward to the OECD ministerial meeting to be held in May 1982, which I will review in some details in the latter part of this chapter.

US Economic Policy Management in the Early 1980s

On January 20, 1981, Ronald Reagan, a Republican, was inaugurated as President of the United States, and on February 18, he announced his plan to rebuild the US economy. To combat the recession, he aggressively cut income taxes from 70 per cent to 50 per cent for the top tax bracket and cut the corporate tax rate from 46 per cent to 34 per cent. He promised to slow the growth of government spending and to deregulate business industries. At the same time, he encouraged the Federal Reserve (Fed) to combat inflation by reducing money supply growth. In May 1981, the Volker Fed raised the Federal funds rate, which further strengthened the dollar and weakened the Japanese yen and the West German mark (Deutschmark, DM).

The WP3 meeting at which US Treasury Under Secretary Beryl Sprinkel made his first appearance was held on 13–14 May 1981. Just prior to it, on 11 May, the BIS monthly G10 central bank governors' meeting was held in Basel. At that meeting, the new US policy of non-intervention in the foreign exchange market, which had been announced soon after the Reagan administration came to power, was officially confirmed by Sprinkel's congressional testimony. There was much criticism of this new US policy in the BIS meeting which Henry Wallich attended on behalf of the Federal Reserve (Fed). There, he made no comment on Sprinkel's testimony, simply reiterating the Fed policy of maintaining emphasis on money supply in domestic monetary policy management.

On the day of the BIS monthly governors' meeting in Basel, François Mitterrand replaced Valéry Giscard d'Estaing as the President of France, and the Bank of France announced higher short-term money market intervention rates and conducted aggressive foreign exchange market intervention to prevent a collapse of market confidence in the French franc.

Following these events in Washington, Basel, and Paris, the WP3 meeting at the OECD headquarters in Paris focused unsurprisingly on the issues of the US monetary authorities' foreign exchange market non-intervention policy, exchange rate levels, and the relationship between exchange rates and interest rates.

At the meeting, Sprinkel introduced himself as a born farmer and not a born monetarist, and then expressed his strong belief in the efficiency of the market. On the other hand, Hayami of the Bank of Japan, Gleske of the West German Bundesbank, and Languetin of the Swiss National Bank, all three just arriving in Paris from Basel, expressed concerns about risks of irrational market expectations, causing panics and turbulences. In this context, the issue of whether the monetary authorities could accurately assess the so-called "fundamentals" affecting the exchange rate was discussed. In Sprinkel's opinion, the authorities were not capable of assessing them. This view was countered by European representatives who argued that the authorities could judge whether a currency was overvalued or undervalued. Gleske stated that the German mark's depreciation was excessive. Michel Camdessus, Directeur Général du Trésor at the French Ministry of Economy and Finance (later Governor of the Bank of France and Managing Director of the IMF), also stated that the selling pressure on the French franc in the first two days of Mitterrand's government was not in line with "fundamentals", which was why the French authorities intervened in the foreign exchange market.

Growing Criticism of High US Interest Rates

Following the WP3 meeting in mid-May 1981, the OECD Economic Policy Committee (EPC) met at the beginning of June, and Murray Weidenbaum, the new Chair of the US President's Council of Economic Advisers (CEA), was elected the new Chair of the EPC, replacing Charles Schultze, former CEA Chair. The meeting opened with a report on the discussions at the WP3 meeting by its Chair McMahon, followed by briefings from Stephen Axilrod, Director of Monetary Policy Division of the Board of Governors of the Federal Reserve System (FRB), and the representative of US Treasury.

Thereafter, a heated debate took place on the problems of high US interest rates, with CEA Chair Weidenbaum joining it from the EPC Chair's seat. Criticism from European representatives was based on the perception that high US interest rates were causing European currencies to depreciate, import prices to rise, necessitating continued or further monetary policy tightening in European countries to defend their currencies and increasing unemployment. They also pointed out that the Reagan government's fiscal policy of tax cuts and spending cuts, which could only be put into place with Congressional approval, placed too much burden on monetary policy, and that such an inappropriate policy mix was problematic.

At this EPC meeting, there was no criticism of Japan's export performance or the weakening of the yen, but only general concern about the risk of rising protectionism associated with high unemployment in Europe. A year later, however, the debate on Japan's economic policy changed dramatically amid persistently high interest rates in the United States, the prospect of accelerated economic growth in Japan due to dependence on external demand and growing criticism of Japan on the trade front, as I will describe below.

Discussion on Money Supply Targeting Policies

The new monetary control method introduced by the Fed in October 1979 did not bring about a noticeable reversal of money supply growth. Short-term market interest rates fluctuated wildly around high levels and the fall of the dollar continued in the exchange market. While these problems were discussed among developed countries in the BIS forum and at the OECD EPC meeting, WP3 was the most suitable forum where senior central bank representatives candidly exchanged views in a small, confidential gathering with those responsible for international monetary issues in the finance authorities of a limited number of OECD member countries.

During the dinner hosted by the WP3 Chairman on the first day of the WP3 meeting in December 1980, it was decided that WP3 should have an opportunity to have an in-depth discussion about the problems associated with the money-supply oriented monetary adjustment approach. Accordingly, I prepared a memorandum entitled "Monetary Control and Exchange Rate Pressures",[2] listing the issues that I thought should be discussed at WP3, and sent it to Chairman McMahon, who promptly forwarded copies to the WP3 representatives of the Fed, the Bank of Canada, the German Bundesbank, and the Swiss National Bank which had set money supply targets, asking them to provide written responses to the issues enumerated in my memorandum.

They included each central bank's assessment of the causes of the fluctuations in short- and longer-term market interest rates since 1980, its assessment of the relationship between money supply targeting and the volatility of market interest rates and exchange rates, its judgement as to the extent to which the central bank adopting money supply targets could tolerate temporary deviations from monetary targets in order to reduce volatilities in market interest rates and exchange rates without undermining market credibility over money supply targets and adversely affecting the public's inflation expectations.

Chairman McMahon later sent his letters (of 25 February 1981) to all WP3 participating countries to inform them of the new WP3 project which turned out to be a major undertaking. The central banks that had set money supply targets, the Fed, the Bank of Canada, the German Bundesbank, the Swiss National Bank and the Bank of England, all responded, while the BOJ and the Banque de France, which had not set money supply targets, also provided their memorandums to the

OECD Secretariat. In addition, the US Treasury Department submitted a congressional briefing by Under Secretary Sprinkel on US monetary policy.

The OECD Secretariat prepared a discussion paper[3] outlining the issues surrounding money supply-oriented policies and a note[4] compiling the responses of these national authorities. After a bit of delay, the Bank of Italy also sent us a paper on the treatment of the monetary base—not money supply—just before the WP3 meeting.

Building on this joint preparatory work by the Secretariat and the national authorities, the WP3 discussions took place over a full day on 9 September 1981. The US delegation had a strong line-up, with Under Secretary Sprinkel from the Treasury Department, Wallich as a member of Federal Reserve Board, Edwin Truman, Director of Fed International Finance Division, and Jerry Jordan, a Member of the Council of Economic Advisors to the President and a noted monetarist who was at the Federal Reserve Bank of St Louis in the late 1960s and 1970s (he served as the ninth president of the Federal Reserve Bank of Cleveland from 1992 to 2003). Furthermore, a research paper on the new monetary procedure[5] written by Stephen Axilrod, who attended the EPC meeting at the beginning of June 1981, was distributed in advance by the OECD Secretariat to the WP3 representatives of each country. Three members of the Secretariat participated in the discussions at the main table at this meeting: Marris, Ostry, and myself.

The debate naturally centred first on the new monetary control scheme in the United States. According to Sprinkel, the problem was that financial markets were still in doubt about the US authorities' willingness to stick to the new monetary policy scheme, and the so far disorderly relationship between the money supply and interest rates should be taken as part of a "transition" towards lower money supply growth and lower price inflation, respectively. He also stated that the sticky expectations mechanism was working very strongly, both in the United States and abroad, and that this was having a significant impact on US interest rates, US and foreign interest rate differentials, and the dollar exchange rates. The US delegation was well aware that this was a major problem for foreign countries, but urged that the current situation should not be confused with the "ultimate outcome" of the new monetary adjustment scheme. It was noted that the most serious short-term domestic cost of the new monetary policy scheme was the damage it had done to the US long-term bond market, which would not recover until market confidence in the new scheme was firmly established.

In the discussions that followed these oral explanations by the US delegation, many participants pointed out that while very short-term fluctuations in interest rates and exchange rates were not a major problem, their ups and downs over a longer period should entail a more serious problem. At the same time, few were of the view that the latter problem was caused by the new US monetary adjustment scheme. Wallich argued that the ups and downs in interest rates in 1980 and 1981 would have occurred even if the Fed had maintained the conventional monetary adjustment approach.

In response to this explanation from Wallich, delegates from other countries expressed the hope that the Fed's policies aimed at price stabilisation would have an effect in calming down expectations of higher prices, and that through this it would not take too long for market interest rates to fall. In this regard, Jordan explained that there was strong pressure on the Fed to ease monetary policy from the US Congress and the private business community, including the housing industry. In response, Wallich expressed the view that if monetary policy were to be eased at this point, expectations of higher inflation would strengthen and market interest rates would rise further.

There was also an in-depth discussion of the United Kingdom and West Germany as countries other than the United States that had set money supply targets. Representatives of both countries expressed the view that "fundamental" factors such as the current account balance and purchasing power parity, which affect expectations, had a greater impact on exchange rates than changes in domestic and foreign interest rate differentials. The ratchet effect of exchange rate fluctuations on prices was not considered important. The UK and German representatives then argued that money supply targeting policies should be managed in a flexible manner, as an overemphasis on stability, whether of interest rates or the exchange rate, would lead to instability in other areas.

In its discussion paper, the OECD Secretariat reported that it had not been able to obtain empirical analysis showing that changes in domestic and foreign interest rate differentials had a significant impact on the exchange rate, but in this connection, Alexandre Lamfalussy, then BIS Economic Adviser, stated that expectations driven by developments such as the current account balance and purchasing power parity had a greater impact on the exchange rate than domestic and foreign interest rate differentials, and in some cases caused exchange rate overshooting. He argued that in such cases, the monetary authorities should signal to the market through policy actions. His view was supported by some national central bank representatives, but was countered by doubts about the authorities' ability to truly identify "market failures". In particular, Sprinkel highlighted the danger of the authorities' errors in intervening in the foreign exchange market, resulting in their losses and great costs to taxpayers.

Fiscal and Monetary Policy Mix in the United States, Japan, and West Germany

Fiscal policy developments in the United States under the Reagan administration, together with fiscal prudence in Japan and West Germany, changed international savings and investment balances within the OECD area. A growing current account deficit of the United States was matched by persistent significant surpluses of Japan and West Germany, and the correction of external imbalances came to the forefront of the international economic policy agenda.

It was pretty obvious what the United States should do. The international consensus was that the United States should reduce fiscal deficits, which should moderate pressure on domestic interest rates; an induced weakening of the dollar exchange rate, together with a shift in domestic savings and investment balances resulting from fiscal consolidation, should reduce its external deficits. On the other hand, it was less clear what Japan and West Germany should do. Different views on this issue emerged within the OECD Secretariat in the runup to the May 1982 meeting of the OECD Ministerial Council meeting.

Before reviewing these views however, it might be worth noting that at van Lennep's meeting with Sir Roy Denman, the European Commission's Director-General for External Relations in Brussels on 27 February 1981, Marris stated that "the Japanese had intervened massively to manipulate the exchange rate and this was something that should be discussed". Denman said that he was not aware of the evidence of the Japanese authorities' manipulation and if there were such evidence he would certainly be prepared to take it up with the Japanese. Ostry received a copy of the compte-rendu of the Brussels meeting[6] circulated by the chief of staff at the Secretary-General's office, and forwarded it to me to ask for my comment. The reported statement of Marris in Brussels was so absurd that, instead of making my personal comment, I simply sent her copies of the articles reviewing the BOJ's foreign exchange market operations published in the quarterly reviews of the Federal Reserve Bank of New York in which it was clearly described that the BOJ had sold US dollars to support the yen in the foreign exchange market rather than bought them as Marris wrongly stated. It was clear to me that Marris had not followed what was going on within the central banking world. Actually, the BOJ and the Federal Reserve Bank of New York were in daily telephone contact to let each other know about foreign exchange market developments in Tokyo and New York (see also Section "Multilateral co-operation for the defence of the yen" in Chapter 8).

Following the Ostry's request, however, I did not send to Marris copies of my memos circulated within the ESD nor the drafts of EPC and WP3 papers prepared under my supervision. It was assumed that Marris as Economic Adviser to the Secretary-General received copies of these draft papers from the Secretary-General's office.

Outside the OECD, Fred Bergsten, a former Assistant Secretary for International Affairs at the US Treasury under the Carter administration and a close friend of Marris, contributed an article titled "The villain is an overvalued dollar"[7] to the March–April 1982 issue of *Challenge* (p. 30), in which he criticised the policy mix of the Reagan administration, running a loose fiscal policy with all the burden of anti-inflation policy on the Fed and driving US interest rates to unprecedented levels in real terms. At the same time, he also criticised Japan, pointing out that it was running the opposite policy mix, which he argued was erroneous from an international standpoint, as it was trying to stimulate the domestic economy by combining a tightening of fiscal policy to close their big budget deficit with a loosening of monetary policy resulting in a weaker yen in the exchange market.

At the WP3 meeting in March 1982, it was noted that Japan's domestic demand recovery was weaker than projected in the OECD Economic Outlook published in December 1981 and that Japanese exports tended to increase noticeably. At the time, the Japanese yen was about 20 per cent weaker against the US dollar than at the end of 1978. According to calculations by the OECD, the nominal effective exchange rate of the US dollar was more than 20 per cent higher than at the end of 1978 while the Japanese yen was about 5 per cent higher and DM was slightly weaker. The effective exchange rate of the UK pound, while not as strong as the US dollar, was still more than 10 per cent higher than at the end of 1978. Following the United States, the United Kingdom had adopted monetarism under Prime Minister Thatcher.

At this meeting, Wallich expressed the view that if the Japanese government sector did not absorb the excess savings of the private sector with a structurally high household savings rate, there would be pressure for capital outflows abroad, resulting in a depreciation of the yen and a persistent current account surplus. As noted in the preceding chapter, at a bilateral meeting with Hayami of the BOJ at the margin of the July 1980 meeting, Wallick had told Hayami that he had no problem with what Japan was doing, but the situation had changed considerably since that time.

Kenneth Cousins, second permanent secretary for international finance at the UK Treasury was quick to echo Wallich's views expressed at the WP3 meeting, pointing out that Japan's economic growth since 1973 had been largely dependent on increased exports. In addition to Cousins, Lamfalussy, then Deputy General Manager of the BIS (later its General Manager), also expressed the view that Japan had room to increase its budget deficit, pointing to the low international level of Japan's budget deficit as a percentage of GNP and the size of total domestic savings. Philippe Jurgensen of the French Ministry of Finance stated that the rate of increase in Japan's fiscal expenditure in 1982 was the lowest since 1956, and that this might put the brakes on the recovery of domestic demand and that low interest rates due to accommodative monetary policy were encouraging capital outflows abroad, resulting in yen depreciation. Furthermore, Flandorfer of the German economic ministry stated that exchange rate adjustment by changing international interest rate differentials should be the most important means for adjusting the current account balance and asked whether, from this perspective, Japanese interest rates could be raised to the extent that this would not impede the recovery of domestic demand.

It was Sprinkel who clearly disagreed with this line of argument and stated that there was nothing wrong with Japan's fiscal and monetary policy mix. From his monetarist point of view, the primary objective of monetary policy should be domestic price stabilisation, and the BOJ should not be pressured to ease monetary policy in order to increase the money supply and refuel inflationary expectations, and it was not right for the BOJ to use monetary policy to manipulate the exchange rate. Moreover, he believed that it was also right for the Japanese government to try to improve fiscal health and that the exchange rate should be left to the market to decide. In Sprinkel's view, the policy problem for Japan was not in the macroeconomic policy area, but delay in its domestic market liberalisation. Within the US Treasury, Mark Leland, Assistant Secretary for International Finance, and others shared Sprinkel's views.[8]

The OECD Secretariat was in the middle of half-yearly economic forecasting exercise around the time of the March 1882 WP3 meeting. Eventually, the Economic Outlook prepared for the April EPC meeting projected that one percentage point of the 4.3 per cent real GDP growth in Japan in 1983 would come from an increase in net exports (Table 9.1).

Internal discussions within the OECD Secretariat on the policy recommendation paper to be submitted to the OECD Ministerial Council meeting in mid-May had started before the WP3 meeting. As already pointed out by Marris at the WP3 meeting in December 1980, he maintained his argument that two policy changes in the United States—a

Table 9.1 OECD Economic Outlook (three largest economies)

	1981	*1982*	*1983*
Gross national product (real, year-on-year, %)			
US	2	−1.5	2.25
Japan	2.9	2	4
West Germany	−0.3	1	3.25
Gross domestic demand (real, year-on-year, %)			
US	2.6	−1	2.5
Japan	0.8	2	2.75
West Germany	−2.5	−1.5	2.25
Current account balance (billion US $)			
US	6.5	11	−5
Japan	4.7	6	21
West Germany	−7.6	2	5
Personal consumption deflator (year-on-year, %)			
US	8.3	5.75	5.5
Japan	4.5	3.75	4.25
West Germany	5.9	4.5	3

Note Forecasts published in the July 1982 issue of the OECD Economic Outlook; Japan's real GDP growth rate for 1983 was revised to 4 per cent from the 4.3 per cent which was submitted to the April EPC meeting. The exchange rates were assumed to remain unchanged at the average levels for the week ending 30 March 1982 (the yen exchange rate was 244 yen to the dollar) reduction in the budget deficit and an easing of monetary policy—should be combined with the opposite policy changes—fiscal expansion and monetary policy tightening—in Japan and West Germany, and such recommendations should be included in the discussion paper for the forthcoming OECD Ministerial Council meeting.

At the WP3 meeting in March, Ostry argued that Japan may have over-adjusted after the second oil crisis and real wages seemed to her to be too low, and if this was the case, this could be one reason why Japan's international competitiveness had over strengthened and why Japanese macroeconomic policy should be changed to adjust for this. Christopher Higgins, who had succeeded the Frenchman Ulmo as Director of the General Economic Branch, initially had ideas similar to those of Marris. He was formerly minister at the Australian Delegation to the OECD on secondment from the Australian treasury, and was a PhD student of Lawrence Klein in econometrics at the University of Pennsylvania.[9]

On the other hand, although I was not a "strong monetarist" like Sprinkel, I was at odds with Marris and Higgins on Japanese fiscal/monetary policy mix even before Sprinkel presented his views at the WP3 meeting in March.

My view was that the current account surpluses of Japan and West Germany should be considered in the global context where, once OPEC oil surpluses were contained, the OECD area as a whole should aim at running current account surpluses matched by sustainable capital outflows coupled with technological transfer to the non-OECD area, and that Japan and West Germany should rather embark on structural reform to strengthen domestic growth potential and, in the case of Japan, also to accelerate domestic market opening.

I thought that it was urgently required for the United States to realise a policy mix of reducing the budget deficit and easing monetary policy which would help correct the strong dollar problem by an induced fall in US interest rates, and that the goal of Japanese monetary policy should not be shifted from domestic price stability to an external objective, nor should the Japanese government's fiscal policy stance be based on too short-term demand management policy perspective. In fact, the Secretariat's discussion paper for the March WP3 meeting, which I oversaw, did not make any recommendations on Japan's policy mix, as Marris had suggested.[10]

On 19 March 1982, I addressed a memorandum "Ministerial Macro-Economic Paper: Outline" (KS/LM (82)55) to Ostry with copies to other ESD directors, where I made the following remarks.

i. In the Ministerial macroeconomic paper, the Secretariat should remind the OECD ministers that "hard-currency" options to cope with domestic inflation pressures are complicating domestic and international adjustment process. Such options may provide a short-run relief on the inflation front, but if they do not go hand in hand with labour market reforms inducing wages and price restraints, it would squeeze profits and weaken investment and international protectionist pressures.
ii. The OECD Ministers should be invited to give some thought to the medium-term appropriate configuration of international trade and current account transactions. Present arguments seem rather narrowly concentrated on the short-term relationship between macro-policies and international trade and employment. The OECD Secretariat should inform the Ministers that they should not be too short-sighted and that in the slightly longer run, it would be beneficial for low-productivity countries to receive real transfer of resources and technology from high productivity countries with some persistent current account surplus in the form of direct investment which would enhance employment opportunities in the longer term.
iii. Export of long-term capital to less developed countries from OECD countries with high savings is a form of international economic co-operation. Japan for example recorded a net direct investment outflow of $5 billion against a current account surplus of the same magnitude, with the World Bank and regional development banks as well as governments of less developed countries as important users of the Tokyo capital market which enjoys a large supply of loanable funds at relatively low interest rates.

In supporting my second point, I referred to a speech made by Kenneth Baker, UK Minister for Trade and Information Technology, made at the British Institute of Management in London, where he called for increasing co-operation between Japanese and British companies in high technology, in third markets and through Japanese investment in the United Kingdom.[11]

On 22 March, the Japan desk in the Country Studies Branch sent an internal note to ESD directors in which it assessed that Japan's current external surplus would widen from $4 3/4 billion in 1981 to $13 1/ 4 in 1982 and to around $25 billion in 1983. At the same time, the desk considered that Japanese domestic demand was recovering and that, given the relatively small external contribution to Japan's domestic output growth, it went too far to say that the Japanese economic growth relied excessively on external demand. The head of the Japan desk was Jean-Pierre Tuveri, a French economist with a PhD from the University of California, Berkeley.

OECD's "Differentiated Approach" versus the US Administration's Views

On March 25, OECD Secretary-General van Lennep had a meeting with Donald Regan, then US Treasury Secretary, in Washington. Regan was an advocate of "Reaganomics" and tax cuts to simulate economic growth and create jobs. The meeting was attended by Under Secretary Beryl Sprinkel and Abraham Katz, US ambassador to the OECD as well as Marris as Economic Adviser to van Lennep. The Secretary-General stated that the OECD Secretariat would propose a "differentiated approach" to economic policy management in OECD member countries at its Ministerial meeting to be held on 11–12 May, one that should result in a more balanced discussion, instead of criticism of one or two major economies. He added that such an approach would point out that all of Europe's problems did not originate in the United States and Japan: the key was their own domestic policies.

Under Secretary Sprinkel argued that the "differentiated approach" suggested by van Lennep contradicted the US administration's view that all OECD countries should give top priority to fighting inflation. On policy priorities in external surplus countries, Sprinkel noted that greater budget deficits for Japan and perhaps more money growth in West Germany were particularly inappropriate policy prescriptions. In reply to Marris' suggestion that Japan should also reduce money growth, Sprinkel indicated that Japanese monetary policy management was good and what he was concerned about was Japanese trade policy.

Without knowledge about the discussion the OECD Secretary-General and Marris had had in Washington, during the internal meeting chaired by van Lennep on the draft economic policy recommendations to be included in the Secretariat's note for the OECD Ministerial Council, Marris and I remained at odds with each other. I made a counter proposal to include the following passage in the draft communiqué for the OECD Ministerial Council meeting, to make the Secretariat's policy recommendation more balanced. The statement I suggested read as follows.

"Lower U.S. interest would help to strengthen the yen; higher Japanese interest rates would help to strengthen the yen. The major question with regard to the latter would be the extent of its contractionary monetary impact on Japanese domestic demand as well as the consequent diversion of output to exports, tending to negate the effects of the yen appreciation on Japanese trade account adjustment. Offsetting significant fiscal expansion in Japan would have undesirable medium-term financial and economic consequences. If U.S. interest rates were to fall and the yen substantially appreciate without a general tightening of Japanese monetary conditions, Japan and the United States would both benefit. So would their trading partners."

In this context, I might recall that, at least in its economic policy recommendation for Japan included in EPC and WP3 papers which were prepared during the periods when I was absent from the OECD Secretariat, it tended to pay less attention to the medium-term supply-side effects of demand management policy than the Japanese authorities.

A typical example is found in the Secretariat paper presented at the September 1977 meeting of WP3 in Washington which was reviewed in Chapter 8. At the time, the OECD Secretariat argued for fiscal expansion through private income tax cuts while the Japanese government increased public works expenditure which was designed to improve social infrastructure with favourable supply-side effects on medium-term productivity performance. As I noted in that chapter, the import content of these two types of expenditures was almost the same.

The provisional ministerial document (dated 9 April 1982) of the OECD Secretariat, entitled "Policy Issues for a Differentiated Strategy", sent to the heads of the delegations of member countries, mixed both Marris' and my proposals. It read as follows:

Ministers will wish to discuss the serious negative international consequences of the current large interest rate differentials between the United States and Japan and the low level of the yen.

- *Would Ministers agree that a general significant tightening of monetary policy in Japan would help to strengthen the yen, but such a policy shift, combined with offsetting substantial fiscal expansion, would have disruptive domestic financial and economic consequences for Japan with the negative impact on the rest of the world as well? Ministers may wish to discuss the possibilities of action to strengthen the yen and thus moderate exports without general tightening of Japanese monetary policy.*
- *Would a shift to relatively tighter fiscal policy in the United States contribute to a better performance for the United States and the membership as a whole? Would it also help to strengthen the yen and reduce international economic tensions more generally?*

On 27 April, just before the EPC meeting on 29 and 30 April, the Nikkan Kogyo Shimbun published an article entitled "Japan asked to raise interest rates – Japan's response at the EPC", in which it reported that European countries had long criticised Japanese interest rate policy, arguing that they were too low and that the Japanese monetary authorities were inducing a weaker yen. The article then reported that experts at the Economic Planning Agency and other institutions who would attend the EPC stated that Japan's interest levels looked relatively high in nominal terms but fairly low in real term with inflation lower than in Western countries, and that the Japanese representative attending the EPC were reportedly planning to refute criticisms from European countries, arguing that the weak yen was basically due to the effect of high interest rates in the United States.

At the EPC meeting, Marris argued that at the then prevailing yen exchange rate of around 240 yen to the dollar, companies of Western countries could not compete with their Japanese counterparts and that at least one of three solutions would be needed to solve this problem: a policy mix of higher Japanese interest rates and fiscal expansion, Japan's introduction of export taxes and import subsidies, or Western countries' restrictions on Japanese exports. WP3 Chair McMahon reported that a good majority of WP3 members were in favour of changing Japan's current policy mix at its March meeting, and Sir Douglas Wass, Permanent Secretary to the UK Treasury, said that a change in Japan's policy mix would be desirable for smaller open economies.

It might be worth noting that four British economists who spoke at both EPC and WP3 meetings—Marris at the OECD Secretariat, McMahon representing the Bank of England and Chair of WP3, Wass representing UK Treasury at EPC, and Cousins representing UK Treasury at WP3—seemed to me to apply the Mundell-Fleming model framework, at least implicitly, to their arguments about the desirable fiscal/monetary policy mix in Japan from a rather short-run international perspective. Unlike Sprinkel who had a monetarist's perspective not only with respect to US domestic economic policy management but also with respect to international monetary and economic policy issues including Japan's fiscal/monetary policy mix, all these British economists adopted an essentially Keynesian approach to international policy discussion without considering its medium-term consequences on the supply side of the Japanese economy and the rest of the world economy. Among the four of them, McMahon and Wass were top UK officials following (or were forced to follow) a monetarist approach to UK domestic monetary and fiscal policies under the premiership of Margaret Thatcher. The economic policy known as "Thatcherism" was implemented under her government which came into power in 1979, and the UK government's Medium-Term Financial Strategy for fiscal spending and taxation in 1980–81 was designed to help achieve the money supply target.

While there was a clear inconsistency in the UK government's domestic and international policy approaches, at least its international policy approach was consistent: at the subsequent OECD Ministerial Council meeting, Geoffrey Howe, UK Chancellor of the Exchequer, expressed the same view as those three senior officials of the UK government, as will be reviewed below.

At the EPC meeting, the Japanese delegation, headed by Tsutomu Tanaka, Director-General of the Research Department of the Economic Planning Agency, did not point out self-contradictions in the UK representatives' policy approach in a straightforward manner. However, Yoshio Suzuki, a Tokyo University PhD economist and Deputy Director-General of the BOJ's Research Department (later Executive Director of the Bank), remarked that changing Japan's policy mix for the sake of fine-tuning would have longer-term negative effects on the supply side of the Japanese economy and harm public confidence in Japan's economic policy. There was also a counterargument by representatives from the United States, West Germany, Australia, and other countries in general terms that short-sighted policy management should be avoided. In addition, Nagaoka, Deputy Director-General of the International Finance Bureau of the Japanese Ministry of Finance, argued that private-sector excess savings in Japan would disappear once private business investment recovered under easier monetary conditions and disagreed with the arguments by Wallich and others that Japan's budget deficit should be increased to absorb structural private excess savings.

The EPC discussion on the state of Japan's policy mix ended without a consensus. In its 1st May evening edition, the Nihon Keizai Shimbun, on the basis of information obtained from diplomatic sources, reported that Toshio Kômoto, Minister of the Economic Planning Agency, criticised the US government's economic policy, saying that high US interest rates were constraining economic management in its partner countries and that he was the first Japanese government leader who "officially and by name" suggested that the US government's fiscal deficits should be reduced. The report also stated that the Japanese government was planning to suggest a reduction in the BOJ's official interest rate on the basis of the need to use interest rate policy in a flexible manner. To me at the OECD Secretariat, this report was a big surprise.

At the OECD Ministerial Council on 10 and 11 May, US Treasury Secretary Regan, the US chief representative, said that his country was aware of the problem of too large a budget deficit in the United States and that the current high interest rate risk premium would dissipate in the coming months and a downward trend would become clearer. He did not make a recommendation on Japan's policy mix. UK Chancellor of the Exchequer Geoffrey Howe, who prefaced his remarks by saying that he was not part of the much-criticised "locomotive theory", argued that the yen's depreciation should be corrected by raising Japanese interest rates, as the UK delegation had already done at the EPC, and called for fiscal policy stimulus to boost domestic demand in Japan.

The key issue at this OECD Ministerial Council meeting was what expressions to be employed in the communiqué under the heading "High Interest Rates and International Tensions".[12] Normally, the draft communiqué used to be pre-cooked behind the scenes at the deputy ministerial level and then agreed upon smoothly at the Council of Ministers. But their deputies' negotiations on how to deal with most European countries' request for Japan to change its policy mix in the opposite direction to that of the United States failed. This led to a heated debate over the communiqué text in English during the negotiations between ministers in plenary. In the end, US Treasury Secretary Regan stated that the OECD's decisions needed to be taken by consensus and that the draft text on the exchange rate of the yen and Japan's policy mix should be deleted as there were divergent views. His proposal was adopted. Thus, the final version of the communiqué[7] only pointed out in general terms the importance of US fight against inflation and fiscal austerity, the use of adjustment mechanisms through exchange rates, and the reduction of trade friction through these measures. On the issue of high US interest rates and international tensions, the following statement was adopted in the communiqué of the OECD Council meeting issued on 11 May 1982.

"*Contrary to previous expectation interest rates have remained high relative to inflation, thereby adding a new factor to public sector deficits and restraining demand in the private sector. Ministers recognised the variety of reasons for currently high interest rates noting the impact of large budget deficits and uncertainty about the future course of fiscal and monetary policies. A durable reduction in interest rates ultimately rests on a durable reduction in inflation and inflation expectations. Ministers recognised the importance and results of anti-inflationary policies in the United States because of the key role of its economy and the dollar in the world economy. Many felt that more action should be taken to ease the pressure on interest and saving flows.*

Ministers recognised the importance of a smoother working of the exchange rate adjustment mechanism. Ministers agreed that under present circumstances improved co-operation with regards to convergence of economic policies to reduce excessive exchange rate fluctuations, such as have occurred in recent years, is necessary. Ministers noted, among the complexity of high interest rates stemming from the desire to avoid currency depreciation and its unwelcome consequences. Ministers took the view that the economic performance of the OECD as a whole would benefit, and current international trade tensions be lessened, if interest rates came down, and if opportunities for trade, capital flows and investment were increased".

From the point of view of an outsider who did not know OECD Ministers' inner work at the Council meeting, the communiqué's wording was unremarkable.

Following the discussions that took place on the first day of the OECD Ministerial Council meeting, there were no in-depth discussions on the global economic outlook at the IMF Interim Committee and the G10

Finance Ministers and Central Bank Governors meeting held in Helsinki on the following day. As these meetings coincided with the second day of the OECD Council meeting which van Lennep had to attend as OECD Secretary-General, he asked me to participate in them on his behalf.

In the communiqués of these two meetings in Helsinki, the sections on economic policy management in advanced economies were, unsurprisingly, in the same vein as the OECD Ministerial Council communiqué. As a side note, the first paragraph of the communiqué of the G10 Finance Ministers and Central Bank Governors' Meeting included the specific names of the OECD, IMF, and BIS representatives sitting at the main table of the G10 meeting. A senior BOJ official who read the communiqué gave me a strange compliment, saying that it was a great achievement that my personal name was included in the communiqué of the G10 Finance Ministers and Central Bank Governors' meeting, while the individual names of G10 Finance Ministers and Central Bank Governors were not specified in it.

In the margin of the Helsinki meetings, BOJ Governor Mayekawa asked me to explain about discussions that had taken place at the OECD ministerial meeting in Paris on the previous day. He had been concerned about the yen weakness and wished the BOJ's Market Operations Department (*Eigyou-kyoku*) to conduct operations to push upward pressure on short-term money market interest rates, although there were people within the Bank who were afraid that such action might weaken domestic demand recovery. Besides, the BOJ as the agent of the Japanese government sold dollars and bought yen in the foreign exchange market to support the yen exchange rate, but such intervention proved ineffective in reversing market trends.

Saving–Investment Balance and Balance of Payments Adjustment

Looking back on the discussions at the series of international meetings and conferences in 1982, it is regrettable that I did not participate in discussions at the EPC and WP3 meetings on the policy implications of Japan's high saving for its balance of payments adjustment when Wallich and others used the framework of the savings–investment balance and argued as if there were a unilateral causal relationship running from Japan's high savings to its current account surplus. In fact, the limitation of such framework was not discussed in depth. Given the hierarchical structure of the OECD Secretariat which was certainly less rigid than that of the BOJ, I could not make oral intervention at EPC and WP3 meetings during my second OECD service, which I did from time to time during my third service and frequently during my fourth service at the OECD in later years.

The debate about Japan's savings–investment balance re-emerged in the latter half of the 1980s and the 1990s. My arguments at OECD meetings and other international fora in my capacity as the BOJ Chief Economist and subsequently as OECD Chief Economist will be reviewed in the following chapters. Among them was my bilateral discussion with John Taylor, then Professor at Stanford University, later Under Secretary of US Treasury, on the topic of "How to use Japan's savings", in which he and I as BOJ Chief Economist discussed the implications of ageing population in Japan for its savings–investment balance and external adjustment process among others (Chapter 12).

Kit McMahon and Stephen Marris

The outbreak of the Mexican debt crisis in the summer of 1982 and the withdrawal from the new US monetary policy management scheme in October 1982 further increased the significance of policy discussions at WP3. The WP3 meeting in September 1982, held in conjunction with the IMF's Toronto Annual Meetings, was the last meeting I attended as Deputy Director of the General Economics Department. In his concluding remarks at the meeting, McMahon added his kind words of appreciation about my service for the WP3. I asked my personal assistant to record his oral remarks on a separate tape from the one to be kept in the Secretariat's archives, and I took it back to Japan as a memento of my work for WP3. McMahon and his wife came to Tokyo to participate in international meetings held in the following year and gave a beautiful English-made porcelain decorative small dish depicting the BOE building to my wife Akiko and me as a gift.

After the closing of the Toronto WP3 meeting, Marris, Ostry, and I went out to a coffee shop for a rest. Marris told me that the OECD Secretariat papers for WP3 that I had worked on over the past two years were really good. Even though Marris and I had at times been in sharp disagreement on some crucial policy issues, my relationship with him continued with occasional contact.

Towards the end of van Lennep's third term of office as the OECD Secretary-General (September 1984), Marris left the OECD to move to Washington to work at the Institute for International Economics founded by Fred Bergsten. He sent me in Tokyo a copy of his farewell speech made at the EPC meeting just before his departure from the OECD. During the time I was General Manager of the BOJ's Nagasaki Branch, Marris and his wife Margaret came to Japan on a trip from Washington, and stayed two nights at the official residence of the BOJ Nagasaki Branch Manager for sightseeing around Nagasaski city (Photo 9.1). About a year after my fourth and last departure from the OECD, Akiko and I invited Stephen and Margaret Marris as well as Stephen and Anne Potter to dinner at a restaurant in Paris. On that occasion, I suggested to Marris that he should write his memoirs on his long work as a prominent leader of OECD economists, playing an outstanding role in stimulating economic policy analysis within the OECD Secretariat and policy debates at OECD EPC and WP3 meetings for decades since the 1960s. But, to my regret, he did not follow my suggestion.

In January 2011, I sent an e-mail to Marris from Tokyo, attaching a copy of the paper I co-authored with Paul Atkinson "Surveillance by international institutions: Lessons from the global financial crisis" which was to be presented at a seminar at the OECD headquarters in Paris in February. A reply e-mail arrived from Margaret, saying that her husband had passed away in the previous year, and that she had been lucky in her life to have spent fifty-six years with such a wonderful companion.

Margaret and Akiko met each other for the first time when we were invited by the Marris for dinner at their house in Meudon on the outskirts of Paris when I was Head of the OECD Monetary Division in the early 1970s. Having received the sad news about Stephen's passing, on the occasion of our stay in France in 2011, Akiko met with Margaret who said that she was continuing her life alone in the house she lived with Stephen in Meudon, doing much more painting as well as other activities to keep her busy.

Margaret passed away in 2021.

Notes

1. OECD, "Recycling", Note by the Secretariat, CPE/WP3(81)5, 29 April 1981.

Photo 9.1 Kumiharu and Akiko Shigehara, Stephen and Margaret Marris, at the Peace Memorial Park in Nagasaki (© Kumiharu Shigehara)

2. Kumiharu Shigehara, "Monetary Control and Exchange Rate Pressures", OECD internal note, KS/LM, 12 February 1981.
3. OECD, "Interest Rate Variability, Exchange Rate Pressures and Monetary Control", Note by the Secretariat, CPE/WP3(81)7, 10 July 1981.
4. OECD, "Interest Rate Variability, Exchange Rate Pressures and Monetary Control", Notes by National Authorities, CPE/WP3(81)8, 13 July 1981.
5. Stephen Axilrod, "New Monetary Control Procedure: Findings and Evaluation from a Federal Reserve Study", Board of Governors of the Federal Reserve System, 2 February 1981.
6. OECD, "Record of a discussion between the Secretary-General and Sir Roy Denman, Director General for External Affairs at the Commission of the European Communities, in Brussels on Friday 27 February 1981", 2 March 1981.
7. Fred Bergsten, "The Villain is an Overvalued Dollar", Challenge, March–April 1982. pp. 30–31.
8. Richard Kirkland, "Are the Japanese Rigging the Yen?", Fortune, 31 May 1982.
9. Higgins eventually returned to Australia and rose to the position of Secretary of the Treasury. He was rumoured to be a candidate for Governor of the Reserve Bank of Australia, but passed away suddenly right after my meeting with him in Tokyo in December 1990.
10. When I was appointed Head of the OECD Economics Department in 1992, the Financial Times reported in an article introducing me that "Shigehara is known to have argued that the Bank of Japan's policies should not be too US-friendly". Apparently, this episode was one of the reasons for this comment by the Financial Times reporter.
11. Kenneth Baker, UK Department of Industry press notice 54, 3 March 1982.
12. OECD Council communiqué, C(82)57(Final), 11 May 1983, "High Interest Rates and International Tensions", para. 13 and para. 14.

CHAPTER 10

The Plaza and Louvre Accords and Japan's Balance of Payments Adjustment

Main topics in this chapter are my recollections and reflections as a former Bank of Japan official on the Plaza Accord to correct the excessive strength of the US dollar and the Louvre Accord to deal with its subsequent excessive fall, Japan's balance of payments adjustment, and the concomitant formation of a bubble in Japan. But I will begin with a short description of my first work on return to the Bank of Japan in late 1982.

Bank of Japan Institute for Monetary and Economic Studies

1 October 1982 marked the centenary of the Bank of Japan (BOJ)'s commencement of its central banking operations. At the centenary celebrations, Governor Mayekawa stated that "monetary stability" is the Bank's most important mission.[1] He then pointed out that in the conduct of monetary policy, emphasis should be placed on monetary aggregates and at the same time due consideration should be given to the exchange rate.

I returned to the BOJ from the OECD soon after its centenary celebrations (Photos 10.1 and 10.2). One of its commemorative projects was the establishment of the Institute for Monetary and Economic Studies. It was tasked to function as the BOJ's important vehicle for co-operation with academic circles in Japan and abroad and to provide

K. Shigehara, *The Bank of Japan, the OECD, and Beyond*,
https://doi.org/10.1007/978-981-97-5307-9_10

the results of such collaborative work for the BOJ's policy deliberation and sharing them with the public at the same time. I was appointed the first Head of Research and Coordination Division and assigned to oversee the functioning of this new institution including its personnel policy management.

By the time I arrived at the Institute, its Japanese name had already been fixed in the Statute of the BOJ as "*Kinyuu Kenkyuu Sho*", whose literal translation into English is "Monetary Research Institute". My view was that the Institute's research should not narrowly focus on monetary issues, but it should cover a wider range of macro- and microeconomic issues such as the monopoly powers of firms and unions, product and labour market rigidities, and many other non-monetary issues which may have significant implications for using monetary policy to achieve and

Photo 10.1 The head office of the Bank of Japan taken around the time of its centenary celebrations in 1982 (*Source* The Bank of Japan, "One Hundred Year History of the Bank of Japan", Vol. 6. © Bank of Japan)

Photo 10.2 The head office of the Bank of Japan taken around 1910 (*Source* The Bank of Japan, "One Hundred Year History of the Bank of Japan", Vol. 2. © Bank of Japan)

maintain price stability. With this consideration in mind, I proposed "Institute for Monetary and Economic Studies" (IMES), which was readily accepted within the Bank.

The first issue of the English edition of the Institute's flagship publication "Monetary and Economic Studies" (MES) was published in June 1983. It included the full text of Governor Mayekawa's speech "The Way back to the Growth of the World Economy" which was delivered at the International Economic Forum attended by members of G30 in Tokyo in April 1983. Mayekawa in person asked me to prepare the draft text in English and I decided on the title of his speech and wrote the draft text putting myself in the position of BOJ Governor with knowledge of OECD Secretariat work on structural policy issues and some European academics' analysis on Keynesian unemployment versus "classical" unemployment. Mayekawa read the text without any amendment.[2]

In drafting this speech for him, I made more explicit comments about a wide range of policy requirements than in Arthur Burns' lecture "The Anguish of Central Banking" delivered in Belgrade in September 1979 (see Chapter 5). After offering basic viewpoints for appropriate policy options, I stressed the importance of the need for an international perspective in national policy-making and discussed a programme for a global approach with specific comments on monetary policy, fiscal policy, microeconomic policy, capital flows to developing countries, the international trading system, and exchange rate stability. I was told that Alden Clausen, World Bank President, praised Mayekawa's speech. It has been a practice for the BOJ Institute for Monetary and Economic Studies to include a session "the Mayekawa Lecture" in the programme for each of the annual international conferences it organises. In this session, distinguished foreign economists are invited to give stand-alone keynote speeches, without being told about the true name of the author of the text of "the Mayekawa Lecture".

In fact, I oversaw the planning of the programme of the Institute's first International Conference which was held in June 1983. The conference began with an opening speech by Governor Mayekawa, followed by keynote speeches by Milton Friedman and James Tobin, two overseas advisers to the Institute. Friedman heavily criticised the US Federal Reserve System (Fed), saying that in rhetoric the Fed claimed to be conducting monetary policy based on monetarism, but it was only following opportunism in practice. Meanwhile, Tobin observed that "Fed suspended its monetary targets, to nearly universal relief" but "no coherent philosophy of monetary control, no systematic strategy has yet replaced them" and proposed changing its monetary policy target from money supply to nominal GNP. Stephen Axilrod, who represented the Fed at the conference, spoke against this proposal, saying that by adopting nominal GNP as a monetary policy target, the Fed would become entangled in politics and its independence would be undermined.

Invited to this conference were leading economists at the central banks of G10 countries, chief economists of the BIS, the IMF, and the OECD, and leading economists from Asian central banks. To my knowledge, this first international conference organised by the BOJ's Institute was also the first occasion for the economists from Asian central banks to engage in discussions with monetary experts of G10 central banks. They were invited to comment on the papers presented by prominent scholars in Japan and abroad. I sat next to the chairperson of each session, helping to keep the proceedings moving and participating in their discussions. The proceedings of the conference were eventually published by the MIT press.[3]

Around the time when I was completing my one-year work at the Institute, Christopher Higgins,[4] Director of the General Economics Branch of the OECD Economics and Statistics Department visited me at the Institute. The main purpose of his visit was to inquire as to my willingness to succeed him in his post at the OECD. He mentioned OECD Secretary-General van Lennep's wish for my return to the OECD. When I immediately informed Higgins that I had no desire to do so, he was surprised and looked disappointed. At the time, my promotion at the BOJ in the near future was almost on the table, and I could not let this slip.

Soon after Higgins' visit to me, I was appointed General Manager of the BOJ's Nagasaki Branch. Among the individuals who were already mentioned in the previous chapters of the book, or whose name will appear in later chapters, Haruo Mayekawa, Masaru Hayami, Toshihiko Fukui, and Masaaki Shirakawa joined the BOJ immediately after graduating from the University of Tokyo, and spent their entire careers at the BOJ without having worked in other organisations, and were promoted steadily internally and, after working their way up through the BOJ's key departments, became members of its Executive Board, then Deputy Governors, and eventually Governors. And, at some point in their careers at the BOJ, each of them had, without exception, spent two years or so at least as the head of one of its local branches.[5] I was expected to gain such experience.

Some months after my move to Nagasaki, van Lennep appointed Masaru Yoshitomi, Deputy Head of the Research Institute of the Economic Planning Agency of the Japanese government to the post of Director of the OECD General Economics Branch. At the specific request made by van Lennep, Yoshitomi flew from Tokyo to Nagasaki. He had been asked to be posted to Paris after being well briefed by me on the management of the OECD General Economics Branch, in particular its personnel policy. It thus became clearer that Higgins' visit to me at the BOJ Institute for Monetary and Economic Studies in Tokyo some months ago reflected van Lennep's strong wish to recruit me as Higgins' immediate successor.

OECD EPC Discussion on the US Economy

In the July 1983 issue of Economic Outlook, the OECD noted that "(I)n Japan the desire to minimise protectionist pressures that a weak yen could exacerbate has perhaps been more important than inflation considerations in the authorities' reluctance to see interest rates fall further".[6]

At the OECD Economic Policy Committee (EPC) meeting in November that year, when I was posted to Nagasaki, concerns were expressed about medium-term growth constraints through persistent high interest rates and crowding out amid accelerating growth in the US economy.

The following May 1984 EPC meeting was the last one attended by OECD Secretary-General van Lennep, who was nearing the end of his 15-year tenure. By this time, economic recovery had taken hold in almost all OECD member countries, led by the rapid expansion of the US economy. Yoichi Ōshima, Deputy Director-General of the BOJ Research Department, who attended the meeting, informed me at the Nagasaki Branch that unlike previous EPC meetings, member country representatives generally stopped criticising the economic management of other countries as they openly did in the previous EPC meetings. He observed that there was at least no overt criticism of the situation of the Japanese economy which recorded large current account surpluses under price stability, and that there was some approval of the positive aspects of Japan's large current account surplus combined with the outflow of long-term capital to countries with insufficient domestic savings.

More noteworthy was the discussion of the US economy at the EPC meeting in November 1984. At the time, the US economy was showing a noticeable growth slowdown after a period of rapid expansion, but the US representatives were bullish, explaining that there was no danger of recession, that the steady inflow of foreign capital was based on a solid foundation of high rates of return and safety of real assets in the United States which would not be easily dampened, and that the US dollar would therefore not fall sharply and any reversal would be moderate. Martin Feldstein had resigned as Chair of the US President's Council of Economic Advisers (CEA), so the EPC meeting was attended by William Poole from the CEA, David Klock from the Treasury Department, and Henry Wallich from the Fed.

The Plaza Accord and the Louvre Accord

In December 1984, Satoshi Sumita, a former finance ministry bureaucrat, succeeded Mayekawa as BOJ Governor.

The dollar had been softening since March 1985, but remained well above a level justifiable by "fundamentals". Correction of this abnormal currency situation was the purpose of the meeting of G5 Finance Ministers and Central Bank Governors at Hotel Plaza in New York on 22 September 1985. In their communiqué, it was stated that in addition to concerted action in the foreign exchange markets to strengthen non-dollar currencies, the United States would reinforce its efforts to reduce its fiscal deficits and Japan and Germany would make efforts to encourage domestic demand growth. Finance Minister Takeshita and BOJ Governor Sumita attended the meeting from Japan. It was on 18 September, only four days before his participation in the Hotel Plaza meeting that Tomomitsu Oba, then Vice Minister of Finance for International Affairs, informed Sumita about the results of the preparatory work that had been carried out by the deputies of G5 finance ministers, such as David Mulford (then Assistant Secretary for International Affairs at the US Treasury) and Hans Tietmeyer (then State Secretary at the West German Ministry of Finance) as well as Oba from Japan, without participation of the deputies of G5 central bank governors. While the former attended the Hotel Plaza meeting of G5 Finance Ministers and Central Bank Governors, the latter did not.

I was very surprised when I learnt in Nagasaki of the news reports that concerted action to correct the strong dollar had been agreed at the meeting. This reaction of mine was based on my understanding of the discussions on the US economy at the EPC meeting in November 1984 which were not in line with the announcements at Hotel Plaza that "some further orderly appreciation of the non-dollar currencies is desirable" and that G5 countries participating in the Accord "stand ready to cooperate more closely to encourage this when to do so would be helpful".

Under the Plaza Accord, G5 countries conducted the concerted intervention in the foreign exchange markets from September 23, 1985. The dollar exchange rate dropped sharply against the major currencies including the yen, falling from ¥242 to the dollar (September 20) just before the Plaza Accord to ¥211 to the dollar on October 4. However, the dollar sometimes rebounded towards late October. Meanwhile, the long-term interest rates dropped sharply in Japanese markets partly due to growing anticipation for monetary policy easing. However, in late October the BOJ Market Operations Department (*Eigyô-kyoku*) conducted money market operations "to leave short-term interest rates at a higher level". This surprised the officials at the Japanese Ministry of Finance as well as those of other G5 countries. In his book "The Yen and the BOJ: Recollections of a Central Banker", Ogata recalled that while a number of his central bank colleagues abroad received news about the BOJ's money market operations favourably, at the subsequent BIS monthly meeting he attended, Fed Chairman Volker vehemently condemned the operations which had caused an unexpectedly sharp decline in the dollar exchange rate.[7] Ogata did not elaborate on reasons for Volker's criticism. When I read about this episode in his book, I thought that Volker must have been concerned about the risk of interest rate hikes in Japan triggering the dollar's "fee fall" and a revival of inflationary pressures in the United States. As a matter of fact, the BOJ's money market stabilising operations continued until mid-December 1985.

As noted in a fairly extensive survey paper "The Japanese bubble and international politics - Those that put the Bank of Japan into a corner" written by Shigeyoshi Miyakawa, professor of economics at Kyoto Advanced Science University,[8] it was after US Treasury Secretary James Baker had a meeting with Noboru Takeshita, then Japanese Finance Minister, on 8 April 1986 and another with Sumita, then BOJ Governor on the following day that both BOJ and Fed cut their policy rates by the same 0.5 per cent on the same day (21 April 1986).

Kiichi Miyazawa replaced Takeshita as Japanese Minister of Finance in July 1986. Following his bilateral meeting with Baker on 22 January 1987, Japanese newspapers began to report that the BOJ would reduce its official discount rate to coincide with the next G5 meeting. Immediately after the newspaper reports were published, I travelled from Nagasaki to Tokyo at the end of the month to attend the BOJ Branch Managers' meeting, where Governor Sumita told us quite frankly that he would decide about the BOJ' official discount rate after considering the domestic and international economic and financial situation including exchange rate trends as well as the G5 agreement. In the end, the BOJ decided on the fifth cut in its official discount rate on Friday 20 February, just before the Finance Ministers and Central Bank Governors of the six major economies (Canada, France, West Germany, Japan, the United Kingdom, and the United States) met at the Louvre Palace in Paris on 22 February and reached an agreement (the so-called "Louvre Accord") to halt the depreciation of the dollar that had started with the Plaza Accord. Italy was invited to sign the agreement but declined.

The BOJ's official discount rate was reduced five times to an unprecedentedly low level of 2.5 per cent from 5.0 per cent. During this period, some members of the BOJ Policy Board suggested that closer attention should be paid to developments in the money supply. In fact, in its Economic Survey of Japan published in November 1986, when Japan's official interest rate was still 3 per cent, the OECD stated that "(S)ince end-1985, monetary policy has been significantly eased, with monetary growth substantially exceeding that of nominal income and the discount rate being reduced in steps to 3 per cent, its lowest level ever. Further relaxation may risk triggering excessive monetary growth and rekindling inflationary pressures in the future. There is perhaps somewhat greater scope for fiscal policy".[9] However, the OECD's warning was ignored by the BOJ and the Japanese government.[10]

The circumstances surrounding the successive reductions in the BOJ official discount rate are described in a well-crafted paper, "Monetary Policy of the Bank of Japan (1984–1989): The Plaza Accord and the Creation of the Bubble" by Akio Kuroda, who worked at the BOJ Institute for Monetary and Economic Studies during the time I was Head of the Research and Coordination Division there, and later became a professor of monetary economics at Meiji University.[11] I would add that according to the confidential record I received from Michio Fukai, who was Director-General of the Coordination Department of the BOJ at the time, it is written that Volcker, then Fed Chairman, repeatedly asked Governor Sumita, through Shijuro Ogata, then BOJ Deputy Governor on International Affairs, to make co-ordinated interest rate cuts.

In his book "International Finance: Testimonies from the field", Takeshi Ota, who succeeded Ogata as BOJ Deputy Governor on International Affairs, wrote that at Sumita's meeting with Volcker in Washington in April 1987, the latter asked Sumita to reduce the BOJ official discount rate further down from 2.5 per cent, which Sumita declined. Ota also wrote that after their meeting, Sumita told him: "Enough is Enough". Ota also wrote that the US authorities continued to put pressure on the BOJ after the Sumita-Volcker meeting of April 1987, but the BOJ resisted them.[12]

The joint statement issued after the meeting between Prime Minister Yasuhiro Nakasone and US President Reagan in May 1987 referred to the low interest rates achieved by the BOJ in the context of Japan's efforts to stimulate domestic demand. This reinforced financial market participants' expectation that Japanese monetary conditions would remain easy for a sustained period.

According to Akira Aoki's testimony, on 30 September 1987, Manuel H. Johnson Jr., then Fed Vice Chairman, contacted Tomomitsu Oba, a key figure in the 1985 Plaza Accord as Vice Minister of Finance for International Affairs, and asked him to share with the BOJ the US wish that the BOJ should keep interest rate differentials between Japan and the United States unchanged.[13] Aoki was BOJ Executive Director in charge of domestic monetary policy management from 1985 to 1989. Thus, pressure on the Bank of Japan came not just from the US government but also from the Fed Chairman and Vice Chairman.

I might add that the German Bundesbank had made its position clear in the summer of 1986 that it could not accept the US demand that the Bundesbank should take additional monetary policy action to boost domestic demand in West Germany. For example, Helmut Schlesinger, then Vice-President of the Bundesbank reportedly remarked in his speech at a seminar organised by the Sparkasse Bonn over the last weekend of July 1986 that Germany's domestic interest rates were already low internationally and historically, and US demands for a further lowering of German interest rates were not acceptable. He also reportedly said that while there was a strong argument in the United States that West Germany and Japan should work to reduce their current account surpluses and facilitate the adjustment process in current account deficit countries, the United States itself was responsible for solving the problem. He pointed out that the international competitiveness of the US industrial sector had weakened since 1985, and if the structural strengthening of the US economy were not realised, the current account surpluses of Japan and West Germany would persist as a counterpart of the US current account deficit.[14]

Japan's Balance of Payment Adjustment under Price Stability

Following the successive cuts in the BOJ official discount rate, city banks increasingly stepped up their lending offensive. In Nagasaki Prefecture, their aggressive lending policy, backed by the huge amount of funds available through low interest rates in the financial markets and collection of new types of time deposits developed under the Japanese government scheme for financial liberalisation, started to affect the attitude of local banks which had been traditionally very cautious in their lending operations. As the General Manager of the BOJ Nagasaki Branch, I exercised moral suasion on the chairmen of the two large local banks with their head offices in Nagasaki prefecture, and they co-operated to moderate their lending to some doubtful areas, but such action was of limited effect when the Bank rate remained at such a low level. Local bankers unanimously complained about the "excessive" competition with the Nagasaki branches of the so-called "city banks" with their head offices in the Tokyo area and nation-wide branch networks.

Japan's subsequent growth performance was striking. Expansion of real total domestic demand, which had averaged an annual rate of 2.7 per cent between 1973 and 1983 and remained within a 3 per cent range in the following three years, accelerated to 5.3 per cent in 1987 and 7.3 per cent in 1988 and maintained a high pace of above 5 per cent in both 1989 and 1990. The real imports of goods and services increased at a double-digit annual rate between 1987 and 1989—11.3 per cent in 1987, 19.5 per cent in 1988 and 15.7 per cent in 1989—and continued to expand at a high rate of 7.0 per cent in 1990. On the other hand, the real exports of goods and services declined by 5.5 per cent in 1986 and 0.5 per cent in 1987, and their growth in the subsequent years remained well below the OECD average. Japan's current account surplus as a percentage of GDP thus declined from a peak of 4.2 per cent in 1986 to 1.5 per cent in 1990.

A spectacular growth acceleration was clearly reflected in labour market conditions. Japan's traditionally low unemployment fell even further from 2.8 per cent in 1986 to 2.1 per cent in 1990, while the annual increase in employment accelerated from 0.8 per cent in 1986 to 2.0 per cent in both 1989 and 1990, with the annual growth rate of labour force rising from 1.0 per cent to 1.8 per cent and the labour force participation rate from 72.2 per cent to 74.1 per cent between 1986 and 1990. A notable feature of this high growth period was developments in unit labour costs. They declined both in 1987 and 1988 as a combined result of sharp increases in labour productivity and firms' efforts to contain increases in wage costs in the face of a substantial weakening of their international competitiveness associated with the yen appreciation. A softening in unit labour costs, together with declines in import prices brought about by the high external value of the yen, contributed to a remarkable stability in consumer prices over the second half of the 1980s.

Another striking feature of this high growth period was the combination of huge increases in land prices with general price stability. Unlike the land price hikes in the early 1970s that was a nation-wide phenomenon, they were limited basically to the Metropolitan Tokyo and commercial areas of other very large cities. They were explained at that time by perceived increases in land productivity associated with a huge demand for office space by Japanese and foreign firms in the context of the globalisation of the Japanese economy. Thus, unlike the nation-wide real estate boom of the early 1970s which was clearly a manifestation of excess domestic liquidity created by the BOJ in an attempt to offset the deflationary impacts of the yen appreciation after the Smithsonian agreement in late 1971 and the subsequent general currency floating starting in the spring of 1973, the BOJ's easy monetary policy was not considered as the main culprit of the real estate boom at that time.

Having said that, it was a factor contributing to the asset market bubble, another dimension of which was found in the equity market. Indeed, the values of Japanese equities continued to rise even after the collapse of the New York market on the "Black Monday" of 19 October 1987. Growth euphoria then prevailing in Japan and huge unrealised profit gains arising from the values of firms' land holdings above original purchase prices were considered to sustain unprecedentedly high price earnings ratios. Overall, the low cost of capital contributed to booms in business fixed investment and residential construction as well as speculative purchases of real estates, paintings, and other precious assets not only in Japan but also abroad.

The literature on sequencing of structural reform, though dealing largely with developing economies, suggest that reform should start with labour and product markets, and trade. Domestic financial market liberalisation should then be introduced to be followed by the liberalisation of international capital transactions. In many OECD countries, reform was implemented in the reverse order. Japan was no exception. Liberalisation of international capital transactions proceeded gradually after the start of the yen floating in 1973 and by the end of the 1980s exchange controls were almost completely lifted. A series of domestic financial market liberalisation measures were taken during the 1980s. The BOJ's quantitative controls, an instrument frequently used in the past periods of restraint, were abandoned. The new financial environment, coupled with the expectation of continued monetary ease, intensified competition among financial institutions facilitated the financing of the "bubble" economy at a time of lax prudential control by the authorities. Japan–US Structural Impediments Initiative Talks (SII) was started in September 1989 to discuss a broad range of issues about Japan's economic structure including land problems. But, overall, product market and land reforms were slow and incomplete. Labour market reform also remained as an unfinished business. I was not involved in SII as I was at the OECD at that time.

I would finish this chapter by referring to the report of the Study Group on Economic Structural Adjustment for International Cooperation, a private advisory body to the then Prime Minister Nakasone, which was published in April 1986. This came to be generally known as the "Mayekawa Report", named after the chairman of the study group, Haruo Mayekawa.

The report stated that the continuation of Japan's large current account imbalance was undesirable from the perspective of Japan's economic management and the harmonious development of the world economy, and advocated expansion of domestic demand, market opening, and financial liberalisation as solutions to the problem. Specifically, in response to US demands, the report called for an expansion of public spending, centred on public investment amounting to ¥430 trillion over 10 years, and the promotion of deregulation to promote domestic private investment and consumption.

Ryutaro Komiya, then professor of economics at the University of Tokyo, criticised the authors of the "Mayekawa Report", stating that:

1. In economics, current account balance is equal to a balance of national savings and national investment, which is obtained from the national income identity and merely the result of the behaviours of individual economic agents chosen as most advantageous. As such, current account imbalances are neither adverse nor unhealthy, even if they are persistent. The twin deficits of the United States were not caused by Japan's trade balance surpluses, but were the result of the actions of US economic agents at the time. The idea that a country's balance of trade or current account deficit is detrimental to that country is a typical heavy mercantilist fallacy and an elementary economic error.
2. Japan's large trade surplus with the United States is not due to Japanese market closures. The consequences of changes in trade barriers affect medium- and long-term terms of trade, which are offset by changes in exchange rates under a floating exchange rate system, and therefore do not affect the trade balance.

My assessment of the macroeconomics aspect of the Mayekawa report was like Komiya's.

Reginald Dale, who spent the majority of his career as a journalist, working as an international economics, wrote: "Washington should give Japan credit where it is due, refrain from encouraging the idea that trade problems are all Japan's fault and stop basing its policy on bluster and mistrust" in his article "Advice to U.S.: Stop Demonizing Japan", published in a column Thinking Ahead/Commentary in the International Herald Tribune of 11 July 1997.

Notes

1. In an article "Monetary Stability: Threat and Proven Response" in "Fifty Years of the Deutsche Mark: Central Bank and the Currency in Germany since 1948" (edited by the Deutsche Bundesbank, Oxford University Press, 1999), Manfred Neumann wrote: "(T)he pre-eminence of the goal of monetary stability can also be derived from its importance for the effective functioning of the competitive

system and, in the final analysis, for guaranteeing social security and social peace".

2. Haruo Mayekawa, "The Way Back to the Growth of the World Economy", Monetary and Economic Studies, Vol. 1, No. 1, Bank of Japan, June 1983, pp. 69–80. https://www.imes.boj.or.jp/research/papers/english/me1-1-3.pdf.
3. "Monetary Policy in Our Times", Proceedings of the first international conference held by the Institute for Monetary and Economic Studies of the Bank of Japan, MIT Press, Cambridge, Massachusetts, 1985.
4. See Note 9, Chapter 9.
5. At the present time, the Bank of Japan has 32 local branches. The Osaka branch is the largest and most important, and headed by a member of the Executive Board. The second largest is the Nagoya branch, headed by a very senior official at the level of the director-general of a key department in the head office in Tokyo. Several other local branches (such as Hiroshima Branch) are headed by senior officials who had experienced managing branches in some other large local cities (such as Nagasaki Branch). The Bank's credit operations to commercial banks whose head offices are located outside the Tokyo area, and which do not have nation-wide branch networks (the so-called "local banks") are conducted by the business divisions of the Bank's local branches under the direction of their general managers in consultation with the Market Operations Department (*Eigyô-kyoku*) in the head office in Tokyo.
6. OECD Economic Outlook, July 1983, p. 14.
7. Shijuro Ogata, "*En to Nihonginkô* (The Yen and the Bank of Japan)", (in Japanese), Chuo-Koron-Shinsho, 1996, p. 23.
8. Shigeyoshi Miyakawa, "The Japanese Bubble and International Politics—The Backdrops That Put the Bank of Japan into a Corner (in Japanese)", The Journal of Economics, KGU, Vol. 24, No. 2, March 2015.
9. OECD Economic Surveys, Japan, 1986, p. 93.
10. Masanao Itoh, Ryoji Koike, and Masato Shizume, "Bank of Japan's Monetary Policy in the 1980s: A View Perceived from Archived and Other Materials" (Monetary and Economic Studies, November 2015, Bank of Japan, https://www.imes.boj.or.jp/research/papers/english/me33-5.pdf) provides useful summaries of the views held by the BOJ or in the 1980s regarding economic

conditions and monetary policy formulation, perceived from the BOJ archives and other materials from the period. However, it does not cover the OECD's recommendations on the conduct of Japanese monetary policy made and published during the 1980s.

11. Akio Kuroda, "Monetary Policy of the Bank of Japan (1984–1989): The Plaza Accord and the Creation of the Bubble" (in Japanese), Meiji University Social Science Research Institute Review, Vol. 47. No. 1, pp. 213–231.
12. Takeshi Ohta, "*Kokusai Kinyuu – Genba karano Shôgen* (International Finance: Testimonies from the field)" (in Japanese), Chuo-Koron-Shinsho, 1991, pp. 111–112.
13. Aoki's testimony is included in a voluminous book "Record of the Japanese Economy- Collection of testimonies from the bubble period" compiled by the Economic and Social Research Institute of the Cabinet Office of the Japanese government in March 2011. He was interviewed by a Japanese academic historian and two economists in March 2010, and the interview record was published in the book. Among former BOJ officials, Yoshio Suzuki (as former Executive Director in charge of economic research) and I (as former OECD Chief Economist rather than a former BOJ official) accepted to be interviewed and our testimonies were included together with Aoki's in the collection. Yasushi Mieno and Toshihiko Fukui declined to be interviewed.
14. Report of the Bank of Japan Frankfurt Office to the Head Office, issued 29 July 1986.

CHAPTER 11

Black Monday, 19 October 1987, and its Aftermath

Emile van Lennep had completed his 15-year term of office as the OECD Secretary-General in May 1984, and was succeeded by Jean-Claude Paye, a former high official of the French foreign ministry. On accepting Paye's invitation for me to assume the post of Director of the General Economics Branch of the OECD Economics and Statistics Department as from September 1987, I was determined to revive the work of WP3 which appeared to have lost ground as a forum for discussing international monetary management issues. According to Stephen Potter, then Deputy Director of the General Economics Branch, WP3 Chairman Geoffrey Littler, UK treasury official, had set out a policy that discussions on exchange rate policy should take place at the G7 deputies' meeting, and not be dealt with at WP3. I alone flew to London to have a tête-à-tête meeting with Littler as the first step to embark on the reform of WP3. I explained to him my view, as a Bank of Japan official who had been involved in the activities of IMF, OECD, and BIS as well as G5, G7, and G10, that OECD WP3 should be revived as a body for frank discussion of all matters including foreign exchange rate policy issues which were deeply related with domestic monetary and fiscal policy management. My view was that, while WP3 and G10 deputies have the same country composition, policy discussions at WP3 should be more informative than those held in other bodies, as long as they are based on well-targeted discussion papers to be prepared by the OECD Secretariat on monetary, fiscal, and foreign exchange rate policy issues of international importance. I told him

K. Shigehara, *The Bank of Japan, the OECD, and Beyond*,
https://doi.org/10.1007/978-981-97-5307-9_11

that I would do my best as the person responsible for running WP3 from this perspective. Littler agreed with me that there should not be restriction on the issues to be discussed at WP3.

Black Monday—19 October 1987

In September 1987 I began my third period of service at the OECD. Around that time, both the Bank of Japan (BOJ) and the German Bundesbank were faced with a difficult internal/external dilemma: how to balance their twin objective of domestic price stability and exchange rate stability. Both banks cut interest rates in the first half of 1987 to cope with strong buying pressure on the Japanese yen and the Deutsche Mark.

Later, in the summer, when downward pressure on the US dollar eased somewhat, the BOJ and the Bundesbank moved to absorb the liquidity they had previously released into the market. Money supply growth in Japan had accelerated to an annual rate of more than 10 per cent. Together with the recovery of domestic demand, speculative activity in various asset markets and price increases in some sectors were observed in Japan. Under these circumstances, the BOJ moved to put the brakes on private bank lending through the so-called "window guidance"—essentially moral suasion—exercised by the BOJ Market Operations Department (*Eigyou-kyoku*), without resorting to the official discount rate hike.

The OECD Secretariat judged that the economic recovery in West Germany was on a less firm footing than in Japan. But central bank money (Zentralbankgeltmenge—the sum of cash currency and bank reserves against domestic liabilities) had remained well above its targets for two consecutive years, which had become a major matter of its concern for maintaining price stability in the medium to long term.[1] Thus, despite the strengthening of the Deutsche Mark against the US dollar in September 1987, the Bundesbank took a tighter monetary stance and moved to raise short-term money market rates at the beginning of October. Media reports of a policy dispute between the US and German authorities inflated speculation that Germany may prioritise domestic price stability over its external commitment to co-operate for the correction of the US dollar's excessive depreciation against the German mark made in the Louvre Accord. On top of that, on Friday 16 October, the US trade balance was reported to have worsened, and on Monday 19, the New

York Stock Exchange opened with a flood of selling, with the Dow Jones Industrial Average falling 22.6 per cent from the level of the previous weekend. This unprecedented rate of decline was almost double the 12.8 per cent fall on Thursday in 1929, which triggered the Great Depression. The US stock market crash quickly spread to Japan and European countries.

In the face of this unprecedented event, I quickly drafted a note on emergency measures that I thought the monetary authorities of major OECD countries hit by the stock market crash should take and submitted it to Paye. In my view, while supplying liquidity to financial markets promptly and adequately after the Black Monday shock was a pressing issue for all the central banks concerned, what would be more difficult should be their exit policy—how much liquidity to absorb from the markets afterwards and at what timing to prevent the rekindling of inflation. I suggested to Paye that he should address his confidential letters to the Finance Ministers and Central Bank Governors of the OECD WP3 participating countries individually, in which he should express his hope that the key issues I identified in my note should be discussed at the forthcoming OECD WP3 meeting.

This action seemed unusual to some of the recipients of Paye's letter. But it reflected my wish for the WP3 to be revitalised as a unique international body in line with my agreement with WP3 Chairman Littler noted above. Following the dispatch of Paye's confidential letter, I added the following paragraph in the Introduction titled "Achieving a sustained reduction of international economic tensions" of the OECD Economic Outlook (EO) published in December 1987.[2]

"The stock-market crisis has added to the tasks of monetary policy, which was already over-stretched in some countries by conflicting domestic and exchange-market objectives. Monetary authorities are now faced with the task of gauging and responding to the demands for extra liquidity arising from financial unrest while ensuring, over a slightly longer-term horizon, that liquidity increase are not such as to give rise to an upsurge of inflation. Preventing a resurgence of inflation expectations is necessary if damaging increases in long-term ineptest rates are to be avoided. International monetary cooperation can and should contribute to orderly conditions in exchange markets".

Furthermore, the following comment was made on the management of Japanese economic policy: "major uncertainties remain about the possible

Table 11.1 Outlook for short-term money market interest rates in Japan

(Call money rate, per cent, annual interest rate)					
1987/1stH	3.6	1988/1stH	3.4	1989/1stH	3.7
1987/2ndH	3.3	1988/2ndH	3.6	1989/2ndH	3.8

Source OECD Economic Outlook, December 1987, p. 12

impact of lower world demand and about future exchange-rate developments. The Japanese authorities will need to remain vigilant to ensure that domestic activity remains on an appropriate growth path conducive to non-inflationary external adjustment. The prospective strength of demand in the immediate future underlines the need for control of domestic liquidity as well as import liberalization. … In particular, the time is ripe for land-use reform to encourage more efficient use of limited space".[3]

In line with these remarks and given a need to reduce the excessive growth of money aggregates, Japanese short-term interest rates were projected to rise by a half percentage point from the first half of 1988 to the second half of 1989 (Table 11.1).[4]

Asset Price Hikes and the Yen Depreciation

Growth in Japanese broad money supply accelerated from an annual rate of 8–9 per cent at the beginning of 1987 to 12 per cent in the first quarter of 1988. Stock prices began to show significant increases, and land prices in Tokyo doubled in 1987 and then somewhat settled down in 1988. On the other hand land prices in the rural areas showed a noticeable increase in that year.

Under these circumstances, the OECD EO published in June 1988 assumed that the increase in short-term money market interest rates would be brought forward slightly from the path assumed in the EO published at the end of the previous year.[5] As for inflation outlook, GNP deflator was projected to rise from −0.2 per cent in 1987 to 1.75% in 1988 and 2.5 per cent in 1989 respectively (Table 11.2).[6]

The rise in asset prices in Japan was discussed at the OECD Economic and Development Review Committee (EDRC) meeting for the annual economic review of Japan and at WP3 meeting, where the representatives of the Japanese government took the view that it could not be described as a bubble, as the increase in asset prices reflected higher

Table 11.2 Outlook for short-term money market interest rates in Japan

(Call money rate, per cent, annual interest rate)

1987/1stH	3.6	19881stH	3.5	19891stH	3.9
1987/2ndH	3.4	1988/2ndH	3.7	1989/2ndH	3.9

Source OECD Economic Outlook, June 1988, p. 17

expected economic growth in Japan over the medium term. This view was challenged by myself and William White, then Deputy Governor of the Bank of Canada, at WP3 meetings. Both argued that the Japanese delegation's explanation was not plausible, and more cautious policy management was in order. Takeshi Ohta, who replaced Shijiro Ogata as the Bank of Japan representative at the WP3, expressed some concern about the overall Japanese economic situation but stopped short of clearly distancing himself from the view taken by the Japanese government representatives at WP3 and indicating the need for correcting the fundamental stance of the BOJ's monetary policy.

Around that time, there was an argument in Japan known as the "Bank of Japan anchor theory", according to which the BOJ as a leading central bank in the world should keep Japanese interest rates low and act as a monetary anchor for the stable running of the global economy.[7] I thought this did not make sense.

A slight change in the Japanese media debate appeared after the turn of the year. In a commentary article entitled "Will the Bank of Japan Anchor Theory Collapse?" published in the 18 March 1989 issue of the *Syukan Tôyô Keizai* (Weekly Oriental Economy), it was noted that Japan had achieved "super-stability" in prices as the only one among G7 countries which had recorded a decline in wholesale prices in 1988, while keeping the BOJ's official discount rate unchanged at a very low level. The article then pointed out that, with the introduction of the consumption tax system on 1 April 1989, the spring wage round and rising oil prices, the "Bank of Japan Anchor Theory" which argued that interest rate hikes in Japan were taboo was likely to collapse.

In May 1989, the BOJ finally raised the official interest rate from 2.5 per cent to 3.25 per cent. I wrote in its preface of the June 1989 issue of OECD EO: "(T)he challenge for Japan is to maintain strong domestic demand growth within the inflation-free range. This will lead to higher living standards and an improvement in the balance of payments.

Achieving these domestic and foreign economic objectives will be aided by a gradual appreciation of the yen in line with developments in domestic and foreign price conditions. The key will be the strong will of the monetary authorities to keep the rate of price increases low". This was one of the final contributions I made as Director of the General Economics Branch of OECD Economics Department to the half-yearly issues of the OECD EO published in 1989, before I returned to the Bank of Japan later that year.[8]

In the OECD Economic Review Survey of Japan issued in November 1989, following the 0.5 per increase in the BOJ's official interest rate in October 1989, it was stated that "(A) further depreciation of the yen must be avoided, as a fall in the exchange rate of the yen may threaten domestic price stability and at the same time impede the adjustment of the balance of payments. As long as Japan's cost inflation is fundamentally below the average of its trading partners, a gradual increase in the effective exchange rate of the yen is appropriate to stop the rate of price inflation at a low level and to achieve external adjustment. The fiscal policy stance should be neutral".

At the end of November 1989, the BOJ Institute for Monetary and Economic Studies held a meeting of a group of academic monetary experts to discuss "Asset Price Fluctuations and the Japanese Economy". The meeting was chaired by Ryuichiro Tate, Emeritus Professor at the University of Tokyo and Special Advisor to the Institute, and moderated by Junichi Miyake, Director-General of the Institute, with the participation of BOJ officials, including Yasushi Mieno, then Deputy Governor, and Toshihiko Fukui, Executive Director in charge of domestic monetary policy management. Among academic monetary experts who presented papers for discussion were Kazumasa Iwata, associate professor at the University of Tokyo (later BOJ Deputy Governor), Kazuo Ueda, associate professor at the University of Tokyo (now BOJ Governor), Yasuhiro Horie, associate professor at the University of Tsukuba, and commentator Akiyoshi Horiuchi, professor at the University of Tokyo. The main points for discussion were the mechanism of rising asset prices and its impact on the financial system and the real economy, and their implications for the management of monetary policy.

On return to the BOJ after the meeting, I read the papers presented to the meeting and the summary of discussions that had taken place there. What caught my attention most was Professor Horiuchi's argument that the surge in asset prices such as stock prices and land prices in Japan appeared to be based on the assumption on the part of investors including financial institutions that asset prices would continue to rise, and that once these assumptions were reversed, financial institutions would be particularly hard hit, and that a reversal of financial intermediation could have a major deflationary effect on the real economy as a whole.[9] The participants considered resort to taxation and other measures for possible measures to stabilise land prices, while they argued that selective policy measures such as restrictions on land-related loans would have loopholes and it was questioned whether they would be really effective. It was also pointed out that in order to achieve land price stability through monetary policy, it would be necessary to raise interest rates significantly.[10]

In the context of the study on the Japanese economy and economic policy during the bubble/deflation period (commonly known as the "Bubble/Deflation Study") planned and supervised by the Economic and Social Research Institute of the Cabinet Office of the Japanese government, Japanese academic experts conducted interviews with 13 people selected from those Japanese politicians, finance ministry bureaucrats, BOJ officials, and some others who were involved in economic policy-making during the period of Japan's bubble formation. The records of these interviews were included as a series of "oral history" in the Institute's report published in March 2011.[11] Three former senior BOJ officials who agreed to give testimony were Akira Aoki, Yoshio Suzuki, and myself. The former two were key members of the Bank of Japan's Executive Board around the time of Japan's bubble formation. Aoki left the BOJ in 1989 to become Deputy Governor of the Export–Import Bank of Japan, and Suzuki left the BOJ to become Vice-President of Nomura Research Institute and subsequently its President in 1991. On the other hand, I was interviewed on the understanding that for most of the period covered by the oral history, I was in a position to make policy recommendations to the Japanese authorities from the OECD and was critical about the conduct of Japanese monetary policy as noted above.

Satoshi Sumita, who was BOJ Governor from December 1984 to December 1989, had passed away in 2008. Yasushi Mieno, who was BOJ Deputy Governor for these five years and its Governor for the subsequent five years, declined to be interviewed by Japanese academic experts. Reportedly, he had been interviewed by a BOJ insider on the understanding that the record could be made public after 30 years. Toshihiko Fukui, who succeeded Aoki's post as BOJ Executive Director in charge of domestic monetary policy, and later became its Deputy Governor and then Governor, also declined to be interviewed by the Japanese academics. The record of a BOJ insider's interview with him is also reportedly to be published 30 years after the interview took place.

In his book "The Japanese Banking Crisis" (Palgrave Macmillan, January 2021), an open access book in English translation, Ryozo Himino, former Commissioner of the Financial Services Agency and presently BOJ Deputy Governor, provides a readable narrative of the bubble and the banking crisis that Japan experienced during the two decades between the late 1980s and the early 2000s.

Notes

1. OECD, Economic Outlook, No. 42, December 1987, p. 13.
2. Ditto, p. VII.
3. Ditto, p. X.
4. Ditto, p. 14.
5. OECD, Economic Outlook, No. 43, June 1988, p. 17.
6. Ditto, p. 51.
7. Naoki Tanaka, "*Nichibei Keizai Masatsu* (Japan-US Economic Frictions)" (in Japanese), NHK Book 573, May 1989, pp. 207–208; Economic and Social Research Institute, Cabinet Office of the Japanese government, 'The Japanese Economy and Economic Policy during the Bubble/Deflation Period', History Part 3, Testimonies (in Japanese), p. 193, p. 196, and pp. 597–639.
8. OECD, Economic Outlook, No. 45, June 1989, p. VIII.
9. Bank of Japan Institute for Monetary and Economic Studies, "Asset Price Fluctuations and the Japanese Economy" (in Japanese), Part 1 "Summary", Monetary and Economic Studies, Vol. 9, No. 1, May 1990, p. 6.
10. Ditto, p. 7.
11. The Economic and Social Research Institute, Cabinet Office of the Japanese Government (planner and supervisor) and Shigeru Matsushita and Harukata Takenaka (editors), "Records of the Japanese Economy - Decision-making Processes Regarding Economic Policy in the Bubble and Deflation Era: Testimony of Policymakers" (in Japanese), March 2011.

CHAPTER 12

Dealing with Domestic and International Economic Policy Issues as Bank of Japan Chief Economist

Halfway through the third period of my service at the OECD, Secretary-General Paye asked me to take up the position of OECD Chief Economist. However, I knew that David Henderson wished to remain in this position until his retirement age of 65 at the OECD. I also consulted with Bank of Japan Deputy Governor Mieno, who was widely expected to be the next Governor of the Bank, and was told to return to the Bank at the originally planned time. Thus, I returned to the Bank in December 1989 and was appointed the Director-General of the Institute for Monetary and Economic Studies. The Director-General of the Bank's Research and Statistics Department at the time was an official who had joined the Bank one year earlier than I, but Mieno told that he wanted me to function as the Bank of Japan Chief Economist in Japan and abroad. As such, I was invited to present papers to, or participate as a discussant in, important international conferences organised by foreign central banks such as the Jackson Hole symposiums of the Federal Reserve Bank of Kansas City and a colloquium of the Reserve Bank of Australia as well as workshops of academic institutions and private research institutes in Europe, not just on monetary but also economic growth, international balance of payments adjustment and trade policy issues. In this chapter, however, I will focus on my involvement in planning the conduct of Japanese monetary policy since my return to the Bank of

K. Shigehara, *The Bank of Japan, the OECD, and Beyond*,
https://doi.org/10.1007/978-981-97-5307-9_12

Japan, after which I will describe my participations in international debates on Japanese trade issues and some aspects of external imbalances and trade issues.

Domestic and International Policy Requirements for Price Stability

The Bank of Japan (BOJ) Institute for Monetary and Economic Studies used to hold an international conference every two years (see Chapter 8), and by the time I was appointed its Director-General, preparations had already begun for its fifth conference. I was told that the aim of the original plan was to help foreign central bankers and academics understand the background to Japan's economic performance in the 1980s which was generally considered to be more successful than in most Western countries. However, I personally had serious doubts about its sustainability and thought that the fifth international conference of the institute should be a more down-to-earth event rather than the one where even the BOJ Institute of Monetary and Economic Studies might be seen as if it were drunk on the bubble economy, celebrating the apparent success story of the Japanese economy to the rest of the world. The theme I chose on my own was "Price Stabilization in the 1990s: Domestic and International Policy Requirements". With regard to domestic policy requirements, there were basic issues such as how to define price stability and how to assess the costs of price stabilisation. On the international side, I thought deep discussion on the costs of exchange rate stability and short- and longer-run relationships between monetary policy aimed at domestic price stability and exchange rate stabilisation measure should take place at the fifth conference.

Before my arrival at the Institute, its consultation with its two Honorary Advisors Allan Meltzer, professor at Carnegie Mellon University, and Stanley Fischer, professor at the Massachusetts Institute of Technology, had already taken place on the initial proposal based on the theme of Japan's economic success. However, it had not started negotiations with Japanese and foreign scholars, asking them to contribute discussion papers. The two Honorary Advisors (Photo 12.1) readily agreed to my suggested change in the conference programme.

Following my idea, the conference, held on 24–25 October 1991, was composed of three sessions. The first session reviewed how non-monetary forces working on the process of wage and price formation in different economies developed and how monetary policy affected inflation in the 1980s. The second session addressed the following two sets of issues: (i) conceptual and practical issues concerning the correct measurement of overall inflation and (ii) the usefulness of indicators or information

Photo 12.1 Akiko Shigehara, Rhoda and Stanley Fischer, Kumiharu Shigehara, and Allan Meltzer at a reception on the occasion of the 5th international conference of the Bank of Japan Institute for Monetary and Economic Studies in October 1991 (from left to right) (© Kumiharu Shigehara)

variables in assessing inflationary pressures. The third and final session considered macroeconomic and structural policy issues under the two headings: (i) medium-term price objectives and domestic policy requirements for non-inflationary growth and (ii) external policy requirements and international co-operation for non-inflationary growth.

Professor Robert Gordon of Northwestern University wrote an interesting paper on the fundamental issues regarding the definition of "price stability" and what price data should be used for achieving and maintaining "price stability" as the objective of domestic monetary policy. The measurement biases in price statistics are now well known, but at the time they were rarely discussed in Japan and abroad, and I believe that this one paper alone would have been significant in my suggesting the change in the main theme for the conference. The conference ended with the general discussion which centred on (i) pros and cons of a zero inflation target, (ii) an international framework for price stability, and (iii) the independence of central banks in the context of the fight against inflation.

The proceedings of the conference, covering papers presented to the conference and an excellent summary of the discussions on them prepared by John Taylor, professor of Economics at Stanford University and former member of the US President's Council of Economic Advisers, were edited by me and published by Macmillan in the United Kingdom.[1]

Revival of "Elasticity Pessimism" and the "Saving–Investment Balance" Approach

As noted in Chapter 9, the argument linking Japan's current account surplus to excessive household savings was made by Henry Wallich of US Federal Reserve Board in the March 1982 meeting of WP3 meeting. But, such an approach to Japan's external imbalance was not limited to him only, but was taken by many other Keynesian economists around that time.

This argument was revived in the late 1980s when the decline in Japan's trade surplus was slow to diminish, despite all the relative price adjustments made through large exchange rate changes following the Plaza Accord. As noted in Chapter 5, before the 1967 devaluation of the UK pound, British scholars such as Roy Harrod proposed the theory of "elasticity pessimism", which argued that a devaluation of the UK pound would not improve the trade balance as the price elasticities of UK exports and imports were low.

This theory of elasticity pessimism was revived in the United States in the late 1980s. The argument that the effectiveness of the price mechanism of exchange rate changes in balance of payments adjustment led, on the one hand, a call for a direct regulation of imports and exports (see below a Supplementary Note on "Japan Bashing"), and, on the other hand, to an argument based on the "saving–investment balance" framework that Japan's budget deficit should be expanded to absorb excess savings in the private sector and reduce the current account surplus savings in the private sector.

As John Taylor was scheduled to participate in the above-mentioned international conference of the BOJ Institute for Monetary and Economic Studies, I seized the opportunity to discuss this issue with him in a dialogue format in Tokyo.

My argument was that the life-cycle hypothesis suggested that with the ageing of the Japanese population which was predicted to develop most rapidly among the OECD economies, the household savings rate would fall as the proportion of the retired population in the working population increased, and that some of Japan's household savings could be usefully devoted to finance foreign direct investment with technological transfer and other longer-term capital outflows to facilitate economic development in the rest of the world, particularly in developing countries, and that the fruits of such capital outflows at the current time could be returned to Japan as overseas investment earnings after a time lag. This would help to maintain the standard of living of the Japanese people at a stage when the working population was to decline. From a medium- to long-term, global perspective, taking into account the differences in demographic trends across countries, current account balance positions among developed countries should not be regarded as a zero-sum game. Instead, developed countries in the process of rapid population ageing should, as a whole, aim at high national savings rates. In this context, it would be wrong for Japan to be asked to increase fiscal deficits to reduce Japan's national saving associated with its currently high private saving rate in order to reduce its current account surplus. At the same time, I argued that if private saving and investment decisions in Japan were subjected to microeconomic distortions, then the proper policy response would be to remove these distortions. I also argued that with a movement towards more integrated capital markets, the current account would become more of a residual factor that reflected the net effect of agents' decisions, and would diminish its role as a policy objective, and that if private saving and investment decisions in Japan were subjected to microeconomic distortions, then the proper policy response would be to remove these distortions. While Taylor expressed some reservation about the implications of Japan's population ageing on its national saving trends, he also thought that Japan's most urgent task was to eliminate remaining structural impediments to international trade and capital transactions rather than assigning fiscal policy to the objective of reducing Japan's current account surplus.

This dialogue, conducted in English, was translated into Japanese by the publisher, edited by me, and published in the 23 November 1991 issue of the *Syukan Tôyô Keizai* (Weekly Oriental Economy).[2]

On top of this action, I took various opportunities to communicate my views on the issue of Japan's high household savings and current account surpluses abroad. For example, I sent a letter to Hans Tietmeyer, Vice-President of the Bundesbank and Chairman of WP3, and to OECD Secretary-General Paye, suggesting that the issue of balance of payments adjustment among OECD countries should be examined at WP3 from a medium- to long-term perspective, taking into account different patterns in the ageing of populations in OECD countries and OECD countries' role in facilitating economic development in the non-OECD area with sustainable capital outflows with technological assistance.

Assessment of the Japanese Economic Situation after the Bubble Burst

The land price issue was discussed at a meeting of the BOJ Executive Board in late March 1990, shortly after I returned to the Bank, based on materials prepared by its Research and Statistics Department. At this meeting, it was pointed out that there had been not a few cases overseas where land prices had soared and then plummeted, leading to the failures of financial institutions and crises in the financial systems. It was then noted that, in addition to lending to the real estate industry and non-banks, Japanese financial institutions had seen significant increases in lending against real estate collateral, making them that much more vulnerable to a fall in land prices. This confirmed the need to avoid a further rise in land prices from a financial perspective.

The BOJ Executive Board meeting to discuss land price issues was held in the form of a one-off special event. On the other hand, the Board discussion on a wider range of economic and financial issues used to take place once every quarter on the basis of the report prepared by the Research and Statistics Department.

The Winter 1991 edition of the Department's quarterly report entitled "Analysis and Outlook of Japan's Financial and Economic Situation" was discussed at the Board meeting held in late January 1991. At the beginning of the meeting, the Director-General of the Research and Statistics Department gave a verbal explanation of the main points of the material, after which Governor Mieno asked for my opinion. It was judged in the report that the downturn in the inventory investment cycle had come to an end and the Japanese economy was turning into a new recovery phase. The report added that a similar phenomenon was seen during the "Izanagi boom"[3] of the early 1960s, which suggested that the current economic upswing might have considerable underlying strength despite more than four years of expansion. It concluded that the risk of a sharp decline in capital investment growth in the near term was extremely small and that in view of the underlying strength of Japan's real economy supported by technological innovation, the outlook for output growth centred on domestic demand was unlikely to change significantly.[4]

I expressed my doubt about the optimistic judgement of the Research and Statistics Department, noting that the ratio of private fixed capital investment to GDP had risen to 20 per cent, the highest level since 1970, and the Japanese economy seemed to me to be entering into an adjustment phase in the capital stock that had been built up.

Subsequently, in the Research and Statistics Department's Autumn 1991 report compiled on 23 October 1991, its judgement on the inventory cycle was revised. It was stated in the report that industrial production was expected to remain suppressed for some time, partly due to the adjustment of inventories that had been building up recently and that there was a strong possibility that the economy would continue its gradual deceleration trend.[5]

Furthermore, in the Winter 1992 report compiled on 30 January 1992, the Research and Statistics Department revised its assessment of the economy, stating that the degree of deceleration in final demand had increased and output activity had entered a phase of deceleration, with growing signs of downward inventory adjustment.[6] By this statement, the Research and Statistics Department completely reversed its assessment of Japan's inventory investment cycle made exactly one year earlier.

In the Spring 1992 report assessment report compiled on 17 April 1992, just before I started the fourth period of my service at the OECD, it was stated that Japan's economy was still in a phase requiring considerable adjustment, centred on inventory adjustment. It was judged that in the manufacturing sector, the year-on-year growth rate of private capital stock had reached a fairly high level of 8 per cent over the previous year. A reversal of private capital stock formation would exert downward adjustment pressure on the economy for some time to come.[7] Broadly speaking, these were the scenarios I had put forward at the Bank's Executive Board meeting in late January 1991, in opposition to the then optimistic assessment of the Research and Statistics Department.

While the overall assessment of the Japanese economy made in the Department's report of Spring 1992 was more cautious than in its report presented to the Executive Board meeting of late January 1991, it still looked fairly optimistic in my view at the time. It was stated in the Spring 1992 report that since an increase in output activity was expected in large non-manufacturing enterprises such as electric power companies, a significant fall in private capital stock formation would be still unlikely.

In any case, as will be found in the next chapter in which I will describe the views I expressed on the Japanese monetary and economic situation and the conduct of economic policy, the BOJ's overall assessment of the economic situation remained more sanguine than mine after I left the BOJ.

+++++

Supplementary Note on "Japan Bashing"

Below is the oral report made to the Bank of Japan's Policy Board by Kumiharu Shigehara, Director-General of the Institute for Monetary and Economic Studies on 17 September 1991.

On 26 August 1991, the New York Times, the International Herald Tribune, and other leading foreign newspapers reported that a proposal to keep Japan out of the world trading system was discussed at an international conference organised by the US Federal Reserve Bank of Kansas City, shocking those in attendance. On the following day, the Asahi Shimbun, a leading Japanese newspaper, also published the same story. Today, I would like to report on debates at this international symposium and those that took place at an international conference "Japan in the Global Economy" which was held immediately afterwards in Stockholm, both I attended as a Japanese speaker.

The Kansas City Fed conference, which is held each year at a mountain lodge in Jackson Hole, Wyoming right after the August meeting of the Federal Open Market Committee (FOMC), brings together the Chairman and some other members of the Federal Reserve Board, district Fed presidents as well as central bank governors and other senior officials from other major countries, heads of leading private research institutes in the United States, prominent academics, and some journalists.

This year's symposium, held on 22–24 August, was the last one before Roger Guffey, President of Kansas City Fed retired in September, and was chaired by Chairman Alan Greenspan on the first day and Bank of Canada Governor John Crowe on the second day, with unusually big names as speakers including former Chairman Paul Volcker. The main title of the symposium was "Policy Implications of Trade and Currency Zones" and discussions in its first session centred around a paper "The Move toward Free Trade Zones" submitted by Paul Krugman, Professor at the Massachusetts Institute of Technology.[8]

Krugman has been the focus of attention in recent years for his so-called "New Trade Theory", which argues against the traditional free trade theory that has prevailed since Adam Smith, and theorises that managed trade can increase economic welfare, assuming imperfect competition and the existence of economies of scale. He is an up-and-coming scholar who has attracted attention for his advocacy.[9]

In his paper presented to the symposium, he argued that:

1. A free trade regime is best, but the GATT regime has collapsed;
2. There is one country that does not abide by the rules of free trade itself but is a free-rider to the international trade system—Japan;
3. There is a deep-seated distrust of Japan in the West. Japan is fundamentally different from countries (Krugman, ditto, p. 41, footnote 7);
4. Whether this is true or not is not the issue. Japan's perceived heterogeneity alone should be enough to kick Japan out of the Western club;
5. A major benefit of a regional trading bloc is that Japan can be excluded (Krugman, ditto, p. 31). We should then trade according to the rules of the regional trading bloc, which are accepted within the West.

Acting as a commentator on the Krugman paper, Fred Bergsten, Director of the Institute for International Economics and former Assistant Secretary of the Treasury in the Carter Administration, stated[10]:

1. Many Americans and Europeans certainly do deeply distrust the Japanese, as Krugman asserts;
2. However, it would be a mistake to institutionalise this distrust. This distrust must be fought; and
3. World history has taught us that attempts to exclude, rather than accommodate, countries that are gaining power will lead to major conflicts.

Jacques de Larosière, Governor of the Bank of France, was not an invited discussant for this session, but was present on the floor and specifically asked to speak. In fact, Krugman's paper presented to the symposium included an observation that "Nobody likes the French. However, it is not that other Western countries have an irrepressible distrust of the French (these words were later deleted in the published proceedings of the symposium). With the Japanese, however, they are completely different".

De Larosière seized on this and remarked: "Distrust ultimately arises from a lack of understanding [ignorance]. There has long been a relationship of hatred between France and Germany. What fundamentally changed this relationship was the Franco-German line of cooperation that de Gaulle and Adenauer set out after the Second World War. The leadership of political leaders is of utmost importance in excluding deep-seated mistrust between states. Yet for a leading academic like Krugman to make such claims is politically exploitable and extremely dangerous".

As a regular invitee to the Jackson Hole symposium since I was Director of the General Economics Branch of the OECD Economics Department, I had a lot to say about Krugman's paper, but I consciously kept quiet on the first day when I was on the floor and waited for my turn as a scheduled speaker on the second day.

As for the content of the second to fourth sessions, few issues directly related to Japan were raised, and due to time constraints at this meeting today, I will omit them. I might only mention that many US economists expressed considerable doubts about the economic significance of European Monetary Union.

To address the fifth session on "Implications of trade and currency areas for the global economy", a paper was presented by Professor Alan Meltzer of Carnegie Mellon University. Meltzer is the chairman of the Shadow Open Market Committee (SOMC) and a strong monetarist. My friends at the US Fed described this paper by Meltzer as his first contribution to political economy issues. Karl Otto *Pö*hl (Poehl), then President of the German Bundesbank, and myself from Japan were invited as two preassigned discussants in this session. But, just before the symposium, Poehl unexpectedly stepped down as the Bundesbank president due to his opposition to the government's intention to exchange East German marks for West German marks at a ratio of 1:1. His role as a discussant from the German side at the symposium was subsequently replaced by Leonhard Gleske, former member of the Board of the Bundesbank in charge of international affairs.

Meltzer's arguments were approximately as follows.

1. The prosperity of the free world after World War II came about under the global political, military, trade, and monetary system created by the United States as a hegemonic power.
2. But the relative economic strength of the United States has declined. The United States is still powerful in military terms, but inferior to Japan and Germany in terms of currency stability. On the other hand, Japan and Germany are reluctant to play a policing role for world peace and to defend and promote the free trade regime, especially when it involves a cost.

3. In order to maintain the prosperity of the free world in the future, the United States, Japan, and Germany will have to create new rules and share costs in three areas: international political and military, trade and monetary regimes.

However, Meltzer did not specify what he envisaged as these new rules.

Following this, it was my turn to speak. John Crowe, Governor of the Bank of Canada, who sat next to me on the stage and acted as the chairperson, had told me beforehand that, "Everyone is paying attention to what you are going to say today, partly because of the first day's discussion on Krugman's paper about shutting Japan out of our system. Your speech will be the highlight of the day", a role which I was not happy to play.

In my speech,[11] I put the arguments of Krugman and Meltzer into perspective and discussed issues such as Japan's roles in both international politics and economic policy co-operation, how to deal with issues surrounding regional integration, and how Japan's high savings rate and current account surplus should be viewed in relation to international trade frictions.[12]

Fortunately, my speech was well received by many participants. Right after the session, de Larosière even went out of his way from the floor to shake hands with me with his words of congratulations, and on return to Tokyo after the symposium, I received a letter of congratulations from John Hyman, former US Comptroller of the Currency and currently Chairman of Merrill Lynch, in which he, as a participant in the symposium, wrote that my speech had "grace and style".

A part of my speech was reported in the International Herald Tribune, and the essence of it was reported on two pages in the "Finance and Public Finance" edition of Jiji Press last Thursday (12 September), which you may have seen. I would like to add, however, that the headline in the Jiji Press article was not quite right, as it stated that I had argued about the "usefulness of Japan's surpluses", which was not what I meant. The "usefulness of Japan's savings", subsequently introduced in the English Nikkei, was what I argued about in my speech at the Jackson Hole symposium.

The final session was a panel discussion between Paul Volcker, de Larosière and Lawrence (Larry) Summers who is World Bank chief economist.

During its question-and-answer time, Yoshio Suzuki, Vice-President of Nomura Research Institute and former Executive Director of the Bank of Japan, raised his hand from the floor and said, "There is an idea to create a group to negotiate trade issues in East Asia. This is not to create a trade bloc, but a kind of negotiating group to defend the GATT system. But if the West becomes protectionist, East Asia will be forced into a bloc whether it wants to or not".

In response, Bergsten immediately noted:

1. The very move to create such a negotiating group is dangerous,
2. It would make the originally inward-looking European Community (EC) even more inward-looking.

Summers, on the other hand, stated that, in practical terms, regional integration was an unavoidable option, and the two sides remained at loggerheads.

For my part, I am keenly aware that there are also difficult issues in the way East Asian countries interact with Japan.

******

After returning from the Kansas City Fed symposium in Wyoming and spending a few days in Tokyo, I attended another international conference, this time on "Japan in the World Economy", organised by the Stockholm School of Economics at the initiative of its President, Staffan Burenstam Linder, and Professor Thomas Andersson. The Stockholm School of Economics, a prestigious institution having produced many leaders in the Swedish government and business worlds, is currently raising funds in Sweden and Japan to establish a research centre on the Japanese economy, which is intended to serve as a bridge to Japan in Europe. The conference, organised as part of this campaign, consisted of an open discussion session and an academic session.

The open discussion session took place in the auditorium used by the Nobel Prize winners for economics where they give their commemorative speeches after Prize award ceremonies. The opening address was given by His Royal Highness Crown Prince Bertil of Sweden. This was followed by keynote speeches from the European and Japanese sides, followed by questions from the floor, which were answered by the keynote speakers.

Political leaders from Europe and Japan were to attend from each side, and Kiichi Miyazawa, former Japanese Prime Minister, was originally scheduled to participate in it, with me as the other Japanese keynote speaker. However, it turned out at the last moment that Miyazawa could not make it, and Ryutaro Komiya, Professor Emeritus at the University of Tokyo, who had originally planned to speak in the academic session only, became one of the two keynote speakers on the Japanese side.

The first speaker was Andreas van Agt, former Dutch Prime Minister. He had been EC Ambassador to Japan for two and a half years from 1980 and currently EC Ambassador to the United States. He stated:

1. Europeans have mixed feelings about the Japanese.[13] They have feelings of respect, fear, envy and jealousy that Japan, reduced to ashes by the Second World War, has achieved so much economic development.
2. However, he believes it is wrong to exclude Japan. In any case, He believes that Europe's criticism of Japan over the recent expansion of its trade surplus with the EC and the one-way flow of direct investment flows from Japan to EC is often unjustified, but not all of Europe's criticism of Japan is unfounded.
3. In any case, it is important for Europe and Japan to understand each other and learn from each other.

Looking back on the development of the Japanese economy in the post-war period, Professor Komiya, using quite harsh terms in English, refuted the US bashing of Japan and criticised Europe's lack of understanding of Japan.[14]

In addition, Bertil Hagman, a leading figure in the Swedish business world[15] and Erik Asbrink, Swedish Undersecretary of Finance (later Minister of Finance), gave speeches that were considerably more diplomatic towards Japan, and the atmosphere was very different from the Jackson Hole Conference at the Federal Reserve Bank of Kansas City.

I gave a speech of about 30 minutes on new developments in the international trade and monetary regime and policy issues,[16] bearing in mind foreign media reports on "Japan bashing" in Europe.[17]

Fortunately, van Agt and other European and Japanese scholars who participated in the conference appreciated my speech. Among them, van Agt asked me for a copy of my speech immediately after it was delivered.

A Japanese scholar in the audience told me later that Komiya's speech sounded a little too "nationalistic". During the subsequent panel discussion, he said: "I included a fair amount of self-criticism of Europe in my speech, but listening to Professor Komiya's speech, I got the impression that he was arguing that there was nothing in Japan that needed to be improved". In response, Komiya again strongly and for quite some time expressed his view that the West was making no effort to understand Japan.

The academic session was attended by Japanese, European, and US academics on various aspects of the Japanese economy, and Japanese academics said they had never participated in an international conference dealing with such a broad range of issues concerning Japan. Indeed, the Swedish hospitality was very impressive.

On return to Tokyo, I visited the Swedish Ambassador to Japan last week to say that I would like to be of some assistance in the establishment of the Japan Economic Centre. In this respect, I must act a bit more as a Japanese citizen with some international experience, although this may be a little beyond the scope of central bank business.

I am going to send the essay which I wrote in my personal capacity to my friends in international organisations, including the Secretary-General of the OECD, and to some leaders of governments and central banks of major countries, in order to obtain their comments, which I intend to use as a basis for further exchange of views. At the same time, I would like to have a discussion with key figures in the Japanese Government on issues including regional integration of trade and currencies.

Notes

1. Kumiharu Shigehara, ed. "Price Stablization in the 1990s: Domestic and International Policy Requirements", Macmillan Press, 1993.

2. John Taylor and Kumiharu Shigehara, "*Nihon no Chochiku wo Dôtsukauka* (How to Use Japan's Savings)" (in Japanese translation), *Syukan Tôyô Keizai* (Weekly Oriental Economy), November 23, 1991.
3. The so-called "*Izanagi* boom" lasted for 57 months from November 1965 to July 1970, the longest high growth phase in the post-War Japan.
4. Bank of Japan Research Monthly Report, Analysis and Outlook of Japan's Financial Economy—Situation Assessment Materials (Winter 1991), February 1991.
5. Bank of Japan Research Monthly Report, Analysis and Outlook of Japan's Financial Economy—Situation Assessment Materials (Autumn 1991), November 1991.
6. Bank of Japan Research Monthly Report, Analysis and Outlook of Japan's Financial Economy—Situation Assessment Materials (Winter 1992), February 1992.
7. Bank of Japan Research Monthly Report, Analysis and Outlook of Japan's Financial Economy—Situation Assessment Materials (Spring 1992), May 1992.
8. Paul Krugman, "The Move toward Free Trade Zones", Federal Reserve Bank of Kansas City, "Policy Implications of Trade and Currency Zones", the proceedings of a symposium held at Jackson Hole, Wyoming, August 22–24, 1991, pp. 7–41.
9. Owing largely to this new theory, Krugman was subsequently awarded the 2008 Nobel Prize in Economics.
10. Fred Bergsten, "Commentary: The Move toward Free Trade Zones", ditto, p. 52.
11. Kumiharu Shigehara, "Commentary: Global Implications of Trade and Currency Zones", ditto, pp. 267–274.
12. See also footnote 2 of this Chapter on my discussion with John Taylor on the domestic and international use of Japan's high savings.
13. Andreas van Agt, "Europe-Japan: Conflict or Cooperation?" in "Japan: A European Perspective", edited by Thomas Andersson, St. Martin's Press, 1993, pp. 3–10.
14. Ryutaro Komiya, "Some Thoughts on the Future Development of Japan-Europe Economic Relations", ditto, pp. 11–25.
15. Bertil Hagman, "Europe-Japan: Strengthened Relations", ditto, pp. 27–37.

16. Kumiharu Shigehara, "Evolving International Trade and Monetary Regimes and Related Issues", ditto, pp. 39–50. https://www.imes.boj.or.jp/research/papers/english/me9-2-1.pdf.
17. William Drozdiak, "Europe's New Rage: Japan Bashing", The Washington Post, June 16, 1991. https://www.washingtonpost.com/archive/politics/1991/06/16/europes-new-rage-japan-bashing/0b9b1f7b-e578-4aae-926b-e2bdd6809f68/.

CHAPTER 13

Coping with the Bursting of Japan's Bubble and External Shocks

The OECD announcement in early 1992 that I would succeed David Henderson as OECD Chief Economist and Head of the Economics Department was welcomed by Cristopher Dow and Sylvia Ostry, both former OECD Chief Economists, as well as many central bank economists and some academics of Western countries. Among them was Wolfgang Rieke, head of the International Department at the Bundesbank. In his letter of congratulations on my appointment, he expressed his wish to strengthen our co-operation in the area of WP3 activities. At the time, the chair of WP3 was Hans Tietmeyer, Vice-President of the Bundesbank, whom I met in his office at the Bundesbank's headquarters in Frankfurt on my way from Tokyo to Paris in the spring of 1992 to attend OECD high-level monetary experts meeting as the Bank of Japan (BOJ) representative and discussed my ideas on how to strengthen WP3 activities. It was agreed between us that Rieke would act as a liaison officer when Tietmeyer was busy with urgent matters at the Bundesbank.

Prior to my decision to return to the OECD, I was well aware that dissatisfaction with the activities of the EPC had been widely shared among senior government and central bank officials participating in its meetings. In his letter of congratulations on my appointment as OECD Chief Economist, Mervyn King, then Executive Director and Chief Economist of the Bank of England, noted that he and Alan Budd, Chief Economic Advisor at UK Treasury, hoped that with their co-operation, I would endeavour to

K. Shigehara, *The Bank of Japan, the OECD, and Beyond*,
https://doi.org/10.1007/978-981-97-5307-9_13

strengthen EPC activities. Moreover, just before I was to fly from Tokyo to Paris to start my work at the OECD in May 1992, I received a faxed letter from Michael Boskin, then Chair of the EPC and Chairman of the US President's Council of Economic Advisors, in which he expressed deep concern about the EPC which he thought had lost sight of what it should work for, and suggested that he and I should get together with the chief EPC representatives from the other G7 countries at a meeting in Washington to discuss how to revive the EPC before the start of my work at the OECD. I therefore changed my flight schedule and flew from Tokyo to Washington on my way to Paris. The Washington meeting was indeed held with participation of all chief EPC representatives of G7 countries, but was cut short as, in the course of our meeting, Boskin was suddenly summoned by the President. Even so, the messages from this meeting were clear to me, and on arrival in Paris, I started my work for the reform of EPC as one of my priority tasks. In this chapter, I will review how my policy recommendations and those of the OECD Economics Department evolved and what discussions took place at the meetings of revitalised WP3 (Photo 13.1) *and EPC on the management of Japanese economic policy after the bursting of Japan's bubble in the early 1990s and in the wake of the East Asian financial crisis in 1997–1998. My and the Department's views and WP3 and EPC discussions on other important policy issues will be described in Part 3 of this book.*

Dealing with the Aftermath of the Bursting of Japan's Bubble

In May 1992 when I started to work as OECD Chief Economist, Takatoshi Ito, then Professor at Hitotsubashi University, contributed an article to the Nihon Keizai Shimbun in which he argued that for correcting Japan's structural current account surplus, it would be desirable to bring the yen exchange rate to a high level by tightening monetary policy and adopting expansionary fiscal policy.[1] The view I had expressed during my previous services at the OECD was fundamentally different from this monetary/fiscal mix theory.

In the main issues paper prepared for the WP3 meeting to be held in March 1992, before I took up the post of OECD Chief Economist, the Secretariat asked whether Japan's growing trade surplus might increase protectionism, whether the Japanese economy, if it continued to falter while the US economic recovery progressed, would not exert upward pressure on the yen/dollar exchange rate, and whether, in that case,

Photo 13.1 Participants of OECD Working Party No. 3 meeting: (from left to right) Laurence Summers (US Treasury Under Secretary), Edwin Truman (Director of Fed International Finance Division), William White (Deputy Governor of the Bank of Canada), Scott Clark (Associate Deputy Minister of Finance of Canada), Jürgen Stark (State Secretary of the German ministry of finance), Jean-Claude Paye (OECD Secretary-General), Hans Tietmeyer (OECD Working Party No. 3 Chairman, Deputy President of the German Bundesbank), and Kumiharu Shigehara (OECD Chief Economist and Head of Economics Department) (the positions mentioned in parentheses are those held at the time the photo was taken in 1993) (© OECD-OCDE)

Japan's economic recovery would require fiscal rather than monetary policy support.

As noted in Chapter 8, the argument for increasing Japan's domestic demand through fiscal expansion was put forward by a number of the OECD Secretariat papers in the late 1970s when I was back at the BOJ. In Chapter 9, it was also noted that, in 1981–1982, Stephen Marris, then Economic Advisor to OECD Secretary-General van Lennep advocated the mix of monetary tightening and fiscal expansion in Japan on which I disagreed as Deputy Director of the General Economics Branch of the Economics and Statistics Department, and the Secretariat could not present a united view on how Japanese economic policy should be managed to the OECD ministerial meeting of May 1982.

Such arguments for monetary and fiscal policy mix disappeared from the Secretariat recommendations after my arrival as OECD Chief Economist. The staff economists' work on the June 1992 issue of the OECD Economic Outlook (EO) was almost completed just before my arrival at the OECD in May that year. However, it was possible for me to add to the final text my words about policy recommendations on Japanese economic policy management in its Introduction. There I wrote that "(A)t first glance, given the low level of net outstanding government debt and the general budget surplus, Japan appears to have room for expansionary fiscal policy. However, the actual room for expansionary fiscal policy in the future will be limited, given that fiscal expenditures are expected to increase significantly with the ageing of the population and that it would be politically difficult to reverse a policy of fiscal expansion intended as a temporary measure in a timely manner".[2]

At my first press conference as OECD Chief Economist, held to launch this issue of EO, the first question was raised by Carl Gewirtz, a Paris correspondent for the International Herald Tribune. It was about my definition of "price stability". After explaining that published official price statistics were subject to various measurement biases, my response to his question was that in terms of the consumer price index, an annual increase of up to around 2 per cent should be considered to be consistent with "price stability", although the precise number might vary among countries.

This was the first occasion for an OECD official to make a public statement on the numerical definition of "price stability". Its implication for the conduct of Japanese economic policy management was that, given the outlook for the Japanese economy contained in the EO, there was considerable scope for monetary policy easing to restore domestic demand growth.

The OECD Economic Survey of Japan published in October 1992 drew attention to the balance-sheet problems of Japanese financial institutions with bad loans and the fact that the plunge in share prices, which began in early 1990, had led to a substantial decline in the unrealised profits of Japanese commercial banks subjected to the Bank for International Settlements (BIS) capital adequacy rules. It was indicated in the report that further declines in share prices would entail further declines in their capital ratios, discouraging them from extending loans to non-financial business firms and consumers, thus weakening the stimulatory effect of monetary policy easing.[3]

In commenting on Japan in my opening remarks at the WP3 meeting on 3 December 1992, I said that the weakness of the Japanese economy suggested the need for further monetary easing which would have an impact on the exchange rate. However, I argued that concerns that further monetary easing in Japan would lead to a weaker yen, leading to trade frictions between Japan and its trading partner countries were mitigated by recent developments in the foreign exchange market. Using monetary policy to support domestic demand to the extent that price stability was maintained would be in the interest of Japan as well as its trading partners. If there were a lack of Japanese policy response in the face of weak domestic demand, there would be a risk that Japanese demand for foreign goods and services would soften. I added that particular attention should be paid to the actual borrowing costs of small and medium-sized companies when determining whether Japan's short-term interest rates were low enough.[4]

In my opening statement at the press conference held shortly afterwards on 17 December to launch the new EO, I stated that Japan's monetary policy should be such that "accommodative measures are taken without compromising the objective of maintaining low inflation".[5] As noted earlier, my view that the monetary policy objective of price stability should not be zero inflation, but "low inflation" had been made clear when I replied to the first question raised by Gewirtz at my press conference introducing the June 1992 issue of EO. But, this time, my opening statement was faxed to the central bank governors of the WP3 participating countries and others as soon as my press conference ended. I was later informed by Eddie George, then Governor of the Bank of England, that many recipients had read my opening statement made at the press conference.

Over my five years as OECD Chief Economist, I made official trips to Japan twice a year in principle, meeting with the vice ministers and other senior officials of the Ministry of Finance, the Economic Planning Agency and the Ministry of Trade and Industry as well as the Ministry of Foreign Affairs. And at the BOJ, I had *tête-à-tête* meetings with the Governor, Deputy Governor and some other members of the Executive Board as well as the Director-General of the Policy Planning Department.

On my first official visit to the BOJ in late 1992, Yutaka Yamaguchi, then Director-General of the Planning Department (later Executive Director and subsequently Deputy Governor), said to me: "Why are you so pessimistic about the outlook for the Japanese economy? I am uncomfortable with your view". Earlier when he was Director-General of the Research and Statistics Department, Yamaguchi was responsible for its quarterly economic assessment report presented to the last Executive Board meeting that I attended as the Director-General of the Bank's Institute for Monetary and Economic Studies. The differences of views on the outlook for the Japanese economy I expressed at the meetings of the Executive Board meetings from those included in the reports of the Research and Statistics Department were described in Chapter 12 of this book.

Commenting on the slow recovery of the Japanese economy in the June 1993 issue of EO, I warned that business investment was likely to be weaker than previously expected due to the appreciation of the yen, and that commercial banks' lending could remain subdued for several years to come because of their non-performing asset problems.[6]

Around this time, at the EPC as well as WP3 meetings, representatives of the Bank explained that the reason for the lack of growth in money supply and bank lending in Japan was weak demand for funds. In contrast, my argument was that at least one reason for the weak demand for funds was that the level of real interest rates was still too high due to low current and expected inflation rates, even though the level of nominal interest rates was very low. I argued that the relatively high level of real interest rates in Japan was one of the reasons why the yen had appreciated, even though it was the currency of a country with a collapsed bubble.

At the wrap-up session of EPC meeting in November 1993 to discuss a desirable set of monetary, fiscal, and structural policies in OECD member countries, I stressed the importance of comprehensive structural reforms as well as more active use of fiscal and monetary policies in Japan (see Box 13.1, my remarks on desirable policies in Europe made at that meeting are found in Chapter 15 of this book).

Some Thoughts on a Domestically and Internationally Desirable and Consistent Set of Monetary, Fiscal, and Structural Policies by OECD Member Countries: My intervention at the wrap-up session on the second day of the Economic Policy Committee, 10 November 1993

*****

Origins of the Current Problems

The balance-sheet problems currently faced by Japan are deep-seated. A number of macroeconomic and structural factors have contributed to this. Some of them are:

1. *Excessive reliance on monetary policy in coping with current account surplus in the second half of the 1980s; in particular a delay in the timing of the reversal of the stance of monetary policy towards restraint.*
2. *Inadequate strengthening of prudential controls at a time of deregulating financial markets.*
3. *Only very limited attempts made for land reforms, particularly in urban areas:*
    - *No wonder the perception persisted that the collateral value of land would continue to rise;*
    - *This led to the laxity at commercial banks' internal control on lending policy in deregulated credit markets.*
4. *Very little progress in structural reforms in the sheltered sectors of the economy:*
    - *Differentials between the equilibrium exchange rate for highly efficient sectors producing traded goods and the equilibrium exchange rate for the sheltered sectors producing non-traded goods and services have widened, with adjustment burdens concentrating on industries engaged in international trade.*

Looking ahead

Japan may have to undergo another year of extremely slow growth. The GDP growth rate for 1994 could be well below one per cent. I must add that a point forecast is a particularly difficult business for Japan at this stage.

So what policy messages?

1. *Perhaps a bit of further active use of fiscal and monetary policy would help, but the backlog of balance-sheet problems and very weak confidence in both the business and household sectors, their effectiveness may be more limited than the past average record suggests.*

2. *Even with more active macro-policy, time is required for balance-sheet adjustment to run its course: it may take several years for banks to restore their earlier solid positions and resume normal risk-taking as financial intermediaries. In the meantime, however painful the domestic adjustment process may be, one must not have an overdose of macro-policies which would worsen the medium- and long-term performance of the Japanese economy. Deterioration of the medium-term performance of the second largest economy would also do harm to other countries.*
3. *Now is the time for comprehensive structural reforms, including the opening of the rice market. In macroeconomic terms, its effect should be very small. But symbolically it would be an important step in demonstrating Japan's resolve to integrate itself further into the open, multilateral system without which particularly countries like Japan, lacking in indigenous natural resources, cannot survive.*
4. *A crucial component in a desirable package of macro and structural policy measures to be adopted by Japan would be land reforms to promote the construction of more spacious houses in urban areas. Housing construction and related spending on consumer durables rather than non-durable consumption should be a main source of sustained domestic demand growth. These are demand components which should facilitate the transfer of savings from the current to future generations in real assets that would alleviate some of the burdens of the working populations in supporting the aged, dependent people in the future.*

Yen Overshooting

Signs of a recovery in domestic demand in Japan, which had been appearing modestly from the end of 1993, were dampened in 1995 by the supply bottleneck caused by the Great Hanshin-Awaji Earthquake (initially called abroad as "the Kobe Earthquake"), as well as the accelerating appreciation of the yen, which worsened business sentiment severely. The yen exchange rate appreciated to ¥79.75 to the dollar at one point in April 1995, breaking through the 80-yen mark.

Under these circumstances, commenting on the Japanese situation in the preface to the EO published in June 1995, we used the expression "yen overshooting", and argued that in view of the wide supply–demand gap in the Japanese economy, the weak outlook for domestic demand,

and ongoing bank credit retrenchment (see Section "Banking problems and the introduction of public funds" below), further cuts in short-term interest rates would be needed unless the yen overshooting was corrected by the market forces.[7]

At the WP3 meeting in July 1995, Lawrence Summers who succeeded Andrew Crockett as WP3 chairman (Crockett, who had followed Tietmeyer as WP3 chairman, was subsequently appointed BIS General Manager) noted the danger of a vicious cycle in which a strong yen would further aggravate deflation in the Japanese economy, which would raise real interest rates and further weaken the real economy. At that meeting, following my remarks made at the EPC meeting of November 1993 (Box 13.1), I observed that Japan needed "a comprehensive, coherent strategy" to overcome its economic woes, and that within this framework, the Japanese monetary authorities should conduct "non-sterilised" foreign exchange market intervention to ease domestic monetary conditions further and at the same time encourage financial institutions to quickly complete the process of disposing their non-performing loans. I added that of these, the latter would be expected to have more lasting effects on the Japanese economy. I also argued that fiscal measures might be necessary in the short term, but they would not be as effective as they used to be. Furthermore, I stated that the sheltered services sector, which had been isolated from market competition and suffering from low productivity, was urgently in need of adjustment, but that given the weakness of Japanese political leadership, it would not be easy for the Japanese economy to get out of its difficulties, and that it would remain in a state of muddling through for at least several more years to come. In response, Takatoshi Kato, then Vice Minister of Finance for International Affairs, and Akira Nagashima, Executive Director of the BOJ, argued that there were substantial structural changes taking place in the Japanese economy.

At the WP3 meeting held in Rome at the invitation of the Italian government in September 1995, the stance of Japanese monetary and fiscal policy to expand domestic demand was again a major topic for discussion. At the meeting, Summers as WP3 chairman observed that the OECD Secretariat's assessment on the effects of Japanese fiscal policy seemed to be different from that of the IMF. I responded by noting that for the past three years, i.e., since my arrival as OECD Chief Economist, the OECD Secretariat had been consistently recommending that the Japanese authorities should move more aggressively and earlier on the monetary policy front to increase domestic demand.

My argument was that further expansionary fiscal measures in addition to those that had been taken by the Japanese government since Japan's bubble burst might be less effective as Japanese taxpayers would become increasingly concerned about their future tax burden needed for fiscal restoration. IMF chief economist Michael Mussa agreed with me that Japan should adopt bolder policies, but added that further expansionary fiscal measures could still be effective if carefully designed. On the other hand, William White, who became BIS Chief Economist after serving as Deputy Governor of the Bank of Canada, agreed with me that Japan may have been approaching a situation where the Ricardian equivalence theory would apply.

On my observation on the urgent need of further monetary policy easing, BOJ Executive Director Nagashima admitted that money supply growth had become low, but argued that its annual growth rate of around 3 per cent was sufficient for economic growth under virtually zero inflation in Japan. In response, I suggested that instead of being satisfied with an annual money supply growth of 3 per cent, the BOJ should aim at higher monetary growth. At the time, Japan's potential output growth was considered to be around 2 per cent per annum. If James Tobin were at the WP3 meeting, he might have argued that the BOJ should set a nominal income growth target of 4 per cent or so with a tolerable inflation rate of some 2 per cent per annum (see his argument on nominal income growth targeting in Chapter 10).

Foreign Exchange Market Intervention and Monetary Policy

In the OECD Secretariat document prepared for the Rome meeting of WP3, we stated that "a further decline in the yen would be clearly helpful to the recovery of the Japanese economy". We argued that the correction of the strong yen would contribute to a recovery in domestic demand by raising Japanese stock market prices which would result in a lower cost of capital, as well as alleviating Japanese banks' balance-sheet problems by an improvement in their capital ratios through a restoration of unrealised profits on their shareholdings, leading to a stronger appetite for their credit extension. In addition, if Japanese nominal GDP growth rate recovered to 6 per cent in 1997, as in the alternative projection published in the EO of December 1995, it would bring about progress in fiscal consolidation, given the income elasticity of tax revenues. An upturn in asset prices as a result of the correction of the strong yen would contribute to fiscal consolidation also through increases in capital gains tax revenues.

Following this line of argumentation, we recommended that the BOJ should intervene by buying dollars and selling the yen if foreign exchange market forces were insufficient to alleviate the yen's strength.

At the WP3 meeting in Rome, a question was raised about the effectiveness of the authorities' intervention in the foreign exchange market (on the WP3 discussion about this issue at its May 1981 meeting, see Chapter 9). In response, I argued that although there were various opinions regarding the effectiveness of the authorities' *non-sterilised* intervention in the foreign exchange market in influencing the exchange rate,[8] the OECD Secretariat's document clearly stated that in order for the Japanese monetary authorities' dollar-buying/yen-selling operations to have lasting effects on the yen exchange rate, they must conduct *non-sterilised* interventions, meaning that the yen funds released by these interventions should be left in the yen money market and the reserve positions of Japanese banks should be allowed to increase. I also pointed out that the secretariat's document had commented that, apart from the policy of further depressing short-term market interest rates through *non-sterilised* interventions in the foreign exchange market, a stronger yen could be corrected also through more aggressive buying operations by the BOJ in the open market for the yen-denominated Japanese government bonds.[9] During this debate Chairman Summers remained silent and no other WP3 members spoke.

The results of the OECD Economics Department's econometric analysis on the effects of the yen depreciation were published in the December 1995 issue of EO, see Table 13.1.

Table 13.1 Effects of a 10 per cent depreciation in the effective exchange rate of the Japanese yen

	Baseline projection		*Alternative projection*	
Exchange rate assumption	*103.7 yen to the dollar*		*115 yen to the dollar*	
	1996	*1997*	*1996*	*1997*
Real GDP growth (%)	2.0	2.7	2.8	4.2
Real gross domestic demand growth (%)	2.6	2.9	2.9	4.2
Nominal GDP growth (%)	1.5	3.0	2.6	6.0
Current account balance ($bn)				
Japan	93	95	86	96
United States of America	−161	−155	−160	−156
OECD Europe	72	75	72	75
Asia (excluding Japan and South Korea)	−27	−29	−21	−30

Source OECD Economic Outlook, December 1995, p. 9

According to this work using the OECD Interlink model,[10] *a correction of the yen overshooting would initially reduce Japan's current account surplus in dollar terms through the J-curve effect. The current account balance of Japan's trade partner countries in Asia would slightly deteriorate in the second year following the yen rate correction, while current account balances of the United States and OECD Europe would remain virtually unchanged. We also pointed out in the EO that a correction of the excessively strong yen would lead to a fall in local currency prices of Japanese goods imported into Asian countries, contributing to lower inflation in these countries. The EO also noted that a reduction in the risk of further yen appreciation would have the effect of lowering medium- and long-term interest rates in the United States, as international investors would feel more comfortable returning funds to the United States. However, the impact of these effects on the US economy and the rest of the world was not measured numerically in this analysis.*

In the WP3 paper submitted to its Rome meeting, we added that an excessively weak yen should be avoided, even if it had positive effects in the short term from the perspective of Japan's economic recovery. In particular, we expressed concern that a weak yen could have an unfavourable impact on Japan and its trading partners if it undermined the Japanese government's efforts for structural reform and market opening. We also warned that if the yen's depreciation were to coincide with a deterioration in the US current account balance, there would be a risk of heightened international trade friction, whether or not the former was a major cause of the latter.[11]

The Nihon Keizai Shimbun, in the morning edition of 24 October 1995, reported my comment that the BOJ should act more aggressively to cope with the prevailing deflationary circumstances. It was made at my press interview during my stay in Tokyo to participate in the international conference held by the BOJ's Institute for Monetary and Economic Studies on 26–27 that month.

The subject of this international conference was "Towards more effective monetary policy".[12] Besides Japanese and foreign central bank economists and academics, the conference was attended by BOJ Governor Yasuo Matsushita and Deputy Governor Toshihiko Fukui.

Among the proposals for Japanese monetary policy management made at the conference, most noteworthy were those made by Mervyn Goodfriend[13] as a discussant of a paper presented by Kazuo Ueda, then professor at the University of Tokyo, now BOJ Governor.[14] Goodfriend argued that, with short-term interest rates in Japan close to zero, it would be desirable for the BOJ, through its open market operations, to increase the prices of yen-denominated stocks, bonds, and other assets, thereby increasing demand for dollar-denominated assets and raising the dollar exchange rate against the yen. This would reduce Japanese demand for imports from abroad and increase domestic and foreign demand for cheaper Japanese goods, thereby stimulating domestic production. This policy would also lower long-term interest rates, and thus stimulate domestic spending and output activity in Japan. Furthermore, Goodfriend argued that a rise in the prices of yen-denominated equities would have the effect of lowering the cost of capital for Japanese companies and increasing demand for durable goods with an expansionary impact on aggregate output. It would also have the effect of reinforcing Japanese commercial banks' equity capital by restoring their unrealised profits on equities. Goodfriend's argument was consistent with the policy recommendations for Japan contained in the OECD Secretariat discussion paper submitted to the Rome WP3 meeting. Goodfriend was then Director of

Research at the Federal Reserve Bank of Richmond. I was unsure whether he had read the OECD WP3 documents.

In the Ueda paper, the BOJ's policy management towards the end of the 1980s was characterised as its second monetary policy mistake, following its failure to prevent inflation in the early 1970s under the government of Kakuei Tanaka who succeeded Eisaku Sato as the Japanese Prime Minister.

In this regard, Goodfriend, drawing on the 1994 OECD Economic Survey of Japan,[15] wrote in his paper that after the 1985–86 recession, real GDP growth averaged 4 per cent per year during the 1987–91 recovery and expansion period, during which the GDP gap as measured by the OECD turned from −4 per cent to +4 per cent; the real short-term interest rate fell from 2.5 per cent in mid-1986 to 1 per cent in early 1989; inflation in terms of the consumer price index began to pick up, rising from below 1 per cent in early 1989 to nearly 4 per cent by mid-1990; more pronounced was the uptrend in the unit labour cost in manufacturing, which rose from an increase of 2 per cent in 1989 to over 7 per cent in 1992; long-term interest rates rose from around 4 per cent in the first half of 1989 to 9 per cent in mid-1990, probably due to heightened inflationary concerns reflected in long-term interest rates; the Nikkei Stock Average rose from a little above 20,000 in early 1988 to nearly 40,000 in early 1990, before falling sharply to 25,000 at the end of 1990 and below 20,000 in 1992. After summarizing these developments in Japan, Goodfriend observed that the Bank of Japan began to raise the real short-term interest rate as late as in late 1989 by which time the real GDP gap had disappeared,[16] and that the delay in monetary tightening under the governorship of Satoshi Sumita led to doubts about the BOJ's commitment to low inflation.

I would note that the BOJ at the time had no legally established independence from the government and was severely constrained by domestic and international policy agendas set under the Plaza and the Louvre Accords as well as bilateral political deals between Japan and the United States. It is striking that around that time, none of high BOJ officials made critical comments about US economic policy management like those expressed by Bundesbank Vice-President Schlesinger (see Chapter 10).

While Goodfriend did not mention this aspect in his paper, Alan Meltzer, one of the overseas advisers to the BOJ's Institute for Monetary and Economic Studies, in his oral comment at the BOJ's conference noted that one of the reasons for the difficulties in money supply-oriented policy management during the period of sustained yen appreciation in the late 1980s was the importance attached to international policy co-ordination regarding the yen-dollar exchange rate.[17] This aspect was stressed in my paper submitted to the 1997 Annual Meeting of the European Economic Association comparing the monetary policy performance of Japan and the United States (see Chapter 16).

The real effective exchange rate of the Japanese yen in the first quarter of 1996 was 24.5 per cent higher than in 1991. During the same period, the real effective exchange rate of the US dollar depreciated by 7.8 per cent. Against this backdrop, I contributed an article to the 3 August 1996 issue of a Japanese weekly economic journal "*Tôyô Keizai* (Oriental Economy)", once again stressing the importance of monetary policy for Japan's economic policy management in expanding domestic demand.

In the preface to the EO published in June 1996, we acknowledged that the fiscal measures adopted until then to boost economic activity had contributed to the recovery of domestic demand in Japan, but recommended that Japan should move as quickly as possible to reduce the budget deficit as long as domestic demand remained strong, as both the large budget deficit and high government debt balance were unsustainable and their correction was desirable in the medium term.[18] The OECD Economic Survey of Japan published in November 1996 also recommended that fiscal consolidation should be strengthened in the medium term as long as the underlying strength of domestic demand permitted, and that any negative effects on domestic demand that would arise in the course of the implementation of the programme for fiscal consolidation should be dealt with through further easing of monetary policy. It was also suggested that monetary easing would help stimulate business activity and restore the health of Japanese financial institutions, which would contribute to supporting economic growth.[19]

Banking Problems and the Introduction of Public Funds

Since around 1992–1993, I had been thinking that public funds would probably have to be injected in order for Japanese financial institutions to quickly complete the process of disposing their non-performing loans, and to encourage them to engage in normal risk-taking in lending activities required to support the recovery of the Japanese economy. While

I expressed such views at confidential WP3 meetings, I hesitated to make candid statements on the need to inject public funds into Japanese financial institutions at my press conferences and interviews, fearing that ringing the alarm bell there might be counterproductive, given the public opinion then prevailing in Japan that neither zombie firms nor problem financial institutions should be bailed out by the injection of public funds.

For example, my remarks made at a press interview in Tokyo in October 1992, i.e., five months after my appointment as OECD Chief Economist, were reported by the Nihon Keizai Shimbun (14 Oct 1992, morning edition, p. 7) under the title "Slow improvement in bank assets" as follows.

"The current banking difficulty in Japan is not a credit crunch like the one that occurred in the US, and is not a problem for the banking system as a whole. However, as a problem specific to Japan, due attention should be paid to the fact that the fall in stock prices has resulted in a decline in banks' capital ratios. As for the use of public funds, I can't say that they should never be released. In some cases, the cost of injecting public funds to problem banks to protect the financial system could be lower than the damage to the economy and society of doing nothing with problem financial institutions. However, the risk of moral hazard cannot be ignored, and it would be preferable for the public authorities to intervene as little as possible".

Inside the OECD Secretariat, however, I more candidly expressed concern about the issue of the procyclicality effect of the BIS capital adequacy rules, which I had referred to at the press interview in Japan. From Paris I carefully watched the evolution of the extremely difficult problems involved in Japanese authorities' dealing with individual cases of insolvent banks and specialised housing finance institutions. In the EO published in June 1993, we again warned that bank lending could be curtailed for several years to come because of the bad asset problem.[20]

The OECD Secretariat discussion paper prepared for the Rome WP3 in September 1995 also raised the issue of the merits and demerits of injecting fiscal funds, rather than BOJ funds, to enable Japanese financial institutions with large amounts of non-performing assets to restore normal lending behaviour, while pointing out the problem of moral hazard associated with the introduction of public funds.[21] The meeting was attended by Kato and Nagashima from Japan.

On the issue of dealing with problem financial institutions, Nagashima made the following comments:

1. The main objective should be to remove depositors' concerns and the authorities will act only when the financial system as a whole is considered to be at risk;
2. Problem financial institutions to be bailed out by the authorities must be liquidated and that other financial institutions must be asked to co-operate; and
3. All parties must be held accountable in order to avoid moral hazard

The OECD Economic Survey of Japan published in November 1995 after the WP3 Rome meeting stated that "further monetary easing could have the effect of helping private banks adjust their balance sheets through higher asset prices. However, it would not be sufficient to restore stability to the financial system". The report then identified three policy options. The first was a policy of forbearance, which was in place at the time. The second was to provide support measures to merge the problem financial institutions with other financial institutions. The third was the injection of public funds. And we argued that the third option was necessary.

The EO published in December of the same year pointed out that "the difficulties in the financial sector, such as the recent setbacks of weak financial institutions and the huge amount of non-performing loans, must be resolved as soon as possible. This will require an injection of government funds, but care must be taken not to create a moral hazard".[22]

The following July 1996, a basic agreement was reached for private financial institutions to contribute to a financial stabilisation contribution fund to cover secondary losses arising from the disposal of non-performing loans of specialised housing finance institutions which were subsidiaries of Japanese commercial banks. In November the same year, Hanwa Bank, which was in financial difficulties, was ordered by the Japanese government to suspend banking operations. This was the first case of a bank failure in the post-war Japan.

The OECD Economic Survey of Japan published in November 1996 pointed out that the amount of burden incurred by private financial institutions was left unclear with regard to the disposal of non-performing loans of specialised housing finance institutions, and raised the question of whether the disposal of non-performing loans could be carried out efficiently. The importance of decisions by bank supervisors on the operation of the deposit insurance system and the triggering of early corrective measures were also discussed.[23]

Reportedly, public opinion in Japan was confused by the mix-up between the protection of depositors, the preservation of the financial system as a whole and the bailout of individual banks. Apart from the discussions at WP3 and my statements in English as OECD chief economist at press conferences on EOs, the question I had was when to present my recommendations in Japanese. As I will describe later, I decided to do this on my official business trip to Japan after I became OECD Deputy Secretary-General in May 1997.

The East Asian Financial Crisis

The EO published in December 1996 issued one important warning. We stated there that if economic growth in non-OECD Asian countries (i.e., excluding Japan and Korea) were to develop at a lower rate than the OECD basic projections, weaker import demand in these countries would lower exports and economic growth in OECD countries, with Japan likely to be most adversely affected.[24]

The EO published in June 1997, shortly after I became OECD Deputy Secretary-General, presented a relatively positive assessment of the Japanese economic situation. In 1996, aggregate domestic demand grew by a high 4.5 per cent in real terms compared with the previous year. Aggregate output growth of 0.6 per cent in 1994 and 1.4 per cent in 1995 was followed by more solid growth amounting to 3.6 per cent in 1996, in the face of the negative contribution of the decline in Japan's external surplus amounting to 0.9 percentage point. For 1997, despite fiscal restructuring, output growth of 2.3 per cent was projected, supported by firm capital investment and export growth.[25]

The initial budget for 1997 was the first austerity-type budget since 1988 with a meagre 1.5 per cent increase in general expenditure, and the consumption tax rate was raised from 3 per cent to 5 per cent in April. All these fiscal actions were taken into account in the EO projections of June 1997.

A few months later, the East Asian financial crisis broke out. This was followed by a major shock in the New York stock market on 15 August when the dollar's depreciation triggered a sharp fall in share prices, the second biggest crash in history after Black Monday. In November 1997, the collapse of Hokkaido Takushoku Bank, one of 12 city banks with a large branch network in Japan and several branches abroad, and Yamaichi

Securities, a leading security firm with an international branch network, shocked the Japanese people and global financial markets.

Unlike in other OECD countries such as the United States, the United Kingdom, and some Nordic countries that had suffered from the fragility of financial institutions earlier than Japan, private consumption never contracted on an annual basis for several years until the private consumption tax was raised in 1997. While the unemployment rate began to pick up in 1993 from a low of 2.1 per cent in 1991, the subsequent yearly rises were limited until 1998 when the unemployment rate jumped to the 4 per cent mark. Japanese firms tried hard not to shed surplus labour in the face of continued weak activity, hoping for a turnaround of the economic climate.

The financial crisis broke out in Thailand in July 1997 and soon spread to Malaysia, Indonesia, the Philippines, Hong Kong, and Korea. They saw their currencies depreciated substantially against the US dollar and the yen. Between 1997 and 1998, the Thai baht fell by about 30 per cent against the Japanese yen. During the same period, the Korean won deprecated by some 50 per cent against the yen.

The June 1997 issue of the EO published the results of the OECD Interlink model simulation exercise for measuring the impact of the strong yen on the Japanese economy (Table 13.2).[26]

Table 13.2 Effects of a 10 per cent appreciation in the effective exchange rate of the Japanese yen[27]

Deviation from the basic forecast				
	1997	*1998*	*1999*	*2000–2002 (average)*
Real GDP growth (%)	−0.2	−0.7	−1.0	−0.2
GDP deflator increase (%)	−0.2	−0.5	−1.0	−1.4
Current account balance (in % of GDP)	0	−0.2	−0.5	−0.9
Current account balance ($bn)				
Japan	5	1	−17	−39
US	−1	1	4	12
EU	1	0	4	11
Non-OECD area	−4	−2	7	10

Source OECD Economic Outlook, June 1997, p. 4

In the preface to the EO published in December 1997, unprecedentedly in-depth comments were made on the management of the Japanese economy.[28] On top of the negative economic impacts of the consumption tax hike and other fiscal consolidation measures that had been factored in, the combination of the emergence of domestic financial risks, the unexpected deterioration in overseas export market conditions, and the yen's sharp appreciation against Japan's trading partners in Asia led to a significant deterioration in the outlook for the Japanese economy. We therefore pointed out that, in addition to supporting the economy from the monetary policy side, temporary measures were also needed from the fiscal side. Specifically, we recommended tax cuts that would contribute to reforming the economic structure, while subsidies and other measures should eventually be reduced so that the fiscal position would not be adversely affected in the medium term (Table 13.3).

At the WP3 meeting on 9 June 1998, the deteriorating state of the Japanese economy was a major theme of discussion. Japan was represented by Eisuke Sakakibara, Vice Finance Minister on international finance, and Masayuki Matsushima who succeeded Akira Nagashima at the BOJ.

The discussion on Japanese economic policy management was started with comments by Bank of Canada deputy governor Paul Jenkins. He attributed the downturn in the Japanese economy to the combination of several factors: a loss of confidence across the private sector, depressed

Table 13.3 OECD Projections on Japanese Economic Growth (per annum, per cent)

	1997	*1998*	*1999*	*2000*	*(Yen rate)*
Real gross domestic demand					
December 1996	1.6	3.5	...	...	(114.10)
December 1997	−0.5	1.5	2.0	...	(121.00)
December 1998	−0.5	−3.3	-0.1	0.6	(119.30)
December 1999	0.1	−3.5	1.5	1.2	(106.00)
Real GDP					
December 1996	1.6	3.7	...	...	(114.10)
December 1997	0.5	1.7	2.1	...	(121.00)
December 1998	0.8	−2.6	0.2	0.7	(119.30)
December 1999	1.4	−2.8	1.4	1.4	(106.00)

Source Economic Outlook, December 1996, December 1997, December 1998, and December 1999

labour market conditions, domestic financial instability, and financial crises elsewhere in Asia. He then pointed out, with the benefit of hindsight, that the Japanese economy had not been prepared for the withdrawal of fiscal stimulus that had occurred in 1997. On the fiscal side, he stated that tax rebates on consumer or investment goods and hikes in unemployment insurance benefits, rather than conventional stimulus measures, would be preferable. In terms of monetary policy, he pointed out that the biggest effect of further monetary easing would be the yen depreciation, and that although concern had been expressed abroad, this should not be seen as a problem to the extent the Japanese authorities were taking the appropriate steps to boost domestic demand. However, in concluding this discussion at the WP3 meeting, Chairman Summers observed that the positive effects of a weaker yen on the Japanese economy must be balanced against the negative effects on overseas economies.

Two months after the discussion of Japan's problems at the WP3 meeting in June 1998, US academic and monetarist Alan Meltzer pointed out, in an interview in the Nihon Keizai Shimbun (2 August 1998), that the only way to stop deflation in Japan was to let the yen fall and that "currency intervention is the best way".

Volatile Movements in the Yen Exchange Rate

1998 was a period of unprecedented volatility for the yen/dollar exchange rate which started at around ¥131 to the dollar on 1 January. In that year, there were major unilateral interventions by the Japanese monetary authorities to support the yen on 9 and 10 April (selling more than 20 billion dollars all in all) which resulted in the yen appreciation against the dollar from ¥132 to ¥128 during Tokyo trading. But it fell back over the next few days to its pre-intervention level. On 17 June, a co-ordinated intervention by the Japanese and US authorities to sell the US dollar and buy the yen was conducted in the New York market.[29] While it appeared to have had some short-run positive effects, downward pressure on yen persisted, bringing it further down to ¥147 on 11 August, an eight-year low against the dollar. Its turnaround occurred on 17 August when Sergei Kiriyenko, then Prime Minister of the Russian government announced the abandonment of its defence of the rouble exchange rate against the dollar,[30] default on government domestic debt forcing its restructuring, and a 90-day moratorium on commercial external debt payments. Subsequently, the increased fears of international investors who had been assuming the exchange risk involved in the so-called "carry trades"[31] reversed the course and strong upward pressure on yen developed. By September 1998, the yen rose to about ¥130 to the dollar, and then appreciated by 14 per cent on 6–8 October, reaching ¥111. This appreciation of the yen was its largest two-day move since it began to float in February 1973, as a result of the collapse of the Bretton Woods system. The yen/dollar rate ended the year at ¥114 intraday.

The US Treasury Department's involvement in Japanese policy around the time was described by US academic and monetarist Alan Meltzer in a speech he gave at Harvard University in June 2001.[32] There he remarked:

"The Japan problem is primarily, but not entirely, created within Japan. This is because the US Treasury also played a role. The US Treasury recommended that Japan should rely on fiscal stimulus and avoid monetary easing sufficient to depreciate the yen against the dollar. These recommendations were made publicly, and I have been personally informed of such facts. In 1998, there were signs that monetary easing was causing the yen to fall: in June, the exchange rate of the yen against the dollar fell to ¥145 from around ¥100 a few months earlier. At that point, Deputy Treasury Secretary Summers went to Tokyo to call off the policy. The yen quickly rose to ¥105. It was a massive and foolish change for an economy with falling prices and rising unemployment. The policy was mistaken, wrong and it failed. The major mistake was not recognising that the yen was overvalued. If Japan cannot reduce the nominal value of the yen, then without a fall in prices, Japan cannot achieve a real exchange rate for the yen that is compatible with steady growth and stable prices. Such a fall in prices would take time, and this is what is happening now".

I was not surprised by Meltzer's observations, as I had been in occasional correspondence with him, an old acquaintance and overseas adviser to the Bank of Japan's Institute for Monetary and Economic Studies. While the main title of his speech was "International Economic Policy in the Clinton Administration", he could have also added comments about the international ramifications of economic policy management under the previous US administrations in the 1980s and Fed Chairman Volcker's frequent approaches to the BOJ, asking it to ease its monetary policy in the latter half of the 1980s (see Chapter 10). Meltzer passed away in 2017, and Goodfriend (see above) served as the Friends of Allan Meltzer Professor of Economics at Carnegie Mellon University from 2005 until his death in 2019.

Disposal of Non-performing Assets and Introduction of Public Funds

It was not clear to me how discussions at the OECD meetings on the use of public funds to deal with Japanese financial institutions' non-performing loans and to restore their health after the bursting of the bubble were reflected in the Japanese authorities' internal deliberations. In a situation where there was strong resistance among the Japanese public regarding the use of public funds, however, it was not an easy task for me as an international civil servant working in Paris to convey my opinions to the Japanese people clearly unless I were to go back to Japan and express my views directly to the Japanese press. I therefore decided to go on an official trip to Tokyo in December 1997. After my tête-à-tête meeting with Tadayo Honma, Executive Director in charge of prudential policy, and other senior officials of the Bank of Japan as well as the Ministry of Finance, I had separate press interviews with the three major newspapers, the Nihon Keizai Shimbun, the Yomiuri Shimbun and the Asahi Shimbun on 26 December 1997, the day before my departure from Tokyo to return to Paris. All three newspapers reported my remarks with my photograph in their morning issues of the following day.

In these press interviews, I recommended that the injection of public funds should not be limited to weakly capitalised financial institutions, but should also be injected to relatively healthy ones, because the latter should not be put at a competitive disadvantage. Under normal circumstances when money market interest rates are well above zero, the BOJ can provide support to financial institutions on equal footing through policies that will improve the cost environment for banking institutions as a whole, such as by significantly reducing money market interest rates and bank reserve requirement ratios, but these policies were no longer readily available with money market interest rates close to zero at the time. My view was that the strengthening of banks' capital base by the injection of public funds on an equal footing, combined with fiscal and structural policy measures to pave the way for "growing out of debt", would be less costly even from a fiscal perspective over the medium- to long-term term.

The OECD Economic Survey of Japan published in November 1999 judged that the economic downturn that began in 1997 with a combination of fiscal austerity measures, domestic instability in the Japanese financial system and the outbreak of the East Asian crisis had apparently bottomed out around the end of 1998, and that it was desirable to maintain monetary policy in its current stance for the time being. It was then pointed out that one idea would be to facilitate the BOJ's external communication by setting an inflation target when a time came to eventually break away from the zero-interest-rate policy.[33]

******

Notes

1. Takatoshi Ito, "*Ohaba Keijô Kuroji to Seisaku Unei: Genshô he Endaka Yuudô wo* (Large current surplus and policy management—Needs to induce yen appreciation for its reduction)", in Japanese, Nihon Keizai Shimbun, 22 May 1992 (morning edition).
2. OECD, Economic Outlook No. 51, June 1992, p. xi.
3. OECD Economic Surveys, Japan, 1992, pp. 106–107.
4. Kumiharu Shigehara, "Statement on the General Economic Situation and the Policy Challenges in Europe", OECD Working Party No. 3, 3 December 1992, mimeo.
5. Kumiharu Shigehara, "Introductory Statement: Press Conference—OECD Economic Outlook 52", 17 December 1992, mimeo.
6. OECD, Economic Outlook No. 53, June 1993, pp. 62 and 66.
7. OECD, Economic Outlook No. 57, June 1995, p. xiii.
8. See Philip Jurgensen, "Report of the working group on foreign exchange market intervention", US Treasury Department, 1983. See also John Williamson, "The Case for Roughly Stabilizing the Real Value of the Dollar", The American Economic Review, Vol. 79, No. 2, "Papers and Proceedings of the Hundred and First Annual Meeting of the American Economic Association", May 1989. In this paper, Williamson wrote that it sterilised intervention plus "jawboning" can have a substantial effect on exchange rates.
9. OECD, "Policy Management in the Current Situation", Working Party No. 3 of the Economic Policy Committee document No. 1, 13 September 1995, Section II "Broad Policy Considerations and Issues for Discussion", para 6.
10. T. Dalsgaard, C. André and P. Richardson, "Standard Shocks in the OECD Interlink Model", OECD Economics Department Working

Papers, No. 306, 2001, OECD, https://doi.org/10.1787/000706200171.
11. OECD, "Policy Management in the Current Situation", Working Party No. 3 of the Economic Policy Committee document No. 1, 13 September 1995, Section II "Broad Policy Considerations and Issues for Discussion", para 7.
12. Bank of Japan, 7th International Conference, "Towards a More Effective Monetary Policy" (held 26 and 27 October 1995), Journal of Financial Research, Vol. 15, No. 1, March 1996.
13. Marvin Goodfriend, "Comments" in "Towards More Effective Monetary Policy", Macmillan, 1997, pp. 291–295.
14. Kazuo Ueda, "Japanese Monetary Policy, Rules or Discretion? A Reconsideration" in "Towards More Effective Monetary Policy", Macmillan, 1997, pp. 253–279.
15. OECD Economic Surveys, Japan, 1994, p. 12.
16. Ditto, p. 37.
17. Bank of Japan, Institute for Monetary and Economic Studies, "The 7th International Conference", Kinyuu-Kenkyu (in Japanese), Vol. 15, No. 1, p. 14.
18. OECD, Economic Outlook No. 59, June 1996, p. xii.
19. OECD Economic Surveys, Japan, 1996, pp. 3, 4.
20. OECD, Economic Outlook No. 53, June 1993, p. 66.
21. OECD, "Policy Management in the Current Economic Situation", Working Party No. 3 of the Economic Policy Committee document No. 1, 13 September 1995.
22. OECD, Economic Outlook No. 58, December 1995, p. xii.
23. OECD Economic Surveys, Japan, 1996, pp. 6–7.
24. OECD, Economic Outlook No. 60, December 1996, Table 6 "Impact of a 1 per cent slower growth rate in 1997–98 in non-OECD Asia", p. 8.
25. OECD, Economic Outlook No. 61, June 1997, p. 49.
26. OECD, Economic Outlook No. 62, December 1997, p. xii.
27. The yen's effective exchange rate was assumed to appreciate by 10 per cent from the 1 May 1997 level.
28. OECD, Economic Outlook No. 62, December 1997, p. xii.
29. Media reports that in his 11 June 1998 congressional testimony, US Treasury Secretary Robert Rubin sounded reluctant for the US authorities to intervene in the foreign exchange market led to market participants' speculation that the yen's depreciation would

be left unchecked. There were also media reports about criticism in China that the United States, along with Japan, was neglecting the yen depreciation and the speculation of a devaluation of the Chinese yuan was developing. On June 17, US President Clinton, who was preparing for a visit to China, and Japanese Prime Minister Ryutaro Hashimoto had a telephone talk during which Hashimoto expressed his intention to expand Japanese domestic demand and accelerate the disposal of Japanese banks' bad loans. On the same day, the US–Japan foreign exchange market intervention was implemented in the New York market to shore up yen. See Nihon Keizai Shimbun, "Japan and US concerted intervention", 18 June 1998 (morning edition), in which it was reported that on June 12, the day when the yen hit a low of ¥144 to the dollar, Japanese Prime Minister Hashimoto instructed Eisuke Sakakibara, then Vice Minister of Finance for International Affairs, to negotiate for Japan–US concerted foreign exchange market intervention to support the yen. It was also reported in the article that some members of the Japanese Ministry of Finance were sceptical about the effectiveness of Japan's unilateral foreign exchange market intervention to support the yen in the light of its experience in April 1998 when it sold more than 20 billion dollars to support the yen in vain. See also and Daniel Sanger, "U.S. joins Japan in surprise move to shore up yen", The New York Times. 18 June 1998, Robert Rubin with Jacob Weisberg, "In an Uncertain World: Tough Choices from Wall Street to Washington" (Random House, 2003), Chapter 7.

30. In early summer 1998 when Ivan Materov, First Undersecretary of the Ministry of Economy, visited me at the OECD Paris headquarters to discuss the Russian economic situation, the author of this book suggested that the government, which was formed in April of that year, should not hesitate to devalue the rouble. At that time, the author was OECD Deputy Secretary-General and responsible of its programme of co-operation with Russia (see Part IV of this book).
31. A "carry trade" is where an investor borrows money in yen at a low Japanese interest rate and then invests this money in dollars at a higher interest rate; it is possible to make large profits if the yen does not appreciate.

32. Alan Meltzer, "International Economic Policy in the Clinton Administration" prepared for "American Policy in the 1990s", Harvard University, 27 June 2001.
33. OECD, Economic Survey of Japan, 1999, p. 16.

CHAPTER 14

Japan's Economic Policy Management since the Beginning of the Twenty-First Century

Before May 1997 when the OECD Council appointed me as its Deputy Secretary-General at the request of Donald Johnston who succeeded Jean-Claude Paye as the Secretary-General in June 1996, I had personally told him that I would not wish to stay long in the post, as my elderly mother, who lived alone in Tokyo, was eagerly awaiting my return. After having worked for nearly 17 years on four different occasions at the OECD, I finished my career as an international civil servant to return to Tokyo in late 1999.

I had long been enthralled by a semi-autobiographical book written by the British writer George Gissing in his final years, "The Private Papers of Henry Ryecroft",[1] *in which he described, in elegant classical English, Rycroft's life in his old age when he spent most of his time on contemplating the changing seasons in the beautiful countryside of southern England, reading and writing not under pressure to maintain his life, as he had done in his youth, but occasionally as he felt like it.*

I dreamt of such a lifestyle. But, my real life after my final departure from the OECD did not evolve in such a way. As soon as I returned to Japan, I as a free man was invited to speak at conferences and seminars in Japan and abroad. Besides, I founded the International Economic Policy Studies Association (IEPSA), with several of former OECD economists who were keen to continue their intellectual activities after their retirement (Photo 14.1). *I became president of the Association, and from time to time, organised seminars and other activities with my base in France to discuss the results*

K. Shigehara, *The Bank of Japan, the OECD, and Beyond*,
https://doi.org/10.1007/978-981-97-5307-9_14

Photo 14.1 Kumiharu Shigehara's former colleagues at the OECD Economics Department: (from left to right) Andrew Dean, Nicholas Vanston, Robert Price, the author, Jeffrey Shafer and Paul Atkinson (© Kumiharu Shigehara)

of our co-operative work and eventually had them published in books and papers. After the failure of Japanese Prime Minister Juinichiro Koizumi to appoint me as the Bank of Japan Governor in the spring of 2003 (see Chapter 1 "Introduction"), I actively contributed short articles to major Japanese and foreign newspapers and periodicals on economic and non-economic issues, no longer constrained by the shackles I had as the prime minister's preferred candidate for the post. Besides, with the technical assistance of Hiroaki Shigehara, my son living in Tokyo, I set up my own personal website having both the Japanese and English versions,[2] so that I can freely communicate my personal opinions to the outside world. As there are few Japanese people presenting their opinions in foreign languages, I recognised the importance of my speaking out abroad as someone with a long history of international experience.

In this chapter, I will focus on my activities as a free man relating to the management of Japanese economic policy. Those on other issues will be briefly reviewed in Parts 3 and 4.

Japan's Economic Policy Management after the Bursting of the "Dot-Com" Bubble

The December 1999 issue of the OECD Economic Outlook (EO), published just before I left Paris to return to Japan, showed a relatively positive outlook for the OECD economy as a whole. In particular, the US economy was expected to continue to grow above 3 per cent in 2000, after a high growth rate of close to 4 per cent in 1999, mainly due to a sharp increase in investment in information and communication technology (ICT)-related industries. In Japan, although the downward trend in prices was expected to continue, the recovery in output activity that began in early 1999, partly due to the effects of fiscal measures, was forecast to continue in 2000, with real GDP growth at 1.4 per cent in both years. In the foreign exchange market, however, the yen continued to appreciate against the background of Japan's economic recovery and the widening current account deficit in the United States, with the exchange rate against the dollar reaching the ¥103 level in September 1999 for the first time in nearly four years.

In this context, the OECD made the following comments on Japan's economic policy management.

"Should the yen continue to appreciate and/or government bond yields continue to drift up, the recovery could, however, prove to be weaker than currently expected. With short-term interest rates having been driven close to zero, further easing of monetary policy cannot be achieved by standard operations in the money market. However, options still remain in the form of more aggressive intervention in the foreign exchange and government securities markets to hold the yen and long-term interest rates down while accepting any resulting impact on bank liquidity. While this would be unorthodox, there may be no alternative if the economy shows signs of faltering from its recovery course".[3]

This policy message from the OECD was in line with its proposal presented in its document for the WP3 meeting in Rome in September 1995 for which I was responsible as OECD Chief Economist (see Section "Foreign exchange market intervention and monetary policy" in Chapter 13).

Table 14.1 OECD Economic Outlook on Japan

	1997	*1998*	*1999*	*2000*	*2001*	*2002*
	Real GDP growth (%)					
Dec 1999	1.4	−2.8	(1.4)	(1.4)	(1.2)	
June 2000	1.6	−2.5	0.3	(1.7)	(2.2)	
Dec 2000	1.6	−2.5	0.2	(1.9)	(2.3)	(2.0)
	GDP deflator (%)					
Dec 1999	0.1	0.4	(−0.6)	(−0.5)	(−0.3)	
June 2000	0.3	0.3	−0.9	(−0.8)	(−0.1)	
Dec 2000	0.3	0.3	−0.9	(−1.5)	(−0.4)	(−0.2)
Yen/US dollar	121.0	130.9	113.9	107.8	121.8	125.3

Figures in brackets are estimates or forecasts at the time of publication
Source OECD Economic Outlook, December 1999, etc.

In the OECD Economic Outlook published in mid-2000, Japan's real GDP growth rate in 1999 was lowered from 1.4 per cent to 0.3 per cent. But it was expected to recover gradually in 2000 and 2001, with real GDP approaching the level assumed six months earlier by the end of 2001 (see Table 14.1).

On 11 August 2000, shortly after the publication of this Outlook, the Bank of Japan (BOJ) decided to abolish the so-called "zero-interest-rate" policy of keeping the call money rate within a narrow range of 0.25 per cent to 0.15 per cent that had been in place since February 1999 and to raise its target range for the short-term money market rate to 0.25 per cent. On this day, I was staying at Lake Yamanaka Village near Mt. Fuji for a summer retreat with my wife and had lunch with Teruo Fujii, a former senior official of the BOJ, and his wife. Asked about my personal opinion on the announced change in the BOJ's policy, I immediately expressed my frank opinion that the decision had been taken too soon.

Subsequently, the boom which had originated in ICT-related firms in the United States, which was generally referred to in English as the "dot-com bubble", came to an end. This affected the Japanese economy significantly, leading to a downward revision of the economic outlook and increasing deflationary pressure (see Table 14.1).

Under these changing circumstances, the BOJ decided in February 2001 to encourage the uncollateralised overnight call rate to move on average around 0.15 per cent, while reducing the official discount rate to

0.25 per cent. In the following month, it decided to introduce "quantitative easing measures" by changing its operating target for money market operations from the overnight money market rate to the outstanding total amount of financial institutions' current accounts at the BOJ. It announced that it would aim at the average total balance of 4 trillion yen in February 2001 and added that "(A)s a consequence, it is anticipated that the uncollateralized overnight call rate will significantly decline from the current target level of 0.15 percent and stay close to zero percent under normal circumstances".

A Flaw in the IMF World Economic Outlook

In early May 2001, dreaming in Japan of the lifestyle described in Gissing's "The Private Papers of Henry Ryecroft", I retreated to my second house on the Izu Peninsula about 120 km south-west of Tokyo to look out over the fresh green and blue sea facing the Sagami Bay and the island of Izu Ōshima, freeing up time to read the full text of the IMF World Economic Outlook (WEO), which had just been released on the internet. As I studied the IMF's analysis, a sense of anxiety began to grow in my mind as the prescriptions for policy issues for developed countries, including Japan, contained in the WEO seemed to me to be quite unsatisfactory.

One of the key issues the IMF considered regarding the global economy at the time was what policy responses the industrialised countries should take jointly after the "dot-com" crash resulting in a downward revision of growth forecasts for the United States and in the event of a sharp fall in the currency of the United States, the world's largest external debtor.

On this issue, the IMF presented the results of simulations with its econometric model to show the impacts on the global economy of a shock of a simultaneous decline in the US dollar and stock prices in its scenario exercises. It found that, in a scenario based on the assumptions of a 20 per cent decline in the real value of the US dollar against the euro and the yen, and a 20 per cent decline in US stock prices, global and Japanese economic growth would both decline by around 1 percentage point between 2001 and 2002 compared with the baseline projection, even if monetary easing in the United States, Europe and Japan was further pursued.[4] As short-term market interest rates in Japan were already close to zero, the IMF economists involved in this exercise must have assumed that they would be brought down significantly below zero, but their levels assumed in their scenario were not specified in an explanatory note on this IMF work.

In response to my e-mail of enquiry sent to the IMF Research Department, Tamim Bayoumi, then head of division in charge of WEO, sent me an e-mail in which he noted that "there is an inconsistency between the fall in the interest rates in the scenarios and that was reported in the main case". According to his reply, "the scenarios were run on the Fund's MULTIMOD simulation model, which uses an outdated version of the WEO database. As a result, the nominal interest rates in the simulation model were higher than projected in the current WEO database. Hence, while the scenarios do have a constraint that the nominal interest (rates) cannot go negative, they were driven down by more than is likely to occur at the current conjecture". He added that "I apologize for this, and will ensure that it does not occur in subsequent exercises of this type".

I did not send my initial rather embarrassing e-mail of enquiry to my good old friends such as Stanley Fischer, then First Deputy Managing Director, and Michael Mussa, then IMF Economic Counselor. It was my deliberate decision to send it to the IMF Research Department without a specific personal name as its recipient. Nor did I specify my former official title at the OECD as its sender. Bayoumi's reply was sincere, but I was shocked. I thought that the IMF staff's serious mistake would not have been made available to outside readers, if either the members of the IMF management group, its Executive Directors, or officials of the Japanese Ministry of Finance and the BOJ had carefully read the internal version of the IMF paper prepared for discussion at the IMF Executive Board. They could have found such mistakes and have them corrected before the final version was made available to the outside world.

Subsequently, I sent a letter to the Financial Times editor to call for the attention of the international community about the importance of the global policy implications of a zero bound on nominal interest rates under which the BOJ had been operating its monetary policy. My contribution was published in its 15 May issue with a provocative title "Flawed assumption in simulations with IMF model". The original title was "IMF World Economic Outlook and Economic Policy Management in Japan". It was changed to a more journalistic title by the editors of the Financial Times. The original title remained on my website. My contribution was published as a top article in the newspaper's section "Letters to the Editor" under a space constraint. Be that as it may, I thought it was in a sense one of my duties as a former international civil servant to conduct this type of work. It was made possible only after my retirement from the OECD where I had been too busy running its Economics Department to have time to examine the details of IMF work.

In my contribution to the Financial Times, I first stressed that Japanese short-term money market interest rates were already close to zero, and further significant interest cuts in Japan could not be made as assumed in the IMF simulations.[5] I then argued that correct simulations with a zero constraint on nominal interest rates would suggest that the negative global output effect of larger external adjustment associated with a significant US dollar decline and a further fall in US stock prices entailing similar development in the stock markets in the rest of the other industrial countries would call for flexibility in the conduct of Japanese fiscal policy in the short run, at least allowing for the working of built-in stabilisers rather than limiting the maximum amount of Japanese government bond issues to ¥30,000 billion (about 245 billion dollars) in Fiscal Year 2002 regardless of cyclical positions—which was a policy issue then hotly debated in the Japanese parliament.

Measures to Cope with the Global Economic Slowdown

The impression I had from examining the unsatisfactory policy analysis of the May 2001 issue of the IMF WEO was that the IMF had not thought through from a global perspective the question of how to deal with the deflationary pressures that emerged in Japan during the adjustment process following the bursting of the bubble, by failing to promptly implement measures that would help restore the credit supply function of the private financial sector, while increasing aggregate demand to close the output gap. True, it wrote, in the introductory paragraph of Chapter 1 "Prospect and Policy Challenges", that (G)iven the rapid policy response by the US Federal Reserve and a number of other central banks, and with most advanced countries—with the important exception of Japan—having considerable room for policy maneuver, there is a reasonable prospect that the slowdown will be short-lived". But, in the latter part of the same chapter commenting on the alternative scenario, the IMF simply noted that "(W)eaker output leads to a generalized fall in core inflation, and monetary policy is loosened throughout the advanced world" and gave no specific policy advice for Japan to deal with the worsening of deflation in Japan in the wake of the double shocks originating from the United States assumed in its scenario exercises.

Both the US Federal Reserve and the European Central Bank still had room to cut short-term money market interest rates in response to downside risks to the global economy, but the BOJ had exhausted this orthodox measure. My view was that, in order to secure aggregate demand to support output activities and overcome deflation in Japan under these circumstances, it was essential to implement a policy of buying dollars in the foreign exchange market to correct the excessive appreciation of the yen, increase the amount of yen funds released to the money market and let bank liquidity to build up, while gaining the understanding of Japan's trading partners.

My article published in the Financial Times was written with the aim of encouraging domestic and international discussions on the management of aggregate demand policy in Japan which had been constrained by zero interest rates. But the Japanese press did not follow up on my article written in English. I therefore decided to publish a more detailed version of my views on the question of how to deal with the risk of a further slowdown in the global economy, in Japanese as well as in English and French.

From this perspective, I published an article in the 10 July 2001 issue of the Nihon Keizai Shimbun with the main title "Risk of further slowdown of the world economy" and with two subtitles: "Correction of the yen rate needed" and "Trust building in Japan, the United States and Europe urgently needed", all of them were chosen by the newspaper's editorial team, which seemed to have a good grasp of the key aspects of my argument.

I concluded this article with the following sentences.

"The official responsible for international monetary affairs in the Bush administration is a renowned economist. In aiming at better trilateral monetary co-operation for currency stabilization, the first step to be taken by the Japanese authorities should be enhancement of mutual trust with him as well as Chairman Greenspan and other key central bank bankers in the United States and the euro-area".

In order to communicate my personal view in more detail in English to the international community, I published a relatively long article in the 12 July 2001 issue of the Japan Times.[6] A few days later, I published a French translation of the Japan Times article in a leading French economic newspaper Les Echos.[7]

"The official responsible for international monetary affairs in the Bush administration" mentioned in my article published in the Nihon Keizai Shimbun was meant to be John Taylor, Under Secretary of the Treasury for International Finance in the George W. Bush administration. I sent him a copy of my article written in English for The Japan Times, along with a brief personal letter. At the time, I was aware of the delicate relationships that Taylor had with some US Congressional members and others who were critical of the Japanese authorities' intervention in the foreign exchange market to curb the appreciation of the yen. Taylor had lived in Tokyo with his wife as a visiting scholar when I was Director-General of the BOJ Institute of Monetary and Economic Studies. When I was Director of the General Economics Branch of the OECD Economics and Statistics Department, he had moved from being a professor at Stanford University to a member of the Council of Economic Advisers to President under the George H.W. Bush administration, and attended OECD WP3 meetings. He also participated in the Economic and Development Review Committee meetings to discuss the draft OECD Economy Surveys of the United States.

Zenbei Mizoguchi was Director-General of the International Finance Bureau of the Japanese Ministry of Finance and a key person to lead large-scale intervention in the foreign exchange market, selling yen and buying US dollars in order to curb the yen's sharp appreciation at the time. He had been involved in WP3-related work in 1993 when I was OECD Chief Economist. But, neither he nor BOJ Governor Hayami was informed about my personal approach to Taylor.

Hayami had been active in the business world for a long time after ceasing to be a BOJ Executive Director before becoming Governor, so there was a considerable age gap between him and the two Deputy Governors and senior officials assisting him. Under such circumstances, he was always very pleased at my occasional visits at the Governor's office. I did not take such occasions to explain my views on Japanese monetary policy directly to him. Rather, I tried to give him a break with reminding him of the days when I worked for him as Director-General of the Bank's Foreign Department and subsequently its Executive Director for international affairs. My opinion was something that Hayami was already aware of through the articles I published in Japanese newspapers and other publications.

Hayami never showed any sign of being put in a bad mood by my assertions on the yen issue. As already noted in Chapter 3, when the BOJ raised the official discount rate on 1 September 1969 to control inflation pressure amid a growing surplus in the balance of payments under the Bretton Woods system, I opposed this and argued for a revaluation of the yen. In contrast, when Hayami was BOJ Governor, I was opposed to his wish for a strong yen which he expressed at his press conferences and about which he published a book.

On 16 July, immediately after the publication of my article in the 10 July issue of the Nihon Keizai Shimbun, I was invited by Koichi Hamada, Director of the Economic and Social Research Institute attached to the cabinet office of the Japanese government, to a *tête-à-tête* meeting in his office. At that meeting, I explained about the discussions on Japanese economic policy and balance of payments adjustment issues held at OECD WP3 meetings over years and my personal views on Japan's policy challenges. Hamada said he understood my views quite well, adding that while BOJ officials often explained things in a way that was not clear to him, my talk went through his head in the same ways as when he had discussions with economists at Yale University where he taught as professor of economics. Hamada later became adviser to Shinzo Abe, who was Japanese Prime Minister from September 2006 to September 2007 and from December 2012 to September 2020.

Beggar-Thy-Neighbour Policy?

I did not hear any explicit objections to my views expressed in the Nihon Keizai Shimbun, but I did occasionally see comments in the newspapers and elsewhere that foreign exchange market intervention by the Japanese authorities to correct the strong yen was a beggar-thy-neighbour policy, benefiting Japan while harming its trading partners. It is true that under a fixed parity system, a devaluation could cause problems undermining export opportunities for trading partners. However, under a floating exchange rate system, if Japan's trading partners did not wish an increase in imports from Japan due to a weaker yen, or if they did not welcome a fall in the domestic currency prices of goods imported from Japan, then, in order to neutralise such unwanted effects, they could use the remaining scope for monetary policy easing unlike Japan under a zero-interest-rate constraint. In this case where the exchange rates of their currencies against the Japanese yen would not appreciate but remain unchanged, Japan's export volumes would increase not because of the price effect through a weaker yen, but because of the income effect of higher economic growth due to monetary easing in trading partners, i.e., an expansion of Japan's export markets. Faster output growth resulting from the increase in Japanese exports through this mechanism would in due course result in an increase in Japanese imports.

In short, the question was whether the United States, Europe, and other countries that had left room for orthodox monetary policy management under the constraints of zero interest rates, and Japan, which had no room for it, could build a relationship of trust and cooperate with Japan in its overcoming domestic deflation while avoiding trade friction. These issues of international co-operation could not be solved simply by my discussing them within Japan. I wondered, as a free man, how I would act if I were in Governor Hayami's position.

At the end of the summer holiday season, I began an extended stay in Paris, the base of the International Economic Policy Studies Association, to intensify my discourse activities abroad. First, at the invitation of the Bank for International Settlements (BIS), I travelled to Basel on 17 September to talk about the management of the global economy and Japan's deflation problems. My view on the importance of strengthening mutual trust between policymakers in the United States, Japan, and Europe was emphasised at a luncheon meeting that General Manager Andrew Crockett hosted with me as guest of honour.

At this sitting, Crockett said he hoped that I as an internationally minded former Japanese central banker would succeed Governor Hayami rather than Toshihiko Fukui, who followed his career on the domestic side of the BOJ and had been its deputy governor until March 1998. This remark was a bit embarrassing, as Setsuya Sato, a young secondee from the BOJ to the BIS, as well as several BIS economists, were also invited to the luncheon.

Following my visit to Basel, on 24 September I went to London to meet individually with Governor Edward (known as "Eddie") George and Deputy Governor Mervyn King at the Bank of England to explain my views. I had originally made an appointment only to meet King, but George heard about my visit to the Bank and wished to have a separate meeting with me. He and I had about a one-hour-long *tête-à-tête* meeting. I was aware that Hayami, a close friend of George, had proposed my appointment as General Manager of the BIS as successor to Crockett, and George supported it. But the central bank governors of the other G10 countries did not like it, as with my long association with the OECD, my appointment as the BIS General Manager might be seen as if the BIS were taken over by the OECD, so I was later told by Hayami.

As Governor George was chairing the G10 Governors' Meeting at the time, I asked him if he could issue a statement on Japan's deflation problem and the desirability of the correction of the overvalued yen exchange rate from a neutral standpoint as the chairman of the G10 Governors' Meeting. After thinking for a while, George replied that it would be difficult to issue such a statement on exchange rate issues because of the politics involved. With George's approval, the views we exchanged at the Bank of England were promptly notified to Hayami by international telephone, while he was working in his office in Tokyo.

I returned to Paris on the evening of the same day, and on the following day, 25 September, I met with Bank of France Governor Jean-Claude Trichet and Deputy Governor Hervé Hannoun separately in their offices. On that occasion, I handed them copies of my articles which I had contributed to the French newspaper Les Echos.

Furthermore, on 2 October, I flew from Paris for a day trip to Frankfurt to hold a seminar at the European Central Bank (ECB). Due to time constraints, I had initially planned to see my old friend Otmar Issing before the seminar started. At the time, Issing was a member of its Board and Chief Economist. But, hearing of my visit to the ECB, Tommaso Padoa-Schioppa (later Finance Minister of Italy) and Christian Noyer (later Governor of the Bank of France), also members of the Board and my old friends, wished to meet me. Padoa-Schioppa's advice for me to write my memoirs, mentioned in Chapter 1 of this book, was given at this meeting.

I would add that all these appointments with the Governors, Deputy Governors, and the other members of the central bank boards were made entirely by me in person. The BOJ has its European representative offices in London, Paris, and Frankfurt, and I was well aware that former senior officials of the BOJ usually asked its representative offices aboard to make appointments for their meetings with senior officials of foreign central banks. But, as a free man, I never used such channels.

Fiscal Policy Management under the Koizumi Administration

On 8 May 2001, less than a month after the Junichiro Koizumi administration came to power, Martin Wolf, chief economics editor of the Financial Times and a friend of mine, published an interesting article entitled "Why Koizumi will fail?". Just a week after his article was published, in my contribution to the 15 May 2001 issue of the Financial Times entitled "Flawed assumption in simulations with IMF model", I argued that "Japanese fiscal policy should remain flexible in the short run, at least allowing for the working of built-in stabilisers rather than rigidly limiting the maximum amount of government bond issues to 30 trillion yen in coming fiscal years regardless of cyclical positions". Somewhat later, Paul Krugman, professor at Princeton University, questioned the Koizumi government's economic policy line with a sharp tongue (New York Times, 9 July). The common criticism in these articles was that the economic policy line of the new administration was focused too much on measures to improve the supply side of the Japanese economy and not pay enough attention to the importance of aggregate demand management policy.

Krugman reported that when he met with Heizo Takenaka, Minister for Economic and Fiscal Affairs, the minister explained that policies that would encourage supply-side improvements would eventually create demand. He also reported that the minister did not give a clear answer as to what kind of aggregate demand management policy he intended to use to fill the output gap until the demand creation effect of structural policy measures was achieved. Krugman argued that Koizumi's economic policy was not a choice between "no recovery without structural reform" or "structural reform or economic stagnation" as argued by Koizumi, but rather it was following a path of "reform and stagnation".

I thought it would be better to write a rather detailed paper on my views about requirements for demand management policies under the Koizumi government, covering fiscal and monetary policies as well as exchange rate policy, and have it published in Japan.

> In retrospect, in the late 1980s, Japan's international commitments to increase domestic demand were realised mainly through the implementation of expansionary monetary policy, while fiscal consolidation was promoted. In 1990, the fiscal balance of the general government as a ratio

of nominal GDP recorded a surplus amounting to 2.0 per cent, and its structural balance excluding tax revenue increases due to the economic upturn and other cyclical factors recorded a surplus of 2.5 per cent. However, after the bubble burst, the general budget balance continued to deteriorate year after year due to expenditure increases, mainly on public investment, as countermeasures to the economic downturn, as well as reductions in tax burdens on companies and individuals, and tax revenue shortages due to the prolonged economic slump. In 2000, the ratio of the general government fiscal deficit to nominal GDP was 6.0 per cent before cyclical adjustment, 5.2 per cent after it, and the ratio of public debt to nominal GDP rose to 123 per cent, the highest level among developed countries. Moreover, the population was already ageing at the fastest pace among developed countries, and according to the OECD estimate, the ratio of public pension payments to nominal GDP, which was 7.9 per cent in 2000, would be the highest of any developed country by 2050, as the total amount if public pension payments were expected to reach 13.0 per cent of GDP in 2050 if no reforms were made.

While I thought it was quite appropriate for the Koizumi government to take up fiscal austerity as a medium- to long-term issue, I was concerned that its programme of early introduction of fiscal consolidation was running a risk of creating a policy recession from its rigid target for fiscal consolidation. Besides, I was doubtful about the macroeconomic effect of additional monetary policy measures aimed at increasing the monetary base along the line of the argument of strong monetarists who ignored the aggregate output and price effects of fiscal policy changes. I thus decided to write an article in Japanese, somewhat more systematic than my contribution to the 15 May 2001 issue of the Financial Times. While I was in Paris in early autumn that year, I sent an article to that effect to the *Kinyu Zaisei Jijô*, a Japanese weekly financial journal, with the main title "Will the Koizumi government's economic policy succeed?". It was published in full over six pages in its 8 October issue.[8]

In this article, I repeated my argument that, given the zero-interest-rate constraint on Japanese monetary policy, fiscal policy should be managed in a somewhat flexible manner in the short term, rather than being bound by the 30-trillion-yen limit on the maximum amount of government bond issuance. I also pointed out that the policy of increased public investment after the bursting of Japan's bubble played an important role in securing employment in regional economies where private capital investment and housing investment had fallen sharply. At the same time, I wrote that it was important to reflect on the fact that the implementation of such flexible fiscal policy stance would involve a risk of a "haphazard" policy if not implemented with a rigorous examination of its direct and indirect economic and non-economic effects. I also added that public investment that would lead to the enhancement of solid social infrastructure with a long service life should be promoted before the ageing of the population further progressed with a structural shortage of workers, and that the principle of free competition, including open tendering for the government contracts for public works, must be thoroughly enforced.

Breaking the Vicious Circle of Deflation and a Strong Yen

In November 2001, I was privately informed that there was a move within the Koizumi cabinet to make me a "hidden candidate" for the governor of the BOJ to succeed Hayami. This was an unexpected event which happened just a month after the publication of my article critical of the Koizumi government's economic policy management. The final outcome of this unexpected episode was described in Chapter 1 "Introduction" of this book.

Over ten years from 1993—a year or so after the burst of a bubble economy—and 2002, Japan's share in world merchandise exports declined sharply from 10.0 per cent to 6.6 per cent. During the same period, the US share was remarkably stable at around 11 per cent and Germany's remained close to 10 per cent. Japan's poor export performance in the face of weak domestic demand was largely a result of weaker international price competitiveness associated with the excessively high yen value. This export behaviour of Japan was in sharp contrast to that of countries such as Britain, Australia, and Nordic countries. They managed to get out of recessions and to solve balance-sheet problems resulting from sharp declines in domestic asset market prices through export-led recovery induced by sharp currency depreciation. The role of monetary policy in many of these countries was to contain inflationary pressure associated with currency depreciation. They adopted numerical inflation targets and at the same time tightened fiscal policy to improve budget positions and prevent the collapse of the government bond market.

The OECD EO published in June 2002 indicated that Japan's deflation problem was not expected to improve in any way looking ahead to the following year, 2003 (see Table 14.2). It seemed strange to me that despite this, the following comment on the management of Japan's economic policy was made in its Introduction.

"With the effectiveness of demand management policies obviously constrained, the urgent need is to pursue vigorous structural reforms".[9]

The word "policies" here was written in the plural which I took to mean monetary, fiscal, and exchange rate policies, implying that the OECD Secretariat was in support of the Koizumi government's economic policy line focused on measures to improve the supply side of the Japanese economy, and differed from the views of Krugman and myself who argued that aggregate demand management policies were needed at the same time. The OECD EO at the time was compiled under the supervision of Ignacio Visco, my immediate successor as OECD Chief Economist, shortly before he returned to the Bank of Italy after 5 years of service in the post. He later became Governor of Banca d'Italia.

A year later, in the EO published in June 2003, the price situation in Japan deteriorated compared with the projection published in the

Table 14.2 OECD Economic Outlook on Japan

	1997	*1998*	*1999*	*2000*	*2001*	*2002*	*2003*	*2004*
(Date of publication)	Real GDP growth (%)							
June 2002	1.8	−1.1	0.7	2.4	−0.4	(−0.7)	(0.3)	
Dec 2002	1.8	−1.1	0.7	2.6	−0.3	(−0.7)	(0.8)	(0.9)
June 2003	1.8	−1.1	0.1	2.8	0.4	0.3	(1.0)	(1.1)
	GDP deflator (%)							
June 2002	0.4	−0.1	−1.4	−2.0	−1.4	(−1.4)	(−1.7)	
Dec 2002	0.4	−0.1	−1.4	−2.1	−1.2	(−1.0)	(−1.6)	(−1.4)
June 2003	0.3	−0.1	−1.5	−1.9	−1.6	−1.7	(−2.2)	(−1.8)
	1997	1998	1999	2000	2001	2002	2003	2004
Yen/US dollar	121.0	130.9	113.9	107.8	121.8	125.3	115.9	108.1

Figures in brackets are estimates and forecasts
Source OECD Economic Outlook, June 2002, etc.

same period of the previous year, and a fall of around 2 per cent was forecast to continue until 2004. The OECD then made the following recommendation on Japanese monetary policy.

"Continued liquidity expansion is necessary to prevent worsening deflation, including via the purchase of foreign denominated assets".[10]

This recommendation was the same as the argument I made in my capacity as OECD Chief Economist at the September 1995 WP3 meeting (see Chapter 13).

The OECD Secretariat also pointed out that "as long as the monetary policy transmission mechanism is defective, 'quantitative easing' in the form of liquidity injections against domestic collateral will not suffice. Bank balance sheets are saddled with very large amount of non-performing loans".[11]

OECD Chief Economist responsible for June 2003 EO was Jean-Philippe Cotis, whom I had recommended to Secretary-General Johnston as Visco's successor. Cotis had previously Director of the Prevision at the French treasury and Chairman of the Working Party No. I of the OECD Economic Policy Committee. Unfortunately, he passed away in June 2023 after a long illness.

In March 2003, prior to the publication of this issue of the EO, BOJ Governor Hayami stepped down ending his term of office and was replaced by Toshihiko Fukui. For my part, finished with seclusion in France since earlier that year as Prime Minister Koizumi's "hidden candidate" for BOJ Governor, I returned to Japan as a free man again, and visited the new Governor Fukui at the BOJ to tell him what had happened, and then resumed my discourse activities in Japan, which I had been refraining from for some time.

First, the Yomiuri Shimbun, one of Japan's major newspapers that had been following the developments in the BOJ governor appointment, asked me for an interview. The gist of my talk to a reporter of that newspaper was published in its morning edition on 18 March 2003 as the third in a series entitled "What I want to say to BOJ Governor Fukui". In it, I said that I welcomed the appointment of Fukui, because he had not only worked at the BOJ for a long time, but he also had his recent five years of experience in the private sector after his resignation as BOJ Deputy Governor. I noted that it was very important for the Governor to have had the experience of breathing air outside the BOJ. The reporter's article on his interview with me was titled "Correcting the strong yen together with the government" in which he wrote that I had argued that "the BOJ, the

Ministry of Finance and politicians must all work together" to correct the excessively strong yen. In its morning edition of 9 April 2003, the Asahi Shimbun, another leading Japanese newspaper, also published an interview article with me under the title "Need for correcting the excessively strong yen".

However, these articles were written by newspaper reporters, and I considered it to be important to present my opinions accurately in my own wording, given the critical economic situation at the time in Japan. Moreover, I thought it essential to get Japan's trading partners to understand the need to correct the overvalued yen rate and to achieve this with their co-operation without causing trade friction.

I thus wrote a draft op-ed in English and emailed it to the editorial board of the Financial Times. It was immediately accepted for publication and was placed at the top of the economic commentary page on 2 April 2003, with the main title "A weaker currency is the best medicine for Japan" which was chosen by the Financial Times editors.

In the opening section of this article, I wrote that "Japan continues to struggle with deflation, despite monetary policies that have left nominal short-term interest rates virtually unchanged at zero and vastly increased the monetary base. Rehabilitating financial institutions and further fiscal stimulus will not solve Japan's problems. Japan must rely on another effective stimulus package, with the support of its trading partners. That measure is a downward correction in the value of the yen".

I then wrote that the net effect of a weaker yen on the trade balances of trading partners would be insignificant over time as Japan's domestic economic recovery triggered by increased Japanese exports would induce its import growth. My argument was backed up by reference to the results of the OECD work with its Interlink Model for measuring the effect of a 10 per cent depreciation of the effective exchange rate of the Japanese yen which was carried out when I was OECD Chief Economist.[12]

In the draft article I proposed ten specific measures.

First, the BOJ should adopt total bank reserves as its operating target for and set its annual target rate of increase within a range consistent with a desirable nominal GDP growth rate, e.g., 5 per cent per year. However, in the event of an unexpectedly large increase in bank reserve demand, the BOJ should flexibly respond to this so that nominal short-term market interest rates remain near zero.

Second, the Japanese government should announce the target range of the yen exchange rate, say 150 to 160 yen per US dollar. As argued by Lars Svensson, pegging of the yen would be another option.

Third, to avoid tensions with Japan's trading partners, the Japanese government should impose a special exchange rate adjustment tax on Japan's big export companies' "windfall" profits resulting from the weaker yen.

Fourth, the government should encourage competition among Japanese and foreign firms in once protected sectors. Non-viable industries and companies should not be protected by subsidies.

Fifth, increased revenues from the special tax should be used to support those workers who lose jobs.

Sixth, the government should announce a credible medium-term plan for reducing structural budget deficits. Automatic stabilisers should be allowed to work.

Seventh, once these government policies are in place, the BOJ should adopt the price level target to be achieved in a two-year time horizon and announce its intention to move to a regime of inflation targeting once the level target is achieved.

Eighth, Japan should advise Asian partner countries to adopt currency baskets in which the yen's weight is raised to absorb some of the shocks associated with exchange adjustment.

Ninth, the Japanese government should argue that some fiscal flexibility be allowed in the euro-area. This would help prevent the euro-area economy from getting into recession in part arising from weaker exports associated with the recent firming of the euro.

Last, the Japanese government should take a leading role in the post-Uruguay round of trade liberalisation. Further opening of Japanese markets should increase the import elasticity of Japanese domestic demand.

In the draft of my op-ed, I clearly stated that the move to a fixed parity system was proposed by Professor Svensson of Princeton University,[13] but that part was removed by the editors of the Financial Times.

I did not send copies of my Financial Times article to high officials of the monetary authorities such as John Taylor, US Under Secretary of the Treasury for International Finance, as I thought that they used to read the economic commentary pages of the Financial Times. In Japan, the Asahi Shimbun newspaper followed up on my contribution to the Financial Times and published an article of its reporter's interview with me in its morning edition on 9 April 2003, exactly one week after the publication of my Financial Times article, under the title “Correcting the excessively strong yen”. It reported that I stressed the importance of the Japanese monetary authorities that the package of measures I advocated did not represent a “beggar-thy-neighbour policy”. As with the Yomiuri Shimbun’s interview article with me, it was accompanied by my photograph, which appeared to be an indication that the Asahi Shimbun had paid considerable attention to my contribution to the Financial Times.

My op-ed published in the Financial Times was written for an international audience, and I thought it would also be an important task for me to express my views to a Japanese audience in conjunction with some additional information. The article thus written in Japanese was published in the morning 25 April 2003 issue of the Nihon Keizai Shimbun. It had the main title “Correcting the too strong yen to break the vicious circle” and the subtitle “Together with monetary policy, domestic structural adjustment is also indispensable”, as specified by the Nihon Keizai Shimbun’s editorial team.

In this article, I carefully avoided expressions such as “weakening the yen’” and used the phrase “correcting the excessively strong yen”. I also used the expression “yen rate adjustment” and wrote that “‘the view expressed by some people that such an adjustment of the yen’s exchange rate would impose significant costs on Japan’s trading partners is wrong”. I added that Professor Meltzer of Carnegie Mellon University in the United States had pointed out that Japan’s deflation was costly for these countries as well. This information was not included in my Financial Times op-ed.

Subsequently, the Nihon Keizai Shimbun ran an article reporting its interview with me in its morning 20 June issue. It was published in a special commentary page entitled “Deflation is eroding Japan”, under the headlines “Conventional measures cannot overcome the problem” and “A series of bold proposals”. The enclosures summarising my remarks were headlined “Stimulating investment through increased exports” and “The yen rate induced to 150-160 yen”.

On 17 July, about a month after this article was published, the Nihon Keizai Shimbun published the Japanese translation of a contribution from IMF Chief Economist Kenneth Rogoff on the subject “Concern remains about simultaneous global deflation” with the subtitles “Japan needs to get out of the way quickly” and “Strong downward pressure on prices in the United States and Europe”. In this article, Rogoff wrote that the view held by many experts that the only way out of deflation in Japan was a weaker yen was in a sense right. Whether the BOJ would buy Japanese stocks, government bonds, or foreign currency to allay deflationary fears, the yen would plummet. Such an approach could be perceived as a manipulation to the detriment of other countries, but after 5 years of deflation in Japan, other countries (and the IMF) would unlikely complain much.

Rogoff had previously worked as a visiting scholar at the BOJ Institute for Monetary and Economic Studies when I was its Director-General. I had occasionally emailed him my personal views and it seemed certain that he had read my op-ed in the Financial Times of 2 April 2003.

Regarding my contribution to the Financial Times, I received an e-mail from Professor Svensson, who had read it and agreed with me. In addition, Thomas Andersson, Director of the Swedish Institute for Economic Research (IKED), sent a comment to the editor of the Financial Times in support of my proposal, recalling Sweden's experience in dealing with the financial crisis it suffered in 1990. His comment which supported my assertion was published in the Financial Times's "Letters to the Editor" section on 7 May 2003.

All of these led me to believe that my international discourse activities had had some positive response.

Responding to the Global Financial and Economic Crisis

Rogoff's contribution to the Nihon Keizai Shimbun ended with the point that the most desirable external development for Japan would be for the economies of its trading partners to pick up while it was tackling its own problems. However, the softening of the US housing market that began in early 2006 accelerated in 2007, and a similar development began in the United Kingdom in early 2007.

However, the OECD EO published in December 2007 still showed a fairly optimistic outlook for the economies of Japan's major trading partners, including the United States. Based on this outlook for Japan's export markets, its projection for Japan's economic growth was 2.2 per cent in 2006, followed by a gradual slowdown through 2008 (see Table 14.3).

In the spring of 2008, when the appointment of a successor to BOJ Governor Toshihiko Fukui was underway under the Yasuo Fukuda government, Robert Feldman of Morgan Stanley Securities published a report entitled "The Next Bank of Japan Governor - A Comparison

Table 14.3 OECD Economic Outlook on Japan

	2002	*2003*	*2004*	*2005*	*2006*	*2007*	*2008*	*2009*	*2010*	*2011*
	Real GDP growth (%)									
Dec 2007	0.3	1.4	2.7	1.9	2.2	(1.9)	(1.6)	(1.8)		
Dec 2008	0.3	1.4	2.7	1.9	2.4	2.1	(0.5)	(−0.1)	(0.6)	
June 2009	0.3	1.4	2.7	1.9	2.0	2.3	−0.7	(−6.8)	(0.7)	
Dec 2009	0.3	1.4	2.7	1.9	2.0	2.3	−0.7	(−5.3)	(1.8)	(2.0)
Outcomes										
Japan	0.3	1.7	2.3	1.3	1.7	2.2	−1.1	−5.5	4.5	−0.7
US	1.8	2.5	3.5	3.1	2.7	1.9	−0.3	−3.5	3.0	1.7
OECD area	1.7	2.0	3.1	2.7	3.2	2.8	0.1	−3.8	3.2	1.8
	GDP deflator (%)									
Dec 2007	−1.5	−1.6	−1.1	−1.3	−0.9	(−0.5)	(−0.3)	(0.3)		
Dec 2008	−1.5	−1.6	−1.1	−1.2	−1.0	−0.8	(−1.0)	(1.3)	(−0.3)	
June 2009	−1.5	−1.6	−1.1	−1.2	−0.9	−0.7	−0.9	(1.3)	(−1.5)	
Dec 2009	−1.5	−1.6	−1.1	−1.2	−0.9	−0.7	−0.9	(0.0)	(−1.7)	(−0.8)
Outcomes										
Japan	−1.6	−1.7	−1.4	−1.2	−1.1	−0.9	−1.3	−0.5	−2.1	−2.1
US	1.6	2.1	2.8	3.3	3.2	2.9	2.2	1.1	1.2	2.1
OECD area	2.4	2.4	2.6	2.4	2.6	2.5	2.5	1.1	1.3	1.9
	2002	2003	2004	2005	2006	2007	2008	2009	2010	2011
Yen/dollar exchange rate	125.3	115.9	108.1	110.1	116.4	117.8	103.4	93.6	87.8	79.7
Effective exchange rate (2005 = 100)	96.4	99.2	103.1	100.0	92.7	87.7	98.6	113.2	116.7	123.4
GDP gap (OECD estimates, %)	−3.1	−2.1	−0.4	0.2	1.2	2.8	1.0	−5.0	−1.3	−2.8

Figures in brackets are actual estimates and forecasts
Source OECD Economic Outlook June 2007, etc
Definitive figures are from the May and November 2012 issues of ibid

of Candidates", in which he rated the qualifications of 19 candidates for the post (the English version was made available on 25 March and the Japanese version on 26 March) which was reported in an article in the 3 April edition of the Financial Times). According to Feldman's assessment, I was ranked first in terms of the criteria emphasising the importance of the candidates' grasp of macroeconomics and independence from the government. I was also ranked as one of the two highest in terms of the two criteria emphasising the candidates' experience in heading policy-making bodies and domestic and international networks. This report apparently led to expectations for my appointment as BOJ governor among overseas observers.

The three proposed candidates for BOJ Governor presented by the Yasuo Fukuda government to the Diet were all former Ministry of Finance bureaucrats and were rejected one after the other by the House of Councillors, which then had a majority of opposition parties, on ground that their appointment would undermine the BOJ's independence from the government. In this situation, Masaaki Shirakawa, appointed as Deputy Governor as of 19 March, started to serve as an Acting Governor, as Fukui stepped down as Governor on 20 March. Shirakawa was not on the list of 19 candidates in the Feldman Report and his promotion to the Governor's post surprised many former senior officials of the BOJ. In his article commenting on the compromise subsequently made between the majority and opposition parties to officially appoint Shirakawa as Governor, Yasuhiro Tase, then professor of public management studies at Waseda University, referred to the Feldman's report which had not been covered by the Japanese media before the political turmoil relating to the BOJ governor appointment was settled in this way. In response to my e-mail of enquiry, Tase let me know that unlike the Financial Times, the Japanese media followed the policy of not reporting the Feldman report and wrote me that it should be critically reviewed.

In the course of 2008, the debacle in the US and UK housing finance markets which had started in the previous year, became even more serious, developing into a global financial and economic crisis from the collapse of Lehman Brothers and other factors. The resulting contraction of Japan's export markets, coupled with the ongoing appreciation of the yen, caused Japanese exports in 2008 to grow only by 1.8 per cent on a volume basis compared to the previous year, a sharp brake after an 8.4 per cent increase in 2007. As a result, Japan's real GDP in 2008 fell by 1.1 per cent, almost fully reflecting the decline in gross domestic demand.

It was remarkable that in the United States, gross domestic demand fell by 1.3 per cent in 2008, but export volumes rose by 6.2 per cent year-on-year and import volumes fell by 3.5 per cent, with net export volumes contributing to a 1.1 percentage point increase in real GDP growth. Thus, the decline in US real GDP was merely 0.3 per cent year-on-year, far smaller than that in Japan. Indeed, the aggressive monetary easing in the United States following the financial crisis and the resulting depreciation of the US dollar led to a turnaround in US exports, which contributed to a smaller contraction in the real economy following the financial crisis. It was also notable that in the following year, 2009, the continued increase in US net export volumes contributed to real GDP growth by 1.2 percentage points.[14]

In Japan, on the other hand, the decline in net export volumes in 2009 contributed to a decline in its real GDP growth by 1.5 percentage points. As a result, Japan's real GDP fell by a substantial 5.5 per cent, even worse than the 4.0 per cent decline in real gross domestic demand in the previous year.

Before this situation became a reality, I was unsure of when and how to issue my warning. This was because I did not want to get involved in the debate over the BOJ's policy under the governorship of Shirakawa. Both Hayami and Fukui were senior to me at the Bank, and I felt it was my duty, in a sense, to comment, mainly overseas but also occasionally in Japan, on the BOJ's policies during their tenure as Governors, as a former OECD Chief Economist rather than as a BOJ alumnus. However, I was reluctant to make critical remarks about the policies of the BOJ led by Shirakawa, as I was afraid that it might be perceived as bullying one of my former junior colleagues at the BOJ.

I was concerned that deflationary pressure would be exerted on the Japanese economy after the collapse of Lehman Brothers through three spillover channels. The first of these was that the downturn in overseas economies caused by the global financial shock would, through its income effect, push down the volume of Japanese exports and widen the output gap in Japan. Second, if the BOJ did not make its intention to further ease monetary policy clear to the market in the face of such a situation and left the market with continued expectations of an appreciation of the Japanese yen, it would increase the risk of the yen appreciation momentum continuing in a self-fulfilling manner. In such a case, a negative price effect would emerge quite quickly, with a rise in the *nominal* effective exchange rate of the yen pushing down Japanese import prices. Moreover, thirdly, a further rise in the *real* effective exchange rate of the yen, taking into account price and cost differentials between Japan and overseas countries, would further weaken the international price competitiveness of Japanese exports, which would eventually widen Japan's output gap by reducing its share of global export markets, thereby intensifying deflationary pressure in Japan.

At the time of the collapse of Lehman Brothers, there was a general perception that the Japanese financial system was in more solid than those of Western advanced countries, which reduced the risk premium for foreign investors investing in Japanese yen assets and increased the risk that this would act to further strengthen the yen exchange rate. In other words, in addition to changes in domestic and foreign interest rate differentials due to interest rate cuts in major Western countries following the collapse of Lehman Brothers, there was a risk that changes in the relative risk premiums between domestic and foreign currencies would accelerate the appreciation of the yen.

The BOJ under the governorship of Shirakawa did not participate in the co-ordinated interest rate cuts by the central banks of major advanced countries on 7 October 2008 (US time), and my worry about the Bank's slow response to the deteriorating external environment surrounding Japan continued to grow. In his book "Tumultuous Times: Central Banking in an Era of Crisis", Shirakawa provides an insider's account of the Bank's policy at the time and thereafter.[15]

It was pointed out in the OECD's Economic Outlook for 2009 that a substantial decline in exports and falling domestic demand undermining economic activity and increasing deflationary pressures in Japan. In view of this, I decided to express my views to the outside world, first in English rather than in Japanese. My contribution was published in the 25 November 2008 edition of the Financial Times to call for urgent action by the Japanese monetary authorities.

On 1 December of the same year, I contributed an article to the Nikkei Weekly[16] in which I wrote in English that it was necessary to correct the situation where the real effective exchange rate of the yen appreciated by 22 per cent between mid-2007 and October 2008, to a level more than 11 per cent higher than in March 1973 when Japan moved to a floating exchange rate system. Furthermore, I remarked that the decline in the dollar-denominated prices of oil and other primary commodities, combined with the appreciation of the yen, had led to a significant fall in the yen-denominated import prices. Under these circumstances, I argued that correcting the excessive appreciation of the yen in order to prevent the decline in Japanese exports resulting in lower domestic production activity was not a beggar-thy-neighbour policy.

In the section entitled "Time to move", I made specific proposals for action to be taken by the Japanese authorities.

One of these was the Japanese authorities' intervention in the foreign exchange market, following the announcement of concern about recent developments in the yen made in the statement by the Finance Ministers and Central Bank Governors of the seven major economies, released on 27 October.

I also argued that the BOJ's previously implemented zero interest rates and the so-called "quantitative easing" of monetary policy should be immediately reintroduced.

In relation to the latter point, I pointed out that the macroeconomic effects of further monetary easing would not be very large according to the macroeconomic model analysis, but such measurement was mainly based on the spillover effects through changes in the term structure of interest rates, and did not sufficiently take into account the effects of these monetary easing measures on foreign exchange rates, equity, and other asset market prices and the macroeconomic effects of these asset market price changes. I also argued that the increase in the market value of Japanese equities held by Japanese commercial banks and the increase in the yen value of their foreign currency assets would raise their capital ratios and contribute to the enhancement of credit availability as a result of the fall in the yen exchange rate. Finally, I noted that it would be difficult to accurately measure the macroeconomic effects of zero interest rates and so-called "quantitative easing" of monetary policy through these spillover channels, but the BOJ did not have the luxury of not acting until it had measured these effects in the first place.

Another aspect of my discourses during this period was a call for enhancing multilateral surveillance by the OECD WP3 and other bodies to ensure that major countries, including Japan, would not take measures in the conduct of their monetary and exchange rate policies that could be seen as beggar-thy-neighbour policies. With this in mind, I published an article in the Japan Times on 1 December 2008 in which I stressed the importance of promoting the coherent conduct of macroeconomic policies across countries to restore economic growth and boost employment globally. In a nutshell, I attempted to encourage the OECD as well as the BOJ to move proactively.[17]

Japanese export volumes fell by 55 per cent on an annualised basis between July–September 2008 and January–March 2009. This was almost twice the average for OECD member countries and the largest drop among them. In the OECD's short-term outlook released in September 2009, the decline in Japan's net export volumes was expected to contribute to a contraction in real GDP of approximately 2 per cent for 2009 as a whole, and, combined with the decline in domestic demand, real GDP was expected to fall by 6 per cent, the largest decline among the seven largest economies.

One of the main reasons for the significant decline in Japan's exports was the contraction of its export markets. However, according to the OECD data, the size of Japan's export market in 2009 was 16.6 per cent lower than the previous year, not so different from the average decline in the size of export markets for all OECD countries, which was 15.4 per cent. The second reason was that Japan's exports were heavily concentrated on advanced capital goods, such as automobiles and ICT-related items, and the significant reduction in the inventories of such goods in overseas markets put particularly strong downward pressure on Japanese exports. However, in Germany, where the composition of export items was quite similar to that of Japan, the decline in exports was not as drastic as in Japan.

This led to another important reason for the significant decline in Japan's exports: the decline in Japan's international price competitiveness due to the sharp appreciation in the effective exchange rate of the Japanese yen. Its external value increased not only against the currencies of the United States and the United Kingdom where the financial crisis originated but also the currencies of Korea and newly industrialised Asian countries, important competitors of Japan in its export markets. These currencies depreciated not just against the Japanese yen but also against the US dollar. Thus, according to the measurement on which OECD Economic Outlook was based, the average level of the effective exchange rate of the Japanese yen appreciated by 25.1 per cent during 2009, well above the rate of its appreciation against the US dollar which was 18.9 per cent.[18] On the other hand, given the importance of Germany's trade within the euro-area, the appreciation of the euro against the dollar did not significantly alter Germany's overall international price competitiveness.

All in all, the appreciation of the yen acted as a significant brake on Japanese exports, while Korea, which, like Japan, excelled in ITC-related equipment, automobiles, and other industrial goods, increased its share of exports amid the deteriorating global export market conditions.

The BOJ's "Outlook for Economic Activity and Prices" (Outlook Report) published in April 2009 stated that the downward trend in prices was expected to continue in FY2010, as a large output gap was likely to remain, and wages were likely to remain weak. After pointing out that there was a high degree of uncertainty in both the upward and downward direction of prices, the Report went on to state that fluctuations in the yen exchange rate could also cause a commensurate change in consumer prices through changes in import prices, in addition to the channel through its impact on the real economy.

In the wake of the outbreak of the global financial and economic crisis, the Bank of Canada, in its Monetary Policy Report published in July 2009, emphasised the downside risks to prices, stating that the key risk was that a strong Canadian dollar, and its further violent volatility would be highly negative for growth and put downward pressure on prices. The Governor of the Reserve Bank of New Zealand also reiterated the statement to the effect that further appreciation of the New Zealand dollar against the Australian dollar was not favourable. Particularly noteworthy was the Bank of Canada's public statement articulating the risks of a "strong Canadian dollar" in a report prepared at a time when the Canadian dollar had fallen by about 20 per cent against the US dollar since mid-2008 and had stabilised at 0.80 US dollar to the Canadian dollar.

The decline of the US dollar and the British pound against the yen and the euro during this period was probably partly due to a loss of confidence in the currencies of the countries that had experienced financial crises. However, the fall in the exchange rate against the US dollar occurred in Canada, where the financial system was considered to be relatively sound. It seemed reasonable to me to think that market movements under a floating exchange rate system were influenced not only by market participants' perceptions of the stability of their countries' financial systems, but also by bold policy responses after the crisis and credible policy statements that would change market expectations.

To call for the BOJ's aggressive monetary policy, I once again contributed an article to "Economists Forum" of the Financial Times which was published on 26 October 2009.[19] However, unlike the Bank of Canada, the BOJ under the governorship of Shirakawa remained hesitant in its policy conduct and statements on its policy stance. Some BOJ officials with an international background reported to me that there was a growing taboo within the BOJ on discussing foreign exchange rate policy.

In this situation, I decided to express my views in Japanese, which I had refrained from doing after writing an article in English for the Japan Times on 1 December 2008. I first contributed an article to the morning edition on 12 October 2009 of the Nihon Keizai Shimbun, which was entitled "The Bank of Japan needs to be more vigilant against a strong yen". In addition to the main title, it had two subtitles: "Dealing with deflationary pressure" and "Need to take into account bold policy actions taken abroad".

In this article, I emphasised that the change in the exchange rate was not merely a function of actual interest rate differentials between countries, but it would occur as a result of the change in market expectation about the monetary authorities' future actions. In this regard, I pointed to the case of the Bank of Canada, which in April 2009 announced its intention to keep its policy rate at 0.25 per cent until the April-June period of 2010, unless there were major changes in the internal and external environment. In July 2009, the Swedish central bank announced that it would apply a negative interest rate of 0.25 per cent on one-week deposits with the central bank by financial institutions. It was also reported that Mervyn King, Governor of the Bank of England, was taking note of these policy developments.

Such policy developments by foreign central banks were pursued as bold experiments without waiting for empirical analysis to confirm their effectiveness. In the last part of my article, I called for a serious debate on the effectiveness of various possible non-traditional monetary policy instruments, not only within the BOJ but also among academics and other monetary experts outside the BOJ.

Furthermore, my short essay summarising main points of my arguments, first published in the 26 October 2009 edition of the Financial Times (see above), was followed by a more detailed article in the 2 and 3 November editions of the Japan Times.[20] In addition, I published an article entitled "Policy responses the BOJ should take to stabilise exchange rates" in the 3 November issue of *Shukan Ekonomisto* (The Weekly Economist) in Japanese with more space than a newspaper contribution, in which I tried to support my argument by proving a table showing data about the contributions of net export volumes to economic growth in major countries, as well as the changes in the exchange rates of major currencies against the US dollar and their effective exchange rates.[21]

Throughout this period, the BOJ under the governorship of Shirakawa refrained from making statements on how to cope with the strong yen problem.

Abenomics and the Bank of Japan's Failure in Achieving its 2 Per Cent Inflation Target

On 14 November 2012, Prime Minister Yoshihiko Noda, leader of the Democratic Party of Japan, and Liberal Democratic Party (LDP) President Shinzo Abe held the party leaders' debate in which Yoshihiko Noda expressed his intention to hold a general election for the House of Representatives in December 2012. With the LDP expected to gain the upper hand in this lower house election, President Abe repeatedly stated from the day after the party leaders' debate that he would "co-ordinate policy with the Bank of Japan and carry out bold monetary easing" and "have the Bank carry out unlimited monetary easing to achieve the price target", resulting in the emergence of the "Abe trade", which accelerated the yen's depreciation and stock market appreciation.

The second Abe Government, which began on 26 December 2012, positioned its goal as economic recovery and planned to rebuild the Japanese economy through "three arrows", commonly referred to as "Abenomics": (1) bold monetary policy (quantitative easing until deflation is overcome and the 2 per cent inflation target is achieved, (2) flexible fiscal stimulus (mainly for reconstruction following the Great East Japan Earthquake) and (3) a growth strategy to stimulate private investment (deregulation to create growth industries and jobs, and attract investment).

On 22 January 2013, the Japanese government and the BOJ issued a joint statement in which it was stated that they would strengthen policy co-ordination and work in unison to end deflation at an early stage and achieve sustainable economic growth under price stability. In this context, the Bank set the price stability target at 2 per cent in terms of the year-on-year rate of increase in consumer prices. In his book noted above, Shirakawa recounts the long process that led to the joint statement by the government and the Bank.

Shirakawa resigned as BOJ Governor on 19 March that year, pending the expiry of his five-year term on 8 April 2013. On 2 that month,

Haruhiko Kuroda succeeded Shirakawa as BOJ Governor. On the same day, my article "My expectations for BOJ Governor Kuroda" was published by a local newspaper, Jômô Shimbun, in which I expressed my hope that he, in co-operation with the government led by Shinzo Abe as Prime Minister, would succeed in ending deflation and achieving a sustained economic upturn amid a correction of the strong yen.

Kuroda was a former finance ministry bureaucrat who attended OECD WP3 as Vice Minister of Finance for International Affairs and was President of the Asian Development Bank immediately before his appointment as BOJ Governor. In the Feldman report "The Next BOJ Governor – Comparing Candidates" noted above, Kuroda ranked 13th in terms of the criteria emphasising candidates' grasp of macroeconomics and independence from the government, 7th in terms of the criteria emphasising experience as head of a policy-making body, and 13th in terms of the criteria emphasising domestic and international networks.

On his assuming the BOJ Governor's post, I said to Kuroda that I would not comment on his monetary policy in public as I did when Hayami , Fukui and Shirakawa respectively were its Governor. When I said this to Kuroda, I did not expect the Abe government would appoint him as BOJ Governor for full two five-year terms which ended in April 2023. Over this ten-year period, the BOJ failed to achieve its policy target of 2 per cent year-on-year growth in consumer prices in a sustainable manner,[22] and BOJ credibility, which had eroded since the bursting of Japan's bubble, was undermined further.[23]

The IMF's annual surveillance report on Japan based on Article IV of the IMF Articles of Agreement, published in February 2022, stated that, based on the IMF staff's medium-term economic outlook assumption that the GDP gap would be eliminated in 2024 and the GDP gap would be zero from 2025 to 2027, with the unemployment rate remaining at 2.4 per cent, while consumer price inflation would be around 1.0 per cent. According to this outlook, the real GDP growth rate per capita in Japan was expected to remain at around 1.2 per cent.

If this medium-term outlook is considered to be reasonable, it can be said that the BOJ's policy under the governorship of Kuroda over the past ten years of forcibly enforcing monetary easing even after the correction of an excessively strong yen to achieve its 2 per cent inflation target on a sustainable basis was inappropriate. In an article published in the 22 September 2022 edition of a Japanese weekly economic journal, *World Economic Review—Impact*,[24] I argued that the BOJ and the Japanese government should review the basic framework of Japanese monetary policy management described in their joint statement issued in January 2013 in which the BOJ announced its 2 per cent inflation target.[25]

The BOJ adopted a 2 per cent annual rate of increase in the consumer price index as its inflation target without explaining its reasons in detail, simply stating that it is a global standard. On the other hand, the European Central Bank puts forward the reasons for choosing 2 per cent as its inflation target in the following way: an inflation rate of 2 per cent is low enough for the economy to fully reap the benefits of price stability with a sufficient margin to allow for (1) a smoother adjustment of macroeconomic imbalances across euro-area countries, avoiding inflation in individual countries persistently falling into negative territory, (2) downward wage rigidities, which risk raising unemployment excessively, and (3) a positive measurement bias in the price index, which could imply that the true level of inflation is lower than the measured level.

Reason (1) does not apply to Japan. Downward wage rigidities mentioned in (2) above are not so significant in Japan as in the euro-area, as evidenced in Japanese nominal wage developments in the 1990s and in the early two decades of the twenty-first century. The positive measurement bias in the price index, mentioned in (3) above, is not considered to be as large as 2 per cent in Japan. The 2 per cent rule in the United States was simply a result of a compromise between inflation hawks and doves. Three years after Bernanke as Federal Reserve chairman persuaded his colleagues to adopt the target, he said, "I don't see anything magical about targeting 2 per cent inflation".[26] In my article, in addition to these points, I referred to my keynote speech "The Options Regarding the Concept of a Monetary Policy Strategy" delivered at the German Bundesbank's symposium on "Monetary Policy strategies in Europe" in 1996 where I expressed a cautious view on the use of numerical inflation targets.[27]

In April 2023, Kazuo Ueda, former professor of economics at the University of Tokyo, succeeded Kuroda as BOJ Governor. In the Feldman report "The Next BOJ Governor – Comparing Candidates" noted above in which he scored 19 candidates for the BOJ Governor, Ueda ranked the third together with two other candidates in terms of the criteria emphasising candidates' grasp of macroeconomics and independence from the government and the fifth together with two other candidates in terms of the criteria emphasising domestic and international networks. Neither Hiroshi Nakaso, Deputy Governor during Kuroda's first five-year term of office as Governor, nor Masayoshi Amamiya, Deputy Governor during Kuroda's second five-year term as Governor, was appointed as Kuroda's successor. Japanese financial market had viewed both of them as leading candidates to replace Governor Kuroda.

At the first Policy Board meeting of the BOJ chaired by Governor Ueda on 28 April 2023, it was decided to "conduct a broad-perspective review of monetary policy, with a planned time frame of around one to one and a half years".

Notes

1. George Gissing, "The Private Papers of Henry Ryecroft", Archibald Contable & Co Ltd, 2 Whitehall Gardens, England, 1903.
2. Their URLs are http://shigehara.online.fr/jp/ and http://shigehara.online.fr/en/
3. OECD Economic Outlook No. 66, December 1999, pp. 19–20.
4. IMF, World Economic Outlook May 2001, Chapter 1, Fig. 1.17 and Tables 1.12 & 1.13.
5. The Bank of Japan eventually (in 2016) adopted a negative interest rate policy. But the falls in short-term money markets rates in Japan were not as large as assumed in the IMF scenario work of May 2001.
6. Kumiharu Shigehara, "Is the world prepared to deal with the global economic slowdown?", The Japan Times, 12 July 2001.
7. Kumiharu Shigehara, "Comment affronter le ralentissement économique?", Les Echos, 18 July 2001.
8. Kumiharu Shigehara, "Will the Koizumi administration's economic policies succeed?', Weekly Kinyu Zaisei Jijo, 8 Oct 2001, pp. 24–30.
9. OECD Economic Outlook No. 71, June 2002, p. x.
10. OECD Economic Outlook No. 73, June 2003, p. 21.
11. Ibid.
12. OECD Economic Outlook No. 58, December 1992, Table 8, p. 9.
13. Lars E.O. Svensson, "How Japan can recover", The Financial Times, Personal View, 25 September, 2001, https://larseosvensson.se/papers/ft109/, in which he suggested "pegging it (the yen) at a clearly 'undervalued' level, such as 140, 150 or even more yen to the dollar".

14. The figures used here rely on OECD Economic Outlook No. 94, November 2013, Statistical Annexes.
15. Masaaki Shirakawa, "Tumultuous Times: Central Banking in an Era of Crisis", Yale University Press, 2021.
16. Kumiharu Shigehara, "Swift BOJ action is needed to check yen's sharp rise", The Japan Times, 1 December 2008.
17. Kumiharu Shigehara, "Managing the international economic crisis", The Japan Times, 10 December 2008.
18. Calculations based on the assumption that the average exchange rate against the US dollar in 2009 was the same as the mid-year level. Source: OECD Economic Outlook No. 86, June 2009.
19. Kumiharu Shigehara, "Japan needs more aggression in warding off deflation", The Financial Times, 26 October 2009. The article, which was posted on the paper's "Economists Forum", received a large number of responses from its readers. Among them, one economist anonymously posted the final comment recorded on 27 October, saying "(T)his is a fascinating article, probably the most revealing and comprehensive I have read in the realm of international finance".
20. Kumiharu Shigehara, "Japan's demand management and yen rate in the global crisis", The Japan Times, 2 November 2009; "Central banks experimenting to counter deflationary pressure", The Japan Times, 3 November 2009.
21. Kumiharu Shigehara, "Policy responses the Bank of Japan should take to stabilise the exchange rate" (in Japanese), *Shukan Ekonomisto* (The Weekly Economist), Mainichi Shimbunsha, 3 November 2009.
22. See Chart 16 in Masazumi Wakatabe, "Seven Reflections on Japan's Economy, Monetary Policy, and the Bank of Japan", speech at the Center on Japanese Economy and Business, Columbia University in New York, February 27, 2023. https://www.boj.or.jp/en/about/press/koen_2023/data/ko230228a1.pdf
23. See, for example, Stephen J. Cole, Enrique Martínez García and Eric Sims, "Living up to Expectations: Central Bank Credibility, the Effectiveness of Forward Guidance, and Inflation Dynamics Post-Global Financial Crisis", The Federal Reserve Bank of Dallas Research Department, Globalization Institute Working Paper 424, September 2023. According to their study on the effectiveness of central banks' forward guidance, the central banks of the United

States, the United Kingdom, Germany, and other major advanced economies have similar levels of credibility (albeit far from full credibility), but Japan's central bank credibility is much lower.

24. Kumiharu Shigehara, "The Bank of Japan needs to review of the policy management framework" (in Japanese), World Economic Review—Impact, 12 September 2022, http://www.world-economic-review.jp/impact/article2673.html
25. Hiroshi Nakaso, "Evolving Monetary Policy: The Bank of Japan's Experience", Speech at the Central Banking Seminar hosted by the Federal Reserve Bank of New York, New York, 18 October 2017, https://www.boj.or.jp/en/about/press/koen_2017/data/ko171019a1.pdf
26. David Wessel, "Alternatives to the Fed's 2 percent inflation target", Brookings Report, 7 June 2018, https://www.brookings.edu/articles/alternatives-to-the-feds-2-percent-inflation-target/
27. Kumiharu Shigehara, "The Options Regarding the Concept of a Monetary Policy Strategy" in Deutsche Bundesbank, "Monetary Policy Strategies in Europe. A Symposium at the Deutsche Bundesbank", Vahlen Verlag, München, 1996.

PART III

Domestic and International Frameworks for Economic Policy Management

CHAPTER 15

Frameworks and Conduct of Monetary Policy in Europe

Strategies for Lowering Inflation

This chapter provides a brief account of the evolution of frameworks of domestic monetary and foreign exchange rate policies followed in Europe since the 1990s and reviews discussions at OECD meetings on the management of the European Exchange Rate Mechanism (ERM) and the introduction of a single European currency. In this context, it also provides a detailed account of the views the author expressed as OECD Chief Economist, including his specific suggestion about adding some flexibility to the operation of ERM by temporarily widening exchange rate fluctuation bands.

Controlling virulent inflation became a top policy agenda in all OECD countries in the 1970s. In this setting, the choice of an optimal financial target for monetary policy became a crucial matter of practical importance to the monetary authorities and monetary aggregates were adopted as policy targets in the context of inflation control in many OECD countries.[1] However, the reliability of these aggregates as monetary policy targets declined significantly as their relations with prices and other key economic variables such as output and unemployment became unstable due to various factors, including financial deregulation and innovation in the 1980s onwards.

In Europe, drawing lessons from the deceiving experience of the European fixed exchange rates system established in 1992, marked by repeated

K. Shigehara, *The Bank of Japan, the OECD, and Beyond*,
https://doi.org/10.1007/978-981-97-5307-9_15

realignments of the central parities, a new strengthened Exchange Rate Mechanism (ERM) and the related new Common Currency Unit (ECU) were introduced under the European Monetary System (EMS) in March 1979. Member countries of the ERM agreed to limit fluctuations of their currencies relative to those of other members to 2.25 per cent.[2] Thus, for countries other than West Germany participating in the ERM, disinflation by targeting an external nominal anchor, the Deutschemark (DM)—which was the ERM-wide benchmark currency—effectively functioned as an alternative to disinflation by targeting monetary aggregates. However, after the unification of East and West Germany in 1990, expansionary fiscal policy was introduced in Germany, which led to fears of inflation. In view of this, tight monetary policy was adopted by the German Bundesbank, causing interest rates to rise. This led to widespread concern that EMS participants other than Germany would not be able to follow the Bundesbank's high interest rate policy and maintain the ERM.

At the WP3 meeting of 9 September 1992, following Chairman Tietmeyer's suggestion, I commented on the Secretariat's assessment of the overall economic situation and expressed my views on policy issues (Annex 1). I began by pointing out that the Secretariat's projection made in the spring of 1992 before my return to the OECD from the Bank of Japan would likely prove too optimistic, and that most other forecasters had made similar errors. I then noted that OECD economies were behaving in unusual ways, especially in financial markets: it was increasingly difficult for policy to shape expectations; targets for monetary aggregates had been de-emphasised as these aggregates appeared less reliable guides to the economy, perhaps even in Germany; exchange rate objectives had at times implied interest rates otherwise inappropriate for domestic consideration; progress in fiscal consolidation had largely stopped or even reversed by sluggish economic growth; agreement in Uruguay Round of GATT negotiations had not been achieved; and, domestic structural reforms remained incomplete in many instances.

Having made these observations, I suggested that the strategy adopted by countries participating in the ERM might not be the best way to shape policy in the period ahead when policy actually was not entirely on course, and remarked that it was necessary to move back on course decisively and then stay. I added that such a strategy would take time to bear fruits, but that short-term fixes would make matters worse.

The 1992–1993 ERM Crisis

Less than two weeks after I made these remarks at the WP3 meeting, more precisely on September 16, 1992 (later often referred to as "Black Wednesday"), a collapse in the UK pound forced the United Kingdom to withdraw from the ERM.[3] Foreign exchange markets had become unstable in the aftermath of the Danish referendum that took place on June 1992 on the Maastricht Treaty for European monetary unification. In the face of successive speculative currency attacks against the UK pound, the United Kingdom could not prevent the value of the pound from falling below the lower limit specified under the ERM. On the following day, Italy also announced to withdraw from the ERM.

Furthermore, speculation developed that the French referendum on 20 September might also reject ratification of the Maastricht Treaty and the ERM's volatility increased. In the French referendum, the Treaty was approved by only 51 per cent of the voters. This result, known as the "petit oui", along with the Danish "No" vote, increased market doubt about the process of European monetary integration and the ERM crisis continued.

At the start of the EPC meeting on 9 November 1992, I said: "(L)ast week's meeting of forecasters identified downside risks to the projections of both output and inflation, implying a significant downside risk on the growth of nominal income. One does not have to be a fan of nominal income targeting—indeed I have always been sceptical of the idea—to realise that there would indeed be further room for monetary policy actions if the downside risks were to emerge. Such room would be particularly significant in Europe". I did not touch on sensitive issues regarding the management of the ERM in my introductory statement as I thought it would not be appropriate to have in-depth discussion at the EPC meeting with a large number of attendants including officials of governmental agencies that are not involved in sensitive foreign exchange rate policy matters.

Just before the WP3 meeting was held on 3 and 4 December 1992, I gave a telephone call to Jean-Claude Trichet, then Directeur Général du Trésor at the French Ministry of Economy and Finance and the principal delegate of the French government at the WP3 (later Governor of the Bank of France and subsequently President of the European Central Bank), asking him to intervene as the first speaker in response to my introductory statement on the general economic situation and the policy challenges in Europe. I informed him that in my oral statement I would make remarks on some sensitive policy issues which were not described in the Secretariat paper for the WP3 meeting sent to the WP3 Delegates beforehand through the usual distribution channels. Although it was a practice for the Secretariat to send WP3 discussion papers as confidential documents to the WP3 members, given the extreme sensitivity of the issues, I thought it would be wise to discuss them only in my oral intervention. The speaking note prepared for my oral remarks had not been circulated within the Economics Department to avoid the risk of leak to the outside world. I handed a paper copy of my speaking note (Annex 2) to Secretary-General Paye[4] just before the start of the meeting.

In my introductory statement at the WP3 meeting on 5 March, I noted that under the current and prospective circumstances where the fiscal burdens of reconstructing the German eastern Länder were likely to remain large and further cuts in interest rates in Germany would not be propitious, sticking to the strategy that had been adopted by many European countries to move toward price stability by formally tying their exchange rate parities to the DM involved significant downside risks to the economy. Among a series of other policy options that could reduce tensions by decoupling, temporarily, monetary conditions in Germany from those elsewhere in Europe, I mentioned a widening of the ERM bands for France and other narrow-band countries vis-à-vis the DM, while indicating that I saw serious risks in each of these courses of action. In my final remark, I stressed the need to assess the objectives and the risks of each strategy, and said that "none of the choices looks simple, but urgent decisions are nonetheless needed".

Following my statement, Trichet defended his government policy of sticking to the strategy. In this context, it was indicated that the underlying trend in export competitiveness in France was still favourable, even allowing for the effective appreciation of the French franc resulting from the depreciations of the currencies of some European countries such as the United Kingdom, Italy, and Sweden. It was also pointed out that some of this change would probably be absorbed by lower profit margins for French exporters rather than cuts in export volumes.

In the ensuing discussion, a number of Delegates argued that a change in the policy mix to allow a significant fall in interest rates in Germany would be the best means of easing the internal/external dilemma for ERM countries, and avoiding further turmoil on the foreign exchange markets. The representative of the IMF argued that a large cut in German short-term interest rates should take place immediately, given long lags in the transmission of monetary policy and the likelihood that German inflation was set to fall over the coming year.

A related issue that arose in connection with the turmoil on European exchange markets was whether countries that had chosen to float such as the United Kingdom could have lower interest rates than in Germany or whether those countries that had depreciated their ERM parities could narrow interest rate differentials with Germany. Experience was mixed on this issue and no firm conclusions were drawn from the WP3 discussion.

The establishment of new monetary policy frameworks in those countries that, at least temporarily, had abandoned an exchange rate anchor was also discussed at the WP3 meeting of December 1992. The UK Delegate explained how it was hoped to re-establish the authorities' credibility by the explicit announcement of inflation targets. They intended to bolster confidence in this strategy by fostering a process of greater transparency and analysis about the setting of monetary policy. It was recognised, however, that it would take time and evidence of results to overcome market scepticism. Some Delegates even queried the role of greater transparency in the setting of policies, arguing that markets would be inherently sceptical. In this connection, the US Delegate acknowledged that proposals had been made for the adoption of explicit inflation targets for the United States, but he doubted their utility. Some other Delegates suggested that it was important to consider granting formal independence to the central bank as an additional pillar in the UK strategy.

A final theme running through the WP3 discussion on Europe was the degree to which changes in nominal exchange rates had modified competitiveness and export prospects among European countries, thereby providing a source of economic growth in these countries. The Italian, UK, and Swedish Delegates all agreed that export prospects had been improved by the depreciations of their currencies. They also argued that these gains were unlikely to be dissipated quickly in higher inflation. The UK and Swedish Delegates argued that large gaps in labour and product markets would discipline wage demands while the Italian Delegate stressed the role of incomes policy as an additional restraint.

On 17 December 1992, a week after the December 1992 WP3 meeting, I had a press conference occasioned by the publication of OECD Economic Outlook 52. In my remarks on policy requirements for those European countries whose currencies had depreciated, either through devaluations or through floating, I argued that they must urgently develop a new and credible strategy for macroeconomic policies to bear down on inflation and to sustain higher growth of output, noting that the evidence suggested that it would not be easy to re-establish policy credibility quickly (Annex 3).

For Germany, I stressed the importance of further efforts to reduce budget deficits to alleviate burdens on monetary policy and also remarked that if demand pressure proved to be weaker than embodied in the OECD projections, the Bundesbank should reduce interest rates more rapidly than assumed there. For obvious reasons, I did not mention my suggestion about a widening of the ERM bands as a possible option to deal with the ERM crisis which I orally stated at the WP3 meeting of 3 December 1992.

The ERM crisis continued into 1993. In my statement at the beginning of the WP3 meeting on 5 and 6 March 1993, I discussed the pros and cons of three specific options regarding monetary and exchange rate management in Europe: a general realignment of ERM parities, a widening of the fluctuation bands in the ERM, and the temporary float of major ERM currencies (Annex 4).

Delegates participating in the ERM felt that it was necessary to stick to the existing system, with exchange rate pressures likely to dissipate during the year as interest rates came down. Some Delegates suggested that there had been a missed opportunity for an earlier realignment of exchange rate parities at the time of German unification or perhaps for some modification in the ERM, such as widening of the bands, last September. Some Delegates thought the current configuration of exchange rates was appropriate and could be sustained, but others voiced fears about pressures on the system unless interest rates were to come down significantly. North American Delegates raised the issue of whether fixed rate systems could work, given that shocks would occur (such as German unification) and that such systems might—especially in the context of a single fully integrated market—require stronger fiscal centralisation than was allowed for in Europe. If countries had to accept that monetary policy needed to be subordinated to exchange rates in such a system, they should be prepared to accept the short-run costs for longer-run gains, and should not resort to trade protection and other measures to alleviate the pain. In reply, some European Delegates stressed the political as well as economic nature of the commitment to EMU and denied that fiscal policies had to be subject to European-wide control.

In the report of WP3 Chairman Tietmeyer to G10 Ministers and Governors at their meeting on 30 April 1993 in Washington, D.C., he said that an important slowdown in activity in Europe was recognised by everyone and there was concern about serious downside risks, even with German interest rates coming down and there was agreement that the main source of growth needed to be found in Europe itself. He reported that the WP3 discussion focused on the scope for further substantial monetary easing in continental Europe since fiscal action was essentially ruled out by existing budgetary and debt problems. Tietmeyer reported that some Delegates had argued that German short-term interest rates could be cut relatively quickly and substantially, but others had warned that the Bundesbank's credibility should not be jeopardised by over-hasty action, since this would only lead to adverse pressure on long-term interest rates, and that further retrenchment of the German fiscal position was necessary to allow interest rates to come down. Tietmeyer did not mention the WP3 discussion of the three specific options regarding monetary and exchange rate management in Europe that I had suggested at the WP3 meeting of March 1993.

Wider Bands in the ERM

Pressures within the ERM intensified further in July 1993. Eventually, a decision was taken to widen temporarily the bands for mandatory intervention to plus or minus 15 per cent from the central parties (except for the Dutch-German one, that stayed at 2.25 per cent), effective August 2 that year. In his book with narratives about developments in the ERM, Bernard Connolly, who had participated in WP3 meetings as head of the EMS, National and Community Monetary Policies Unit in the European Commission, wrote that "(T)he idea had been floating around for some time: OECD Chief Economist Kumiharu Shigehara had been suggesting it since the previous autumn".[5] Connolly added that the Bundesbank confirmed that, in its Annual Report for 1993 (issued in April 1994), it had been advocating wider bands in the first half of 1993. As a matter of fact, Rieke, head of the International Department at the Bundesbank, gave me a ring from Frankfurt the day after the March 1993 meeting of the WP3 to tell me that my suggestion about the adoption of wider bands in the ERM was much appreciated within the Bundesbank.

At the 10 September 1993 meeting of the WP3, North American Delegates pointed out that in North America there was no consideration being given to going beyond the establishment of a free trade area to the creation of a monetary union. They questioned whether European countries with limited labour market mobility and low-wage flexibility could maintain fixed exchange rate relationships in the face of regional divergences in economic conditions. Many European Delegates, however, questioned this comparison. The European Single Market being more ambitious than the North American Free Trade Agreement, they pointed to the longer-term need for close European monetary co-operation. Given the large number of independent countries of different size—with no country having a dominant influence like the United States—some European Delegates also mentioned the potential dangers of competitive devaluation if countries began to resort to the option of floating.

In response to my question about the possibility of taking advantage of the wider bands in the ERM, North American members felt that high short-term interest rates were a major obstacle to better economic performance, and that good use could be made of the widened ERM bands for more flexible monetary policy management in the ERM counties. A widely, although not unanimously held, European view, on the other hand, was that this must be done very cautiously, taking into account both the immediate economic situation and the longer-term consequences. To some degree, this view attached less weight to the role of short-term interest rates as a cause of the prevailing problems and more weight to structural problems in Europe and to the need to strengthen confidence.

Introduction of the European Single Currency

In January 1994, a few months after the decision was taken to widen the ERM exchange rate bands temporarily, the European Monetary Institute (EMI) was established as the second step towards European monetary union. It was initially located in Basel and moved to Frankfurt one year later. The main objective was to prepare the third stage, the European Central Banking System and the European Central Bank (ECB). Alexandre Lamfalussy, General Manager of the BIS, was appointed as the first President of EMI and Robert Raymond, Director-General of Crédit of the Bank of France, as his deputy. The EMI's operations were supported mainly by staff seconded from the central banks of European countries participating in the EMI.

In the light of these developments in Europe, a momentum grew among the representatives of major non-European countries participating in the WP3 to discuss policy issues related to the introduction of the European single currency at WP3. At the time, the WP3 was chaired by US Deputy Treasury Secretary Larry Summers (former Under Secretary, later Secretary). He was particularly keen to take them up on the basis of a discussion paper to be prepared by the OECD Economics Department at the WP3 meeting in December 1995.

In the official invitation notice sent to the WP3 Delegates, the venue, as usual, was stated to be the OECD Paris headquarters. But it was hastily changed at my suggestion to a meeting room at the BIS headquarters in Basel because of reports of a strike by air traffic controllers at Paris airports on the day of the WP3 meeting. Eventually, the strike was lifted on the morning of that day, and Jean Lemière, then Directeur Général du Trésor at the French Ministry of Economy and Finance and the principal delegate of the French government at the WP3 (and later president of the European Bank for Reconstruction), mildly complained about the change made about the venue, with the WP3 meeting held in the BIS building providing a "sanctuary" of central bankers in Basel.

Besides Raymond from the EMI, active speakers at the meeting included Alan Blinder, Fed Vice Chairman, Paul Jenkins, Deputy Governor of the Bank of Canada, and Nigel Wicks, Second Secretary of UK Treasury, as well as Summers.

In mid-November, just prior to the WP3 Basel meeting, the EMI announced a timetable for the introduction of the euro on 1 January 1999, but there were growing market concerns regarding countries that might have difficulty meeting the Maastricht Treaty criteria required for the introduction of the euro. The German authorities had also put forward a proposal to impose stricter fiscal discipline on countries introducing the euro than was included in the Maastricht Treaty. According to this proposal, the Maastricht Treaty's budget deficit-to-GDP ratio of 3 per cent was to be the upper limit, which could not be exceeded even in recessionary periods, and the deficit ratio should not exceed 1 per cent under normal circumstances. It was also proposed that the ratio of government debt to GDP should be maintained below 60 per cent in the medium term.

The WP3 Basel meeting discussed mainly the issue of coping with local shocks (so-called "asymmetrical shocks") in parts of the single currency area, fiscal norms and mechanisms for financial support between countries in the area, and the costs versus benefits of introducing a single currency. Delegates from European countries aiming to introduce a single currency emphasised the benefits of its introduction. To me, it was striking that many of them said they were not very concerned about asymmetrical shocks. In contrast, in the OECD Secretariat's document we expressed concerns regarding the differences in labour market mobility and nominal wage rigidities in the countries aiming to introduce a single currency, the reduced scope for monetary policy to respond to such shocks after the introduction of a single currency and common monetary policy, constraints on the automatic stabilising effect of fiscal policy, and other factors. The OECD Secretariat's views were shared mainly by representatives from the United States and Canada.

I got the strong impression from this meeting that Germany, in particular, among the countries aiming to introduce a single currency, was more concerned with the issue of how to secure fiscal discipline across member countries of the single currency area than with the issue of how to deal with asymmetrical shocks which can occur within it. I cannot forget the discussions at this WP3 Basel meeting, in relation to the international conference on the euro-area crisis that I presided over in Paris in September 2013, which I will describe in Chapter 18.

Neither the documents nor the minutes of the WP3 meetings were published at the time, as they were classified as confidential. However, the OECD Secretariat's views were described in a paragraph in the Introduction to the December 1995 issue of the Economic Outlook, published immediately after the WP3 Basel meeting, and in more detail in the Europe section of the same issue in the chapter entitled "Policy Considerations in a Medium-term Perspective". Policy issues relating to the introduction of a European single currency were discussed also in the issue of June 1996 in the chapter "Macroeconomic Policy Requirements in the Current Situation". Moreover, well before the WP3 meeting of December 1995, the Secretariat document entitled "Policy Issues in the Transition to a Single Monetary Union (EMU)" was submitted to the WP3 meeting of April 1992.[6] It was not published, but papers produced in this connection were included in the OECD Economics Studies.[7]

Annex 1[8]

Kumiharu Shigehara's Introductory Statement at the Working Party No. 3 Meeting on 9 September 1992

I first want to say how pleased I am to have the opportunity to serve this group again, after the absence of over two years.

In preparing this meeting, our country specialist reviewed the conjunctual situation. It is clear that the forecasts we published in June were too optimistic. The majority of forecasters in the private sector, in government, and in other international agencies have been similarly optimistic and a very pertinent question is why we have all been making such large errors recently.

Part of the answer is that our economies are behaving in ways that we do not fully understand. Nowhere is this clearer than in the credit markets. As the Secretariat discusses more fully in the supplementary note prepared for this meeting, caution and retrenchment on the part of household and firms are depressing expenditures, despite interest rates that, in the United States and Japan, at least, are near historically low levels. Slumping prices of real estate and of equities in some countries are undermining major financial institutions and likely contributing to the failures of household and business confidence to rebound.

Hence, a crucial question facing policymakers is how to stabilise private-sector expectations firmly, and thus boost and sustain confidence. Recent financial market turmoil underlines the unsettled state of their expectations. The forecasting mistakes I referred a moment ago have made it clear that policymakers make errors, and they are learning on the job as they react to novel phenomena. On the side of monetary policies, the plain fact is that the central bankers and government officials responsible monetary policy-making cannot rely on simple indicators such as monetary aggregates to guide policy. The lack of transparent rules for the conduct of policy itself is destabilizing for private-sector agents.

It is easy to criticise the stance of policy taken by the monetary authorities in this environment. But, as Herb Stein[9] recently wrote in connection with criticism from the Whitehouse and others of the Federal Reserve's policy, "More is not a monetary policy, unless one is prepared to say more of what, how much, and for how long, and in what circumstances one would say "less".

It is not only in the United States that the monetary authorities face difficulties in assessing the situation. In Japan, while monetary aggregates have played a role in monetary policy formulation for many years, the Bank of Japan's view on these have always been relatively eclectic. Even so, monetary aggregates have become less reliable in recent years, and monetary policy implementation had accordingly become more complex in Japan too.

Germany is another country where questions can be posed about the appropriateness of monetary setting. The German Bundesbank have always had the greatest confidence in monetary aggregates. Indeed, the rapid growth of M3, its preferred monetary policy target, has reinforced the Bundesbank's commitment to its current tight policy stance. Yet, even in Germany, respected private-sector analysts are questioning the wisdom of the Bundesbank's approach and current policy settings.

Other European countries in the ERM have relied on exchange rate commitments to stabilise expectations. But, with high interest rates in Germany, this "hard-currency" option has tended to sap economic growth and put vulnerable financial sectors at risk in some of them. There is heightened concern about the sustainability of exchange rate commitments.

On the fiscal front, deficit reduction has virtually disappeared from the political agenda in the Unites States. The Maastricht agreement has committed several European countries—Italy most notably—to substantial fiscal reforms, but also raises doubt about their political feasibility. Views that flexibility exists in Japan probably underestimate the difficulties in ensuring that expansionary fiscal measures, such as the recent package, are only temporary. More generally, sluggish growth has interrupted budgetary consolidation in a number of countries. In all these countries, repeated pledges to keep medium-term objectives—inflation reduction, fiscal consolidation, and promoting a stable financial system—may sound hollow to market participants.

Looking beyond the problems of the immediate situation, there are a number of other disquieting features of the economic landscape. At the international level, co-operation has not evolved well. The difficulty in obtaining a satisfactory outcome in the Uruguay Round negotiations is the most obvious example. The ongoing concerns being expressed about the external implications of regional trade arrangements are another manifestation. As for domestic structural reforms, little progress is being made in important areas such as labour markets.

Against this background, how best can we stabilise expectations, boost confidence, and revitalise non-inflationary growth? Some might take issue with the recommendation that the answer is to "stay the course" a little longer until balance sheets are restructured, the Maastricht Treaty is ratified or real estate and equity prices start rising again. But, repeating that we will "stay the course" may be the wrong way of looking at policy requirements. Let me submit to you that, in the fiscal and structural areas, many countries have in fact been well off course and that, in retrospect, monetary policy erred on the side of permissiveness in the late 1980s.

If this premise is accepted, markets can best be stabilised by decisively and convincingly moving fiscal and structural policies back on their medium-term paths, and then "staying the course". But we all know that budgetary policy is paralysed in the United States and many other OECD countries seem to lack the political will to pursue fiscal consolidation. Structural reforms will take time to bear fruits, even if they are accelerated. Political reality is such that over-burdening of monetary policies is the most likely outcome, at a time when there are enormous problems in implementation. But compounding existing mistakes by further mistakes, e.g., by quick fixes or short-term palliative, is not the answer.

The Working Party is not a decision-making body. But I hope this meeting will provide an occasion for a frank exchange of views on how best to overcome the present difficulties.

Annex 2

Kumiharu Shigehara's Introductory Statement at the Working Party No. 3 Meeting on 3 December 1992

Over a number of years, many European countries have sought to move toward price stability by formally tying their exchange rate parities to the Deutschemark or European Currency Unit (ECU). With domestic monetary policy being fixed through an exchange rate target, this has required domestic policies that reinforce the exchange rate commitment and, in brief, "convergence". This is not what we have had. In sum, what we have had in Europe is differing underlying economic performances in some cases, and in some other cases differing cyclical positions and policy mixes which have led to undesirably tight monetary conditions in many European countries.

For some countries, differences in underlying competitive positions had to be corrected by exchange rate adjustment, rather than nominal wage and price adjustment. Over recent months, the lack of convergence in cyclical positions in several countries has also led to developments in foreign exchange markets which are adding to pressure on monetary policy. In particular, countries maintaining exchange rate commitments vis-à-vis the Deutschemark or ECU are having to hold domestic interest rates above German levels, even though inflation performance in certain cases—for instance France, Denmark and Ireland—is better than in Germany and likely to remain so for some time; high interest rates in circumstances where they are not justified by domestic conditions have threatened political support for ERM parities, leading to market doubts about the viability of those parities.

How should policy react to these difficult circumstances?

Current policies and exchange rate arrangements are expected to yield a non-inflationary recovery under our projections. However, this strategy involves significant risks. It depends on governments being able to withstand market pressures—which some to date have not been able to do—but, more fundamentally, may hold problems in store. The fiscal burden of reconstructing the German eastern *Länder means Germany is likely to stay for some time a high (real) interest rate country. Interest rates there may not fall to low enough levels over the medium term to allow other low-inflation countries, linked to Germany, to adopt monetary conditions fully consistent with domestic requirements of recovery and fiscal consolidation. One of the circumstances in which German interest rates might be much lower—recession in Germany—would pose other problems in Europe. Furthermore, our most recent reading of the inflation situation in Germany, as the monetary numbers we have seen in recent months, does not reassure us that further cuts in German interest rates would be propitious. ERM credibility would be further weakened if inflation in Germany rebounded.*

So, what other options are there?

One option would be a variant of this "sticking to it" policy, namely what has been called the "two-speed Europe" approach. This entails fixing exchange rates for a set of hard-ERM countries—the "inner core". France might be able to maintain parities more easily, allowing a lower risk premium with respect to the Deutschemark or ECU and hence lower French interest rates; while countries outside "hard" group could converge at their own pace. However, interest rates in France and elsewhere might not fall sufficiently—unless German rates fell substantially—and France would still be vulnerable to market doubts about the prospects of economic recovery at current levels of interest rates, and hence about the sustainability of current parities.

Beyond this, there would appear to be a series of options which would essentially involve changes to the exchange rate mechanism that could reduce current tensions by decoupling, temporarily, monetary conditions in Germany from those elsewhere in Europe. There is a range of ways of accomplishing this, such as a widening of the ERM bands for France and other narrow-band countries, or floating of the Deutschemark. Let me say that I see serious risks in each of these courses of action. While they could have important advantages if they went well—in particular, allowing domestic monetary policies to be brought more in line with domestic needs and, in best case scenarios, leading to restoration of ERM credibility once short-term adjustments had been made—the outcome might also be the virtual failure of the ERM system, calling into the question the whole Maastricht process. The financial markets could draw the wrong conclusions and we might end up in a far worse position than by "sticking to it".

On the other hand, current and prospective economic conditions—price performance, budgetary positions, competitiveness—in France and Germany are such that, over a period of years, the French franc should be strong against the Deutschemark. Of course, political situations and, to a certain extent, the legacy of the past, mean that this is not currently the way markets view the situation. However, providing market participants with more information about underlying trends in relative inflation performance in Germany and elsewhere might help set the stage for easier monetary conditions in low-inflation ERM countries. If such information were more fully reflected in risk premia on interest rates, market forces would move interest rates, without causing exchange rate pressures, towards levels that could be considered to be more appropriate on domestic economic grounds in these countries. While more information about underlying economic performance is important, there has perhaps been rather too much commentary on exchange rates and monetary policy coming from policy makers. Conflicting signals have sometimes been damaging, because they have given speculators the chance to attack specific currencies. It is important to create the conditions for a two-way market in order to defuse the speculative pressure.

Clearly, we need to assess the objectives and the risks of each strategy. None of the choices looks simple, but urgent decisions are nonetheless needed.

The position of other European countries such as the United Kingdom and Italy, is of course rather different from the position of those countries who have remained in the ERM. These countries no longer have a nominal anchor, and can therefore set interest rates as they feel appropriate for domestic economic conditions. But they also need some self-discipline in order to keep inflation on a downward path. How they might best do this is also a key question we have to discuss.

Annex 3

Kumiharu Shigehara's Statement at the Press Conference on 17 December 1992 to Introduce Economic Outlook 52 (Excerpt)

In the context of discussion on immediate macroeconomic policy requirements in major OECD countries, following comments were made after those on the United States and Japan.

Policy management is more complicated in Europe. Germany's post-unification problems—a large budget deficit, underlying inflation in a range of 4.5 to 5 per cent and high interest rates—have affected monetary conditions and exchange rates in many European countries. In discussing policy requirements, it is useful to distinguish two groups of countries.

- For those countries whose currencies have depreciated recently, either through devaluations of their ERM parities or through floating, gains in international competitiveness and lower interest rates are likely to boost demand in the short run. But these countries must now develop a new and credible strategy for macroeconomic policies to bear down on inflation and to sustain higher growth of output and employment. The evidence suggests it will not be easy to re-establish policy credibility quickly.
- Countries maintaining exchange rate commitments vis-à-vis the Deutschemark or the ECU have maintained domestic interest rates above German levels, even though inflation performance in certain countries (for instance, in France, Denmark, and Ireland) is better than in Germany and is likely to remain so for some time. Over time, their better performance on prices and other fundamentals may permit them to reduce interest rates, without causing exchange rate pressures, towards levels consistent with their domestic objectives. But their policy dilemma would be eased if domestic conditions in Germany allowed lower interest rates there.

In Germany, further efforts to reduce budget deficits, in particular by cutting subsidies, would alleviate burdens on monetary policy. As regards monetary policy, if demand pressure in Germany proves to be weaker than embodied in our projections, this should allow the Bundesbank to reduce interest rates more rapidly than we have projected, a move which should be followed in low-inflation partner countries. But this monetary easing should be carefully timed so as not to reverse progress towards price stability.

Annex 4

Kumiharu Shigehara's Statement at the Working Party No. 3 Meeting on 5 March 1993

Economic and financial developments in Europe remain disquieting. European exchange rate changes since last September have not been conducive to promoting economic stability. In Germany, despite the effective appreciation of the DM, inflation pressures are still strong, particularly in the non-tradeable sector. The high German interest rates that have been needed in order to lower inflation, which have been discussed here on several occasions since reunification in 1990, have faced other European countries with hard choices. Some have been forced to devalue their ERM parities or float. Others have had to accept higher risk premia over German interest rates in order to avoid downward pressure on their currencies. Indeed, among ERM partner countries which are currently experiencing lower inflation than in Germany, only the Netherland has nominal interest rates below German levels. Moreover, with the subdued inflation outlook in most ERM countries, real interest rates have been even higher, particularly at the short end of the market, and this is damaging growth prospects.

The domestic situation in those countries remaining in the ERM requires a significant cut in both short- and long-term interest rates from the current high levels. But this can only occur in the credible anti-inflation policies in such countries. Unless interest rates can be reduced sharply and quickly, it is difficult to see how a recovery strong enough to cut unemployment can get underway in these low-inflation countries. Pressure is already mounting for further easing which would reverse the progress towards budgetary consolidation.

The most desirable scenario to solve the European dilemma would be one in which wage and price pressures in Germany ease quickly and substantially and agreement is reached on a large cut in German fiscal deficit. In this case there would be considerable scope for interest rates to fall to levels that Germany's partner countries in the ERM would find more tolerable. As this would remove the principal source of doubt about those countries' willingness or ability to maintain their exchange rate commitments, it is likely that the risk premia built into short- and long-term market rates would also decline. While the Secretariat foresees a steady easing of German short-term interest rates during 1993, there is a question-mark over whether it can take place rapidly enough and go far enough to relieve pressures within the ERM.

Given this question-mark, it is only prudent to examine whether there are other policy options to deal with the European dilemma and what the pros and cons of such options are. One option would be to a general realignment of ERM parities, in which the Deutschemark would be revalued against those currencies where the pressures are most severe. This would probably ease the immediate pressures, contributing to disinflation in Germany and allowing reductions in interest rates, at least at the short end of markets in other countries which actually enjoy lower inflation than Germany. However, such a general realignment could adversely affect the credibility of monetary policies which have invested a great deal during the past ten years, with considerable success, to build up their credibility. As a result, there is a risk that, under this option, long-term interest rates might rise rather than fall. In addition, devaluation against the Deutschemark would have an adverse effect on inflation prospects in these countries. On the other hand, the appreciation of the Deutschemark alone might not improve inflation prospects in Germany on a durable basis, particularly if large resource transfers continue to be made to the eastern *Länder* over the medium term.

A second option would be to introduce greater exchange rate flexibility by widening the fluctuation band of the Deutschemark vis-à-vis other currencies within the ERM. This option would have the advantage of maintaining the broad structure of existing arrangements, and thus be consistent with plans for the Economic and Monetary Union (EMU). It would be important that the widening of the band for the Deutschemark be sufficient to accommodate depreciations against the Deutschemark that would flow from the desired reductions in interest rates in partner countries. As with the realignment option, the demonstrated willingness to depreciate the currency against the Deutschemark would carry an inflation risk which could lead to higher long-term interest rates. However, if market participants could be convinced that such a depreciation would not reflect accommodation of domestic inflation but rather a shift to more appropriate domestic policies which are justified by fundamentals, there need not be such an adverse impact on credibility. A clear commitment to both short- and medium-term price stability, which could be given concrete expression by the announcement of inflation targets, would do much in this regard; this commitment could be enhanced by increasing central bank independence in some countries. Provided credibility is secured, there would be a strong chance of maintaining better wage and price performance in these countries than in Germany. Once the market became aware of this, the prospect of an eventual appreciation against the Deutschemark might be generated. This would both limit depreciation, even in the short term, despite sharply lower interest rates, and at the same time encourage lower long-term interest rates.

A third option, in some respects similar to the second, would be to temporarily float the major ERM currencies. However, the virtual suspension of the existing European Monetary System might be a more severe blow to European integration than the wider band option. It might well stifle current efforts to achieve EMU along the agreed timetable.

This quick review of options suggests that there is no panacea. One could also argue that the best timing for a substantial change in the exchange rate arrangements for countries remaining in the ERM has already gone. For these countries, there may be grounds for sticking to the chosen strategy, at least for the moment, and hoping for an easing of monetary conditions via early substantial falls in German interest rates. In the meantime, faster growth abroad, or protectionist moves at home, as well as calling for sharp and rapid monetary easing in Germany, may increase market participants' doubts about the sustainability of the current strategy adopted in these countries, widen risk premia on their interest rates, and dampen credit demand and growth.

The experience of countries which have already depreciated their currencies is somewhat mixed. However, on the whole it appears to confirm the view that the alternative of increasing exchange rate flexibility to allow some monetary easing could be counterproductive unless it can be accomplished without adversely affecting the credibility of the authorities' resolve to achieve and maintain price stability as well as to restore fiscal balance. The loss of confidence in the fiscal authorities, which to an important degree precipitated the crisis in Italy, continues to require a large risk premium in the market. In the United Kingdom and Sweden, following sharp declines in short-term rates, long-term rates have also fallen, but they still exceed German levels—an indication of market concern about the future inflation outlook or about fiscal consolidation in both countries given the sharp rise in public sector deficits in the last years. It is important to engineer a significant reduction in the greater risk premia on interest rates which actually exist vis-à-vis German rates. This will require the establishment of an institutional framework conducive to domestic price stability, irrespective of the type of exchange rate arrangements adopted by European countries. It will also require credible medium-term plans for fiscal consolidation.

Annex 5

Kumiharu Shigehara's Statement at the Economic Policy Committee Meeting on 10 November 1993 (Excerpt)

The following remarks on the policy option of widening temporarily the bands for mandatory intervention under the ERM to enlarge the scope for using monetary policy for domestic economic considerations were made after my comments on the role of short- and long-term interests in domestic economic management at the wrap-up session on the second day of the autumn 1993 meeting of the EPC.

In Europe, more precisely in continental Europe, which may have reached the trough, the projected recovery is weak; faster growth would help. The fiscal situation is most serious in Europe. Scope for fiscal stimulus is virtually nil. On the other hand, when it comes to monetary policy, in contrast to Japan, no body expressed doubt about its effectiveness, it was on the scope for action that views somewhat diverged.

- In Germany, long-term interest rates are the most important variables;
- In Belgium, its central bank representative also argues that long-term rates are more important than short-term rates;
- In France, short-term rates are still important (hence, if there is scope for further interest ease, it would have a significant impact on activity).

Another important channel in the open-economy context is the exchange rate. Because this is such a powerful transmission mechanism in EC countries with deeply integrated markets for goods and services, there is heightened concern over competitive devaluations if countries start to make fuller use of the wider band without co-ordination. Having said this, costs involved in maintaining the ERM in terms of lost output and higher unemployment are great, particularly if a cyclical rise in unemployment becomes a rise in the structural component through hysteresis. We must also take into account the costs of trade protection, including EC barriers against products of central and eastern Europe which are harmful to the recovery of these economies.

After the September 1992 crisis of the ERM, which was something we had anticipated but did not lead to lasting solutions, within the Secretariat, we, or at least I, started to argue for wider bands without changing the central parities.

A major question at the time was whether and how the situation could be established in which Germany's partner countries with lower inflation could start the process of monetary easing without creating the perception in the market that these countries are not compromising their inflation objectives, which would increase risk premiums on financial assets of these countries and put downward pressure on the exchange rate.

Could the articulation of inflation objectives, and intermediate monetary targets, as well as full autonomy of the central bank, help enhance the credibility of price stabilisation objectives of Germany's partner countries? If so, exchange rate declines associated with monetary easing in Germany's partner countries might be limited, so long as markets realise that Germany will eventually follow its partner countries in the easing process.

Appreciation of the DM through monetary easing in Germany's partner countries can reduce inflation pressure in Germany and weaken its competitiveness further, hence the scope for German ease will increase. Once this expectation is embedded in the market, then the DM may not rise sharply against its partner countries.

Can such a situation be created? Now that the markets appear to have detected that countries are shadowing the DM, it would be more difficult to do so than several months ago. But I think there is still something the governments and central banks should learn on the job, together with market participants.

Given the time constraints, lwould not elaborate on priority areas for structural reforms in Europe. I might just say that the reform of the labour market is high on the agenda.

Notes

1. In the light of this development, a new volume in the OECD Monetary Studies Series with the title of "Monetary Targets and Inflation Control" was published in 1979. It was followed by another volume titled "Budget Financing and Monetary Control" published in 1982. This focused on the implication of financing high budget deficits for aggregates-oriented monetary policy and the extent to which increased public sector borrowing may constrain the financing of the private sector. The last volume in the OECD Monetary Studies Series "Exchange Rate Management and the Conduct of Monetary Policy" was published in 1985.
2. Margins in the ERM for Italy were set at 6 per cent until 1990 when they were narrowed to 2.25 per cent.
3. The United Kingdom joined the ERM in 1990.
4. Jean-Claude Paye, former French diplomat, had good contact with Pacal Lamy, then chef de cabinet for Jacques Delors, the president of the European Commission (later Director-General of the World Trade Organization), who after the 1992 Danish Maastricht Treaty referendum reportedly remarked that, "Europe was built in a Saint-Simonian (i.e., technocratic) way from the beginning, this was (Jean) Monnet's approach: The people weren't ready to agree to integration, so you had to get on without telling them too much about what was happening. Now Saint-Simonianism is finished. It can't work when you have to face democratic opinion".
5. Bernard Connolly, "The Rotten Heart of Europe: The Dirty War for Europe's Money", Faber and Faber, London, 1995, p.324. Mark Carney, former Governor of the Bank of Canada and former Governor of the Bank of England, reportedly identified Connolly as one of the very few economists who predicted the 2010 era global economic and financial crisis. See: Landon Thomas Jr., "Words of a Euro Doomsayer Have New Resonance", The New York Times, 17 November 2011.
6. OECD, "Policy Issues in the Transition to EMU", ESD/CPE/WP3(92)1, 25 March 1992.
7. Thomas Egebo and Steven Englander, "Institutional commitments and policy credibility: a critical survey and empirical evidence from the ERM", OECD Economic Studies, No. 18, Spring 1992;

Thomas Egebo, "Adjustment under fixed exchange rates: application to the European Monetary Union", OECD Economic Studies, No. 20, Spring 1993.

8. These interventions were made by Kumiharu Shigehara in his capacity of Head of the Economics Department of the Organisation for Economic Co-operation and Development (OECD). The opinions expressed and arguments employed herein do not necessarily reflect the official views of OECD Member countries.
9. Herbert Stein was an American economist and the chairman of the Council of Economic Advisers under the governments of Richard Nixon and Gerald Ford.

CHAPTER 16

Inflation Targeting and Alternative Monetary Policy Approaches

Adoption of Numerical Inflation Targets

This chapter starts with a review of the numerical inflation targets which a number of OECD countries adopted in the first half of the 1990s. It then discusses the optimal rate of inflation and the significance of two per cent as an inflation target, together with the implications for inflation targeting and alternative monetary policy approaches of central banks' errors in forecasting and analysis of root causes of financial and economic shocks. It also describes the author's involvement in international efforts to establish and strengthen central bank independence.

As noted in Chapter 7, one of the conclusions from the series of OECD studies on monetary policy during the 1960s was that the outcome of monetary policy did not appear to depend very much on the choice of instruments or details of the operating procedures. From the 1970s onward, significant convergence of monetary policy instruments occurred across OECD countries, with greater emphasis on the use of market-oriented instruments. The shift was a natural response to the evolution of national and international financial markets induced by deregulation and innovation in a more competitive environment. The experience of OECD economies during the 1970s and the 1980s also led to greater convergence of views on the use of macroeconomic policies. The view came to be shared widely among OECD countries that the ultimate

K. Shigehara, *The Bank of Japan, the OECD, and Beyond*,
https://doi.org/10.1007/978-981-97-5307-9_16

macroeconomic policy objective of raising living standards on a sustainable basis requires the management of macroeconomic policy in order to provide a stable non-inflationary environment. An important conclusion of the OECD Jobs Study (1994) was that credible commitment to non-inflationary monetary policy would favourably influence wage and price formation throughout the economy, and contribute to lower inflation premia in market interest rates. This would provide a favourable backdrop for decisions about current resource allocation and new investment.[1] The use of fiscal policies while fighting inflation with tight monetary policy led to high real interest rates, exchange rate misalignments, rapid increases in public debt, and allocative distortions in the 1980s. These adverse consequences made it difficult to establish the credibility of monetary policy geared to price stability.

In the first half of the 1990s, a number of OECD countries adopted numerical inflation targeting. They were generally countries with a historical record of relatively high inflation, and inflation targeting meant both as a way of communicating the goal of monetary policy to the general public and a guide to assessing central bank performance. New Zealand was the first country which introduced this approach under the policy target agreement between the finance minister and the Reserve Bank governor in 1990. Canada started inflation targeting in 1991 in the form of a joint declaration by the Canadian government and the Bank of Canada. In the United Kingdom, the Chancellor of the Exchequer, who was ultimately responsible for monetary policy until the Bank of England was given independence from the government by the Bank of England Act of 1998, announced the adoption of inflation targets in October 1992. The central banks of Sweden and Finland followed suit in early 1993, the Bank of Spain in the autumn of 1994, and the Bank of Italy in 1995. In Australia, a flexible inflation target was introduced, initially as a broad central tendency for inflation in the early 1990s.

It is interesting to note that, unlike the generalised shift to monetary targeting in the mid-1970s, the successive adoption of numerical inflation targeting by these countries in the first half of the 1990s was not significantly influenced by academic discussion on this targeting rule. Rather, this trend was an outcome of the difficult environment in which central banks found themselves. In fact, in many countries, the introduction of inflation targeting in this period was preceded by difficulties with exchange rate targets, including currency depreciation after withdrawal from the ERM (the United Kingdom and Italy), suspension of the pegging of currencies to the ECU (Finland and Sweden), and devaluations and depreciation under the wider bands (Spain). Having lost the exchange rate as a nominal anchor, these countries resorted to inflation targets to help stabilise inflation expectations. In some other countries which had floating exchange rates, inflation targeting followed a decline in the effectiveness of money growth as an intermediate target or a guidepost to control inflation (Canada and New Zealand).

As with monetary targeting, ranges, rather than points, were generally set for inflation targets at the time of the adoption of inflation targeting (only Finland adopted a point target). These were typically 2–3 percentage points wide. The measures of inflation used for targeting were usually the consumer or retail price index which is released monthly, with a fairly short lag and normally without revision, rather than the GDP deflator which is available only on quarterly basis, with a long lag and is often revised. In some cases, the index was adjusted: for example, the effects of changes in interest rates affecting housing costs may be excluded. In some other cases, "escape clauses" or exemptions to the strict implementation of targets were provided for changes in indirect taxes and commodity prices. It was recognised that there is a trade-off between credibility of inflation targeting and the width of target ranges or flexibility embedded in "escape clauses".

In practice, the conduct of monetary policy did not differ markedly between countries which adopted inflation targets and those which used monetary aggregates or exchange rates as intermediate targets. The German Bundesbank, which adhered to M3 as preferred intermediate target, specified the "unavoidable" increase in prices in numerical terms (usually a maximum of 2 per cent) at the time of announcing monetary targets. Issing wrote that "The Bundesbank never understood an orientation towards a monetary target as meaning that no other factors could be included in its deliberations".[2] Indeed, fairly wide target ranges were set for M3, actual outcomes were allowed to deviate, sometimes substantially, from annual target ranges, and past deviations were not systematically taken into account in setting the annual target for the following year. Yet, the inflation track record of the Bundesbank was, on the whole, good. German inflation in trems of the GDP deflator over the period of 1980-1995 averaged 3.0 per cent.

Even better price performance was achieved by the Bank of Japan, with inflation in terms of the GDP deflator averaging 1.6 per cent over the period of 1980–95. It adopted an eclectic approach, without relying on numerical inflation or monetary targets, as noted in my paper presented to an international seminar organised by the Reserve Bank of Australia in 1990.[3] However, domestic asset prices, in particular real estate prices, rose sharply in the late 1980s, in part as a result of heavy emphasis on monetary easing for the purpose of balance of payments adjustment. In a seminal paper, Alchian and Klein argued that the prices of both current and future goods and services should be incorporated in a correct measure of inflation, and considered the inclusion of asset prices which embody the relative price of future goods and services.[4] But, given far greater volatility in asset prices than other prices in the latter half of the 1980s in Japan, targeting a measure of inflation including asset prices could have caused large offsetting variations in the prices of current goods and services and in output activity, depending on a weight to be attached to asset prices. Leaving aside the issue of including asset prices in a general measure of inflation, the identification of the appropriate level of (or rate of increase in) asset prices remains an unresolved issue.

Like the Bank of Japan, the US Federal Reserve System under the chairmanship of Alan Greenspan did not announce numerical inflation targets. He defined price stability as "price levels sufficiently stable that expectations of changes do not become major factors in key economic decisions".[5] The inflation track record of the Federal Reserve for the fifteen-year period of 1980–95, averaging an annual 3.9 per cent in terms of the GDP deflator, was less satisfactory than those of the Bank of Japan and the Bundesbank. But considerable progress towards price stability was achieved by the mid-1990s. While target ranges of a set of monetary and credit aggregates were announced each year under the Humphrey-Hawkins Act, heavy reliance on such aggregates as a guide-post had long disappeared. Instead, the Federal Reserve operated, like the Bank of Japan, under what Benjamin Friedman called "the information variable approach", looking at a whole range of economic and financial indicators.[6]

Observing inflation performance for the fifteen-year period of 1980–95 in those major countries where the central banks had not adopted numerical inflation targeting and in the light of other relevant evidence, in the concluding part of my keynote speech titled “The Options Regarding the Concept of a Monetary Policy Strategy” delivered at the symposium “Monetary Policy Strategies in Europe” organised by the Bundesbank on 16 April 1996, I remarked:

> (V)arious monetary policy experiments since that period (the 1960s) reviewed in this lecture suggest that there is no single optimal rule for the conduct of monetary policy that would ensure stability of economies which are exposed to a variety of unanticipated financial and real shocks. In no country is knowledge of the transmission process, time-lags and the magnitude of monetary policy effects robust enough to support rigid adherence to a specific monetary rule. In this light, monetary authorities have to act with a certain degree of discretion, while ensuring accountability and transparency which are particularly important in retaining public support for their decision-making based on longer-term consideration of achieving satisfactory price performance.[7]

My lecture was followed by a speech by Mervyn King (then Executive Director and Chief Economist of the Bank of England) titled “Direct Inflation Targets” and another one by Nout Wellink (then Executive Director of De Nederlandsche Bank) titled “The Role of Exchange Rates in Monetary Policy: The European Monetary System”.

The Optimal Rate of Inflation and Two Per Cent as an Inflation Target

Among academic economists, there was much debate on the optimal rate of inflation. One extreme view was that it should be negative. Based on a simple model in which the only cost of inflation arises from the efficiency loss associated with the taxation of money balances, the proponents of this view argue that the incentive to economise on real balances should be removed by negative inflation at a rate that reduces the nominal interest rate to zero. The welfare losses arising from taxing money balances seem to be fairly small relative to the distortionary effects of inflation on nominal contracting arrangements which impair the efficiency of the price mechanism. Inflation also distorts the measurement of taxable income, in particular income from capital, and can discourage capital accumulation. These distortions are eliminated at zero inflation.

Measuring true zero inflation has turned out to be difficult, owing largely to measurement biases in price indices. They have reflected various factors, including insufficient measurement of quality improvement, substitution among products not reflected in fixed-weight indexes, the introduction of new products, substitution among outlets in favour of lower-cost retail outlets, as well as short-run distortion of inflation measures caused by misleading measures of housing costs. While there is uncertainty about the precise size of measurement biases, targeting a zero inflation in terms of the consumer price index has been considered to imply a deflationary bias, and a small, but positive, rate of inflation has generally been regarded zero inflation in reality.

Economists have also debated whether a rate of inflation higher than zero (after adjustment for any measurement biases) is optimal. One argument has been that positive inflation could facilitate a reduction in relative real wages required for efficient resource allocation in the face of downward rigidities of nominal wages and prices. A second argument for positive inflation has been based on the fact that nominal interest rates cannot fall below zero which means that real interest rates could not fall below zero inflation. It has been argued that the zero-interest-rate floor reduces the usefulness of monetary policy in responding to deflationary demand shocks.[8]

In January 2012, the US Federal Reserve under the chairmanship of Ben Bernanke announced that inflation at the rate of 2 per cent, as measured by the annual change in the price index for personal consumption expenditures, is most consistent over the longer run with its statutory mandate.[9]

In January 2013, the Bank of Japan under heavy pressure from the Abe government announced to set "the price stability target" at 2 per cent in terms of the year-on-year rate of change in the consumer price index (CPI). Previously, it had adopted a positive range of 2 per cent or lower in terms of the year-on-year rate of change in the CPI as "price stability goal in the medium to long term" and set "a goal of 1 per cent for the time being".[10]

The price stability mandate of the European Central Bank (ECB) set out in the Treaty on the Functioning of the European Union did not give a precise definition of what is meant by price stability. However, from its start in October 1998, it stated that "price stability" was meant to be an increase of less than 2 per cent in the harmonised index of consumer prices (HICP). In 2003, the ECB's inflation target was set as "less but close to 2 per cent". After concluding its strategy review in July 2021, the ECB's Governing Council announced that price stability should be maintained by aiming for 2 per cent inflation over the medium term. The ECB chose HICP as the appropriate measure for assessing the achievement of the price stability objective, while noting that the inclusion of costs related to owner-occupied housing in the HICP would better represent the inflation rate, and it was working on including those costs in the inflation measure. The ECB's argument for the adoption of the 2 per cent inflation target was described in Chapter 14 of this book.

Errors in Forecasting and Analysis of Root Causes of Financial and Economic Shocks

As a Federal Reserve Director, Donald Kohn (later member of the Board and Vice Chairman) once noted that "making monetary policy is about forecasting".[11] This applies not only to the Federal Reserve, but to all other central banks. In this context, it is notable that central banks in inflation-targeting countries have placed increased emphasis on explicit inflation forecasts. These are published on a regular (often quarterly) basis, normally with a time horizon of two years. Perhaps, increased public attention to these central banks' published inflation forecasts is a key element which in practice distinguishes the inflation-targeting approach. In his capacity of Executive Director and Chief Economist of the Bank of England, King stated that the aim of inflation targeting was to convince private sector agents that the inflation target was credible.

However, inflation forecasting, like any economic forecasting, is subject to considerable uncertainties. Major forecasting errors were made in the runup to and during the global financial and economic crisis that prevailed from mid-2007 to early 2009 and the euro-area crisis which erupted in late 2009. More recently, high inflation far exceeding the price forecasts of most Western central banks upset private economic agents and gave rise to political backlashes against central banks.

Among them, the Reserve Bank of Australia (RBA) came under particular heavy political pressure and in July 2022, the Australian Treasurer Jim Chalmers commissioned the first independent review of the bank since its monetary policy arrangements were instituted in the early 1990s, including looking into the inflation target, monetary tools, board structure, accountability, public communications, and culture. In March 2023, the report prepared by three independent reviewers[12] was delivered to the Treasurer, with 51 recommendations including reforming the board of directors, improving communication, and enhancing the bank's accountability, without recommending major changes in the 2 per cent to 3 per cent inflation target. Treasurer said in a statement: "This review is all about ensuring the RBA has the right processes, structure, culture and objectives to help it make its important decisions independently".

In the United Kingdom, in a speech delivered on 4 January 2023, Prime Minister Rishi Sunak identified a quick decline in inflation as the first among the five foundations on which he wished to build a better future for UK children and grandchildren, saying that "(F)irst, we will halve inflation this year to ease the cost of living and give people financial security". In July 2023, the Bank of England announced that Ben Bernanke, former Chairman of the US Federal Reserves had agreed to lead a review into the Bank's forecasting and related processes during times of significant uncertainty, and that he would be supported by the Bank's Independent Evaluation Office.

Prior to these developments at some central banks in the English-speaking world, I contributed an article to the 22 September 2022 issue of a Japanese weekly economic journal "*Sekai-Keizai-Hyoron* (World Economic Review)" in which I called for a fundamental review of the Bank of Japan's economic forecasting exercise in the light of its unsatisfactory performance. Furthermore, in the summer of 2023, I organised a meeting with two Japanese academic monetary experts to discuss how to improve frameworks for central banking in Japan. The issues covered in our discussion included the needs to correct tendency towards "groupthink" within the Bank, to strengthen the analytical ability of its professional staff resources, and to improve the selection process of the Bank's policy makers and other senior officials.[13]

Around the same time, a group of senior advisers to the Center for Financial Stability (CFS), an independent, nonpartisan, and nonprofit think tank focused on financial markets,[14] undertook an assessment of the root causes of the failures of the three mid-sized US banks: Silicon Valley Bank (SVB), Signature Bank (SBNY), and First Republic Bank (FRB). Their failures had given rise to concern about the safety of bank deposits and the stability of the US banking system. These advisers identified the role played by monetary and fiscal policy in the United States as the first among the root causes of their failures. They noted that the Federal Reserve's "overly accommodative" monetary policy stance for an extended period was followed by an "over-tightening" in early 2023, adding that excessive fiscal stimulus made the Federal Reserve's task harder.

At the same time, they reported that they had not found the word "monetary" once in the text of the combined 171 pages in the Board of Governors of the Federal Reserve System's "Review of the Federal Reserve's Supervision and Regulation of Silicon Valley Bank" and its Office of the Inspector General's "Material Loss Review of Silicon Valley Bank". These reports found faults in SVB management, the supervisory process, and regulation rather than monetary policy. In light of these observations, the Center's senior advisers recommended that the Federal Reserve leadership should actively work to thwart groupthink to diminish the risk of future policy errors.[15]

Central Bank Independence

In preparing the Secretariat's draft policy recommendations for inclusion in the OECD Survey of the United Kingdom for 1995, I as Head of the Economics Department asked the UK Desk in its Country Studies Branch to include a specific paragraph to argue for giving to the Bank of England independence from the British government in the conduct of UK monetary policy in its draft report.

The draft review report prepared along the lines of this argument by the Department are to be discussed by the OECD Economic and Development Review Committee (EDRC), and after its discussion the draft report is to be amended by the Secretariat, taking into account the comments from the country under review as well as those from the other members of the Committee, and to be approved by the Committee before publication. As such, OECD Economic Surveys differ from the OECD Economic Outlook which is published under the authority of the OECD Secretary-General and was effectively under my final editorial responsibility at least during the time I was Head of the Economics Department and Chief Economist.

In the process of preparing the final version of the OECD Survey of the United Kingdom for 1995, the UK government representatives requested that the OECD recommendation that independence should be granted to the Bank of England be deleted. Subsequently, an internal report came to my office that the negotiation between the UK authorities and the OECD Secretariat at the level of the Country Studies Branch of the Economics Department had come to a deadlock. This eventually led to a direct telephone call from me to Alan Budd, then Chief Economic Advisor of UK Treasury and the United Kingdom's principal representative to the EPC, to negotiate. Between us, we were able to reach a compromise agreement on the wording, but Budd asked for some time to make a final deal between us. Because of the politics involved, it appeared necessary for Budd to take the matter up to the Chancellor of the Exchequer and to get his approval on the wording. In the end, Budd called me back to confirm that we could go with the text agreed between us. The OECD Secretariat thus managed to include the following text in the published version of the 1995 Survey of the United Kingdom, broadly in line with my initial suggestion that the Bank of England should be ensured by law to be responsible for its independent operation of monetary policy (operational independence), though the word "possibly" which had not existed in the draft report was added in the final version.

> *Credibility might be further enhanced by giving the Bank responsibility (possibly with legal backing) for determining the size and timing of interest rate changes.*

The OECD Survey of the United Kingdom was published in July 1995. Eventually, in May 1997, Gordon Brown, then Chancellor of the Exchequer, announced that the Bank of England, which had been nationalised since 1946, would be given independence to manage monetary policy. In the following year, 1998, a new Bank of England Act was enacted. This made it the Bank of England's primary responsibility to achieve an inflation target determined by the Chancellor of the Exchequer, and gave it independence from the government in the conduct of its policies. However, it was also stated that the Bank of England was not to be separate from the government's economic policy, and was required to support the government's economic policy as long as price stability was ensured.

Twenty years later, in September 2017, the Bank of England held a conference entitled "Bank of England independence: the last 20 years". It began with a keynote speech by Governor Mark Carney that was followed by discussions among a wide range of speakers on the significance of central bank independence. As a former OECD official who was involved, though marginally, in the process leading to the new Bank of England Act, I watched the London event online from Tokyo.[16]

Exactly twenty years before this event in London, in September 1997, the International Economic Association (IEA) held a conference "Monetary Theory as a Basis for Monetary Policy" in Trento, Italy.[17] In the Introduction of the proceedings of the conference which were subsequently published by Palgrave in 2001, Axel Leijonhufvud, then professor at the University of Trento and the editor of the proceedings, wrote that "the planning for the conference began in the summer of 1996, well before the Asian plunges into depression. But even if the theme did not adumbrate such dramatic developments or their further ramifications in Russia and elsewhere, it concerned related issues. The conference was intended to start a debate over the relationship between current economic theory and central bank practice".

Leijonhufvud also noted that "(M)onetary neutrality has gained a stronger hold over theory since the inflationary 1970s, starting with the monetarist doctrines that the Philips curve is vertical and that inflation expectations explain nominal interest rates, later becoming embedded in more fully articulated models of intertemporal general equilibrium. The theory resulting from this development leaves central banks with nothing useful to do except to stabilize the price level. It is not an altogether unwelcome doctrine among central bankers, as it frees them from responsibility for difficult trade-offs and, in addition, it has become the basis of the recent fashion for giving central banks independence from political authority".

The Trento conference was attended by prominent monetary economists in academia including two winners of the Nobel Prize for economics, Robert Mundell and Robert Lucas, and central bank economists including John Crow (former Governor, Bank of Canada), Dale Henderson (Federal Reserve Board, United States), Otmar Issing (Chief Economist, Deutsche Bundesbank), and Pedro Pou (Governor, Central Bank of Argentina) as well as myself.

In the summer of 1997, Leijonhufvud came to visit me in my office at the OECD and asked me to present a paper to the conference. I hurriedly prepared a paper with the title of "Monetary Policy and Economic Performance: The Recent Experience of the United States and Japan". In this paper, I examined the extent to which the evolution of monetary policy frameworks and actual policy decisions in the two countries contributed to the differences in their macroeconomic performance in the 1980s and 1990s. It considered the extent to which monetary policy decision-making was faulty, and how it might have been done better, given the information available to policymakers at the time. The discussion in it provided some insights into the contribution of academic thinking to monetary making, based in part on my experience as a central banker and a policy adviser in an international organisation engaged in international economic co-operation. My conclusion was that monetary policy frameworks did not differ in most respects between the United States and Japan during this period and that, with one important exception, the difference in policy frameworks that did exist does not explain the differences in macroeconomic performance, the exception being that, under the law then in effect, the Bank of Japan was less independent from the government than the Federal Reserves. I wrote that this constraint, coupled with some errors of judgement, impeded the proper decision-making of monetary policy at a critical juncture during the period reviewed in my paper.

More specifically, I pointed out that the Japanese monetary policy was too loose, leading up to the bubble economy in the latter half of the 1980s, and, despite political resistance and other difficulties, policy makers should have tightened financial conditions earlier than they did to correct the imbalances that were building up. I also argued that monetary policy should have been eased more aggressively in the early stages of the recession in the 1990s, although it would have been difficult for policy makers at the time, with the history of the bubble in their minds, to formulate and justify bold action.

On US monetary policy, I concluded that it was in fact generally well-executed during this period, but it had some help at times from fortuitous movements in asset prices. Thus, I added a caveat that there are pitfalls in an "eclectic" approach in monetary policy, but also there were reasons why neither the Federal Reserves nor the Bank of Japan could not follow a simple rule-based strategy, as advocated by some academics.

In a letter to me on 23 January 1998, Alan Greenspan, then Chairman of the Federal Reserve Board, wrote: "(T)he paper raises a number of important issues for both countries that are pertinent to the conduct of monetary policy. You highlight the operational autonomy for a central bank, including its effect in enhancing credibility. The independence of the Federal Reserve has been an essential element not just in our recent success in achieving sustained growth in a low-inflation environment, but over the much longer run as well. In view of your observation that the Bank of Japan was constrained at times in the past by a lack of independence, the implementation within a few months of the new law that gives the Bank greater operational autonomy should be a very helpful development".

My comments on the conduct of the Bank of Japan's monetary policy since it was given operational independence[18] were described in the latter part of Chapter 13 and Chapter 14.

As to the conduct of US monetary policy from the early part of the 2000s onward, I wrote in a paper co-authored with Paul Atkinson[19] that:

- Debate continues in the United States on the role played by monetary policy in causing the financial crisis. On the one hand, Bernanke (2010) and Greenspan (2010) strongly deny that the low interest rate policy followed by the Federal Reserve during the early part of the 2000s was responsible and posited that the "global saving glut" was the main cause of financial imbalances in the US. On the other hand, Taylor holds the view that easy monetary policy during that period contributed significantly to the housing boom, to excessive risk-taking, and thereby to the financial crisis in the United States. Referring to a Taylor Rule, Gordon puts forward a similar view. Obsfeld and Rogoff also assign some role to monetary policy.

- Bernanke argued that "interest rate increases in 2003 or 2004 sufficient to constrain the bubble could have seriously weakened the economy at just the time when the recovery from the previous recession was becoming established". He also asserted "monetary policy from 2002 to 2006 appears to have been reasonably consistent with the Federal Reserve's mandated goals of maximum sustainable employment and price stability".
- In retrospect, it is clear that the Federal Reserve did not succeed in this regard even during the period preceding the crisis. Overall CPI inflation edged up from relatively low levels to above 3 per cent in 2005, fluctuated around that level in the subsequent two years and rose sharply in 2008 before collapsing in 2009. During this period, the private consumption deflator showed a broadly similar inflation pattern. Thus, monetary policy was too loose even by Bernanke's own standard.

On a critical comment on the conduct of US monetary policy for an extended period which was followed by an "over-tightening" in early 2023, see the report by a group of senior advisers to the Center for Financial Stability noted in the previous section "Errors in forecasting and analysis of root causes of financial and economic shocks" in this chapter.

The Role of Central Banks in Globalised Financial Markets

One interesting international event concerning the role of central banks in which I was involved dates back to 1991, when I was invited to participate in an activity of the InterAction Council. This body was established in 1983 under the initiative of former Japanese Prime Minister Takeo Fukuda, with Helmut Schmidt, former Chancellor of West Germany, as its chairman and Takeo Fukuda as its honorary chairman. It used to hold its general meeting before the G7 Summit each year to present its policy recommendations in the form of a declaration. As a main theme for the Council's declaration in 1991, Schmidt chose "The Role of Central Banks in a Globalised Financial Markets". He initially intended to chair a meeting to discuss issues on this theme with some members of the Council and high-level experts selected from G5 countries as well as central bank governors and other monetary and financial experts of several non-OECD countries. However, because of his health problem, he asked Valéry Giscard d'Estaing, former French President and a member of the Council, to chair a meeting at the Luxembourg Palace in Paris on 19–20 April 1991. It was attended by four other members of the InterAction Council – Maria de Lourdes Pintasilgo (former Portuguese prime minister), Malcolm Fraser (former Australian prime minister), Manuel Ulloa (former Peruvian prime minister), and Olusegun Obasanjo (former Nigerian president).

As experts from G5 countries, Stephen Axilrod (former Staff Director for Monetary and Financial Policy, US Federal Reserve Board), John Heimann (former US Comptroller of the Currency), Norbert Walter (Deutsche Bank Chief Economist), Robert Raymond (Directeur-Général du Crédit, Banque de France) and Michael Hewitt (Director of Central Bank Studies, Bank of England) as well as myself (Bank of Japan Chief Economist) were invited. As experts from Eastern European countries were Victor Gerashchenko (Chairman of the Gosbank of the Soviet Union), Josef Tosovsky (Chairman of the Czechoslovak State Bank), Irme Tarafas (First Deputy President of the Bank of Hungary), and one expert each from India, Pakistan, and Brazil were also invited, but none from China.

It is noteworthy that the importance of central bank independence and inflation targeting was chosen as the first among the ten recommendations included in the report which was sent to the plenary meeting of the InterAction Council and subsequently published. More specifically, it was argued in the report that the European System of Central Banks, the Bank of Japan and the US Federal Reserve all should pursue an identical goal, namely zero inflation, see below:

"*The InterAction Council should send a signal to all the relevant national and international authorities that the time is ripe for the adoption of a comprehensive approach concerning the role of central banks and supervisors in the new financial environment. aiming at stability. transparency and efficiency.*

To this end, the High-level Expert Group formulated a ten-point strategy which the InterAction Council may wish to endorse. This strategy aims at greater transparency, stability and efficiency in financial markets through an adaptation of the role of central banks and other supervisors.

I. Ensuring the Independence of Central Banks

The best encouragement to stability in financial markets and to adequate private savings is the perception of monetary policies steadily oriented toward price stability. This is best accomplished through independent central banks with a clear mandate to that effect. It has been agreed that the new European System of Central Banks (ESCB) should have these characteristics but there is a need to reform accordingly the statutes of individual European national central banks. This is an example to be followed by central banks in Eastern and Central Europe and more broadly by non-OECD central banks.

An important lesson gained from economic policy management over the past two decades is indeed the primary importance of price stability as the ultimate objective of monetary policy, to be conducted by independent central banks taking a long-term view and being immune from day-to-day reactions to economic and financial developments. Another lesson is that a short-run trade-off exists between lower inflation and securing employment opportunities but that central banks should not aim at addressing conflicting goals. Hence, central bank efforts towards price stabilization need to be complemented by governmental fiscal policies and by structural policies to improve the labor and product markets in order to minimize the social costs involved in the process of disinflation. A convergence of objectives for medium-term inflation rates at the lowest possible levels in the United States, the European Community and Japan and the perception of monetary policies steadily oriented towards achieving such objectives will by itself encourage stability in financial markets. To ensure the independence of central banks is crucial in gaining and maintaining market credibility in their task of achieving price stability.

While deregulation makes coordination of monetary and exchange rate policies both more necessary and more difficult, independent national central banks would not necessarily ensure greater coordination between them (although, arguably, they might be more likely to collaborate effectively than Governments). But if the ESCB, the Bank of Japan and the US Federal Reserve all pursued an identical goal, namely zero inflation, equally effectively, their actions would be likely to be more consistent with each other".[20]

Notes

1. Kumiharu Shigehara, "Causes of Declining Growth in Industrialized Countries" in the proceedings of a symposium sponsored by the Federal Reserve Bank of Kansas City "Policies for Long-run Economic Growth", Missouri, 1992. In this paper, I argued that given the inherent uncertainty of our knowledge of the factors underlying productivity growth, a broad-based programme stands a better chance of success than approaches that emphasise more aggressive interventions across a narrow set of policies.
2. Otmar Issing, "Theoretical and Empirical Foundations of the Deutsche Bundesbank's Monetary Targeting", Intereconomics, November/December 1992.
3. Kumiharu Shigehara, "Japan's Experience with Monetary Policy and Financial Liberalisation", in Reserve Bank of Australia "Monetary Policy and Market Operation", 1990.
4. Armen Alchian and Benjamin Klein, "On a Correct Measure of Inflation", Journal of Money, Credit and Banking, Vol. 5, No. 1, pp. 173–191, February 1973.
5. Alan Greenspan, Statement before the Committee on Banking, Finance and Urban Affairs, US House of Representatives, 24 January 1989, Federal Reserve Bulletin, March 1989, pp. 139–142.
6. Benjamin Friedman, "The Role of Judgment and Discretion in the Conduct of Monetary Policy: Consequences of Changing Financial Markets", in "Changing Capital Markets: Implications for Monetary Policy", The Federal Reserve Bank of Kansas City, 1993.
7. Kumiharu Shigehara, "The Options Regarding the Concept of a Monetary Policy Strategy", in the Deutsche Bundesbank, "Monetary Policy Strategies in Europe". Verlag Vahlen, 1996, p. 34.
8. Lawrence Summers, "How should long-term monetary policy be determined?", Journal of Money, Credit and Banking, Vol. 23, No. 3, Part 2, August 1991, pp. 625–631.
9. The Board of Governors of the Federal Reserve System, Historical Statements on Longer-Run Goals and Monetary Policy Strategy.
10. The Bank of Japan, The "Price Stability Target" under the Framework for the Conduct of Monetary Policy, 22 January 2013, https://www.boj.or.jp/en/mopo/mpmdeci/mpr_2013/k130122b.pdf

11. Donald Kohn, "Commentary: The Role of Judgment and Discretion in the Conduct of Monetary Policy", Federal Reserve Bank of Kansas City, 1993.
12. Three reviewers were Canadian central banker Carolyn Wilkins, Australian National University economics professor Renee Fry-McKibbin and former senior Treasury official Gordon de Brouwer.
13. Kumiharu Shigehara, Nobuyuki Kitamura and Kazuhiko Yago, "*Nozomareru Chuôginkô no Arikata wo Megutte* (On what the central bank should be)" (in Japanese), Sekai-Keizai-Hyôron (World Economic Review), January/February 2024, pp. 73–80.
14. About this institution, see: https://centerforfinancialstability.org/about.php
15. Seila Blair, Joyce Chang, Charles Goodhart, Lawrence Goodman, Barbara Novick, and Richard Sandor, "The Role of Monetary and Fiscal Policies in Recent Bank Failures", Center for Financial Stability, 16 October 2023. https://centerforfinancialstability.org/research/CFSMonPaper101623.pdf
16. Bank of England, "Independence – 20 years on", https://www.bankofengland.co.uk/events/2017/september/20-years-on
17. "Monetary Policy and Economic Performance: The Recent Experience of the United States and Japan" in International Economic Association, "Monetary Theory and Policy Experience" (edited by Axel Leijonhifvud), Palgrave, 2001, pp. 36–65.
18. On the revision of the Bank of Japan Law of 1997, see Masanao Itoh, Yasuko Morita and Mari Ohnuki, "Monetary Policy in the 1990s: Bank of Japan's Views Summarized Based on Archives and Other Materials" in Monetary and Economic Policy Studies, Vol. 38, Bank of Japan, November 2020, pp. 109–110, https://www.imes.boj.or.jp/research/papers/english/me38-3.pdf
19. Kumiharu Shigehara and Paul Atkinson, "Surveillance by International Institutions: Lessons from the Global Financial and Economic Crisis" (co-authored with Paul Atkinson, OECD Working Papers No.860, May 2011), https://www.oecd-ilibrary.org/economics/surveillance-by-international-institutions_5kgchzchkvd2-en

20. InterAction Council, "The Role of Central Banks in Globalized Financial Markets", https://www.interactioncouncil.org/index.php/publications/role-central-banks-globalized-financial-markets About the InterAction Council, see: https://www.interactioncouncil.org

CHAPTER 17

Macroeconomic and Prudential Controls on International Financial Markets

Oil Money in the Eurodollar Market

Since its inception, the so-called Eurodollar market has functioned as a global financial market where transactions have been freely conducted regardless of the nationality of its participants without regulatory control. My involvement in policy discussions on macroeconomic policy issues related to this market dates back to the first period of my service at the OECD. In later years, I also dealt with prudential as well as macroeconomic policy aspects of international financial market activities both as a Bank of Japan official and as an OECD economist.

Following the massive increases in oil prices decided by the Organisation of Petroleum Exporting Countries (OPEC) in late 1973, Rinaldo Ossola, then chairman of the G10 deputies' meeting and Deputy Governor of the Bank of Italy, argued that if dollar revenues resulting from the huge external surpluses of OPEC countries were to be invested in the Eurodollar market, a multiple expansion of the global money supply would occur. Deposits placed in the Eurodollar market were free from administrative controls unlike dollar deposits in the US domestic banking system which were subjected to reserve requirements and interest rate ceiling controls. He thus was concerned that the OPEC countries' placement of surplus funds in the Eurodollar market was a new source of global inflation.

K. Shigehara, *The Bank of Japan, the OECD, and Beyond*,
https://doi.org/10.1007/978-981-97-5307-9_17

Not fully convinced by Ossola's argument, Otmar Emminger, Vice-President of the Bundesbank and Chairman of WP3, requested the OECD Secretariat to examine it, and Stephen Marris, then Director of the General Economics Branch, asked the Monetary Division to prepare a paper for WP3. Around that time, the staff resources of the Division which I headed were fully occupied with new work for the Committee for Monetary and Foreign Exchange Matters (established in 1973) on top of ongoing work on OECD Monetary Policy Studies (see Chapter 7). In addition, there was current work for WP3 and EPC. I ended up writing a draft paper myself and sent it first to a meeting of OECD high-level monetary experts to find out their reaction. Stephen Axilrod said it looked like a Ph.D thesis but did not object to the paper's conclusions which were:

- as long as fund flows between domestic money and capital markets rates and the Eurodollar market are determined by free market forces, the OPEC countries' surplus fund management in the Eurodollar market will not in itself lead to an unmanageable expansion of that market; and
- the liberalisation of the US financial system should be encouraged to play a more important place for OPEC countries' financial investments and that the US authorities should adopt more prudent fiscal policy for domestic demand control, while making more important use of monetary policy for exchange rate stability.

My paper was submitted to the WP3 meeting held in Tokyo in the spring of 1974. On that occasion, Chairman Emmiger approached me to tell me in person that he liked my paper and its copies had been widely circulated within the Bundesbank. The paper was then sent to the spring 1974 meeting of EPC, and was published in the July 1974 issue of OECD Economic Outlook under the title "Implications of the Oil Situation for Domestic Monetary Management".

I might note that I was not directly involved in BIS negotiations following a proposal from William Miller, then Chairman of the US Federal Reserve Board, made in the late 1970s (1978–1979) for establishing reserve requirements on Eurodollar deposits which came to nothing. They are described in some detail in Stephen Axilrod's memoirs "Inside the FED" (pp. 83–86).

Bank of Japan Guidance on Commercial Banks' International Financial Market Operations

I was appointed head of the Foreign Currency Operation Section of the Foreign Exchange Division in the Bank of Japan (BOJ)'s Foreign Department in November 1975, after a year's service in its Policy Coordination Department which was described in Chapter 8.

The main task of the Section I headed was to keep abreast of the international financial market operations of major Japanese commercial banks and the Japanese branches of foreign banks and to provide guidance with them as necessary to maintain the soundness of their international activities. For this purpose, some dozen staff members of my section were in daily contact with all of them to monitor their major foreign-currency operations and to check for any irregularities.

At the time, in the aftermath of the first oil crisis, the international financial community was concerned about Japan's foreign currency provisions, as the country had run a large current account deficit, and it became extremely difficult for Japanese banks to borrow funds on the Eurodollar market and elsewhere, with the so-called "Japan premium" attached to their external borrowing rates. In other words, Japanese banks could only procure foreign currency funds at higher rates than their Western counterparts. In some cases, sharp competition between Japanese banks to procure foreign currency funds raised their borrowing cost to an exorbitant level.

When these developments were first observed in the Eurodollar market in London, Reiichi Shimamoto (see Chapter 8), the BOJ's Chief Representative in London, with negotiation with the Bank of England, exercised his shrewd skills in watching Eurodollar transactions by Japanese banks in London and exercising moral suasion to maintaining orderly market conditions in the London market in close contact with the Bank of England. Eventually, my Section in the Bank's head office was charged with systematic surveillance of Japanese banks' international operations in not just London, but also New York and other major overseas markets.

In addition to monitoring their foreign currency procurement operations on a daily basis, my Section was in charge of setting quarterly guidelines for the total amounts of short-term lending abroad in foreign currencies by Japanese banks in order to maintain the soundness of their international credit operations. This guidance was similar to the way in which the BOJ Market Operations Department (*Eigyô-kyoku*) conducted over-the-counter guidance on yen lending by major Japanese banks at the time of monetary policy tightening for domestic demand management. Furthermore, to prevent excessive maturity transformation and help avoid liquidity shortage in foreign currencies, we asked Japanese banks to maintain the ratio of medium- to long-term foreign currency procurements to medium- to long-term foreign currency loans above certain levels specified by my Section.

It is true that such guidance we exercised to individual Japanese banks was to some extent arbitrary. However, it was also true that, at the time when there was intense competition between the Bank of Tokyo, then Japan's only bank specialising in foreign exchange with a worldwide branch network, and major Japanese commercial banks engaged in both domestic and international banking, there was a certain amount of willingness on the part of all these internationally active Japanese banks for the BOJ to act as an arbitrator to prevent excessive competition among them.

Eventually, during the second period of my service at the OECD where I was involved in preparing discussion papers for WP3 on the role of international banks in recycling oil-producing countries' surplus funds after the second oil shock, the opportunity I had had to get closer to the reality of Japanese banks' international financial activities through this work at the BOJ was an advantage over those economists and some of WP3 members who had studied international finance only as a theory.

Establishment of the BIS Committee on Banking Regulation and Supervision

In the aftermath of serious disturbances in international currency and banking markets, notably the debacle of Bankhaus Herstatt in West Germany in June 1974,[1] the BIS Board of Governors decided in December 1974 to establish a standing committee called the BIS Committee on Bank Regulation and Supervisory Practices to enhance financial stability by improving the quality of banking supervision and to serve as a forum for regular co-operation between its member countries on banking supervisory matters.

The Committee which initially comprised representatives from the central banks and regulatory authorities of G10 countries first met in February 1975, and its meetings have been held regularly three or four times a year since. George Blunden, Head of Banking Supervision at the Bank of England (later an Executive Director of the Bank and appointed Deputy Governor in succession to Kit McMahon) was its first chairman (1974–1977) and Peter Cooke, Associate Director at the Bank of England, the second chairman (1977–1988). I was the representative of the Bank of Japan from 1975 to mid-1980 just before the start of my second service at the OECD.

At the outset, one important aim of the Committee's work was to close gaps in international supervisory coverage so that supervision would be adequate and consistent across member jurisdictions. In 1975, as a first step in this direction, the Committee produced the paper on "The Concordat" which set out principles for sharing supervisory responsibility for internationally active banks' foreign branches, subsidiaries, and joint ventures between host and parent (or home) supervisory authorities.

The scandal at the Chiasso branch of Credit Suisse Bank which broke out in the spring of 1977[2] led to a review of measures to be taken on the issue of bank secrecy in offshore centres which was an obstacle to banking supervision by the home-country authorities. The Committee prepared a report which pointed out the importance of banking supervision on the basis of consolidated balance sheets, whereby the accounts of subsidiaries can be monitored by the home-country supervisory authorities. With regard to co-operation with banking supervisors outside the member countries of the Committee, the so-called Enlarged Committee met in London in August 1979.

The Committee was also in the process of reaching an agreement on the minimum capital adequacy ratios to be observed by internationally active commercial banks, which was announced in 1988. On top of the Committee on Bank Regulation and Supervisory Practices, the BIS also hosted occasional meetings of central bank experts on the development of BIS international bank credit statistics and on macroeconomic aspects of international banking credit, and I also attended these meetings as the BOJ representative.

On the evening of the last day of my attendance at the Committee, then chaired by Peter Cooke, René Larre, then BIS General Manager (a former Finance Inspector at the French Ministry of Finance), hosted a farewell dinner inviting all members of the Committee at the BIS Sports Club. I was told that it was the first time he organised such an event. I was a bit uncomfortable, wondering why he had not hosted a farewell dinner with all members of the Committee on the last meeting day of the Committee chaired by Blunden.

Growth of International Bank Credit and the Recycling of Oil Money

The OPEC countries ran a current account surplus of about $ 100 billion in the two years 1974–1975, about 30 per cent of which was invested in the Eurodollar market and about the same amount in the domestic financial and capital markets of the United States and the United Kingdom. On the other hand, oil-importing countries where OPEC countries did not place surplus funds were forced to finance their current account deficits by borrowing foreign currency funds. This led to external debt problems in non-oil-producing developing countries which depended largely on international syndicated bank loans.

In the December 1980 issue of the OECD Economic Outlook, published some three months after the start of my second service at the OECD Economics and Statistics Department, it was noted that "(T)he OECD economy as a whole, and it constituent economies individually, are now gripped firmly by the effects of the increase in world oil prices of around 150 per cent over the eighteen months to mid-1980. In many ways the problem is strongly reminiscent of 1973/74" (p. 9).

At the WP3 meeting in May 1981, when Beryl Sprinkel first appeared as US Under Secretary of the Treasury, the risk of over-reflux of oil money was considered on the basis of a Secretariat discussion paper entitled "Recycling".[3] The question raised in this paper was not so much whether balance of payments deficit countries was easy to finance, thus encouraging inflation, but rather whether they were not financed under appropriate conditions to encourage structural economic adjustments needed to cope with high oil prices. The concern was expressed that countries with balance of payments deficits, without adequate adjustment of their domestic economies, might continue to borrow easily from international banks, impairing their ability to repay funds and causing them to default, thereby creating a problem with the soundness of the international private banking system.

In this connection, it was pointed out that banking supervisors in WP3 countries should put the brakes on excessive reflows, but it was also noted that there would be problems with authorities intervening in individual loan cases. It was also noted that the role of the IMF in maintaining the soundness of the reflux of oil-producing countries' funds through international private banking organisations would be sensitive, as it lied between oil-producing and oil-importing countries. During this period,

Sprinkel argued that the case of Brazil should also be considered, where the exit of private banks encouraged the domestic economic adjustment of the borrowing country, which in turn allowed the return of funds to be restored, albeit on more stringent terms than the original borrowing.

At the WP3 meeting held in July 1982, the issue of whether there was any danger of lemming-type behaviour in private banks' credit activities interfering with macroeconomic management was discussed. In this context, the WP3 also considered the question of what steps should be taken to encourage those in charge of reviewing international loans at private banks to make credit decisions from a global macroeconomic perspective. Some suggested that a kind of information centre on international finance should be set up in co-operation with the private banks. However, some argued that such an information centre might instead encourage collective psychological behaviour. The view was also reiterated that forcing over-indebted countries to make structural adjustments at the initiative of private banks would only lead to unsatisfactory results, and that international organisations, especially the IMF, should take the lead, as was the case during the discussions at the WP3 meeting in May 1981. Assistant Secretary Leland, who attended the meeting on behalf of Sprinkel from the US Treasury Department, pointed out that private banks were rather more active in co-financing between international organisations and private banks, while international organisations were more reticent.

The WP3 meeting, held on 8 and 9 July 1982, did not discuss the 5 July collapse of the US Oklahoma-based Penn Square Bank, but it did lead to more selective lending by private banks. In this context, lower-rated debtor countries began to demand a higher premium for new borrowing, and in August following the July meeting of WP3, Mexico was forced to default on its external debt. And the US experiment with a new money supply-oriented monetary adjustment scheme, which had led to high and volatile interest rates and various external problems since its introduction in October 1979, came to an end in October 1982, not long after the outbreak of the Mexican debt crisis.

At that time, syndicated loans, in which private banks lent to developing countries as a group rather than as individual banks, were becoming increasingly popular. In response to these developments, the BIS prepared statistics on international private-sector credit so that private banks could use them as a reference in their credit activities, but what Japanese banks wanted to know was not the total amount of credit extended by private banks in all countries participating in the BIS statistics, but the total amount of credit extended by US banks as a whole, particularly to each of the Latin American countries.

Basel Capital Accord

The onset of the Latin American debt crisis heightened the concerns among members of the BIS Committee on Banking Regulation and Supervision about the deteriorating capital ratios of internationally active banks of G10 countries. Backed by the G10 central bank governors, the BIS Committee worked towards greater convergence in the measurement of capital adequacy and reached a broad consensus on a weighted approach to the measurement of risk, both on and off banks' balance sheets.

In December 1987, the Committee (then called "Basel Committee on Bank Supervision") published a consultative paper for a multinational accord to remove a source of competitive inequality among internationally active banks which the Committee considered to arise from differences in national capital requirements. Following this process, a document entitled "International Convergence of Capital Measurement and Capital Standards" (the so-called Basel Capital Accord) was approved by the G10 Governors and released to international banks in July 1988.

Although I was not involved in the Basel Committee's work as I was then Director of Policy Studies Branch of the OECD Economics and Statistics Department, some European bankers who were concerned about Japanese banks' aggressive lending attitude in international banking business informally came to ask me about my views on the Committee's consultative paper. While the Japanese supervisory authorities at the time admitted hidden reserves as part of banks' capital, I expressed the view that they should be excluded from the core equity capital element after a certain transitional period.

The Accord of 1988 was intended to have rather modest objective of levelling the competitive playing field by establishing a floor, not necessarily a sufficient level, of capital adequacy for international banks to underpin the soundness of the international financial system.

Policy Implications of Globalised and Deregulated Financial Markets

In an address given at the Economic Council of Sweden in Stockholm on 3 May 1994, I discussed the implications of globalised and deregulated financial markets for macroeconomic policies, prudential polices and structural policy more generally. Among the specific comments I made therein, those related to prudential policy are as follows.

"Considerable progress in improving prudential standards has been made in recent years, most importantly in the area of strengthening capital adequacy with the widespread application of BIS standards. However, it is important to ensure that the strengthening of prudential standards does not lead to a procyclical bias. One risk in this regard is that, in an attempt to satisfy capital adequacy requirements in a cyclical downturn, banks may be induced to restrict their lending to a degree that reinforces cyclical pressures. This problem should not arise if banks normally maintain their capital levels significantly above minimum requirements. However, the fact that the risks attached to loans normally become most apparent in an economic downturn, and other factors such as the inclusion of unrealised capital gains on securities in Japanese banks' capital, clearly expose banks' balance sheets and capital to procyclical forces. More generally. The enforcement of capital standards may be prone to procyclical pressures should be resisted, and cutting resources available to supervisors, as occurred during the mid-1980s in the United States, may offer tempting budgetary savings. On the other hand, when losses emerge during the downswing, supervisors may face excessive pressures to respond.

In the context of the recent unusually severe balance-sheet problems, a number of practical issues have been relevant. One that it is important to ensure the longer-term effectiveness of capital standards. Any measure that are perceived to leave banks permanent scope to operate without meeting them from them would undermine confidence in the system. At the same time, precipitous action may not be wise where banks suffer a sharp erosion of their capital base and fall below the standards. Such situation should be managed pragmatically but with a view toward ensuring that any failure to meet standards will clearly be temporary. Another issue concerns the management of losses once they have been incurred, and the appropriate mechanism for capital to be rebuilt. There is some evidence of banks having widened their profit margins in some countries to help rebuild their capital, but this is a slow process. Requiring financial institutions to contribute more to covering the costs, for example, by increasing fees associated with deposit insurance schemes, raises questions about fairness, since it would tend to penalise the more successful institutions. Moreover, it may not be practical, since it amounts to redistributing losses in a system whose capital base is already weak. It might also make it difficult to attract new capital into the industry. These considerations raise the question of resorting to some public support, as occurred in some Nordic banks and US depository institutions. However, it is important to ensure that such assistance is provided on terms which minimise any incentives for irresponsible financial behaviour.

Finally, all players in financial markets—monetary authorities, supervisory authorities and market participants themselves—have a general need for information on which to base their decisions. It is important to ensure that they do not under-invest in improving the information useful to all players in financial markets. From the perspective of national authorities, there has been a clear deficiency in certain forms of macroeconomic and financial information. Macroeconomic data are often of limited accuracy, not available on a timely basis and subject to substantial revision. Financial data generally consist of detailed balance-sheet information for financial institutions, concerning quantities such as bank lending and monetary aggregates, but contain relatively little about terms and conditions in the bank credit market. In addition, information about corporate and household balance-sheets is inadequate, while in some countries data on land and property price behaviour are available only after a long lag. These deficiencies may have hindered early recognition of the 'credit crunch' phenomenon. They also made it difficult subsequently to address monetary policy response. Improvements in these areas would assist policy formulation and implementation.

I turn, finally, to the international systemic implications of financial liberalisation. The interdependence of financial markets and the sensitivity of exchange rates to any major disturbances throughout the system, raises the question of how great a role should be assigned to international policy co-ordination and what its nature should be. With regards to its role, the primary responsibility of governments to their own electorates should be borne in mind so that expectations about what can be accomplished by co-ordination are not exaggerated.

There would appear to be little case for active policy co-ordination efforts in the sense of attempting to persuade countries to follow policies not in their own interest. Any such efforts are likely to be counterproductive. The greatest contribution that economic policies can make toward enhancing the stability of international financial markets is to ensure that such policies are sound and stable at the macroeconomic level. Since such policies are in each country's own interest, they should not need to be actively co-ordinated.

The emphasis of policy co-ordination should be on surveillance, monitoring, exchanges of information and the search for a common assessment of the domestic and international situations and policy requirements in a globally consistent framework. This requires that there be sufficient information to monitor developments and carry out the surveillance role that is essential if countries are to have confidence in the co-ordination process. In this regard, it is necessary for countries engaged in international policy co-ordination to share up-to-date indicators which provide an early warning of any potential problems and to ensure the domestic and international consistency and coherence of policies. These indicators should be capable of contributing to informed assessment of the longer-term implications of policy changes, so that the risk of short-sighted policy stances can be avoided.

Co-ordination along these lines can provide mutual recognition of the problems that each country faces and an understanding of the most effective national polices to ensure stable medium-term economic developments".

Causes and Implications of the East Asian Financial Crisis

At the French International Forum on Asian Perspective organised by the Asian Development and the OECD Development Centre on "Financial Liberalisation in Asia: Analysis and Prospects" that was held in Paris on 5 June 1998, I delivered a speech entitled "Causes and Implications of the East Asian Financial Crisis". In an article entitled "Don't Blame the Victims of Asia's Crisis" published in a Singaporean newspaper The Strait Times, Anthony Rowley wrote: "It is instructive that a Japanese national (Mr Shigehara) writing from Europe (the OECD offices in Europe) should be able to analyze the situation with such clarity. It seems that the ideological miasma in which Washington-based institutions such as the IMF and the World Bank have become entrapped, by virtue of their proximity to the US administration and Congress, renders such clear thinking impossible on their part. They dare not blame the system of unthinking trade, investment and capital market liberalization to which they have co-opted, so they blame its victims" (via Reuter, OECD Media Relations, 11 June 1998). Below are the main parts of my speech.

"Financial problems have been a prominent cause in the economic downturns in the English-speaking OECD countries and some Nordic countries in the early 1990s, as well as Japan's protracted phase of poor macroeconomic performance in recent years. These problems include: the balance-sheet problems of financial institutions and/or the fragilities of the enterprise or household sector with excessive debt positions associated with declines in equity or real asset prices. They typically arose in the wake or in conjunction with substantial liberalisations in the countries' financial sectors.

The financial structures of emerging market economies in East Asia have generally remained less developed than in the industrial world. Attempts at financial market liberalisation in the 1980s were generally considered to be inadequate. The challenge in the 1990s has been to achieve more liberalised financial systems in the process of further economic development, without incurring the difficulties that the industrial countries have experienced. Unfortunately, the recent events have demonstrated that a number of emerging market economies of East Asia have failed to meet this challenge. The unfolding adverse consequences of the financial crisis in these countries are far greater than those experienced by OECD countries in the 1990s.

It is now a consensus view that financial sector weakness contributed to the economic crisis in emerging East Asia. But many other countries in that region and the rest of the world also have weak financial sectors and have not experienced a crisis. Financial sector weakness can therefore not be considered as the unique root cause of the crisis. It is clear that a number of factors have interacted with each other to bring about the crisis and magnify its severity in emerging East Asia. The precise relationship between them appears to be different in different countries in that region and further analysis is required to determine their causal relationships precisely.

Causes of East Asian Financial Crisis

Given the time limit, I shall be highly selective in discussing the causes and implications of the financial crisis in emerging East Asia.

The first point I would like to make is that the recent financial crisis in emerging East Asia differs from previous crises in developing countries—such as the Mexican peso crisis of 1995 and the Latin American debt crisis of the early 1980s

- Both the Latin American debt crisis and the Mexican peso crisis, with the major exception of Chile's episode, were associated with heavy external borrowing of the public sector. In the case of emerging East Asia, the main source of difficulties lay with the private sector. The budgets were generally balanced in emerging market economies in East Asia, in contrast to many Latin American economies previously hit by the financial crisis.
- Moreover, these East Asian economies were characterised by high private saving rates. Excessive consumption was not a source of external deficits. These economies were also more successful in keeping inflation lower than Latin American economies.

There were also differences in the international environment. World trade remained buoyant in 1997, while interest rates in international capital markets were kept low. In contrast, the Latin American debt crisis of the early1980s occurred against the background of high interest following the Volcker measure of monetary tightening and widening US budget deficits. The Mexican peso crisis occurred after the worldwide rise in long-term rates from the beginning of 1994.

Partly because of these favourable domestic and international factors supporting the emerging economies of East Asia, the depth and breadth of its financial crisis have surprised us. Indonesia's current account deficit was not exceptionally large in the several years before the crisis (it averaged 3.8 per cent of GDP over 1995–1996), although it was rising. And, Korea's deficit had begun to come down in the first half of 1997 from its 1996 level of just under 5 per cent of GDP. True, Thailand was running a large current account deficit—averaging nearly 7 per cent of GDP over 1990–1996 and 8 per cent of GDP in 1995–1996. But, we must remember that Singapore ran a current account deficit about 9 per cent of GDP from 1975–1982, and this period is generally considered as an era of remarkable economic success.

The early diagnosis was that the exchange rates of emerging market economies in East Asia were over-valued. Many observers considered that they had lost international price competitiveness by something in the order of 10 per cent. Then, why did the 20 per cent devaluation of the Thai baht on July 2 last year trigger a fully blown crisis, quickly spreading to other countries in South East Asia and eventually to South Korea? It appears that a self-fulfilling loss of confidence played a key role in deepening and spreading financial crises. Even countries with relatively limited international capital transactions can suffer from sharp outflows of capital in a major confidence crisis. Emerging market economies in East Asia integrated into international financial markets were more vulnerable. The inflow into these economies were around US$ 40 billions in 1994, and doubled to nearly US$ 100 billions in 1996. It reversed to an outflow of around US$ 12 billions in 1997. The volatility of exchange rates was largely with changes in capital flows. The problem was exacerbated by the short-term nature of capital flows and the foreign currency denomination of debt without hedging. The build-up short-term, unhedged debt increased the vulnerability of emerging East Asian economies to a sudden loss of confidence. Once confidence is lost, rushed hedging of short-term foreign currency debt aggravated the situation.

The vulnerability of emerging economies in East Asia is also associated with the fragility of financial sectors, which in turn, at least in part, reflects the effects of earlier large capital inflows. Large inflows led to easy funding for projects and asset prices were bid up. The practice of local banks of relying on the availability of collateral rather than on a rigorous analysis of profitability encouraged huge credit expansion hand in hand with the rise in asset prices and the value of collateral. Such practice also skewed bank lending towards real estate and construction. These problems were exacerbated by implicit or explicit government guarantees which encouraged banks to assume excessive risk, and by lax supervision and regulation, which failed to ensure that banks made adequate provisions against problem loans or to maintain adequate levels of capital. Investors' realisation that these weaknesses in the financial sector were shared by most other countries in the region, as well as emerging economies elsewhere, was a powerful force in generating contagion once the crisis started.

The problems were magnified by inadequate attention paid by external creditors in lending to these countries. They lent despite inadequate information about borrowers or knowledge about their unhedged foreign currency exposure. Was this because of their expectation that they could be bailed out in the event of failure? Or, can it be explained simply in terms of collective "exuberance"? Is it true that foreign investors thought that they were working in a riskless world, and made their investment decisions accordingly, and then suddenly realised the risk and reversed their positions? Further, rigorous analysis is needed to answer these questions. Whatever the final answers are to them, it is clear that private sector lenders from industrialised countries should assume their proper share of the responsibilities for the sound functioning of deregulated and globalised financial markets.

Lessons from the Crisis

An important lesson to be drawn from the crisis in the East Asian emerging economies is that even economies with fairly sound macroeconomic policies can fall victim to a sudden loss of confidence in the new environment of more integrated international capital markets. Emerging market economies with relatively strong fundamentals such as high saving ratios, sound fiscal positions, low inflation, and high growth have often experienced large capital inflows that create problems which increase their vulnerability to an adverse shift in investor sentiment. The inflows add to inflationary pressure under the fixed exchange rate regime. When public finances are in a healthy state and the size of the government is small, it will be difficult to fully offset inflationary pressure by fiscal retrenchment. How about the effect of offsetting monetary action? Sterilised intervention will encourage foreign creditors to continue lending, as it prevents interest rates from falling in response to capital inflows.

Countries such as Hong Kong and Argentina have successfully maintained a currency board system for the past years. But, for a number of countries, the burden of domestic adjustment required for the operation of a currency board would be too great to bear. If so, some flexibility would be needed in the area of exchange rate management as a safety valve. That said, the exit from fixed rate regimes to floating could produce turbulence in markets, unless the timing is well chosen. It would probably be better to shift from a fixed rate to a more flexible regime when macroeconomic conditions are stable, in particular when the current account positions are favourable.

The recent crisis in emerging Asia has clearly demonstrated the importance of the interaction between financial market weakness and economic disturbances. Much has been said about the importance of strengthening prudential regulation and supervision.

The strategy of a number of banks in OECD countries of relying on local banks in emerging market economies for the screening of borrowers and channelling of credit according to their recommendations did not work well, as local banks generally lacked the necessary credit risk assessment skills and operated in a lax supervisory environment. While this episode underscores the importance of emerging countries' adherence to a set of 25 "core principles" set out last year by the Basle Committee on Banking Supervision, it is equally important to consider ways to strengthen the capacity of banks in industrial countries to conduct their international operations with greater prudence.

Over the years, an important device for strengthening the soundness of banks in industrialised countries has been risk-weighted capital adequacy standards. The Basle Accord on capital standards in 1988 was s significant achievement in this respect. But, calls for reform have begun to grow. I shall not go into detailed discussion on this issue, but let me briefly say that the risk-weighting that assigns zero risk to all OECD Member countries' sovereign debt and a reduced weighting (20 per cent) for claims on banks may need to be re-considered. I would also argue that means need to be found to prevent capital ratios from becoming unduly distorted by fluctuations in equity prices and associated unpredictable changes in the valuation of unrealised capital gains counted as part of capital. More generally, the Basle Accord should not prevent banks' efforts to develop and use their own models for measuring and managing risks prudently in their banking operations. It is also worth noting that countries need to apply the Basle standards in a manner that is meaningful based on their particular circumstances. The Asian crisis has underscored that banks in countries undergoing rapid change in their financial systems are likely to need to maintain capital ratios significantly above the Basle minimum if they are to be financially sound.

With respect to the role of credit rating agencies, they apparently led a competitive race to the bottom in reducing ratings after the crisis, but were not of much help in flagging potential trouble earlier on. This is not to disparage the important role that credit rating agencies can play in disseminating information and bolstering market discipline nor the importance of improving their ability to effectively monitor risks in emerging markets. However, a lesson from the Asian crisis is that banks need to improve their own in-house credit risk assessment so that they do not become overly dependent on the views of rating agencies.

Having said so, I must add that rating agencies do not usually have access to any more data than private participants in financial markets generally do. This leads to the importance of greater transparency, as highlighted in the communiques of the recent meetings of various international financial groups and committees. No one would disagree with the assertion that "more information is better than less information". The IMF's Special Data Dissemination Standard and the BIS data on international bank lending are some of the important efforts to provide relevant information to financial market participants. The issue is not whether more information is needed, but "where the crucial information deficiencies lie". There is an urgent need for monetary authorities of both developed and emerging market economies jointly with private sector participants in financial markets to address this issue.

The recent crisis had demonstrated the risk inherent in partial and inconsistent financial market liberalisation. When short-term capital movements were substantially more liberalised than long-term flows and enterprises' capacity to borrow abroad were severely restrained, inflows concentrated on banking channels and the vulnerability of the banking system was magnified. Had financial market liberalisation focused more on equity and bond markets, the banking system would have suffered less damage. A more balanced approach to financial market opening also requires putting appropriate infrastructure and framework conditions in place, including improved corporate governance structures and improved relationships between the government, financial institutions, and business firms.

The crisis in emerging East Asia raises broader issues concerning the management of the international financial system. As was the case in Mexico in 1995, the amount of financial resources that have been disturbed by the IMF and other lending institutions is large. However, it is considerably less than the potential capital movements which the crisis could entail. This has placed responsibility on private creditors to set up refinancing facilities to overcome short-term funding problems, which is reminiscent of the process of Latin American debt rescheduling during the 1980s. Where negotiations prove successful, as with the recent agreement with Korea and major international banks, favourable effects can become visible in financial markets quickly. Having said this, I must add that there are legitimate questions about whether the crisis in emerging East Asia could have been more limited if lenders from OECD countries had paid greater attention to the risks inherent in lending to borrowers in emerging market economies on which they had limited information. In order to prevent the reoccurrence of large-scale international financial crisis, it will be necessary to ensure that participants international capital markets are not sheltered from the consequences of their own actions".

The text of this speech was distributed to the press by the OECD Media Relations. Paul Fabra, an influential French reporter, wrote an article about some critical comments on BIS capital standards made in my speech, which was immediately published in Le Monde. I immediately phoned Andrew Crockett, then BIS General Manager, to explain the background to the speech and my past association with the Basle Committee. He took my explanation calmly.

The Role of Capital Controls

In April 1997, the IMF Interim Committee agreed that there would be a number of benefits from amending the IMF Articles of Agreement to make the liberalisation of international capital movements a central purpose of the IMF and to extend its jurisdiction to capital movements. At an IMF seminar "Asia and the IMF", held in Hong Kong, China on 19 September that year, Stanley Fischer, then First Deputy Managing Director of the IMF, argued in his speech entitled "Capital Account Liberalization and the Role of the IMF" that the proposed amendment to the Articles of Agreement for free international capital movements would be in the interests of all members of the IMF.[4]

In early November 1998, I gave a keynote speech "Towards More Stable Global Finance: Some Issues Concerning Orderly Liberalisation in Emerging Market Economies" at the thirteenth Pacific Basin Central Bank Conference, Los Cabos, B.C. S., Mexico. In this speech, after discussing a broad range of issues concerning orderly liberalisation in emerging market economies, I specifically examined the role of capital controls in promoting financial stability and development. As the first part of this speech is essentially a shorter version of my speech made in Paris on 5 June 1998, already described in the previous section of this chapter, only its second part is shown below.

"The ongoing crisis in a number of emerging market economies associated with volatile capital flows has triggered debate on the rationale, scope and modalities of capital controls. One traditional argument in support of capital controls is made with reference to the 'second-best' principle of welfare economics. It has been argued that, if serious distortions exist in some markets (which is particularly the case in less advanced countries), then some 'optimal' degree of distortions in the operation of financial markets might lead to an overall improvement of welfare. Even proponents of this view have to agree, however, that, from a public policy viewpoint, the 'first-best' solutions to market imperfections would be to address the origin of distortions in all markets—the financial markets in particular.

A further line of argument accept that capital movement controls are basically undesirable but that they may nevertheless play a useful role in preserving domestic monetary autonomy and exchange rate stability at the same time. Over the past two decades, policy requirements in this area in advanced OECD countries had to be adjusted in the light of the evolving exchange rate regimes and global financial markets which increasingly impinge on the determination and transmission of monetary impulses. With a shift to the floating exchange rate regime and the rapid development and greater sophistication of financial markets, and the attendant international orientation of the business community in response to the forces of globalisation, capital controls have been relaxed and then dismantled in advanced OECD countries. Some OECD countries have, at times, relied on selective control measures to alleviate exchange rate pressure associated with capital flows. However, the introduction of new financial instruments has provided channels for capital flows which are frequently outside the scope of existing control, and—in the face of greater substitutability of financial assets—it has become more and more difficult to devise and enforce restrictive measures based on largely theoretical distinctions according to maturities, nature of instruments and their links with trade, commercial or financial operations. The very broad range of decisions taken by internationally-operating domestic enterprises, multinational firms, financial institutions and other private market participants highlights the limitations of exchange controls short of restrictions so severe that they would significantly interfere with normal international trade, investment and financing operations. These observations have become relevant to many emerging economies with economic agents actively engaged in global commerce and finance.

In addition to their overall ineffectiveness, it has been argued that capital controls may at the same time cause severe distortions, as it is difficult to enforce them in a fair and even-handed manner. In particular, restrictive measures inhibit activity by individual investors and small firms, while larger operators can more easily circumvent controls because their business are highly diversified or because they have indirect recourse to a number of foreign and international markets and intermediaries.

Another important argument against controls is that the imposition of restrictions on capital movements and the efforts required by the private sector to comply with them—particularly controls which run counter to market incentives—may lead a considerable waste of resources. Government officials are required to devise elaborate enforcement and surveillance mechanisms and to monitor in ever greater detail the activities of economic agents that are subject to control. Enterprises and other market operators must spend considerable energy in complying with official regulations. Moreover, as the banking system is frequently used as a vehicle for enforcement, the direct costs to the authorities may in fact represent only a fraction the resources of the economy devoted to the enforcement of capital controls.

Among a number of issues which have come to the forefront of public debate in connection with the ongoing crisis in emerging market economies are those which concern selective restraints on certain types of capital movements into and out of emerging market economies. In this context, I shall discuss the case for early liberalisation of foreign direct investment (FDI) flows and the use of control measures on certain other types of capital flows. The debate on these issues is still continuing and, without pretending to give definitive answers, it may be useful to consider them against the background of well-known conditions for achieving successful financial and economic integration I have discussed.

Although sensitivity about foreign penetration in certain economic sectors ('strategic industries' in particular) continue to persist in many countries, it is increasingly recognised that liberalisation of FDI plays a prominent role in their economic development. In particular, allowing the establishment of foreign companies and their participation in local firms can be expected to enhance competition in general as well as to increase the know-how and efficiency of domestic enterprises. Similarly, by removing hindrances for companies to expand abroad, the longer-term possibilities of exploiting foreign markets and allocating international activities more efficiently are also likely to be significantly improved. Freedom of direct investment may thus substantially contribute to the positive impact of liberalisation for the growth of world trade and the globalisation of the world economy as swell as the improvement of the overall allocation of resources.

The specificities of FDI have often been used as an argument for a differentiated treatment relative to other capital flows. Clearly, several considerations militate in favour of such an approach. Thus, for example, the modalities of FDI control can include special procedures for screening, registration, conditional authorization, performance requirements etc. that do not lend themselves to application to other types of capital movements. Also, from the legal point of view, another difference stems from the fact that FDI operations are covered by extensive network of bilateral investment treaties (which in many cases are based on a broad definition of investment, encompassing many forms of capital flows) aimed at ensuring investor protection and providing mechanisms for dispute settlements. Finally, it is true that, from a historic perspective, such a differentiation has been applied in practice, with FDI being often the component of the capital account singled out for early, though not necessarily full, liberalisation. This being said, it is also important to note that the lines of demarcation between FDI and other intranational capital flows have tended to become more blurred.

Although intuitively the concept of direct investment seems straightforward, its operational definition is complex and continues to present a number of grey areas notwithstanding the efforts to improve the methodology by institutions such as the IMF and the OECD. At the same time, the web of "financial relations" among the parties to a direct investment makes it often difficult to disentangle the specific nature of certain types of transactions—a problem which has been more acute as a result of the wave of financial innovations of the past two decades. As a consequence, distinction that may be relevant from a statistical viewpoint may not necessarily reflect the realities of economic relations and it can be misguided to rely on them as a basis for international capital control policy.

The financial crisis has revived interest in the use of selective controls on short-term capital movements as a means of insulating countries from the impact of 'destabilising' international capital flows. This issue is certainly not new and, for example, was the subject of intense debate when European countries moved to a system of full capital account convertibility. Even proponents of restrictions in this field recognise that there are formidable conceptual and practical problems that make it difficult to devise 'economically-sensible' procedures for exerting effective controls on such flows. In this respect, a distinction is often made between the use of *outright prohibitions and quantitative restrictions*, which prevent the execution of specific transactions, *tax-like measures*, including deposit requirements, that mainly impact on the cost of such transactions.

Recourse to quantitative restrictions runs against the principle of convertibility and implies that the authorities have confidence in their ability to segregate certain transactions or, indeed, whole segments of financial markets. In today's financial environment, greater substitutability of financial assets, new technology and financial innovations make it extremely arduous to effectively enforce control systems that permit 'desirable' flows while concurrently limiting the scope for other categories of capital flows. Apart from serious concerns about the effectiveness of controls, the growing difficulty of distinguishing among trade-related, commercial, financial, hedging or purely speculative flows, highlights the risks that recourse to quantitative restrictions may result in severe distortionary effects that would over time impact negatively on the economic welfare of the country concerned.

These considerations lie behind the emphasis put in some circles on the relative benefits of using 'taxes' (e.g. through non-remunerated deposit requirements) to discourage short-term transactions and/or provide an incentive to foreign investors to hold certain assets beyond a given minimum period of time. Through this system, the freedom of transactions is preserved but its costs are affected by time-related parameters to be set by the authorities. In view of its, by now, relatively long experience, the case of Chile has been analysed in considerable detail. From the state of this debate to date, two observations can be made. First, a recent study of the Chilean experience has come to the conclusion that the evidence on the effectiveness of the Chilean controls in reducing the short-term external debt is mixed and, more particularly, that the evidence is somewhat ambiguous. Second, it is important to note that while the Chilean measures initially concerned only foreign loans, the coverage of the deposit requirements had to be extended considerably in 1991–1997 so that by the end of last year it applied to all inflows that do not increase the stock of capital. This lends to the argument that the effectiveness of capital controls can only be ensured if they become pervasive. Irrespective of the view one can have of the usefulness of these controls as a policy instrument in "normal" circumstances, the earlier experience of some OECD countries with similar devices experimented with under the Bretton Woods exchange rate system suggests that they are not effective when the riding gets really tough".

Notes

1. On 26 June 1974, German regulators forced the troubled Bank Herstatt into liquidation. That day, a number of banks had released payment of German marks to Herstatt in Frankfurt in exchange for US dollars that were to be delivered in New York. The bank was closed at 16:30 Frankfurt time, which was 10:30 New York time. Because of time difference between the two cities, Herstatt ceased operations between the times of the respective payments. The counter party banks did not receive their US dollar payments, and the BIS Board of Governors addressed the cross-jurisdictional implications of the Herstatt debacle.
2. The so-called "Chiasso scandal" broke out at the Chiasso branch of Credit Suisse Bank in the spring of 1977. In the 1960s, three executives of Credit Suisse including the deputy manager of its Chiasso branch set up a Lichtenstein company which was used for many years to illegally launder money from Italy without the knowledge of the bank's central management in Zurich. Despite an initial alert in 1968 following a complaint by a manager of another Swiss bank about the methods employed by the Credit Suisse employees, it was as late as in 1977 that the bank's central management found the irregularities in the branch.
3. OECD, "Recycling", Note by the Secretariat, CPE/WP3(81)5, 29 April 1981.
4. Stanley Fischer, "Capital Account Liberalization and the Role of the IMF", IMF Seminar, 19 September 1997, https://www.imf.org/en/News/Articles/2015/09/28/04/53/sp091997.

   See also Jonathan Ostry et al., "Capital Inflows: The Role of Controls", IMF Staff Position Note, 19 February 2010, SPN/10/04, https://www.imf.org/external/pubs/ft/spn/2010/spn1004.pdf.

CHAPTER 18

The Role and Limits of Multilateral Surveillance

In discussing "Macroeconomic and Prudential Controls on International Financial Markets" in Chapter 17, I briefly expressed my views on the role of multilateral surveillance in general terms. In this chapter, I will review the role and limits of multilateral surveillance conducted by the OECD and some other international institutions such as the IMF and the BIS in the 2000s onward.

The Role of Multilateral Surveillance

In his speech entitled "Through the Looking Glass: Reform of the International Institutions" made in December 2006 in Australia,[1] Mervyn King, then Governor of the Bank of England, argued that "(U)necessary duplication is a waste of both time and money" and "it would be better if microeconomic issues were examined within the OECD, and, in turn, issues of macroeconomic spillovers and 'global imbalances' were left to the IMF".

My view on the role of the OECD's surveillance had been expressed in the 1996 Global Finance Lecture which I delivered at the University of Birmingham in October that year. In this speech, I offered my comments on OECD approaches to surveillance, first in the macroeconomic and then structural policy areas, recognising the importance of links between structural impediments, constraints on macroeconomic

K. Shigehara, *The Bank of Japan, the OECD, and Beyond*,
https://doi.org/10.1007/978-981-97-5307-9_18

policies and economic performance.[2] Furthermore, following the lines of arguments in this lecture, I commented on King's suggestion about the division of labour between the IMF and the OECD in a 2011 conference in Paris.[3] In this speech, I argued that utmost care would be required in rationalising the surveillance activities of the IMF and the OECD so that their overhaul should not result in weakening of surveillance on the interaction between macroeconomic and structural policies and that multilateral fora for a coherent review of key economic players' actions or non-actions in these two policy areas are essential for improving overall economic performance.

To make this point clear, in a section of my speech under the heading "Division of labour between the IMF and the OECD?", I pointed out that:

- large rises in unit labour costs in several member countries of the euro-area resulting from labour market rigidities which had persisted even after their participation in the area had weakened their international competitiveness and worsened external current accounts;
- their unsatisfactory economic growth and high unemployment rates combined with the better performance of the German economy had led to the emergence of an underlining threat to the viability of the euro system with adverse consequences for global macroeconomic stability; and
- as euro-area countries competing with Germany could no longer use exchange rate adjustment to narrow their relative cost disadvantages vis-à-vis Germany, accelerated labour and product market reforms in these countries was the only way to prevent a build-up of macroeconomic tensions within the euro-area with possible undesirable secondary effects on the United States, Japan, and the rest of the world.

Based on this analysis, I argued that surveillance of macroeconomic policies—fiscal, monetary, and financial—should go hand in hand with structural policy surveillance within the OECD in order to prevent an anomaly whose underlying cause is the malfunction of structural policies combined with constraints on the use of macroeconomic policy instruments. I asserted that the two types of surveillance should not be separated, and that the OECD should not discontinue macroeconomic analysis and forecasting which is essential for examining the interrelationship between macro and structural economic forces and enabling the OECD to make appropriate recommendations on a coherent set of macroeconomic and structural policies over the medium term.

Lessons from the Global Financial and Economic Crisis

Have the OECD and other international institutions engaged in multilateral surveillance on economic policy management lived up to the billing?

In late 2008, on her visit to the London School of Economics, the Queen of England spoke for many, asking why nobody had noticed the global financial crisis was on its way. In response, the British Academy wrote to her:

> "Many people did foresee the crisis. However, the exact form that it would take and the timing of its onset ferocity were foreseen by nobody".

> "… the failure to foresee the timing, extent and severity of the crisis and to head it off, while it had many causes, was principally a failure of the collective imagination of many bright people, both in this country and internationally, to understand the risks to the system as a whole".[4]

In fact, several international institutions, e.g. the IMF and the OECD, have been tasked for many years to assess the likelihood of risks and events that are potentially dangerous or disruptive to global economic growth and financial stability with a view to calling for preventive action by national authorities. At the IMF and the OECD, officials produce regular reports and analyses on these topics which are discussed, in the case of the IMF, at its executive board in Washington D.C., and in the case of the OECD at meetings of committees and their subsidiary bodies all of which are attended by government and central bank officials coming to Paris from their capitals.

As easier access to information about the surveillance activities of the international institutions has been considered to assist the private-sector actors in conducting their economic and financial transactions in an increasingly integrated world plagued with uncertainties, both the IMF and the OECD have been asked to strengthen their efforts to increase transparency about the results of their work. Thus, initially confidential surveillance reports, to varying degrees, have been made available not only as paper copies but also, and increasingly, on the internet for wider dissemination to outsiders.

Unlike the IMF and the OECD, which are inter-governmental organisations, the Bank of International Settlements (BIS), originally established after the First World War to provide services to member central banks, has not been mandated to conduct surveillance on national government policies, but has over decades widened and deepened its activities to promote co-operation among central banks and other financial authorities on matters of their mutual concern. Among the Bank's publications, the Annual Report has a long tradition of providing the outside world beyond the central bank community with important messages concerning policies required for global financial market and macroeconomic stability.

Against this background, I together with Paul Atkinson, executive director of the International Economic Policy Studies Association, reviewed recommendations that had been published in the flagship publications of these three international institutions about policies relevant to economic and financial stability in the United States, where the global financial and economic crisis originated, and in the United Kingdom, another early epicentre. In our work assessing the three institutions' surveillance activities, Nicholas Vanston, former Head of Division at the Country Studies Division of OECD Economics Department (ECO) and a senior fellow of the International Economic Policy Studies Association, participated in the preparation of a background note "A Review of Early Warnings Prior to the Outbreak of the Current Global Financial and Economic Crisis: Surveillance Documents of Key International Institutions" whose main points were reflected in the draft main paper I co-authored with Atkinson which was entitled "Surveillance by International Institutions: Lessons from the Global Financial and Economic Crisis".

We argued that the usefulness and effectiveness of the three international institutions' warnings about economic and financial developments prior to the crisis and recommendations on policies relevant to its prevention would depend crucially on their timeliness. In addition, desirable features of their warnings and policy recommendations would include:

- clarity of their messages, i.e. the need to go beyond simply citing as a "risk" or as one part of an "on the one hand ... on the other hand" discussion;
- consistency within institutions, i.e. global surveillance reports and bilateral country consultations or surveys should reinforce each other; and
- consistency over time, i.e. the strength and forcefulness of warnings and policy recommendations should have increased with time as the boom became progressively overheated and downside risks increased.

To have been effective, of course, such warnings and recommendations would have had to lead to policy adjustments which might have at least limited the damage that has ensued.

From these viewpoints, we indicated the need for improving the analytical framework for the three institutions' surveillance. Noting that the influence of regulatory and prudential policies is an important element of macroeconomic-financial linkages, we argued that the international institutions ought to improve their own analytical tools to better understand these linkages for more effective multilateral surveillance of both monetary and prudential policy. We also raised a number of issues concerning the institutional frameworks in which surveillance was carried out and staffing and management issues within the institutions. In addition, we stressed the importance of the need to review the dissemination process of their work to private-sector actors with the view to making surveillance more effective.

Specific suggestions about these issues were spelled out in our co-authored paper. Robert Price, former Head of the Monetary and Fiscal Policy Studies Division of ECO and another senior fellow of the International Economic Policy Studies Association, joined us in discussing the issues raised in our draft paper and made helpful comments, in particular about the staffing problem at the OECD Economics Department put under tight budget constraints.

A slightly revised draft paper[5] was presented to an OECD informal seminar in early February 2011, chaired by Andrew Dean. Designated discussants were Robert Raymond and Niels Thygesen (former Chairman of the Economic and Development Review Committee of the OECD). Among others, Emmanuel van der Mensbrugghe (then Director of the IMF Office in Europe) and Adrian Blundell-Wignall (then Special

Adviser to the OECD Secretary-General on Financial Markets and Deputy Director of the Financial and Enterprise Affairs Directorate of the OECD) offered useful comments. After the seminar, Guy Quaden (Honorary Governor of the National Bank of Belgium) offered helpful written comments on this version. The final version was published as OECD Economics Department Working Paper No. 860 in May 2011.[6]

In the course of our work, I learned that a postmortem of the IMF's performance before and during the crisis was under way at its Independent Evaluation Office (IEO). Thanks to the intermediation of Takatoshi Kato, former Vice Minister of Finance for International Affair at the Japanese finance ministry and former Deputy Managing Director at the IMF, I contacted IEO Director Moises Schwartz, sent him a draft of our paper and asked him to comment on it. In his reply, he noted that it was well argued and made a sound case for strengthening surveillance in the three institutions we covered, adding that he did not detect an issue of fairness in our assessments across the three institutions. The IEO's own evaluation report was published in November 2014. It concluded that: "(T)wo reforms would enhance the IMF's ability to warn about emerging systemic risks. First, the IMF needs to consolidate the initiatives aimed at identifying risks and vulnerabilities, and it should better disseminate their findings to authorities. Second, it should focus its financial sector surveillance on the five to seven truly systemic financial centers".[7]

Lessons from the Euro-Area Crisis

Just a few years after the outbreak of the global financial and economic crisis which originated from the US housing market debacle, another financial crisis occurred in the OECD area, this time in the euro-area.

For some time after the outbreak of the euro-area crisis, it was often described as a European sovereign debt crisis in the Western media. It was certainly triggered by a sudden loss of market confidence in Greek government debt in late 2009, which was associated with substantial revisions of Greek government debt statistics and prospects for its financial positions in the future. The crisis soon spread to Ireland and Portugal, and by the middle of 2011 Spain and Italy were also affected by a loss of financial market confidence in their sovereign debt.

However, to me as an outside observer residing in Tokyo at the time, the basic causes of the ongoing crisis in the euro-area seemed to be multifold. My analysis was that it had arisen not only from fiscal imbalances in

Greece and some other member countries of the euro-area, but also from private-sector financial imbalances that in turn resulted, to a significant extent, from structural imbalances in the area.

In fact, for a long time, Greece had been running twin deficits—both fiscal and external current account deficits—with its external deficits being the combined result of unsatisfactory fiscal policy management and low private-sector financial saving and excess fixed investment. Among euro-area member countries with a greater economic size than Greece, Ireland, and Portugal, an example of the association of private-sector financial imbalances and large external imbalances was found in Spain where general government net financial balances had been over years below those of Germany and France. In that country as well as in the smaller countries mentioned above, monetary policy rates determined by the European Central Bank (ECB) for inflation control for the euro-area in its entirety had been far too low for domestic demand management. A result was an unsustainable housing boom and wage and price inflation, which in turn weakened external competitiveness and deteriorated external balances.

Italy also appeared to have suffered from the ECB's one-size-fits-all monetary policy for the euro-area. While the country had not experienced significant housing booms as in Spain and Ireland, price and wage inflation persisted at rates much higher than in the euro-area average, resulting in the erosion of international competitiveness and external positions.

Neither regional surveillance within the European framework nor global surveillance by international institutions such as the IMF and the OECD was effective in preventing such large-scale crises in developed countries. Its outbreak in late 2009, its worsening in the following year and the initial management of the crisis by the euro-area authorities revealed to me, as an outside observer in Japan, not only the limits of surveillance by European and global institutions but also the unsatisfactory analysis and understanding within European institutions of the root causes of the crisis. A prevailing view in Europe, and in particular in Germany, was that it was essentially a sovereign debt crisis and it must be dealt with as such.

On the other hand, my basic argument was that at the root of the euro-area crisis was not only a sovereign debt problem but also a balance of payments disequiblium and, as such, a multifaceted approach was required to restore the euro-area economy back to a sustainable growth path, rather than simply focusing on fiscal retrenchment in the crisis-hit countries as advocated by the government authorities in Germany and some other euro-area member countries at the time.

In early June 2012, at a lunch meeting I had in Paris with Paul Atkinson and Michael Kennedy, former Head of Money and Finance Division of the OECD Economics Department, I told them that as far as I could detect as an outside observer, international institutions with a multilateral surveillance role had not only failed to act effectively to prevent the euro-area crisis but had not yet provided their views on a range of issues concerning its causes and remedies for it in ways clearly understandable to outsiders.

From this viewpoint, I thought that I should prepare an issues paper for discussion at a suitable venue in Europe, and on return to Tokyo, I prepared a draft note in which I discussed not only the root causes of the euro-area crisis and the way to deal with it but also pointed to the limits of surveillance by international organisations, even when the surveillance is well done.

While the records of regional surveillance within the framework of the European community and euro-area based institutions were not accessible to outside observers, surveillance reports by the IMF, a principal global institution engaged in the surveillance of individual member countries and the euro-area as a whole so as to ensure global financial stability and promotion of economic growth, were published. My own review of the back numbers of the IMF flagship publication "World Economic Outlook (*WEO*)" conveyed an impression that the IMF's early warning function in the runup to the euro-area crisis was not satisfactory. In October 2011, a group of outside experts published a report on the postmortem of IMF staff annual consultations with euro-area member countries and supranational institutions in the euro-area and the European Community as well as the IMF Executive Board surveillance.[8] It revealed a number of weaknesses in its exercises before the outbreak of the euro-area crisis.

Another international institution which has been engaged in surveillance of individual member countries and the euro-area is the OECD. Unlike at the IMF, a systematic exercise by outside experts to review the OECD's (published and unpublished) documents for surveillance on euro member countries and the euro-area in its entirety had not been carried out within the OECD. However, my own review of the back numbers of its flagship publication "Economic Outlook (*EO*)" since 2000 suggested that the OECD had issued warnings about some emerging fundamental problems in several euro-area member countries at a fairly early stage. For example, in the December 2001 *EO*, the erosion of Italy's competitive position was discussed as a matter of the OECD's particular concern in the country note on Italy (p. 67). In the subsequent issues of *EO*, the evolution of Italy's competitiveness and related policy issues were highlighted regularly in the country notes, with particular attention paid to divergent developments in relative unit labour costs.

In view of these findings, I called attention, in particular, to three forces which would have been at work regardless of however much the institutions would have improved their own analysis and oversight:

- Limits governments impose on surveillance by international institutions in their "shareholding" capacity, as well as self-restraint by the institutions themselves ("sanitation", self-censorship).
- The reluctance of elected governments to face up to the implications of warnings and alerts if this would be politically unattractive.
- Failure of markets to discipline policies that permit macroeconomic, fiscal, or financial imbalances due, at least in part, to poor assessments of available information, including "sanitised" surveillance reports published by the institutions.

I also referred to the difficulty in designing effective micro- and macro-prudential policies, their mixes and their co-ordination with monetary policies, and the "herd instinct" of financial institutions, moral hazard and the problem of regulatory and supervisory "capture" by large financial institutions.

My draft issues paper was sent to a number of first-class economists with rich experience in domestic and international economic and financial policy-making as well as policy advisory work in Europe and the United States. Stephen Axilrod sent me his written comments. Others provided their oral comments at the international conference I initiated as a non-bipartisan, non-political voluntary activity as president of the International Economic Policy Studies Association. It was held at a magnificent hall in the premises of La Maison de l'Europe de Paris in the heart of Paris with assistance from Robert Raymond, advisor to the Association and treasurer of La Maison de l'Europe de Paris in September 2013.

All of those commentators who made their oral comments at the conference subsequently provided me with written commentary notes.

Besides, Axilrod Charles Goodhart (Professor Emeritus and member of the Financial Market Group at the London School of Economics), and William White (then Chairman of the Economic and Development Committee of the OECD), who could not participate in the conference due to other work or family-related events, provided me with notes commenting on main issues raised in my paper.

The names of authors and the titles of their commentary notes, categorised thematically, are shown below.
On the role of surveillance:

1. André Icard, "Global and Regional Surveillance: Lessons from the Euro-Area Crisis"
2. Leif Pagrotsky, "Surveillance Failure or Systemic Failure?"
3. Val Koromzay, "The Role of Surveillance: Lessons from the Euro-Area Crisis"

On the role of prudential policy:

4. Paul Atkinson, "Beyond Surveillance: Reducing the Risk of Financial Crises
5. Jeffrey Shafer, "How should Microprudential Control be Strengthened to Prevent Local and Global Financial Market Failure?"
6. Carol Sirou, "Financial Market Failure and Their Remedies"

On the role of macro-prudential policy:

7. Stephen Axilrod, "On the Connection between Monetary Policy and the Regulation of Banking and Financial Markets"
8. Adrian Blundell-Wignall and Caroline Roulet, "Macroprudential Policy, Capital Controls and Bank Systemic Risk"
9. Charles Goodhart, "Risk, Reward and Bank Resilience"

On the management of the euro-area:

10. William White, "Can Europe Get its Political Act Together? Alternative Scenarios for the Eurozone"
11. Gunter Baer, "More Effective Management of the Euro-Area"

In addition to these commentary notes, Robert Price and Nicholas Vanston prepared an executive summary and a fuller report about oral discussions by preassigned speakers and other participants at the conference. All of these written contributions were collected and edited by me into a book entitled "The Limits of Surveillance and Financial Market Failure: Lessons from the Euro-Area Crisis" which was published by Palgrave Macmillan in 2014.[9]

Besides compiling this book for its publication in English, which was expected to take some time, I thought I should make my view on the reform of the euro-area known in Europe, in particular in Germany, in the light of the following message I received from a German participant in the conference.

"I would like to thank you once again for your kind invitation to your conference on the limits of global and regional surveillance. I very much enjoyed participating in this conference. Your main issues note and the background papers were excellent. Your chairmanship, the oral presentations of papers and discussions were at high professional level. So, I only can congratulate you to a successful and worthwhile event.

For me personally, the real test of whether I benefited from a conference, is not necessarily whether I got some new answers to a number of questions which have been on my mind before, but frequently much more whether I go home with new ideas and new perspectives. And this was in fact the case. In particular, your thesis that the euro-crisis is basically a balance of payments crisis and not a sovereign debt crisis, which I fully support, was a real eye-opener for me.

If we give the euro-area crisis this interpretation, austerity programs, the banking union, the stability pact and improved surveillance are all to a certain extent necessary steps to overcome the crisis, but they are by far not sufficient. None of these measures will make a major contribution to convergence of productivity levels. Structural adjustment, if ever possible supported by dynamic economic growth, becomes much more important. Moreover, it becomes very much clearer, if one adopts this interpretation of the euro-area crisis that it is illusionary to believe that the main debtor countries will ever be able to repay their debt. If one drives this direction of thought to the extreme, one may even conclude that the euro-area might not have a longer-term future if the Europeans do not get their act together and move to a Federal State. Perhaps one should see whether there are lessons which could be drawn from the early phases of monetary union in the United States."

Inspired by this comment, I approached a Paris correspondent of an influential German newspaper *Frankfurter Allgemeine* to sound about the possibility of an op-ed with the title of "How to run the euro-area". In its draft, I argued that given the underlying threat to the viability of the euro-area as a whole arising in particular from divergences between the economies of the two key partner countries in the euro-area, France and Germany, there was an urgent need for the French government to build public support for fundamental structural reform, including measures for securing a better functioning of labour and product markets. I also remarked that some countries in the euro-area needed to shift resources within public budget expenditures from transfers to productivity enhancing investments, while establishing a reliable legal and regulatory environment and a general economic and social climate conducive to investment, innovation, and risk-taking. Furthermore, I stressed that as creditor countries such as Germany still had high debt/GDP ratios and expected pressure on public budgets to increase in the future, it would not be wise to recommend them to give up on budgetary discipline. Rather, they should be asked to take the lead in microeconomic reform at national levels and in further opening and deepening the Single Market at the European level. As to the role of the European Central Bank (ECB), I argued that its monetary policy could play a major role in facilitating the adjustment process by sticking to a "symmetrical" approach to stabilising price inflation at or around 2 per cent for the euro-area as a whole, avoiding any deflationary bias. This would allow for short-term divergences in cost and price inflation across the region to restore a more sustainable configuration of competitive positions. At the same time, it would reinforce the ECB's credibility and narrow divergences in longer-run inflation expectations in individual countries participating in the euro-area, consequently aligning real interest rates in them closer to the area average.

My draft article written in English was sent to its editor in the Frankfurt head office through its Paris correspondent. As it was not adopted for publication by the German newspaper, I had a slightly revised version published as an op-ed co-signed with Paul Atkinson, Wolfgang Michalski, Leif Pagrotsky, and Robert Raymond in the 21 April 2014 issue of the *Japan Times*.[10] It was a follow-up of my op-ed "Chances of eurozone reform" published in the 24 October 2013 issue of the same Japanese newspaper.[11]

Subsequently, Michalski produced a German version of our Japanese newspaper article with the title of "Wirtschaftspolitik für die Eurozone" and approached another influential German newspaper *Handelsblatt* for publication, but it was not adopted either. In the end, the German version was published in an economic journal *Wirtschaftdienst*.[12]

The Role of Inter-Governmental Institutions in Public Opinion Formation

In the summer of 2016, I wrote an issue paper which reads:

Prior to the United Kingdom's EU referendum (UK referendum) held on 23 June 2016, the Bank of England's Monetary Policy Committee (MPC) stated, inter alia, that:

> *The most significant risks to the MPC's forecast concern the referendum. A vote to leave the EU could materially alter the outlook for output and inflation, and therefore the appropriate setting of monetary policy. Households could defer consumption and firms delay investment, lowering labour demand and causing unemployment to rise. At the same time, supply growth is likely to be lower over the forecast period, reflecting slower capital accumulation and the need to reallocate resources. Sterling is also likely to depreciate further, perhaps sharply.*

The Governor of the Bank of England reportedly added that there were a range of possible scenarios for the economy in the event of UK withdrawal from the UK (Brexit) and these "could possibly include a technical recession"—defined as two consecutive quarters of shrinking GDP.

Brexit campaigners repeatedly accused the Governor of the Bank of England of going beyond his remit for setting out the Bank's view that EU membership was a net benefit to the British economy, and warning of the shock to the economy and financial stability that would follow a decision to leave the EU.[13] Events in the aftermath of the referendum indicate that the Bank of England's warnings about its consequences proved to be justified as far as the immediate consequences on the financial and exchange markets are concerned. Notably, the UK pound hit a 31-year trough on 6 July 2016.

Somewhat earlier, the UK Treasury published a report in which it assessed how much poorer the UK would become in the long run if it left the EU.[14] Its analysis suggested that Brexit would lead to a long-run fall in GDP of 3.8 per cent relative to baseline under the Norway option (UK joins the European Economic Area); a 6.2 per cent fall under the Canada option (UK negotiates a Free Trade Agreement with EU); and a

7.5 per cent fall under the WTO option (UK trades with EU under WTO rules).

Among inter-governmental institutions, both the OECD and the IMF were notably explicit about the potential economic and financial risks involved in Brexit.

In a press release of 27 April 2016 titled "OECD study finds Britons will be paying a heavy 'Brexit tax' for many years if UK leaves EU", the OECD stated that:

> *A UK exit from the EU would immediately hit confidence and raise uncertainty which would result in GDP being 3% lower by 2020, which equates to GBP 2200 per household. The projected hit to living standards would amount in effect to a permanent "Brexit tax" on households.*[15]

In fact, the OECD presented three scenarios: optimistic, central, and pessimistic, to assess the longer-term effects of weaker technical progress, migration, and capital caused by Brexit. In the optimistic projection, the negative impact on GDP is around 2.7 per cent by 2030, but in the pessimistic scenario it would be more than 7.5 per cent. In the central scenario, UK GDP would be more than 5 per cent below what would be expected if the country remained in the EU. This GDP shortfall is equivalent to GBP 3200 per household.

The IMF also explored the potential impact of uncertainty on UK growth during the post-Brexit transition in two illustrative scenarios.[16] In the limited scenario in which uncertainty is relatively moderate and the UK was assumed to negotiate a status similar to that which exists between Norway and the EU, the study found that output would fall by 1.4 per cent by 2019 (compared to the baseline case in which the UK remains in the EU). In the adverse scenario of long negotiations and a default to the trade rules of the WTO, GDP would plunge by 5.6 per cent by 2019 (again compared to the baseline case in which the UK remains in the EU).

Both the OECD and the IMF resorted to a wide range of media communication instruments including speeches by the heads of the institutions as well as press releases for introducing and summarising more technical reports prepared by their staff (in both paper and electronic forms) to publicise these findings.[17] A number of established newspapers and television news reported the key messages in their reports and also reported that they triggered rows with the Brexit camp.[18]

Immediately after the outcome of the referendum was disclosed, in an interview with an economics correspondent of The Guardian, Mervyn King, the former Bank of England governor, argued that exaggerated claims by George Osborne, UK Chancellor, and the Treasury over the Brexit campaign backfired, and that they will need to row back from their claims that left him "baffled". King pointed out that the debate over the Brexit could not be "reduced to a cost/benefit analysis".[19] While he was not explicit about the claims made by the OECD and the IMF, it may be that his comment could apply also to the warnings the two institutions gave in the runup to the UK referendum. King reportedly said: "(I)t would have been enough to say there would be a great deal of uncertainty, but they went way beyond that, using precise numbers to say how much our living standards might fall".

Several inter-governmental institutions have been tasked for many years to assess events or forces that involve significant risks to the management of the global economy and financial stability with a view to calling the attention of national policy makers, financial investors, economic agents and the civil society at large. These institutions' assessment of risks involved in the scenario of Brexit and its publication in the runup to the referendum was their legitimate action and not to be considered as trespassing on UK sovereignty or interference in its domestic policy affairs. That said, it would be important to assess their daunting tasks to conduct analytical work including numerical exercises dealing with economic and so-called "non-economic"[20] policy issues and to distil the results of such work into effective policy messages in terms of clarity and strength needed for going beyond policy makers and reaching out to the general public in order to influence its opinion and thus help good policy making and execution.

This is not the first time that inter-governmental institutions were put into difficulty. A notable case is found in the OECD work on the Multilateral Agreement on Investment (MAI) which was negotiated among OECD member countries between 1995 and 1998. The aim was to set out multilateral rules for ensuring international investment in a more systematic and uniform way between countries. However, when a draft of the Agreement was made public, sharp criticism was directed by civil society and a number of developing countries which argued that the Agreement would make it difficult to control foreign investors. A global campaign against it led to a withdrawal of France, the OECD's host country, from its negotiation. This prevented its adoption by the OECD which follows consensus procedures for the adoption of new rules.

In April 1998, the OECD published a report titled "Open Markets Matter: The Benefits of Trade and Investment Liberalisation"[21] to argue the case for open markets and to discuss market openness and national sovereignty. But it did not prove to be sufficiently effective in diminishing the anxiety of those campaigning against the Agreement.

The OECD has changed greatly since then. It has been more openly encouraging debate to better deal with such global policy issues as economic growth, inequality, employment, financial stability, trade and investment, development, health and social welfare, the environment and climate change as well as public and private governance and regional development.

At the IMF also, efforts have been made to strengthen its surveillance activities notably since the debacles of the US and UK housing markets and the ensuing global financial and economic crisis.[22]

Despite these efforts made by both the OECD and the IMF, it might be useful to discuss the future role of surveillance by these institutions in the light of their experience with policy advice made in the runup to the UK referendum.

It was suggested that pro-EU voters were more likely to shift position in response to a threat to their standard of living, while most Leave voters remained committed even when told they would personally lose out. According to one report (published on 31 May 2016, based on fieldwork between 14 and 25 April), just 7 per cent of Leave supporters surveyed said they would vote Remain if Brexit left them £500 a year worse off. Leave voters were largely those who were unlikely to change their allegiance for financial reasons.[23]

If this report reflects reality, does it imply that the inter-governmental institutions should have more squarely addressed so-called "non-economic" considerations on top of the assessment of the likely macroeconomic costs of Brexit in making their policy advice? While such a task may be beyond the remit of the IMF, should the OECD not have more explicitly discussed major "non-economic" issues involved in the Brexit campaign[24,25]? After all, unlike the IMF, the OECD deals with a wide range of government policy issues including social and employment affairs, inequality, regional development, and so on.[26]

Actually, there is an OECD study in which rising inequality is estimated to have had a significantly negative effect on economic growth in the UK, while the OECD report "Policy Challenges for the Next 50 Years" suggests a possible trade-off between trade exposure and economic growth.[27]

If the OECD and the IMF (and also the Bank of England and the UK Treasury) had taken into account the need for lesser inequality as a policy objective of the UK government, their policy advice would have looked more balanced and more carefully presented than it had actually been prior to the UK referendum.

The making of solid policy advice by the inter-governmental institutions based on their assessment of so-called "non-economic" as well as economic forces working in the policy-making process, with better amalgamation of professional expert resources in economic, social, and other policy areas, should go hand in hand with far more effective dissemination of their policy messages through their interaction with the general public.

****

In his commentary note presented to the workshop held in Paris on 14 December 2016, Wolfgang Michalski remarked that if international organisations want their policy advice to be relevant, they may have to go on a tightrope between general macroeconomic and other policy advice on one side and analysis of country-specific options on how to deal with the economic and non-economic adjustment costs on the other; international organisations have to be extremely careful not to interfere with county-specific problems related to national sovereignty which is easily done when dealing in very concrete terms with distributional issues.

Paul Atkinson doubted that the OECD should have let itself be drawn into the political debate surrounding Brexit. He also endorsed Mervyn King's remarks that the UK Treasury, and by extension the OECD and the IMF, had done itself a disservice by making exaggerated and overly precise numerical assessments of damages from Brexit for which there was no basis. The analytical tools available to these institutions were not designed to analyse the effect of a major structural change such as Brexit in quantitative terms.

Nicholas Vanston noted that policy advice from the IMF and the OECD would certainly be more credible if more holistic, and that the OECD is better placed than the IMF in this respect. This would require closer collaboration between the various OECD Directorates and would profit from public messages that are neither bureaucratic double-speak nor slick slogans. In the end though, credibility depends on analysis and findings that prove to be consistently relevant and accurate. In recent years, the "experts" (not only economic) have too often been proved wrong.

Nicholas Bray (former Head of Media at the OECD) noted that, despite the sincerity of the warnings issued by the OECD, the organisation would have succeeded better in transmitting them by making clear how it had arrived at its forecasts and what margin for error these entailed. The setback underscored a lesson in communications terms that sincerity alone is insufficient to carry the day for a statement whose credibility can too easily be cast into doubt.

John Martin (former Director, OECD Directorate of Employment, Labour and Social Affairs) wrote that the key to success in the policy advice of the OECD is that the work supporting it is painstaking, of a high professional standard and is conducted with the active involvement and support of most member Governments, and with outreach to relevant non-governmental organisations.[28]

****

More than 8 years have passed since I organised the Paris workshop to discuss the role of inter-governmental institutions in public opinion formation in the light of the experience of the IMF and the OECD in the runup to Brexit.

Reviewing their experience at the time and the evolution of social media since then, Charles Goodhart offered the following comments:

"With the benefit of hindsight, the numerical calculations made about the likely economic consequences of Brexit by the OECD and IMF at the time look all too accurate now. Moreover, a large proportion of those in the United Kingdom who voted Leave, now regret doing so. But that does not mean that such external commentary on complex and socially divisive issues is, or was, likely to be welcomed by, or have much effect on, public opinion in recipient countries. To take a current example, national policies with regard to inward migration are likely to loom large in determining political and economic outcomes in member countries. I doubt whether the views of economists at the OECD or IMF would either be welcomed or influential on this key subject. Such policy choices, whether good or bad, are the prerogative of nation states.

When multilateral surveillance might have a more useful role would be in reviewing international macroeconomic measurement issues. For example, housing expenses are treated in different ways in the calculation of price indices in separate countries. What difference does that make to the relative assessment of inflation? Another example is the measurement of productivity, which has been subject to huge bias over time, e.g. overstating productivity gains, 1950–2000, as married women's unpaid household work got replaced by consumer durables; and understating productivity gains recently, as mobile phones, e-mail and Zoom, replaced postal services and other less efficient means of communication (comment received 4 March 2024)".

****

Notes

1. Meryn King, "Through the Looking Glass: Reform of the International Institutions", Inaugural International Distinguished Lecture to the Melbourne Centre for Financial Studies, Australia on 21 December 2006, https://www.bis.org/review/r061221a.pdf.
2. Kumiharu Shigehara, "Multilateral Surveillance: What the OECD can offer", the 1996 Global Finance Lecture at the University of Manchester, 16 October 1996, OECD Publications, Paris.
3. Kumiharu Shigehara, "Multilateral Surveillance: the IMF, the OECD and G-20", la Ligue Européenne de Cooperation Economique in Paris on 1 February 2011, http://shigehara.online.fr/en/index.html, https://www.dailymotion.com/video/xh5xan.
4. British Academy, "Letter to Her Majesty the Queen", London, 22 July 2009.
5. The first complete draft paper of 15 November 2010 was initially circulated to a small number of experts for commenting on analysis and views as well as checking factual information contained in it. We received helpful written comments from Stephen Axilrod (former Staff Director for Monetary and Financial Policy and Staff Director of the US Federal Reserve Board), Jean-Claude Chouraqui (former Head of Monetary and Fiscal Policy Studies Division of ECO), Andrew Dean (then Director of Country Studies Branch of ECO), Jorgen Elmeskov (then Deputy Chief Economist of the OECD and Director of Policy Studies of ECO), Graham Hacche (former Deputy Director, External Relations Department of the IMF), André Icard (former Deputy General Manager of the BIS), Jean-Claude Paye (former Secretary-General of the OECD), Robert Raymond (former Director-General of

the European Monetary Institute and advisor to the International Economic Policy Studies Association), and Philip Turner (then Deputy Head of Monetary and Economic Department of the BIS).

6. Kumiharu Shigehara and Paul Atkinson, "Surveillance by International Institutions: Lessons from the Global Financial and Economic Crisis", OECD Economics Department Working Paper No. 860, 17 May 2011, https://www.oecd-ilibrary.org/economics/surveillance-by-international-institutions_5kgchzchkvd2-en.
7. IMF, "IMF Response to the Financial and Economic Crisis", IMF, 2014, https://ieo.imf.org/en/our-work/Evaluations/Completed/2014-1027-imf-response-to-the-financial-and-economic-crisis.
8. Jean Pisani-Ferry, Andre Sapir and Guntram Wolff, "An Evaluation of IMF surveillance of the Euro Area" 31 October 2011, https://www.bruegel.org/sites/default/files/wp_attachments/BP_14_IMF_website.pdf.
9. Kumiharu Shigehara ed, "The Limits of Surveillance and Financial Market Failure: Lessons from the Euro-Area Crisis", Palgrave Macmillan, 2014, https://link.springer.com/book/10.1057/9781137471475.
10. Robert Raymond et al., "How to run the euro area", The Japan Times, 21 April 2014, https://www.japantimes.co.jp/opinion/2014/04/21/commentary/world-commentary/run-euro-area/.
11. Kumiharu Shigehara, "Chances of eurozone reform", The Japan Times, 24 October 2013, https://www.japantimes.co.jp/opinion/2013/10/24/commentary/chances-of-eurozone-reform/.
12. Paul Atkinson et al., "Wirtschaftspolitik für die Eurozone", "Wirtschaftspolitik für die Eurozone", Wirtschaftdienst, Vol. 6, 2014, https://www.wirtschaftsdienst.eu/inhalt/jahr/2014/heft/6/beitrag/wirtschaftspolitik-fuer-die-eurozone.html.
13. FT View, "This is no time to attack the credibility of the Bank of England", The Financial Times, 29 June 2016, http://www.ft.com/cms/s/0/8ef26a24-3de3-11e6-9f2c-36b487ebd80a.html#axzz4DL0lw6M9.
14. HM Treasury "Analysis: the long-term economic impact of EU membership and the alternatives", April 2016, https://www.gov.uk/government/uploads/system/uploads/attachment_data/file/517415/treasury_analysis_economic_impact_of_eu_membership_web.pdf.

15. OECD, "Brexit tax" for many years if UK leaves EU", 27 April 2016, http://www.oecd.org/newsroom/oecd-study-finds-britons-will-be-paying-a-heavy-brexit-tax-for-many-years-if-uk-leaves-eu.htm.
16. IMF, "If the U.K. leaves the EU: substantial negative effects" in IMF Survey Magazine "Uncertainty Clouds the United Kingdom's Economic Prospects", 17 June 2016、http://www.imf.org/external/pubs/ft/survey/so/2016/car061716a.htm.
17. For example, OECD website: http://www.oecd.org/unitedkingdom/the-economic-consequences-of-brexit-a-taxing-decision.htm and Angel Gurría, OECD Secretary-General, "To Brexit or not to Brexit: A Taxing Decision", London, 27 April 2016, http://www.oecd.org/about/secretary-general/to-brexit-or-not-to-brexit-a-taxing-decision.htm as well as "IMF Executive Board Concludes 2016 Article IV Consultation with the United Kingdom", IMF Press Release No. 16/286, http://www.imf.org/external/np/sec/pr/2016/pr16286.htm and IMF Magazine, 17 June, 2016, http://www.imf.org/external/pubs/ft/survey/so/2016/car061716a.htm.
18. For example, see: The Guardian, "Christine Lagarde urges UK to stay in the EU", 17 June 2016, https://www.theguardian.com/business/live/2016/jun/17/eurozone-finally-approves-75bn-greek-loan-business-live?page=with:block-5763bbfbe4b0a88a1c8731bf#block-5763bbfbe4b0a88a1c8731bf, and the BBC, "EU referendum: OECD warning of 'Brexit tax' sparks row", 27 April 2016, http://www.bbc.com/news/uk-politics-eu-referendum-36148316.
19. Phillip Inman, "Mervyn King: Treasury's exaggerated Brexit claims backfired", The Guardian, 27 June, 2016, https://www.theguardian.com/business/2016/jun/27/mervyn-king-brexit-treasury-claim-backfired-osborne. The relevance of claims based on precise numbers was criticized in a more provocative manner by Anne Pettifor Anne Pettifor, "Brexit: economists dangerously irrelevant", Blog "Prime", 24 June, 2016, http://www.primeeconomics.org/articles/brexit-economists-dangerously-irrelevant.
20. L. Alan Winters argues that, on close examination, the so-called "non-economic" objectives of agricultural support such as income distribution through income stability, the preservation of rural

communities, family farms and the environment, and national security turn out to be economic and its objectives are "amenable to measurement in money terms", see Winters, A., (1990), "The so-called non-economic objectives of agricultural support", OECD Economic Studies 13, pp. 237–266, https://www.oecd.org/eco/outlook/34318482.pdf.

21. OECD, "Open Markets Matter: The Benefits of Trade and Investment Liberalisation", 19 May 1998, https://www.oecd-ilibrary.org/trade/open-markets-matter_9789264162938-en
22. See Note 5 above.
23. Ipsos MORI, "Two thirds of Britons think their standard of living won't be affected by Brexit", 31 May 2016, https://www.ipsos-mori.com/researchpublications/researcharchive/3740/Two-thirds-of-Britons-think-their-standard-of-living-wont-be-affected-by-Brexit.aspx.
24. Following Winters (see Note 20 above), it might have been useful to examine whether Brexit would be an efficient way in achieving its so-called "non-economic" objectives such as restoring UK sovereignty and regaining control over the borders.
25. In the UK House of Lords debate on the EU referendum, Justin Welby, the Archbishop of Canterbuy, argued that widening inequality was the most pressing issue in the UK, http://www.archbishopofcanterbury.org/articles.php/5745/archbishop-speaks-in-lords-debate-on-eu-referendum.
26. Note that the Independent Evaluation Office (IEO) of IMF examined the IMF's involvement in social protection issues across its main lines of business—surveillance, lending, and capacity development. See "IMF and Social Protection: Issues Paper for an Evaluation by The Independent Evaluation Office (IEO)" (May 2016) where it is stated that: "(W)hile not an explicit part of its mandate, the IMF has addressed social protection issues" (page 1).
27. Increased inequality between 1985 and 2005 was estimated to have knocked about 9 percentage points off the 1990–2010 growth rate of GDP growth. See Federico Cingano, "Trends in Income Inequality and its Impact on Economic Growth", OECD Social, Employment and Migration Working Papers No. 163, 2014, https://www.oecd.org/els/soc/trends-in-income-inequality-and-its-impact-on-economic-growth-SEM-WP163.pdf.

28. John Martin cited two leading examples of such successes. First, beginning with its landmark publication "the Growing Unequal" in 2008, the OECD published a succession of reports detailing the causes and consequences of growing inequality and policy reforms to tackle it. This work helped push the topic of inequality higher on the policy agenda of many member countries. A second example he cited was the OECD's Programme for International Student Assessment (PISA) which assesses 15-year-olds abilities in reading, mathematics and science. PISA started assessing student performance in 2000 and it currently covers more than 70 countries/regions throughout the world. As such, PISA has had a major impact on education systems and pedagogical methods worldwide.

PART IV

New Challenges for the Global Economy

CHAPTER 19

Regionalisation, Globalisation, and Social Cohesion

The 1990s is often characterized as the decade of globalisation, when free international flows of goods and services and factors of production such as capital and technology became more widespread than ever before. But, around the start of the decade, there was increased concern that the expanding number of participants in negotiations on global frameworks for such flows, and the growing diversity of their interests, points of view and technical capabilities tended to reduce the efficacy and usefulness of global negotiations. bilateralism and regionalism appeared as an increasingly attractive alternative to globalism. This chapter focuses on my involvements in debates on these issues that developed in the 1990s. As it is important to distinguish the implications of globalisation for economic and social policy matters such as employment and equality from those of new technology, a supplementary note "New Technology, Innovation and Employment" is provided at the end of this chapter.

External Dimension of Europe 1992

From 31 December 1992, the twelve countries of the European Community (EC) comprised an area without internal barriers, the called "the European Single Market" in which the free movements of goods, services, labour, and capital was ensured. In advance to its establishment, I as a non-European economist was asked to present a paper to discuss the

K. Shigehara, *The Bank of Japan, the OECD, and Beyond*, https://doi.org/10.1007/978-981-97-5307-9_19

external aspects of this development in Europe to the Annual Congress of the European Economic Association which was held in Lisbon on 13 August–2 September 1990. I was then Bank of Japan Chief Economist.

While numerous studies had been carried out about the internal aspects of the creation of a Single European Market by the end of 1992—"Europe 1992", no systematic efforts had been made to assess the implications of Europe 1992 for the EC's external policy and the relationships between Europe, the United States, and Japan. Indeed, no light was shed on the external aspects of Europe 1992 in the so-called Cecchini Report[1] on the benefits of the European Single Market, nor in the EC Commission's complimentary publication on the economics of 1992.[2]

In my paper,[3] I briefly examined some broad policy areas in which the relationship between Europe, the United States, and Japan might be affected significantly by the EC initiative of Europe 1992. I then assessed its implications for extra-EC trade and foreign direct investment flows, after which I examined the external financial aspects of Europe 1992, as the liberalisation of financial services was estimated in the Cecchini Report to play a major role in boosting economic gains from Europe 1992.

The major conclusions of my paper were as follows:

- Trade diversion is an unavoidable consequence of Europe 1992, even if the average level of EC protection for extra-EC trade is not raised. Whether or not, and the extent to which the United States, Japan, and for that matter the other trading partner of the EC, will benefit from Europe 1992, will depend crucially on the magnitude of extra-EC trade expansion through its domestic growth bonus in the EU. They are also contingent on the actual course of EC protectionist policy with regard to its trade with the rest of the world;
- There may be strong domestic political obstacles to internal industrial reorganisation which may also make it difficult for the European Commission to stick to its declared intention of not raising the average level of protection for the EC, especially if macroeconomic conditions start to deteriorate. Transparency about protection through non-tariff barriers should be increased so that multilateral surveillance of protectionist moves can be carried out more effectively;
- While increased efficiency in the manufacturing sector can come importantly from scale economies, there is some evidence that the

economic gains through financial market integration arise overwhelmingly from increased competition among financial institutions, and not much can be expected from economies of scale and scope. This finding lends weight to the view that free provision of financial services by US and Japanese financial institutions will add to economic gains for the EC;

- Closer co-operation and co-ordination among the responsible authorities are required to prevent increased international competitive pressure from eroding the soundness of financial institutions, and narrow disparities between tax systems which distort the allocation of investment and savings across countries; and
- In the longer run, all trading partners will benefit from *multilateral* and *unilateral* trade liberalisation and the free movements of capital on the basis of the *erga omnes* principle applied on a worldwide basis. The EC, the United States and Japan should cooperate to work out a better multilateral framework for global market integration.

Policy Implications of Trade and Currency Zones

In addition to the EC's programme for internal market integration by the end of 1992, the United States, Canada, and Mexico started negotiations for a proposed free trade zone, building on the US-Canada Free Trade Agreement which went into effect in January 1989. It was against this background that the symposium entitled "Policy Implications of Trade and Currency Zones" was organized by the Federal Reserve Bank of Kansas City at Jackson Hole, Wyoming in late August 1991. As described in the supplementary note on "Japan Bashing" included in Chapter 12, I was asked to act not only as a discussant of Alan Meltzer's paper "US Leadership and Postwar Progress" but also give my own views on policy issues concerning the regionalisation of the world economy.[4]

After a review of the broad evolution of intraregional and interregional trade patterns which suggested the importance of interregional trade, Meltzer argued that it would not be in the interest of either the United States or Japan to develop intraregional trade as a substitute for open, multilateral trade. In my comment in which I agreed with Meltzer's view about the importance of multilateral trade, I noted that one could probably argue that the EC typically represented the case of "natural integration". At the same time, I remarked that for the original EC group, intraregional trade had tended to stagnate in relative terms since 1970. While the apparent loss of momentum in integration had been cited by the European Commission as reason for initiating the programme for completing internal market by the end of 1992, I argued that removing trade barriers with the rest of the world should be a top priority of the EC, if the main competitive pressure—a principal source of greater economic efficiency—should come from the rest of the world rather than from within the EC, as suggested in a study by European economists.

Aa a concrete policy proposal, I said that major trading partners including Japan should strengthen collective efforts to measure and reduce the *effective* degree of trade protection. I stated that as a result of growing resort to non-tariff measures, such as voluntary export restraints, import quotas, local content requirements, and subsidies to domestic industries, data on *average* tariffs no longer precisely measured the *effective* degree of trade restriction. In this context, as former Director of the General Economics Branch of the OECD Economics Department, I referred to the OECD's work on the quantification of agricultural protection,[5] and to its attempt to collect data on industrial subsidies in various forms.

I also noted that in East Asia, diversity in the stage of economic and financial development as well as historical and cultural background in individual countries, and the absence of institutional arrangements for economic integration, would limit the development of an EC-type of monetary integration. Currencies of most of East Asian economies other than Japan were not completely convertible for capital transactions, and the Japanese capital market was not used as actively by private economic agents in these Asian economies as those in the OECD area. While the absolute value of Japan's direct investment that went to Asian countries tripled between 1983 to 1989, and accounted for a substantial portion of total direct investment inflows into these countries, the share of Japan's total direct investment that Asian countries accounted for declined by half during the same period by half from 28 per cent to 14 per cent. According to an IMF study, the yen's share in the official reserve holding of Asian countries rose to about 18 per cent in the late 1980s, but a far greater share (56 per cent) was held in US dollars, and a significant portion (15 per cent) in German marks.

I then argued that Japan should strengthen efforts to make its capital market more efficient and more readily accessible to foreign investors and borrowers on an erga omnes principle, by further financial liberalisation and increasing transparency of its market.

In early September 1991, the Stockholm School of Economics organised a conference "Japan in a Global Economy, a European perspective" in Stockholm, which is also mentioned in a supplementary note "Japan Bashing" in Chapter 12. At that conference, under the main title of "Evolving International Trade and Monetary Regimes and Related Policy Issue", I discussed the roles of both Japan and Europe in realising better global economic performance.[6] Below are some specific comments I made on the European agenda.

- A key question for producers outside the European Single Market is the extent to which its trade-diverting effect will be offset by an expansion of extra-zone trade resulting from faster income growth within the zone through its internal integration. The net result for producers in the rest of the world may be influenced not only by the "static" trade effect but also the long-run "dynamic" effect which a larger, integrated regional market can have on investment and income growth. It is because of this that countries outside the trade zone should be concerned about the process of internal industrial reorganisation in the enlarged regional market, as well as the course of the trade policy to be adopted under the regional trade arrangement.
- An important question in this respect is how industrial reorganisation will proceed within the EC. Greater scale economies will be an essential source of increased efficiency and international competitiveness for the industrial sector, but this means that the number of firms must be reduced. There is a risk that long-run efficiency considerations will be subordinated to short-run sociopolitical pressures to reduce conflicts of interest within member countries where losers are likely to be many. Political pressure may mount to offset the competitive threat to domestic losers by protectionist measures against producers outside the EC region, especially if macroeconomic conditions deteriorate within the region. This points to the importance of good macroeconomic policy management in the process of industrial reorganisation.
- Adoption of a common currency within the EU could foster regional economic integration. It could increase wage and price flexibility if the central body for monetary policy decision-making gains the

credibility of its commitment to price stability, as the experience of a "hard currency" in smaller countries neighbouring Germany has typically shown. But we must recall that during the gold standard period resort to trade policy was frequently made as an adjustment mechanism alternative to exchange rate changes. Too early attempts to introduce a common currency in a trade zone may lead to increased use of trade restrictions as an alternative adjustment mechanism, if such a zone covers a wide range of countries including those where institutional factors are such that wage and price flexibility is likely to remain more limited than in the other member country.

- As structural reform proceeds, trade conflicts arising from greater multipolarity and interdependence should weaken. In the context of non-inflationary growth, it should be easier to absorb changes in competitive advantage which characterize a dynamic economy. Nevertheless, powerful pressure groups will continue to seek protection from international competition. The future of the multilateral trading system will depend on the resistance of trade policy to such sectoral interests. In any democratic society, policy-making will be influenced by the reaction of the electorate. Consumer organisations must be mobilsed in opposing protectionist measures which would reduce their welfare. Economists must play an important role in this regard by offering a thorough and objective assessment of the costs and benefits of protection.

Globalisation, Employment, and Social Cohesion

Free movement of goods, services, capital, technology, and information between more should help to accelerate economic growth and improve material standards of living worldwide. For businesses, costs become reduced through greater profits of scale through trade with global markets as a sales channel. For consumers, goods become available at lower prices, and they have greater choice. In addition, investment gets directed to areas of the world with the highest profit potential. This leads to new capital investment and technology transfer, which increases labour productivity, benefiting workers as well as savers and investors.

However, as globalisation developed, especially after China's accession to the WTO, concern grew that globalisation has negative impacts on employment and wages, especially for unskilled workers, increasing income inequalities in OECD countries. In fact, globalisation led to a growing trend to shift production of goods with unskilled labour components, such as textiles and other light industrial products, and more recently more sophisticated industrial goods, from OECD member countries to non-OECD regions. In addition, globalisation came increasingly to be seen as limiting national sovereignty. For example, when dealing with issues such as taxation, the multinationalisation of corporations narrowed the scope for individual action by national governments. In relation to the implementation of social security systems and environmental policies, it came to be argued that the globalisation of companies that bear the costs of these systems had encouraged competition between nations to "devalue" minimum social standards. It was claimed that the tax systems of non-OECD countries with lower tax burdens and social security costs were creating "fiscal dumping" and "social dumping" by encouraging multinational companies' international re-location of production bases away from the OECD area to the non-OECD area.

Against this backdrop, the OECD Economics Department headed by me pointed out that, although it was generally accepted at the time that the widening income gap was largely due to globalisation, it was actually more due to the widening gap between those with special skills and those without, which was caused by the rapid development of new technologies, including information and communication technologies and robotics. The point was made that this was largely due to the widening gap between those with special skills and those without. It was noted that there was a widening income gap between those with and without special skills acquired after school education among those with the same educational background. There was also a noticeable trend towards long-term unemployment among those without skills, a development common to all OECD countries. In fact, these developments were occurring at the same time in the newly industrialised countries and in developing countries that were opening up more and more to the outside world. Simon Kuznets had argued that income inequality increases at the beginning of economic development and decreases as the economy matures. In the 1990s, as trade and direct investment coupled with technology transfers between low-wage newly industrialising and developing countries and OECD countries, a widening of wage inequalities became a major social issue both in the OECD and non-OECD areas. It was around that time that Richard Freeman, a labour economist and professor at Harvard University, wrote an article entitled "Are Your Wages Set in Beijing?".[7]

In July 1997, shortly after my appointment as Deputy Secretary-General, I wrote a short article in English on the implications of globalisation under the original title "Globalisation, Technology and Employment". Its copies were distributed by the Communications Division of the OECD Secretariat to the media. My article was published first by the *Journal of Commerce* in the United States with a title of "Good new on globalization". Subsequently, a Spanish newspaper *Cincodias* published its Spanish translation the title of "Globalización, tecnología y empleo" (Globalisation, technology and employment), adopting a direct translation of the original title and the main text into Spanish. Likewise, a French newspaper *Le Figaro* published my article with the title of "Mondialisation, téchnologie et emploi", using a direct translation of the original title into French. On the other hand, a German newspaper *Handelsblatt* published it with the title of "Die negative Einstellung zur Globalisierung überwinden" ("Overcoming the negative attitude towards globalization"). Finally, the Japanese version was published by *Yomiuri Shimbun,* a newspaper with the largest circulation in Japan in February 1998. Its title (according to my translation into English) was "Globalisation – Benefits for all countries".

These media activities were preceded by my speechmaking at the International Workshop, which was held at Palazzo Farnese, Piacenza, Italy on 11–12 April 1997. Below is the full text of my speech which was reflected on my media activities mentioned above.

"The title of this workshop, "Globalisation and Employment: A Possible Resolution?" is a topical theme. Let me start out by saying that globalisation—that is to say free international flows of goods and services, and factors of production such as capital and technology—is, overall, a positive development that is to be welcomed. Increased trade between the OECD and non-OECD areas as well as within each of them helps both areas to realise real income gains through specialisation and intensifying competition, and thereby raising efficiency and productivity economy-wide. At the level of firms, trade tends to reduce costs through economies of scale as well as those of scope. At the level of consumers, trade increases the variety of products available at lower prices. And free international movements of capital allow investment to take place in the regions of the world where its return is highest, benefiting savers, investors and the workers whose productivity is increased through new capital stock accumulation embodying new technology, typically through foreign direct investment and associated international transfer of technology. As such, globalisation is nothing but the broadening and continuation of trends which have contributed greatly to the rising prosperity of OECD countries over the last half-century. When discussing problems related to globalisation, it is important to keep in mind that, at the end of the day, this process is something that we will benefit from.

Why are we then concerned about the impact of globalisation on employment? The first point to note is that globalisation is often blamed for developments which are not truly global. In Europe, regional integration is leading to profound structural change. The Single Market project of the European Union is essentially aimed at reaping the efficiency gains associated with having one large unified market. But in the process of achieving that, a great many firms and jobs have been lost already and will be lost in the future. Let me give you a few simple examples: In the early 1990s, the United States had two producers of electric locomotives whereas the then 12 EU countries had 16 such producers. Some adjustment has taken place since then to achieve scale economies in one enlarged and unified market, but the European production remains fragmented.

Another example: in a report published in 1988, the European Commission estimated that 207 out of 739 European footwear firms would have to disappear as a result of industrial reorganisation in the context of the single market. While one should be cautious about exact numbers, this would suggest that more adjustment remains in the pipeline. I say this not to suggest that there is something wrong with the Single Market initiative but to illustrate that a lot of the adjustment burdens being put on businesses and workers are not the result of globalisation per se but the result of regional integration introduced at the initiatives of European governments to achieve efficiency gains. The corollary is that globalisation is often blamed for developments it did not cause, and that resistance to globalisation often arises from such misperceptions.

This is not to say that globalisation, in the true sense of the word, is problem-free. In the rest of my speech, I will concentrate on some of the problems associated with globalisation and what can be done about them. To do so, I will narrow my focus down to the impact on employment and wages in OECD countries of increased trade with non-OECD countries.

One argument often heard these days is that increased trade with the non-OECD area tends to reduce demand for low-skilled workers in OECD countries. The argument rests on unskilled labour making up a larger proportion of labour forces and therefore receiving proportionately lower wages in non-OECD countries than in the OECD area. A prevalent trade theory then tells us that non-OECD countries will typically tend to specialise in goods produced using low-skilled, low-cost labour whereas specialization in OECD countries will move towards goods produced by more highly-skilled labour at higher wages. As a result of trade with non-OECD countries, therefore, the demand for low-skilled labour will fall in OECD countries, in those countries where labour markets are flexible, the relative wages of low-skilled workers will fall sufficiently to maintain their unemployment low. In other OECD countries where wages are rigid, unemployment among unskilled workers will rise.

Whatever the merits of this argument, it is a fact that the demand for low-skilled labour has shrunk in OECD countries. In some of them, low-skilled workers have experienced a significant decline in relative wages, in others a more than proportional increase of unemployment, and in a quite a number of countries a combination of the two. This has happened despite the on-going upskilling of labour forces in OECD countries which has significantly reduced the relative, and in some cases the absolute, supply of low-skilled labour over recent decades. It is not too much, therefore, to speak about a collapse in demand for low-skilled labour in the OECD area.

As part of the work for the OECD Jobs Study, we have reviewed the empirical evidence on the notion that increased trade with non-OECD countries has triggered this collapse in demand for low-skilled labour. The evidence does not point to international trade as being the main culprit. If anything, there is more evidence pointing to technological change as a cause for lower demand for low-skilled labour in the OECD area. More recent as well as on-going work comes up with the same conclusion. But I would not over-emphasise the allocation of blame between technology and trade.

The two developments have been closely inter-connected. Technological development, not least in the form of falling international transportation costs, has encouraged trade. And competition through trade has spurred technological development and diffusion of new technologies across countries both within the OECD area and between the OECD and non-OECD areas.

One methodological objection to both our own work and that of most others in this field also deserves mention. Analysis in this field usually considers the direct effect of trade patterns, or prices of traded goods, on employment and wages in the economy. However, one of the reasons that we welcome globalisation is that we expect it to boost real incomes. Higher real incomes will have impacts on our consumption and production patterns which are usually not taken into account when considering the effects of trade on demand for different kind of labour.

Even if technological progress rather than trade has been the main cause behind the collapse of demand for low-skilled labour in past decades, it is far from certain that the relative importance of technology and trade in influencing demand for OECD workers—both skilled and unskilled—will remain the same in the future. Developments in telecommunication and computing technologies have already allowed firms in the OECD area to outsource accounting and other tasks using relatively highly skilled labour in non-OECD countries. Globalisation and technology might conceivably interact with many other unpredictable results even for skilled workers in the OECD area.

What we do know, however, is that it is important that new opportunities for production, arising as a result of globalisation and technological change, are exploited. This points to the need for flexible and competitive product markets. Governments have an important role to play here in undertaking regulatory reform in order to ensure that excessive and repressive regulation does not stifle entrepreneurship in the business sector.

As regards labour markets, the uncertainty about the future impact of globalisation and technology on various types of labour demand points to the need for flexibility. To reap the full benefits of globalisation and technological change, it is important that labour is reallocated, and is capable of being reallocated, as swiftly as possible when there are shifts in demand. The alternative, where unemployment goes up and remains high as a result of demand shifts, is both socially troubling and economically wasteful.

It is important, therefore, to have in place the mechanisms necessary to achieve a swift reallocation of labour supply in the face of changes in demand. One important aspect of this is to avoid impeding the role of wage adjustment in balancing the supply of and demand for different kinds of labour. But there are other important issues. For example, excessive job protection makes firms reluctant to hire and thereby to absorb workers laid off by other firms. And overly generous income transfers make unemployed workers reluctant to accept available jobs. In the past, labour market policies have often taken the "passive" form of compensating income losses of the unemployed by unemployment benefits etc. Instead, the so-called active labour market policies, such as measures to assist job search, training and re-training as well as employment subsidies, can sometimes help people back into employment more quickly and may also prevent their skills from decaying during a spell of unemployment. Education also has an important role to play. By equipping workers with a solid and sufficiently broad basis, it will increase their versatility in the case of job-shifts. Similarly, by allowing people to return to the education system, it will increase their flexibility. While so-called 'lifelong learning' may sound like no more than a catch-phrase, it covers the reality that shifts in labour demand create needs for re-tooling of labour which the education system needs to be able to respond to. In the cases of both initial education and re-tooling, it is important that the wage structure gives workers the appropriate incentives to engage in such activity".

As noted above, it was in the mid-1990s that Richard Freeman wrote an article entitled "Are Your Wages Set in Beijing?". His extensive analysis assessed inter alia the argument set out in a 1994 landmark book "North–South Trade, Employment and Inequality: Changing Fortunes in a Skill-Driven World" by Adrian Wood, a Professorial Fellow at the Institute of Development Studies at the University of Sussex. Wood's research had led him to the conclusion that trade in manufactures with countries in the South was bound to reduce demand for low-skilled labour in the North, requiring targeted policies to assist the people and places affected.

While Freeman could find no evidence when writing in 1995 that trade with developing countries (with China as a proxy) had influenced wages or employment in OECD countries, he concluded by saying: "(I)n the future, I expect that (other) factors will continue to be more important. I could, of course, be utterly wrong. The best we can do is probe and poke at the evidence and arguments, and present our analyses and prognostications with appropriate humility", implying that while at the time of his writing (1995) neither unskilled workers' wages nor their employment in the United States were being set in Beijing, at some time in the future they might be.

That is precisely what has become a huge political issue in the United States. In the decades after China's admission to the WTO in 2001, a number of Western researchers came to find empirical evidence of the significant impact of a "China Shock" on low-skilled workers in the US mid-West, even as sectors using high-skilled labour had deprived great benefits in other sectors of the US economy, with a net creation of jobs.[8]

Both China and the United States have benefited enormously from their economic interaction. But, the adjustment costs in the United States for low-skilled labour were neither assessed properly nor responded to with adequate domestic adjustment policies. This can now be seen as a major policy failure with serious political consequences in present times, contributing to fundamental changes in trade and industrial policies in the United States.

Setbacks in Multilateral Negotiations on International Investment and Trade

As noted in Chapter 18, the OECD decided at its 95th Ministerial Council Meeting in 1995 to launch negotiations for a Multilateral Investment Agreement (MIA) aimed at a high level of liberalisation and protection of international capital investment and effective dispute settlement procedures. Following this decision, international negotiations got underway with the aim of reaching an agreement by the Ministerial Council in 1997 (Photo 19.1). They involved not just OECD countries, but also several emerging economies. As will be described in the next chapter, as OECD Deputy Secretary-General whose area of responsibility included OECD dialogue with non-OECD countries, I visited Russia, the Baltic States, and elsewhere to meeting presidents, prime ministers, ministers of economic affairs, ministers of foreign affairs, and other cabinet ministers of these countries. One of their key concerns was how much direct investment OECD countries would be willing to make in their countries if they became OECD member countries, and a number of them asked me about the ongoing MIA negotiations. It was around that time that France announced that it would no longer participate in MAI negotiations. It was decided at informal MAI consultations in December 1998 that MAI negotiations in the OECD would no longer take place.

In December 1999, the ministerial meeting of the World Trade Organisation (WTO) was held in Seattle, with the aim of launching a new post-Uruguay round of trade negotiations. At that meeting, there was intensive criticism from developing countries that the trade liberalisations to date had prioritised the interests of developed countries. Moreover, there were violent protests against the acceleration of globalisation from

Photo 19.1 Participants of OECD Ministerial Council meeting of June 1997: (from left to right) Renato Ruggiero (Director-General of the World Trade Organisation), Erik Asbrink (Swedish Minister of Finance), Leif Pafgrotsky (Swedish Minister of Trade) and Kumiharu Shigehara (Deputy Secretary-General) (© OECD-OCDE)

non-governmental organisations on the side of developed countries. In the end, the meeting failed to achieve its aim.

Long before setbacks in these multilateral negotiations, the OECD had undertaken a number of empirical analyses of the labour market impacts of trade with low-wage non-member countries in OECD countries in the course of its research on unemployment issues, concluding that the widening wage gap and rising unemployment in OECD countries was due not to increased trade with non-member countries, but to the labour supply side's inability to respond quickly to the technological innovations occurring within OECD countries. In May 2000, a lengthy report entitled "Social Dumping in Europe", produced with the participation of parliamentarians, was submitted to the lower house of the French Parliament, and subsequently published. The conclusions of this report, like those of the OECD study, were that, from a macro perspective, trade with other countries and foreign investment were not the main causes of the widening of wage gap and high unemployment in France. However, the findings of these studies were not effective in influencing public opinion in France.

In the communiqué of the April 1997 meeting of the IMF Interim Committee it was noted that there would be a number of benefits from amending the IMF Articles of Agreement to make the liberalisation of international capital movements a central purpose of the IMF and to extend its jurisdiction to capital movements (see Chapter 17). But its work for amendment was put on hold due at least in part to the growing caution in view of experiences such as the East Asian financial crisis. In fact, I expressed scepticism about the idea of liberalising capital transactions in non-OECD countries as a matter of principle, when I was invited from the OECD side to an expert meeting chaired by Michel Camdessus, then Managing Director of the IMF, at its Washington headquarters. At the time, I was concerned that many non-OECD member countries had not established solid domestic financial infrastructures to be able to cope with external financial shocks. This cautious view of mine was also reflected in my speech at a conference organised by the OECD Development Centre and the Asian Development Bank on "Financial Liberalisation in Asia" in June 1998,[9] in which I noted that many OECD member countries, including Japan, had experienced financial crises during the wave of financial liberalisation, partly due to the failure of prudential policies. I stressed the importance of balanced liberalisation and micro- and macro-prudential policies in terms of both domestic finance and international capital transactions. I expressed the same view in a French economic newspaper *L' Echo*[10] as well. Furthermore, in my keynote speech on issues surrounding financial globalisation in emerging market economies at the Pacific Rim Central Banks' Conference in Los Cabos, Mexico at the beginning of November 1998, I pointed out the risks of rapid financial liberalisation in countries that had been implementing fixed exchange rate policies without a solid prudential policy framework.[11] And, in my speech at the International Finance Conference held in Istanbul in late November 1998, I said that in order to promote globalisation smoothly, it would be important to ensure the soundness of corporate sector governance as well as the soundness of the financial system, and pointed out the role of the OECD in addressing these issues.[12]

Thus, I stressed the importance of paying attention to the increased risk of instability of the financial system and social justice issues that would arise in the process of globalisation and increased competition, while remaining basically in the position of advocating the merits of economic and financial integration on a global scale, encompassing both developed and developing countries (see Supplementary Note 2 "A View of the Global Economy in the Twenty-First Century" below).

Supplementary Note 1: New Technology, Innovation, and Employment

A keynote speech by Kumiharu Shigehara, Head of the OECD Economics Department, at the Conference on Creativity, Innovation and Job Creation, Oslo, 11–12 January 1996.

At the outset of this conference, it is important to ask the question: "Why are we here?" That is, what makes technology and innovation both so important and so controversial that we want to hold a conference on these issues? In this speech I will focus first on the costs and benefits of technological change. Second, I will consider the role of policies in affecting the pace of technological progress. Third, I will consider policies to assist adaptation to technological change. In addressing these issues, I will adopt an economy-wide perspective. At the OECD we combine this overall perspective with work on more detailed and specific issues.

The Costs and Benefits of Technological Change

In the debate on the costs and benefits of technological change, two extreme views can be distinguished:

One view is that technological progress is always beneficial and should proceed as fast as possible. The other view is that too rapid technological progress carries high costs and is a threat to individual and social welfare; its speed should therefore be moderated. The extreme positive view of technological progress emphasises the importance of technology for generating overall income growth. At some basic level, the mastering and development of technology is one of the main features that set man apart from animals. The story of mankind has to a large extent been driven by improved technology. It is the main factor accounting for rising living standards over the course of history. In this large historical perspective, it seems obvious that we should welcome faster technological development.

Taking the negative view on new technology, some would argue that it inevitably leads to higher unemployment, as new technology raises productivity, fewer workers are needed to achieve the given level of output and therefore unemployment rises. However, this argument overlooks that the demand for output is likely to rise as a result of technological progress. It is actually striking that unemployment in the OECD area began rising at the same time as productivity growth started to slow down in the early 1970s. This historical relationship during the 1970s and 1980s alone cannot of course provide answers to how new technology of the 1990s and onwards will affect employment and unemployment.

The extreme negative view of technology is right in emphasising that new technology can cause dislocation, affecting both individuals, firms and social structures. Moreover, technology often requires organizational change as exemplified by the buzzwords "down-sizing" and "delayering", which raise anxieties about job stability and precariousness of employment. There is also a presumption that technological change affects the demand for different types of labour differently. In some cases, valuable assets including human capital may become obsolete and worthless. In other cases, the return on human capital may increase strongly. Many people have to go through agonising shifts, and some end up as unemployed losers in the process. Nevertheless, most of those who complain about the negative aspects of technological change recognise that while innumerable industries have disappeared as a result of technological progress over the course of history, other industries and other jobs have sprung up.

Their complaint appears to centre on the speed of adjustment, which they claim has become so high that individuals cannot live up to the demands and is likely to become even higher in the future. Back in history, generations followed generations doing the same work.

Until recently, people would still mostly do the same work in their whole active life, though one generation would not necessarily do the same work as the preceding generation. But now, people may have to change work several times during their active life in ways that are difficult to foresee.

The argument is also made that we have entered a new paradigm where globalization and technological development have mutually reinforcing effects. With more effective means of transport and communication, and free capital flows, competition from the non-OECD area is becoming fiercer and firms have greater flexibility in relocating production from one country to another. There is probably something in this, even if one can disagree on the strength of these trends, with trade between the OECD and the non-OECD area remaining small compared to the intra-OECD trade.

Technology is also perceived as a threat against the welfare state. Because new technology is seen to raise unemployment, the fear is that associated public expenditure and deficits will be unsustainable and will lead to cutbacks on welfare spending. This argument overlooks three things. First, as I already noted, it is not obvious that new technology raises unemployment. Second, by raising real incomes, technological progress will also raise the tax base. Third, in some cases social programmes can be re-designed so that they can continue to meet genuine social needs and goals, while mobilising the available labour supply to the maximum and avoiding excessive and possibly unsustainable budgetary pressures.

Perceived risks and pressures arising from rapid changes in technology threaten social cohesion. A decline in cohesion is not just bad in itself, though it obviously does affect the quality of life. It is also bad for the economy. Trust is a very important asset for the workings of an economy. Where trust breaks down, the costs of economic interaction go up, as increased resources have to be devoted to the enforcement of contracts. Resistance to change becomes more entrenched and what one could call social speed limits to change become lower.

This discussion leads me to the following conclusions. We need rapid technological progress. Its benefit is not just higher overall income growth, which in itself is good. But it also generates the resources necessary for measures to help people to adapt and adjust. By strengthening people's inherent capacity for adaptation and by extending direct help to them when that is needed, such support measures, if appropriately designed, will reduce the costs of adjustment to technological progress and thereby raise social speed limits. In the rest of this speech, I will focus on both policies to enhance technological development and those which help adaptation to it.

Policies to Establish a Proper Framework for Innovation

An innovator typically does not receive the full returns to innovation. Part of the returns has a public good character and spill over to society as a whole. The usual policy instruments to compensate for this problem are direct subsidisation or tax rebates.

But efficient subsidisation of R&D, whether direct or through tax breaks, is difficult. We know little about the size of benefits that technological innovation will bring to society. In this situation subsidies are often wasted on activities that would have taken place in any case. The innovator in some cases finds it difficult to realise the full private returns to innovation, for example because competitors will exploit the innovator's new technology. The usual policy instrument to deal with this problem is the innovator's intellectual property rights, including patents.

The costs of innovation relate not least to the costs of finance. Governments can influence the private-sector's financing costs indirectly through the role of fiscal deficits in determining real interest rates in capital markets. Moreover, failure to control inflation also seems to be reflected in a real interest rate premium. For these reasons, maintaining a stable macroeconomic framework with a focus on price stability and long-term sustainability is likely to be the most helpful background governments can provide for encouraging private investment in innovation and its diffusion.

Governments have often intervened more or less directly in the financing of innovation. But typically, much less attention has been paid to the role of government in distorting capital flows in ways that prevent private financing of innovative activities or make it more costly than it ought to be. I will not attempt to be comprehensive, but just point to the role of governments in shaping financial systems through tax policies, regulations on institutional Investors, bankruptcy regulations, accountancy standards, stock-exchange regulations, and so forth.

Turning then to the diffusion of innovation, returns and costs are again of paramount importance. The returns to diffusion, and indeed pressure on firms to introduce innovations, seem to be strongly influenced by the degree of competition. More competition increases the pressure on firms to adapt quickly to new products and new production techniques. One sometimes hears the argument that because competition leads to faster diffusion of innovations, the returns to innovation itself are reduced, discouraging innovation. Let me say that both our own research and our reading of the literature suggest that there is little evidence that "too much" competition is harmful to innovation. Competition seems to be unambiguously positive for innovation and diffusion taken together. Among the main policy instruments for strengthening competition are open trade policies and free access for foreign direct investments. Regulatory reform more generally has an important role to play.

The inherent monopolistic nature of markets is usually invoked to justify restrictive regulatory regimes, which include restrictions on access, ownership and prices. But such regulations tend to make firms fall asleep. And, the increased potential for internationalisation together with innovation itself have made competition possible in a number of markets. Governments should therefore constantly review their regulatory policy to ensure that existing regulations are warranted.

The costs of innovation depend importantly on the extent of property rights to innovations. Such property rights raise the costs for firms of obtaining the newest technology and thereby reduce the rate of diffusion. The policy dilemma is that once an innovation has been made, it is in society's interest that it is diffused as quickly and broadly as 'possible, but doing away with such property rights would, as I argued previously, reduce the return to innovation. From a policy perspective, the way forward would seem to be to separate the income earned from innovation from the use of the innovation through arrangements like licensing, etc.

Adapting to a More Innovative Society

Let me now focus on the issue of how to enhance adaptation to a more innovative society. I see three purposes of policies in this area: First, the mere knowledge that people can receive assistance when forced to adapt, in my view, people's sense of security and attachment to the society. Second, a more cohesive society, where people know that assistance to adapt will be forthcoming, will be less resistant to changes that will raise welfare in the society.

What are the implications for policies? The answer is that they are probably not so different from the requirements needed in any case to bring down unemployment durably. These requirements were discussed in great detail in the OECD Jobs Study.

This Study stressed that the ability to adapt and adjust should be enhanced at the same time as the skills and competences of the work force should be upgraded. Policies in these areas are highly interdependent, but let me nevertheless focus in turn on:

- regulatory policies in the labour market;
- tax and transfer policies; and
- policies regarding training and education.

Faster introduction of innovation is likely to involve a more rapid pace of job-shifts, as new more productive jobs are created and old less productive jobs disappear, the point I discussed in the early part of this speech. This process must be allowed to proceed unhindered by rules and regulations, which may be aimed at preserving old jobs but in fact make firms hesitant to establish new ones. At the same time, the reinsertion of unemployed persons into the work force should not be hindered by excessively high minimum wages. Minimum wages may not be a very effective instrument for pursuing social policy objectives by suppressing low-wage jobs they prevent people from getting a foothold in the workforce, which could serve as a basis for future advances to better-paying jobs.[13]

Tax and transfer systems should protect people against unnecessary hardship. At the same time, they should be designed to give the right incentives to move on from old disappearing jobs to new jobs being created. Among the issues to consider is the need to avoid poverty and unemployment traps which arise when social transfer and tax systems interact so that people get little reward from taking a job or moving to a better paid one. Also, unemployment-related transfers should be paid only when justified, so as to avoid labour market disincentives and excessive fiscal burdens and to ensure continued public, support to such schemes. Active labour market policies have an important role to play in verifying availability for work and active job search effort among recipients of such transfers. Greater reliance on in-work benefits, be it in the form of transfers or tax credits, may also be worth considering.

With old jobs disappearing or being redefined at a faster rate, the need to re-equip members of the labour force with new skills will increase.

A lot has been said about the ideal of moving towards lifelong learning. This is not a very well-defined concept, but progress in the direction indicated by that concept is likely to be required. Moves in this direction will occur spontaneously, because firms and individuals have incentives to act. But, there is probably a strong case for government involvement in this area, given that a substantial part of the benefits from training efforts accrue to society at large.

A faster pace of job-shifts and faster changes in the content of jobs will call on the labour force to be more flexible. With future changes likely to be both many and difficult to foresee, it would seem natural for the basic education system to focus on equipping the labour force with generic skills that can quickly be adapted as new opportunities arise. At the same time, efforts must be made to ensure that all those who leave the education system are equipped with skills that allow them to exploit the new opportunities.

Supplementary Note 2: A View of the Global Economy in the Twenty-First Century

A keynote speech by Kumiharu Shigehara, OECD Deputy Secretary-General at the Ambrosetti Conference on Market Conference on Market Leaders and Scenario for the 21st Century, "Villa d'Este"—Cernobbio (Come), Italy, 26,27, and 28 March 1999.

(Excerpt)

"The world has undergone impressive political and economic transformation in the past quarter century. The widely used term "globalisation" describes the forces that have produced rapid growth in world trade (at twice the rate of world output growth), even faster expansion of international capital flow, the integration of the world financial markets, and the apparent acceleration in global diffusion of new technologies. Important policy and institutional changes, notably declining barriers to trade, the creation of a multilateral trade regime and the dismantling of capital controls, have been a driving force behind globalisation. Remarkable changes in technology which have sharply reduced costs of transport and communication have also promoted greater trade and financial integration, and international transfer of technology. While global integration was in a sense quite advanced in the late 19th and early 20th centuries, the current phenomena of globalisation is different in several respects:

(i) the ratio of trade to world GDP is now well above its pre-Depression peak;
(ii) the scale of capital flows has reached unprecedented levels;
(iii) communication, information and transport technologies are contributing to a major change restructuring/decentralisation of production structures;
(iv) multinational corporations have achieved a truly global presence, and the number of countries with home-grown multinationals has increased significantly; and most importantly
(v) globalisation now involves many more—and an increasing number of—countries (most of which did not exist as independent nation-states during the earlier globalisation era).

Pursuit of open trade and investment policies would contribute to faster economic growth. Indeed, there is evidence that benefits of open trade and investment for faster development holds for countries at all levels of development. Such benefits are greater when it is part of a coherent and mutually reinforcing set of policies and reforms, including institutional and legal frameworks, and a consistent set of macroeconomic and structural policies, and a growing human capital base. The OECD is contributing to this endeavour through many areas, including the "OECD Development Partnership Strategy", which seeks to help developing countries and OECD Member countries work together towards developmental goals for economic well-being, social and political development, and environmental sustainability".

Notes

1. Paulo Cecchini, Michel Catinat, and Alexis Jacquemin, "The European Challenge 1992: The Benefits of a Single Market", Broookfield, Vt., Gower, 1988.
2. Commission of the European Communities, "The Economics of 1992: An Assessment of the Potential Economic Effects of Completing the Internal Market of the European Economy", European Economy, No. 35, Brussels, Commission of the European Communities, March 1988.
3. Kumiharu Shigehara, "The External Dimension of Europe 1992: Its Effects on Relations between Europe, the United States, and

Japan", in "Europe after 1992: Three Essays" (Tommaso Padoa-Schioppa, editor), International Finance Section, Department of Economics, Princteon University, Essays in International Finance, No. 182, May 1992.

4. Kumiharu Shigehara, "Commentary: Global Implications of Trade and Currency Zones" in Federal Reserve Bank of Kansas City, "Policy Implications of Trade and Currency Zones", the proceedings of a symposium held at Jackson Hole, Wyoming, August 22–24, 1991, pp. 267–274. https://www.kansascityfed.org/Jackson%20Hole/documents/3762/1991-S91SHIGE.pdf.
5. The results of OECD modelling of the costs of agricultural protection are reported in a series of articles in *OECD Economic Studies*, Vol. 13, Winter 1989–1990 issue.
6. The full text was published in BOJ Monetary and Economic Studies, Vol. 9, No.2, September 1992, https://www.imes.boj.or.jp/research/abstracts/english/me9-2-1.html.

   It was later included in the proceedings of the conference "Japan: A European Perspective" edited by Thomas Andersson, then Director of International Research Programme at the Industrial Institute for Economic Research, Stockholm, and published by St. Martin's Press, New York, in 1993.
7. Richard Freeman, "Are Your Wages Set in Beijing?", Journal of Economic Perspective, Vol. 9. Summer No. 3, Summer 1995, https://www.aeaweb.org/articles?id=10.1257/jep.9.3.15.
8. D. Autor, D. Dorn and G. Hanson, "The China Shock; Learning from Labour Market Adjustments to Large Shocks in Trade", NBER Working Paper no. 21906, January 2016, https://www.nber.org/system/files/working_papers/w21906/w21906.pdf.

   Robert C. Feenstra, Hong Ma &Yuan Xu, "US Exports and Employment", NBER Working Paper no. 24056, November 2017, https://www.nber.org/system/files/working_papers/w24056/w24056.pdf.
9. Kumiharu Shigehara, "Causes and Implications of East Asian Financial Crisis", a speech at the Fourth International Forum on Asian Prespectives organised jointly by the Asian Development Bank and the OECD Development Centre on "Financial Liberalisation in Asia: Analysis and Prospects", at the French Ministry of Economy, Finance and Industry, Paris-Bercy, 3 June 1998, OECD Press Release of 5 June 1998.

10. Kumiharu Shigehara, "Faut-il controller les mouvements de capitaux?", L'Echo, 5–7 December 1998.
11. Kumiharu Shigehara, "Towards More Stable Global Finance: Some Issues Concerning Orderly Liberalisation in Emerging Market Economies", a keynote speech at the Thirteenth Pacific Basin Central Bank Conference, Los Cabos, B.C.S., Mexico, 9 November 1998, OECD Press Release of 9 November 1998.
12. Kumiharu Shigehara, "Financial Crisis: Causes and Implications of Recent Episodes", a keynote address at the Istanbul Finance Conference, Istanbul, Turkey, 21 November 1998, OECD Press Release of 21 November 1998.
13. More recent reviews of international evidence suggest a more positive role of minimum wages. See Chapter 1 of OECD Employment Outlook 2015, OECD Publishing, Paris, and Taeyoung Doh and Luca Van der Meer, "The Employment Effects of an Increase in the National Wage: Review of International Evidence", The Federal Reserve Bank of Kansas City, 9 March 2023, https://www.kansascityfed.org/Economic%20Review/documents/9401/EconomicReviewV108N2DohVanDerMeer.pdf.

CHAPTER 20

OECD Co-operation with Non-members

The OECD started out with 20 member countries (18 European countries, the United States, and Canada) in 1961, and subsequently four new members joined intermittently, Japan in 1964, Finland in 1969, Australia in 1971, and New Zealand in 1973. With this line-up, the OECD seemed to be comprised of all democratic societies and significant players of the global market economies at the time. For about 20 years, starting from the mid-1970s, OECD membership remained unchanged.

In March 1990, after the fall of the Berlin Wall, the OECD established the Centre for Co-operation with European Economies in Transition to manage its policy dialogue with and assistance to central and eastern European countries as they undertook a process of transition to market economies. With the dissolution of the Soviet Union in 1991, its co-operation programme was extended to the Russian Federation and the other Newly Independent States. The OECD Centre for Co-operation with European Economies in Transition was later renamed as the OECD Centre for Co-operation with Non-Members and expanded to encompass OECD relations and work with other regions in the world.

In May 1994, Mexico, which had launched the North American Free Trade Agreement (NAFTA) with the US and Canada on 1 January of the same year, achieved OECD membership with strong US support. The Czech Republic joined the OECD in 1995, followed by Hungary and Poland in

K. Shigehara, *The Bank of Japan, the OECD, and Beyond*,
https://doi.org/10.1007/978-981-97-5307-9_20

1996. In Asia, South Korea became the second country to join the OECD after Japan at the end of 1996. With further membership enlargement in the two first decades of the twenty-first century, the OECD is comprised of 38 countries at the time of writing.

My role in this process as an OECD official was a fairly limited one. Be that as it may, below is a summary of my activities related to OECD enlargement and outreach.

*****

Co-operation with China

The OECD-China co-operation programme was developed following the requests made at the 1994 and 1995 OECD Ministerial Council meetings for the Secretariat to work towards establishing mutually beneficial co-operation between the OECD and China.[1] This process differs fundamentally from Eastern European countries' active approach to Western Europe and to the OECD following the collapse of the Soviet Union. The OECD's co-operation programme with China started on the principle that costs should be shared equally between the two sides.

The fist senior-level mission of the OECD visited Beijing in July 1995, headed by Secretary-General Jean-Claude Paye, with Makoto Taniguchi, Japan's first Deputy Secretary-General, as its deputy head. I participated in the mission as OECD Chief Economist. The mission members included William Witherell, Director of the Directorate for Financial, Fiscal and Enterprise Affairs, and some other senior officials of the Secretariat. André Barsony, assistant to Taniguchi, played a major role in liaising with officials of the Chinese Ministry of Foreign Trade and Economic-Co-operation.

Our meeting with Premier Li Peng was the first of a series of meetings with Chinese Cabinet ministers. From my perspective as OECD Chief Economist, however, I was dissatisfied with the arrangements that had been made for our visit, as no meeting was set up with the Minister of Finance nor with the Governor of the People's Bank of China. According to what we were told, Wu Yi, then Minister of Foreign Trade and Economic-Co-operation (later a vice premier between 2003 and 2008) was the key person at ministerial level in the Chinese government dealing with China's relations with the OECD. She was known to be a tough negotiator internationally and a protégé of Zhu Ronji, a member of the Poliburo Standing Committees of the Chinese Communist Party from

1992 to 2002 and Premier from 1998 to 2003. We were told that she did not like OECD mission members to have direct contact with persons ultimately responsible for China's macroeconomic policy at the ministerial level, although this interpretation might well have been unfounded. In any event, following some negotiations that took place after our arrival in Beijing, a compromise was reached whereby the Deputy Governor of the People's Bank of China would come to our hotel to meet with me. It was agreed that the Deputy Governor would show up in a taxi instead of an official car and that the OECD would pay for the taxi fare.

Three years later, in 1998, I as Deputy Secretary-General in charge of OECD programmes of co-operation with Non-Members, led a second OECD high-level mission to Beijing at the invitation of the Chinese government.[2] The main purpose of the mission was to assess progress in OECD-China co-operation.

At a meeting of the OECD Council preceding my visit to China, I told OECD ambassadors that if I failed to have meetings with Chinese Finance Minister and the Governor of the People's Bank of China in Beijing this time again, I would propose that the future OECD co-operation programme with China be scaled back at the next budget planning session. Indeed, one of the main aims of my second visit to Beijing was to provide a springboard for OECD Economic Surveys of China. To this end, I asked Val Koromzay, Deputy Director of the Country Studies Branch of the Economic Department to join the OECD Delegation. Another aim of my meetings with Chinese Finance Minister and the Governor of the People's Bank of China was to pave the way for the OECD Secretariat's occasional invitation of their deputies as observers at WP3 meetings. To this end, it was essential to have tête-à-tête meetings with the heads of these two institutions, in addition to my meeting with Wu Yi.

In July 1998, I flew from Paris to Tokyo before going to Beijing and stayed at the Hotel Okura, where I unexpectedly met Dai Xianglong, Governor of the People's Bank of China, in a corridor of the hotel. He knew that I had previously worked at the Bank of Japan. Thus, my meeting with him took place in his hotel room, which meant that my visit to the headquarter of the People's Bank during my stay in Beijing was only for my giving a lecture on monetary policy issues at an auditorium in the Bank's main building.[3]

Finance Minister at the time was Xiang Huaicheng. I had met him during my first visit in Beijing in July 1995 when he was deputy director of State Administration of Taxation and Secretary of the Communist Party's Committee. China's State Tax Administration had previously received technical advice from OECD tax experts and had maintained friendly relations with them. As such, Huaicheng was very co-operative, and agreed to meet with me in his office between his meetings with Premier Zhu Rongj. I thus succeeded in having a positive discussion about building co-operation with the OECD in the macroeconomic policy area, as I did in our meeting with Governor Dai at the Hotel Okura in Tokyo.

In the area of structural policy, although the ageing of China's population was expected to start later than in OECD countries, there were concerns that the social and economic consequences of population ageing would be incomparably more serious in China where the social security system remained less developed than in OECD countries. In light of this, in my speech at the Development Research Centre of the State Council of China, I explained the 1998 OECD Ministerial Council Report "Maintaining Prosperity in Ageing Societies" which had been prepared under my direction as Deputy Secretary-General (see Chapter 21). There, I stated that the OECD would be ready to advise China in this area of structural policy issue.[4]

After returning to Paris, and with the approval of WP3 Chairman Summers, I sent letters to Chinese Finance Minister and the Governor of the People's Bank of China to invite their deputies to a special session of WP3. In response, Lou Jiwei, Deputy Director-General of China's Ministry of Finance, attended a special session of WP3 meeting in the following year, 1999. Also in the same year, Long Yongzu, Deputy Director of China's Ministry of Foreign Trade and Economic Cooperation, attended a special ministerial-level meeting with non-member countries of the OECD, and Secretary-General Donald Johnston was invited by State Councillor Wu Yi to attend an international investment fair in Xiamen, China, and to meet China's First Deputy Premier Li Ranqing in Beijing. Personal exchange relations between OECD top officials and Chinese leaders at the ministerial level in China thus deepened gradually. However, it was not until 2005, five years after I left the OECD, that the OECD's first Economic Survey of China was published.

The OECD Council at the Ministerial level adopted a resolution on 16 May 2007 to strengthen the co-operation with China, as well as with Brasil, India, and South Africa through a programme of enhanced engagement. In July 2015, exactly 20 years after the first senior-level OECD mission visited Beijing, Premier Li Keqiang visited the OECD headquarters in Paris, on the occasion of China's joining the OECD Development Centre.

Co-operation with the Russian Federation

The Soviet Union was one of the original six countries to participate in the activities of the OECD Centre for Co-operation with Economies in Transition, upon its creation in March 1990. Co-operation with the Russian Federation began after the dissolution of the Soviet Union in December 1991. Until mid-1994, co-operation with the Russian Federation was carried out in the context of the OECD programme of Technical Assistance with the Newly Independent States of the former Soviet Union, approved by the OECD Council at the end of 1991.

The OECD and the Russian Federation signed a Declaration on Co-operation in June 1994 in order to enhance policy dialogue and assist the Federation in building a market-based economy. Consequently, a country programme was designed and through its evolution, activities concerning the Russian Federation received increased focus and its programme became by far the largest for a non-member.[5] However, the Russian Federation's approach to the OECD was not as active as that of Eastern European countries, and the first OECD Economic Survey of the Russian Federation was published as late as in 1995 under President Boris Yeltsin.

In May 1996, the OECD received a letter from Prime Minister Viktor Chernomyrdin requesting membership in the OECD. In response, the first high-level OECD mission headed by Secretary-General Johnston and myself as Deputy Secretary-General responsible for OECD co-operation with non-members visited the Kremlin Palace in Moscow on 5–8 October 1997. Preceding our visit to Moscow, on 1 October 1997, the delegation of the Russian Federation led by Ivan Sergeyevich Materov, First Deputy Minister of Economy, visited me in my office at the headquarters of the OECD in Paris. At that meeting, I expressed the hope that our visit to Moscow would provide a good opportunity for Russian policy-makers to develop a better understanding of the work of the OECD, and would give them a clear comprehension of the technical requirements for membership. At the same time, I remarked that it would be stressed during our mission in Moscow that the Russian Federation did not yet qualify for OECD membership on technical grounds; considerable work remained to be done; and, discussions in Moscow would focus on policies that the Russian authorities would need to undertake in order to come fully prepared for negotiations for accession with the OECD. I also said that in our meeting with President Yeltsin in Moscow, our questions would centre on the reform of the government structures and practices, the implementation of the rule of law, and the problems created by the Duma to slow these reforms. Materov responded that the Russian authorities had developed a medium-term programme of economic and social reforms and that it would be natural to use this as a basis for our discussion of future work in Moscow.

Secretary-General Johnston and I were accompanied by William Witherell (see above), Val Koromzay (see above), Christian Schricke, legal adviser, and Eric Burgeat, Head of the Centre for Co-operation with Non-Members. We were received by many influential ministers, starting with Prime Minister Viktor Chernomyrdin and Foreign Minister Yevgeny Primakov (later appointed as Prime Minister in September 1998). In addition, we had a series of meetings with cabinet ministers responsible for a wide range of specific policy areas. We also met Governor Sergei Dubinin at the Central Bank of Russia. On 11 October 1994 (the so-called Dark Tuesday), when the Russian ruble collapsed against the US dollar, President Yeltsin had dismissed Dubinin, then acting Minister of Finance, together with then Central Bank Governor Viktor Gerashenko, but Dubinin was subsequently reinstated as Governor of the Central Bank. Before our departure from Paris, it had also been planned for us to meet President Yeltsin, but our meeting with him did not take place.

Throughout our meetings with Russian cabinet ministers, we insisted on the importance of democratising the Russian Federation and ensuring the principle of the rule of law as a precondition for concretising the OECD programme of co-operation with Russia. We also said that the Russian authorities might wish to design its economic policy, making use of the OECD's multilateral approach covering a wide range of macroeconomic and structural policy issues. Among the Russian ministers we met in Moscow, it was Anatoly Chubais, First Deputy Prime and Minister of Finance, who seemed most keen to reform Russia into a member country of the liberal economic camp and interested in OECD membership (Photo No. 20.1). In fact, Chubais, who had been President Yeltsin's Chief of Cabinet before his appointment as Minister of Finance, asked us about our views on the order in which Russia, already a member of the

IMF at the time, should consider joining three international institutions: the OECD, the EU, and the WTO. As there was no immediate reply from Secretary-General Johnston, I expressed my opinion that Russia should first aim at its membership at the WTO, then at the OECD, and finally at the EU.

Another Russian reformer who particularly impressed me was Boris Nemtsov, the second most powerful after Chubais, and fairly young and energetic politician. He was also First Deputy Prime Minister in charge of housing construction policy and anti-monopoly policy, and at the same time Minister of Fuel and Energy, a position he held as a very influential man. However, as a liberal, he lost his political position under Putin's presidency, and eventually he was assassinated on a bridge near the Kremlin in Moscow in February 2015. He was reportedly in the capital, helping to organise a rally against the Russian military intervention in Ukraine.

Photo 20.1 Kumiharu Shigehara as OECD Deputy Secretary-General shaking hands with Anatoly Chubais, First Deputy Prime and Minister of Finance of the Russian Federation at the Kremlin Palace in Moscow in October 1997. At the centre is Donald Johnston, OECD Secretary-General (© OECD-OCDE)

After Secretary-General Johnston's return to Paris, I remained in Moscow as the head of the OECD mission to continue meetings with key cabinet ministers A young reformist who left a lasting impression with me was Alexei Kudrin. He graduated from the Leningrad University of Economics and President Boris Yeltsin appointed him as First Deputy Finance Minister under Finance Minister Chubais. Kudrin became Deputy Prime Minister and Finance Minister as an economic technocrat from his native place, St Petersburg, after Vladimir Putin became President, despite being close to Chubais. In my tête-à-tête meetings with Kudrin and a similar meeting with Sergey Aleksashenko, First Deputy Governor of the Bank of Russia, I explained about the important role played by the OECD WP3 in its multilateral surveillance of macroeconomic policy management in key member countries.

In the follow-up to my return to Paris, with WP3 Chairman Summers' agreement, I sent letters of invitation for both Kudrin and Aleksashenko to come to Paris to attend a special session of the WP3 meeting. Kudrin who thus got acquainted with Summers at the WP3 meeting, later became Deputy Prime Minister and Finance Minister in Mikhail Kasyanov's cabinet after Putin took office as President of Russia in 2000. Kudrin remained Deputy Prime Minister and Finance Minister in Putin's cabinet under President Medvedev in 2008. However, when Putin announced his candidature in the 2012 presidential election, Kudrin indicated that he would not join the new government if Dmitry Medvedev's cabinet was formed under Putin's presidency. He was asked by Medvedev to resign from his position as Deputy Prime Minister and Minister of Finance. Kudrin thus parted company with Putin.

Among the Russian ministers dealing with policy areas other than the economy and finance, the most impressive was Viktor Danilov-Danilyan, Minister of Environmental Protection and Natural Resources. A graduate of Moscow State University's Faculty of Physics and Mathematics with a PhD in economics, he was active as an economist, computer scientist, politician, and environmental campaigner. He wished the OECD to make a credible assessment of environmental problems in Russia.

In March 1998, the OECD organised a symposium entitled "The Rule of Law and the Development of a Market Economy in Russia" at its Paris headquarters. This brought together key figures from the Russian Government with attendees from OECD member countries for frank exchanges of views. In my opening speech at the symposium, I stressed the importance of the rule of law as an important precondition not only for the development of the market economy in Russia, but also for the success of Russian companies in the global market.[6]

In 2007, the accession process of the Russian Federation was opened at the same time with Chile, Estonia, Israel, and Slovenia. The terms, conditions, and process for the accession were set out in roadmaps for each country.[7] Four of these countries excluding the Russian Federation are now Members of the OECD. On the hand, on 12 March 2014, the OECD decided to postpone activities related to the accession process of the Russian Federation to the OECD for the time being.[8] On 8 March 2022, in response to Russia's large-scale aggression against Ukraine, the OECD decided to immediately suspend the participation of Russia and Belarus in OECD bodies.[9] At the same time, OECD Member countries agreed that the OECD should respond positively to Ukraine's request to further strengthen existing OECD—Ukraine co-operation to take advantage of the OECD's expertise to address the public policy challenges it faces.

Co-operation with the Baltic States

The Nordic countries of Sweden, Denmark, Norway, Finland, and Iceland, all member countries of the OECD, form the Nordic Council, and these five countries signed a co-operation agreement with three Baltic States—Estonia, Latvia, and Lithuania—in 1992. This was shortly after these three countries became independent again, following the dissolution of the Soviet Union. The Nordic countries promoted a campaign to support the Baltic States accession to the OECD. However, the OECD Secretariat was cautious about accepting invitations from the Baltic States for the Secretary-General, Deputy Secretary-Generals and others to make official visits to these countries, taking into account the balance with the development of OECD programmes for co-operation with other non-members. After the first official high-level mission of the OECD Secretariat led by Secretary-General Johnston and me to the Russian Federation, and my visit to China, it was considered within the OECD Secretariat, that the time was right for me to make an official visit to the three Baltic States in October 1998 in my capacity as Deputy Secretary-General responsible for OECD programmes for co-operation with other non-members. Prior to my visit to these countries for which I was accompanied by John West, head of my front office and a former senior economist at the ECO, each of their ambassadors to France invited me to lunch meetings to help me prepare for my trips to their capitals. They were all newly appointed ambassadors, young, intelligent women, symbolising the countries that had just been freed from the fetters of the Soviet Union. It was clear that the governments of the countries had rushed to establish their bureaucracy after independence.

There were no flights between Paris and Vilnius, the capital of Lithuania, the most southerly of the three countries, at the time. Thus, the Lithuanian ambassador to France accompanied me to Vilnius via Copenhagen. President Valdas Adamkus, who had worked for many years as Regional Director of the Environmental Protection Agency in the United States, returned to Lithuania in 1997 and won the presidential election, showed strong enthusiasm for Lithuania's accession to the OECD.

I then headed for Riga, the capital of Latvia. While the three Baltic states border each other, there were no direst fights between the capitals, and I crossed the Baltic Sea from Vilnius to Stockholm and then entered Riga by a fight from there.

President Guntis Ulmanis was born in 1939, the same year as me, and was interned in Siberia with his family during the Second World War. Returning home after the war, he was elected leader of the Peasant Party, like his great uncle Kārlis Ulmanis, who was president of the Republic of Latvia before the war.

Finally, we visited Tallinn, the capital of Estonia, the most northerly of the Baltic States. Again, as there were no direct flights from Riga, the capital of Latvia, I first travelled from Riga to Helsinki and then arrived at Tallinn Airport with the Baltic Sea in my sights. President Lennart Meri was 10 years older than me. He was interned in Siberia with his family from 1941, forced to work as a forest logger, returned to Estonia after the end of World War II, and eventually became a writer, film director, and leader of the Estonian independence movement in 1992, serving as President from 1992.

Through individual meetings with the presidents of these three Baltic countries, and a series of meetings with their prime ministers and other key ministers and central bank governors, it became clear to me that these three countries were eager to join the OECD not only because of their desire to strengthen relations with the Western economies in their proximity, but also because of their desire to achieve economic development in a global market. As we had done in our visit to Moscow, I stressed we recognised the willingness of the Baltic countries to realise economic development within a global framework, respecting values such as democracy, the rule of law, and liberalism shared by the entire OECD membership, which includes the United States, Western European countriss and Japan as key members. I then informed the leaders of these countries that the OECD Economics Department was carrying out an economic review to help their economic development and the OECD was ready to hold further dialogue with the governments and central bank authorities of the three countries on the policy options on the occasion of its completion.

Thus, the main theme of the talks in the Baltic States was to strengthen co-operation with the OECD, but at the same time the economic difficulties in Russia were also a topic of discussion, as Estonia was unable to break away from its economic relationship with Russia. Against this backdrop, the press release[10] issued by the Presidential Office after my meeting with Estonian President Meri stated in the last paragraph that "the OECD Deputy Secretary-General discussed the situation in Russia with the President", indicating President Meri's strong concern about Russia. In fact, I got the impression that President Meri had an outstanding sense of diplomacy in approaching the OECD, which was established with only Western European countries and advanced liberal countries as members, while also taking care of Russians residing in Estonia and striving for good-neighbourly diplomacy with Russia.

At the end of my visit to the Baltic States, a conference entitled "Economic Development of the Baltic Region: the Way Forward" was held in Tallinn with the participation of the foreign ministers of the three countries. I delivered a keynote speech[11] after Estonian Prime Minister Mart Sierman gave an opening address. In this speech, I remarked:

> The OECD does not offer a single model, but rather a framework for countries to develop their own institutions and approaches. The OECD's co-operative activities open up a wealth of experience and expertise from OECD Member countries, and the OECD Secretariat, in developing the institutions and policies for a well-functioning market economy and social stability. These activities are based on policy dialogue with experts from OECD Member countries and also other international organisations, and involves sharing experiences, using 'sounding boards' for policy proposals and undergoing peer reviews. ....
>
> In this context, the OECD Secretariat has made various policy recommendations to Member countries that contribute to sustainable economic growth and social equity in the OECD region, which accounted for about

> 60 per cent of the global economy at the time, and there is a common recognition across member countries that dynamic economic growth in non-member countries is also important for the OECD economy, I hope the conference will be an opportunity to strengthen the policy dialogue between the OECD and the Baltic States.

In concluding the conference, a joint press conference was held with the foreign ministers of the three countries and myself as main speakers. In my opening remark, I stated that "the OECD attaches importance to the regional programme of co-operation between the OECD and the three Baltic States in the context of facilitating the full use of the market economy and their integration into the global economy on the basis of the respect of human rights and pluralistic democracy".

In my reply to a question raised by a local journalist about my view on the impacts of Russian economic problems on the Estonian economy, I said that progress in the reforms of the three Baltic States and their growing integration into the global economy had helped to weaken the undesirable economic effects on these states of the unfortunate developments in the Russian Federation. At the same time, I indicated a number of areas where further reform efforts were needed including the strengthening of the banking system.

Another journalist asked me about the timing of OECD membership of the Baltic States. Naturally, while trying not to be discourteous, I said that decisions on OECD membership were to be taken by Member countries as a whole on a consensus basis, and not by the OECD Secretariat. I added that while there were no numerical criteria for OECD membership, all these countries considered themselves as "like-minded", in a word, committed to democratic values based on the rule of law and respect for human rights. It would be important for new member countries to be judged as such and at the same time to be at or close to the level of a developed country in a number of individual areas of government policies and activities such as acceptance of the OECD tax model that is standard in OECD member countries, and the satisfactory compilation and publication of economic and financial statistics including data on national income and balance of payments as well as various individual aspects of government policies and activities including environmental standards. I added that the results of the OECD Secretariat's Economic Survey of the Baltic States, which was being conducted by its Economics Department would provide important information in these respects.

Following my mission to the three capitals of the Baltic States, the OECD started its co-operation programme for these countries as a group. Among them, Estonia was the first to join the OECD in December 2010, followed by Latvia in July 2016, and Lithuania in May 2018.

****

Notes

1. OECD, "OECD-China Co-operation: The First Ten Years", November 2005.
2. OECD, "OECD Deputy Secretary-General Kumiharu Shigehara to visit China, 15–17 July 1988", OECD News Release, 7 July 1998.
3. Kumiharu Shigehara, "Targets and Indicators for Monetary Policy: Observations from OECD Countries' Experience", a lecture delivered at The People's Bank of China, Beijing, 15 July 1998, OECD Press Release of 15 July 1998.
4. Kumiharu Shigehara, "Policies for Dealing with Population Ageing in the Global Context", a speech delivered at The Development Centre of the State Council of China, Beijing, China, 17 July 1998, OECD Press Release of 17 July 1998.
5. OECD Centre for Co-operation with Non-Members, "OECD and Russian Federation Co-operation 1992–2000", https://www.oecd.org/countries/russia/37082763.pdf.
6. Kumiharu Shigehara, "The Rule of Law and the Development of a Market Economy in the Russian Federation", Opening Statement at an OECD Symposium on 23–24 March 1998.
7. OECD Council, "Road Map for the Accession of the Russian Federation to the OECD Convention, C(2007)10/Final", https://www.oecd.org/legal/41463285.pdf.
8. Statement by the OECD regarding the status of the accession process with Russia & co-operation with Ukraine, 13 March 2014.
9. Statement from OECD Secretary-General on further measures in response to Russia's large-scale aggression against Ukraine, https://www.oecd.org/newsroom/statement-from-the-oecd-council-on-further-measures-in-response-to-russia-s-large-scale-aggression-against-ukraine.htm.
10. Press service of the Office of the President of the Republic of Estonia, "President of the Republic had a Meeting with the Deputy Secretary-General of the OECD", October 19, 1998.

11. Kumiharu Shigehara, "The Path Ahead to High and Equitable Growth for the Global Economy: The Role of the OECD", a keynote speech given at the Conference "Economic Development in the Baltic Region: The Path Ahead", Tallin, Estonia, 20 October 1998. See page 7 in OECD, "Baltic Programme: Annual Report, October 1998–September 1999", CCNM/BALT(99)9, https://one.oecd.org/document/CCNM/BALT(99)9/en/pdf.

CHAPTER 21

Welfare, Global Order, Environment, and Climate Change

My involvement in international considerations and discussions on issues regarding new challenges for the global economy has not been limited to those described in Chapter 19. Around the time when my OECD career was finally coming to an end, population ageing was increasingly recognised in some policy quarters as a potentially very serious risk factor undermining economic performance and adding to social strains in most OECD countries starting in the early decades of the twenty-first century. I worked on a new OECD project in this area which highlighted the challenges posed by this major demographic shift and suggested ways to alleviate them.

Moreover, recognition grew among international observers about the waning of the structures of global governance that had been dominated by OECD countries for most of the second half of the twentieth century and of the urgent need to build new structures more fitted to the shift of power from OECD countries to new significant players in the global economy starting from the last decade of the twentieth century. Indeed, the evolution of geopolitical factors in different regions of the world has since then come to be regarded as a potential threat to peace and economic prosperity. One must add to this list the growing recognition of the implications of climate change for the economic and social wellbeing of humankind. Since the first year of the twenty-first century, liberated from the shackles I had as a senior OECD official (see the introductory note in Chapter 14), I have been invited occasionally to give speeches at international conferences and seminars abroad

K. Shigehara, *The Bank of Japan, the OECD, and Beyond*, https://doi.org/10.1007/978-981-97-5307-9_21

and contribute papers to foreign journals and newspapers on these and other non-economic as well as economic issues.

Below are descriptions (rather detailed in some places) of such activities of mine on four topics: (1) population ageing, (2) the need to establish a new order for global economic governance, (3) peace and economic prosperity in East Asia as a regional challenge of global concern, and (4) the domestic and international economic and social policy implications of climate change.

How to Deal with Population Ageing?

One of my responsibilities at the final stage of my career at the OECD was to direct the OECD's multidisciplinary project on the ageing of populations which involved the staff of the Economics Department, Directorate for Education, Employment, Labour and Social Affairs, Directorate for Financial, Fiscal and Enterprise Affairs, Directorate for Science, Technology and Industry, Public Management Service, and Development Centre. The main report "Maintaining Prosperity in an Ageing Society" was presented to the OECD Ministerial meeting on 27–28 April 1998[1] *and subsequently published by the OECD. Below is my summary of the main points in the report.*

"In most OECD countries, population ageing will cause economic, social, and political strains. A vital element in dealing with these strains is improved economic and financial market performance. And policies should increasingly be seen from the "life-course" perspective, taking people's entire lives into account. The policy response to ageing thus involves cutting across traditional boundaries of economic, financial, and social disciplines, and across the customary areas of responsibility of government administrations.

During the years 2010 ~ 30, the baby-boom generation now in their working-age years will reach retirement age. This development, together with increased longevity and declining birth rates, will reduce the ratio of the number of people of working age (15 ~ 64) to the number of old people (over 65). In addition to these demographic factors, recent trends towards shorter periods in work through longer school and earlier retirement, if continued, would further reduce the overall supply of labour, even though the labour market participation ratio of women may continue to rise.

Higher economic growth will ease the constraints faced by society in general and particularly the problems to be caused by ageing. If overall incomes are rising fast, taxes levied on the young to support the retired will be easier to bear, and will therefore be politically more practical. With economic growth, the material living standards (that is, real consumption of goods and services) of the retired can be protected while the young can look forward to rising prosperity.

But if the sort of low-productivity growth that has been experienced in the past 25 years continues, and if the trends towards increased unemployment and social marginalisation continue, the outcome may be very different.

How can higher economic growth be achieved? There is some hope that the information revolution, increased world trade and capital mobility, and the introduction of reforms of product and labour markets will all help to boost economic growth in the years ahead. Good macroeconomic policy is a prerequisite, and cutting government budget deficits and maintaining low inflation are therefore high on the policy agenda.

The OECD Jobs Study developed policies to improve labour market performance. In addition, the OECD has undertaken work on the creation and diffusion of new technologies and on the role of entrepreneurship. All of these should help to achieve higher growth, or shape the policies that will foster it. Yet, even as such reforms are being carried out, societies must remain concerned about protecting the employment opportunities and income of the most vulnerable among the young as well as the old who may not directly benefit from such reforms. Analysis by the OECD published last year already addressed many of the policy issues associated with population ageing:

- although higher labour productivity is central to increasing the living standards of the whole population, it does not directly address the fiscal dimensions of ageing; higher productivity also results in higher future pension costs since under current schemes pensions are generally related to wages. Existing public pension programmes must be reformed if they are to be made sustainable;
- policies will have to be developed to ensure the continued integration of the old into society, including an increased emphasis on measures early in life that allow people to respond better to changing circumstances; and,

- the presence of increasingly older workers will require improved learning and training opportunities throughout life.

One particularly clear policy conclusion emerged from the OECD analysis: it is imperative that steps be taken soon to reverse the trend towards earlier retirement. In particular, policies that encourage or subsidise early retirement should be reformed. It is clear that older workers can be productive members of the economy, and making pension arrangements more flexible for those who wish to continue work would ease the financing problem of pension programmes. Early retirement has political appeal at times of high unemployment, but such policies will only create expectations for today's workers that cannot be fulfilled.

New Policy Proposals

The OECD has undertaken further study of the reform of social security, including the option of increased reliance on private pensions. Important aspect of pension reform is the implications for intergenerational equity: current programmers imply a transfer of income from the current young to the current old. And even with funded systems, material goods and services have to be transferred in this way. There is much merit in this approach in addressing the anti-poverty objectives of pensions. It is more problematic in earnings-related pensions where, in some countries, high benefits and other design features encourage early retirement and living standards among the retired are reaching those of the population as a whole and are exceeding those of young families with children. It would make more sense to use collective resources for areas that have higher priority and to allow individuals more choice on when to retire and on the kind of income they want in retirement. More reliance on private pensions and savings can be a step in this direction.

The consequences of ageing on capital markets have also been explored. Ageing will change saving and investment patterns nationally, not least through the build-up and subsequent unwinding of private pension assets.

Differences in ageing patterns across countries particularly between the OECD and the non-OECD regions will give rise to shifts in patterns of saving, investment and international capital flows. All these movements will be mediated through international capital markets, and their improved functioning will contribute to higher output growth and higher returns on pension funds by efficient allocation of savings.

So that capital markets can fulfil this enlarged role, the legal and regulatory infrastructure for securities markets will have to be strengthened. Rules governing insider trading and take-overs should enhance the capability of the capital markets to provide discipline over corporate entities. Measures should be introduced to protect the rights of minority investors, including those that enable investors to exercise corporate governance. Accounting and disclosure rules should promote transparency and accountability. The regulatory and supervisory framework for pension schemes should be modernised, with the use of the latest techniques of risk-management encouraged. At the very least, measures inhibiting the development of innovative financial instruments should be reviewed carefully—although governments may also wish to consider giving some support to the development of instruments that are useful in providing retirement income (index-linked instruments, for example).

In addition to putting a premium on raising productivity growth, policy development should address the lifelong requirements of the voters and taxpayers in the OECD countries. These initiatives involve measures to encourage the employment of older workers; reforms to the provision of long-term health care and of retirement income; reforms to education and changes to the provision of social services.

**

The OECD analysis of the determinants of health, learning, productivity, and the economic and social well-being of the old has been developed in the context of the "life-course" perspective of decisions on education, work, and retirement. For example, young people's educational experiences are a central determinant in work decisions, productivity, and well-being later in life. It also emphasises the importance of co-ordinating policies across traditional departmental responsibilities in government. Finally, it makes clear that the timeframe for policy analysis and decision-making must be considerably lengthened.

The agenda that emerges—policies that can deliver higher growth, increase the emphasis on individuals' life-courses, and enhance the role of capital markets allocating long-term savings efficiently, as well as reforms to pension and other transfer programmes—may seem a tall order. But if action is taken now first to develop and then put in place the right package of policies, social, and economic stresses that will inevitably accompany such a historic demographic shift can be mitigated. The

OECD will continue to assist its member governments in designing and implementing the requisite action in both economic and social disciplines, with due regard to political dimensions, in both OECD and non-OECD countries."

As noted in Chapter 20, *I explained the 1998 OECD Ministerial Council Report "Maintaining Prosperity in Ageing Societies" in my speech at the Development Research Centre of the State Council of China in July 1998. On 26 November that year, on behalf of His Majesty the King of the Belgians and the Government of the French Community of Belgium, the University of Liège awarded me the degree of Doctor Honoris causa (Photo* 21.1*). The topic of my special lecture, given in French at the university's main auditorium prior to the honorary doctoral ceremony, was "Policy Implications of Population Ageing".*

Photo 21.1 Honorary Doctor of Economics award ceremony at the University of Liège in November 1998, Belgium: (from left to right) Akiko Shigehara, the author, Bernard Jurion (Doyen de la Faculté d'Économie, de Gestion et de Sciences sociales at the University of Liège) and Guy Quaden (then Executive Director, later Governor of the National Bank of Belgium) (© TIL/LLG-DR)

New Order for Global Economic Governance

In the light of the changing relative economic power of countries around the world, it has been generally felt important to establish a new order for global economic governance. At the invitation of Robert Rubin, then US Treasury Secretary, and Alan Greenspan, then Chairman of the Board of Governors of the Federal Reserve, the Finance Ministers and Central Bank Governors of G7 countries and a number of significant new players in the global economy, together with the leaders of the IMF, the World Bank, the OECD, and the Bank for International Settlements, met in Washington on the 1st October 1998 to review progress made in efforts to strengthen the international financial system in the aftermath of the East Asian financial crisis. It was an exceptional meeting chaired by US President Clinton with Rubin sitting next to him. I attended this meeting as OECD Deputy Secretary-General,

In the following year, the Group of Twenty Finance Ministers and Central Bank Governors (G20) was created as an informal forum comprising finance ministers and central bank governors from 19 countries and the EU (represented by the rotating European Council presidency) and the European Central Bank.[2] *The G20 chair rotates between members, and is selected from a different regional grouping of countries each year. The G20 has no permanent staff of its own. The G20 finance ministers and central bank governors have tended to meet once a year with two preceding deputies' meetings and a follow-up meeting. The focus of these meetings has been to discuss key issues surrounding the promotion of global economic stability. The G20 was upgraded to the level of Heads of State/Government in the wake of the global economic and financial crisis of 2007, and, in 2009, was designated the "premier forum for international economic cooperation".*

Below are excerpts from my speech "Multilateral Surveillance: the IMF, the OECD and G-20" delivered at an international conference "Outlook for the European Union in 2030: Between Emerging Countries and North America" organised by la Ligue Européenne de Cooperation Economique in Paris on 1 February 2011.[3]

"The OECD strictly views surveillance as a peer review process. Members of the OECD Working Party No.3 are deputy finance ministers and deputy governors of central banks of G10 countries who gather at the OECD's Paris headquarters, as such they directly participate in policymaking in capitals. The OECD Secretariat independently prepares analytical reports and policy recommendation papers for their meetings.

After the meetings, it routinely deletes politically sensitive information from reports before they are released to the public. It also allows national officials greater involvement in the preparation of country-related reports.

Compared with the IMF, the OECD has been considered to have some other advantages as a mechanism of peer review: the smaller size and relative homogeneity of membership in addition to the wider coverage of policy issues beyond the macroeconomic area.

But, increased membership over the past decades (from 20 member countries in 1960 when the OECD started to 34 countries now) has eroded these comparative advantages.

Moreover, despite enlargement of its membership, the relative weight of the OECD area in the world economy has been steadily declining. In 1975, the OECD area accounted for 65 per cent of world GDP. In 2015, its share in world GDP is projected to decline to about 50 per cent. On the other hand, the total size of the economies of Brazil, China, India, Indonesia, Russia and South Africa accounts for 25 per cent of world GDP.

Thus, the role of OECD multilateral surveillance has become less effective in the task of promoting global economic prosperity with financial stability. Fundamental restructuring of the OECD whose membership does no longer reflect reality of the global economy is urgently required on the occasion of its 50th anniversary this year.

G20 has the same size of membership as the OECD when it was created in 1960. A major difference is country composition. The OECD initially comprised of the Unites States, Canada, and 18 European countries which were all members of OEEC, and there were no members from Asia–Pacific and Middle and South Americas. G20 includes a number of countries in these regions while a number of European member countries of the OECD are not included in the G20.

As already said, at the OECD, a subsidiary group of fairly small membership called as Working Party No.3 was created to exercise most intensive peer review on international payments adjustment. This body, which is G10 based, did function as the most active multilateral surveillance forum until non-Japan East Asia gained significance as an economic and financial power. G20 Mutual Assessment Process is designed as "country-led, consultative" peer review process. Whether G20 would need a smaller subsidiary group to exercise effective peer review like at the OECD remains to be seen.

Another major issue is whether the G20 process can function effectively without a permanent secretariat. The OECD has a permanent secretariat with professional staff of high quality which conducts independent analysis, prepares economic forecast and makes policy recommendations.

In the age of globalisation with ever growing international spillovers from the interplay of macro and structural policies and such forces in individual countries, no matter how good analytical work on macro and structural issues is individually, multilateral surveillance cannot be effective without systematic interdisciplinary work such as to synthesize opposing political constituencies, essentially spending and non-economic considerations vs. budget control ministry concerns to protect taxpayers and to achieve sustained macroeconomic stability and prosperity.

In concluding, I would stress that it is only with the strong political will of key players at leadership levels in the world economy that we can succeed in a radical reform of international institutions to make them more relevant to the new circumstance."

A special publication entitled "The OECD at 50: Better Policies for Better Lives" was issued by the OECD on the occasion of its 50th anniversary in 2011, and I was asked to contribute an article to it in my capacity as a former Chief Economist and Deputy Secretary-General. The title I chose for my contribution was "The Way forward: Streamlining policy discussions for more effective multilateral surveillance".[4] In this article I wrote that the OECD's Working Party No. 3 on Policies for the Promotion of Better International Payments Equilibrium (WP3)—traditionally the most important peer review group for international macroeconomic co-operation—was particularly active in influencing international policy-making during the first quarter of its existence. I then noted that "(T)oday, WP3 continues to operate as an exclusive club whose meetings are attended by deputy finance ministers and deputy central bank governors involved in macroeconomic policy making in capitals. But its membership remains essentially G10-based, with heavy representation of European countries. To allow the WP3 to retain its effectiveness, its structure should be streamlined to keep the total number of participants within single figures. Similar subsidiary bodies, in which participation is limited to a small number of key players, should be envisaged in other areas. Such an approach would contribute to the efficient functioning of plenary Committee meetings and the entire process of OECD multilateral surveillance more effective. In 1998, as Deputy Secretary-General responsible for OECD relationships with non-member economies, I wrote to

China's finance minister and central bank governor inviting them to send their deputies from time to time to WP3 meetings. Since then, China has attended WP3 meetings on several occasions. Now the time has come to open these meetings to other key non-OECD countries.

The OECD has a strong Secretariat equipped with professional staff of high quality versed in the interplay of macroeconomic and structural forces and policies. It could, if G20 leaders so desire, perform a similar function for the G20. But only the strong political will of key players at global leadership levels will succeed in carrying through the radical reform of international institutions that is needed to make them more relevant to new global circumstances".

At the 2013 Annual Conference "Retrospect and Prospect: Reigniting the Strength of Opening Up", organised by Liu Hongru Financial Education Foundation, Shanghai Institute of Finance and Law (SIFL), and Reniventing Bretton Woods Committee in Shanghai o 1 November 2013, I gave a speech entitled "Interdependence, International Policy Spillovers and Global Governance - An Insider's Views" (4).

In the ending part of this speech, I remarked:

1. Delayed dollar parity changes, both upwards and downwards, under the fixed exchange system run the risk of entailing large long-run economic costs both at home and abroad.
2. Foreign exchange rate management policy geared to the stability of bilateral currency relationships vis-à-vis the US dollar under the floating rate system can distort international resource allocation significantly, particularly in Asia where trade patterns are increasingly diversified with lessening of the relative importance of trade relationships with countries in the US dollar zone. Trade-weighted effective exchange rates should be given greater importance in exchange rate management.
3. Misalignment of effective exchange rates cannot be effectively checked by unilateral foreign exchange rate intervention; multilateral action involving all major trade partners with short-run adjustment costs shared among them could bring about longer-run benefits to all of them.
4. Ad hoc multilateral efforts to stabilize effective exchange rates under the floating rate regime at the sacrifice of domestic price stability can entail significant long-run costs for all partners.

5. Compared with international spillovers of inflationary impulses, those of deflationary impulses would be more difficult to neutralize in countries where the initial levels of inflation are very low and policy interest rates are already close to the zero bound. In such a situation, international policy co-ordination of not just macroeconomic but also structural policies among countries concerned would be urgently required.
6. Multilateral surveillance by the IMF and the OECD should be strengthened to find out suitable ways of such policy co-ordination so as to realize better economic performance in all trade partner countries in the longer run, preventing them from adopting myopic "beggar-thy-neighbour " policies to bring about short-run benefits at home at the sacrifice of partner countries with longer-run economic damages to all concerned.

In my article "New Challenges and a Search for Better Global Governance", which was published in the Boao Review issued in Beijing in April 2014,[5] I wrote that "(G)iven the increased economic weight of emerging market economies, the management of foreign exchange rate policy by them as well as advanced countries can have significant international ramifications. For such action not to become "beggar- thy-neighbor " policy, well–established frameworks of international policy co-operation are essential".

At the time of this writing, the G20 has been in existence for more than a quarter of a century outside the multilateral surveillance frameworks of the IMF and the OECD. However, this body without a permanent and independent secretariat has remained ineffective for multilateral surveillance. A new order for global economic governance is yet to be established.

Peace and Economic Prosperity in East Asia

In 2002, the Barcelona Centre for International Affairs (CIDOB) launched an annual series of international seminars on "War and Peace in the 21st Century" under the sponsorship of the Mayor of Barcelona and under the direction of Javier Solana, former Spanish Minister of Foreign Affairs, former Secretary-General of the North Atlantic Organization (NATO), and Honorary President of CIDOB.

CIDOB chose "Peace and prosperity in East Asia: A regional challenge of global concern" as the main theme of the 12th seminar and Solana invited me to participate as a main speaker in it. Its purpose was to assess to the economic and geopolitical situation in East Asia and to discuss the main challenges the region was confronting in order to ensure peace and economic prosperity. It was held on 18 January 2014 at the Palau de Pedralbes in Barcelona. A summary of the CIDOB's conference report is reproduced below with some abbreviations.[6]

"Xavier Trias, Mayor of Barcelona, opened the seminar highlighting the 'undeniable growing relevance of East Asia'. This region was recognized particularly important for Barcelona as 'the Port of Barcelona is one of the main gateways for China in Europe and in the Mediterranean.' The city has strong economic, commercial and cultural links with Asia, particularly with China and Japan, although, as the Mayor pointed out, Asia is not only about these two economic giants but also about countries like the Philippines, Vietnam, Indonesia, India, Australia and others with an undeniable economic and political relevance.

Mr. Trias concluded his opening speech by remarking his will and confidence in the possibilities to increase Barcelona's collaboration with East Asia. Carles A. Gasòliba, Chairman of the board of CIDOB, made a general introduction to the seminar underlying that growing political tensions and deep regional economic integration are simultaneous processes in East Asia and both have a global impact and reach. CIDOB, stated Mr Gasòliba, aims to explain and to analyse what happens in the world contributing, from Barcelona, to international debates and efforts to ensure peace and prosperity worldwide.

Javier Solana, Honorary Chairman of CIDOB and Former EU High Representative for the Common Foreign and Security Policy stated that peace and prosperity in East Asia is without a doubt one of the most relevant issues the international community may face, as "the central gravity of the world is moving to Asia". Mr. Solana pointed out that while "economic prosperity is assured in East Asia, we cannot say the same on the security field".

Regional Economic Integration In East Asia

Kumiharu Shigehara, President of the International Economy Policy Studies Association and Former Deputy Secretary-General of the OECD, centred his intervention on the transformation of the economic panorama in East Asia in the last decades and its implications for Japan.

Mr Shigehara emphasized that the sizes of the economies surrounding Japan have grown dramatically, but that this has not significantly altered the patterns of Japanese external trade as the country still basically imports raw materials and exports finished products. Mr Shigehara referred to the differences between the economic integration of East Asia and the EU integration process. According to him, the main difference is that the Asian process is driven by market forces and no steps have been taken on currency issues, including the lack of swaps between East Asian central banks. Besides, unlike what happened in Europe in the 1980s, there haven't been serious debates among Japanese trade unions on the potential problems related to "social dumping" resulting from the growth of imports from China.

Mr Shigehara also referred to Japan's outflows of direct investment abroad which are highly diversified, and which aim for long-run returns. As he stated, the Netherlands and Belgium together account for 15 per cent of Japan's direct investment which is more or less the same amount of Japan's direct investment to China.

Françoise Lemoine, Senior Economist in CEPII and Associate Researcher, Centre d'Études sur la Chine contemporaine, started her presentation insisting on the differences between the processes of economic integration in East Asia and the EU process that was built upon political will and common institutions and policies. As she stressed, the East Asian economic integration completely lacks this institutional dimension and is driven by market forces that rely on long-term structural complementarities in key industrial sectors resulting in strengthened interdependence, trade flows and transfers in technology.

Ms Lemoine pointed out that globalization gave a new twist to East Asian dynamics and its vertical division of labour. East Asia's fast growth, as she reminded, has been based on massive demand from outside the region, mainly from US and the EU. However, as Ms Lemoine remarked, China has proven to be resilient to the 2008 global crisis and the collapse of Western demand. In fact, East Asia's trade and large economies are increasingly dependant on China's domestic market and activity. As she indicated, exports to China represent 13% of the GDP of South Korea and 30% of the GDP of Taiwan.

Seeking A New Security Framework For East Asia

Lanxin Xiang, Professor of International History and Politics at the Graduate Institute in Geneva, opened the second panel with a particularly thought-provoking presentation. He warned of the risks stemming from the lack of mechanisms to deal with any security crisis that might erupt in East Asia. As he emphasized a regional collective security system has historically been absent in East Asia and is currently still missing. Professor Xiang considers that "the so-called 'rise of China' is an invention" and he prefers to talk of China's "re-rise or 'restoration' as Mr Xi Jinping does". From this perspective, China is somehow "returning to its normal place". Indeed, as he recalled "China hasn't had trade deficit since the times of the Silk Road". As an overall assessment Professor Xiang considers that "there is no reason for China to challenge the [international] rules of the game". However, he lamented the US believes that China is going to challenge their predominant position and it seems that this is the prevalent view "in their geopolitical calculus".

Professor Xiang focused as well on the rise of nationalisms in East Asia and the territorial disputes. On the Senkaku/Diaoyu issue, he indicated that "Japan should be considered more responsible for the recent deterioration in the light of current security context". "What worries me"—he said—"is an accidental crisis, as the lack of crisis management mechanism makes the scenario riskier".

Ron Huisken, Senior Fellow at the Strategic and Defence Studies Centre at the Australian National University started his presentation highlighting that during the Cold War period, Asia lost the opportunity to arrange a regional security system and he noted that when the Cold War ended nothing happened in East Asia. As a result of this, "East Asia is strategically less stable". Unlike Europe, that had two powerful institutions like NATO and the EU, there was/is nothing remotely comparable in East Asia, he pointed out. And similarly to the concerns expressed by Professor Xiang, Mr Huisken wondered "whom should be addressed in case of a security crisis in East Asia? No institution, no process has a significant track record".

Takashi Inoguchi, Emeritus Professor at the University of Tokyo, had a more optimistic point of view and suggested that confrontation and tensions between China and Japan "should not be exaggerated". In his opinion despite the lack of a regional security mechanism East Asians - Chinese, South Koreans and Japanese - "have achieved a long-lasting stability". Mr Inoguchi claimed that in spite of all tensions and unresolved issues an armed conflict between major powers "is unlikely in East Asia".

During the debate, Professor Xiang didn't dispute the "relative optimism" of Mr Inoguchi, but he showed some concern for the arms race in all areas, including in space, taking place in the region. Professor Xiang agreed with other speakers that maybe "East Asia does not need multilateral abiding rules like the EU" but he asserted that "surely China and Japan can learn a lot from the Franco-German relationship". In the same line, Mr Solana underlined that after World War II France and Germany reconciled while China and Japan have neither then nor now implemented such a rapprochement process.

Miquel Nadal, Economist and Former Secretary of State for International Affairs, asked the speakers to what extent they believe that there is a perception of being a region among Asian countries and populations.

Mr Inoguchi suggested that "Asia is too big and too diverse that it is too ambitious to consider it under one single scheme". Professor Xiang even considered the very notion of Asia as "non-existent and a mere European invention". Ms Lemoine pointed out that "there is not a clear definition of East Asia, nor defined borders or limits". Professor Xiang also referred to the internal sources of instability in China. He suggested that "the Communist Party of China might be facing the most serious legitimacy crisis since 1949". According to him, "corruption, economic slowdown and demographic crisis" are the three most serious issues China must face. Professor Xiang considers that "Xi Jinping, unlike Jiang Zemin and Hu Jintao, understands these problems".

Among the audience, Pere Vilanova, Senior Research Fellow Associate at CIDOB, mentioned that "in the Post-Cold War world the nuclear issue has moved from Europe to Asia". Emilio Lamo de Espinosa, President of the Real Instituto Elcano, called the attention of the participants on the fact that in more than two hours of discussion on East Asian security the UN had not been mentioned even once. Mr Lamo de Espinosa wondered how we should interpret this absence. Jane Marie Hardy, Australian Ambassador to Spain, suggested the need to consider a wider region and explore the conceptualization of the Indo-Pacific basin instead of a narrower East Asian framework. The necessity of including India in the general scheme of Asia's economic integration and geopolitical stability was vividly supported by Mr Shigehara".

Economic Growth, Environmental Protection, and Climate Change

The French-Japanese Business Summit 2021 entitled "Visions for 2050: A Path towards an Imaginative and Sustainable Future" was held at Nikkei Hall, Tokyo on 9 November 2021. Below is my keynote speech entitled "Is Global Green Growth Achievable?".

"In discussing "Visions for 2050", in other words visions for the next three decades, let us first recall main features of the economic performance of major players in the global scene over the past three decades during most of which high economic growth has been the dominant goal of economic policy, and the principal measure of an economy's success.

Back in 1997, Paul Samuelson, a distinguished American economist and a Nobel Prize laureate, wrote an article titled "For Japan, a message of optimism".[7] There, he first commented on the poor performance of the Japanese economy after the burst of its bubble at the beginning of the 1990s. He then went on to write: "Japan workers still have the work ethic. Skills have not been rusting away. Class warfare and trade-union bad feelings have not been spawned by its long stagnating economy." … "Once its wheels of commerce again spin at a normal rate, Japan will probably astound the world and itself by a catch-up and acceleration in Japanese production."

Did Samuelson prove to be right in this observation about Japan? Shortly after his article was published, the Asian financial crisis broke out and severely curtailed Japan's exports to the region. In the second half of the 2000s, the US housing market debacle led to the global financial and economic crisis. Due largely to the mismanagement of Japanese monetary policy to cope with it, economic recovery in Japan in its aftermath remained more hesitant than in the United States. As a result, real gross domestic product (GDP) per capita in Japan, which had stood at 85 per cent of the US level in 1990, declined to 76 per cent of the US level in 2000 and to 73 per cent of its level in 2010. Despite some recovery of the Japanese economy, achieved largely as a result of aggressive monetary easing under the government of Shinzo Abe who started his second term as Japan's prime minister in December 2012, Japan's GDP per capita stood at 70 per cent of the US level in 2019, the year before COVID-19 hit the world economy. In a nutshell, Paul Samuelson's note of optimism proved to be wrong: rather than Japan catching up to the US level of material living standards in terms of this economic output measure, the gap between the two countries widened significantly over the past three decades.

Economic growth performance in several high-income countries in Europe over the past three decades has not been satisfactory either. For example, real GDP per capita in Germany, the largest European industrial power, declined from 87 per cent of the US level in 1990 to 82 per cent of its level in 2019. France's real GDP per capita declined from 81 per cent of the US level in 1990 to 71 per cent of its level in 2019, virtually the same as Japan's level in that year. And, in Italy, a country devastated severely by the euro-area crisis that started in late 2009, real GDP per capita declined from 86 per cent of the US level in 1990 to 64 per cent of its level in 2019.

That said, real GDP per capita alone is not adequate for the international comparison of living standards across countries, as this measure does not fully reflect the adverse effects on human well-being of the interaction between economic output activity and environmental and other factors. In fact, according to the 2021 version of the OECD report "Going for Growth",[8] greenhouse carbon (GHC) emissions per capita in the United States have remained far above the OECD average in recent years while those in Germany have been on a par with the OECD average. Over the same period, GHC emissions per capita in Japan have not decreased, though they have been somewhat below the OECD average, while they have continued to decrease below the OECD average in France. I would add that in Sweden where environmental policies have been used actively, GHC emissions per capita continued to decline to reach a level less than half of that in Germany, while its real GDP per capita has been on a par with that in Germany.

I would also add that, fortunately, a very low share of the population in the United States is exposed to the harmful effects of air pollution whereas more than three-quarters of the populations in Japan, Germany and Italy and two-thirds of the population in France are exposed to such adverse effects.

The rise of China was a topic Samuelson discussed also in his 1997 article. He wrote: "Now that the Soviet Union has collapsed, it is mainland China that is occupying people's mind. We read headlines about more than 10 percent growth rates in mainland China. … (However), China's level of per capita living is only about one-six that of Japan. It will be a long time until China's entire civilian population comes anywhere near its present military might. But then, with some luck, perhaps China will have evolved into a stable multiparty democracy."

China's level of real GDP per capita rose to about 24 per cent of Japan's level in 2010 and to 38 per cent of Japan's level in 2019. While this is a remarkable achievement, Samuelson was right to say that it would take a long time as China's entire population enjoys high living standards. Moreover, GHC emissions per capita in China have been on a rising trend. They were 2.7 times higher than the level in 2000. And Samuelson's hope for China evolving into "a stable multiparty democracy" has remained far from reality.

Looking forward, raising real GDP per capita in China to the OECD average level without entailing significant further increases in GHC emissions per capita would be far more difficult than raising per capita living in Japan and EU economies towards the US level,[9] while aiming at the same time to hit net-zero carbon emissions and limit global warming to a "safe"1.5°C above pre-industrial levels, in line with the Paris Agreement adopted by 196 parties at COP21 in Paris in December 2015 and put into force in November 2016.

Both real GDP per capita and GHC emissions per capita have been on a rising trend in India as well. India has a much further way to go to reach living standards and environmental quality existing in developed economies. India is expected to overtake China as the most populous country by the year 2025. Both of them are crucial partners in determining the future course of the planet.[10]

In the most impoverished regions of the world, including much of Africa and Latin America, the greenhouse gas emissions have been generated primarily for the production of commodities distributed to developed countries. Those regions often lack electrical installations, transportation, schools, health care, housing, and the most basic social services. They are in desperate need of economic development.

It is in this context that David Klein, professor of mathematics at California State University, argued that "global sustainability and basic principles of justice call for selective de-industrialization, especially in the dominant capitalist centres, combined with sustainable industrialization focused most intensively on the parts of the world that have borne the brunt of imperialism." He noted that "to save the planet, we must discard capitalism and develop a better alternative through democratic cooperation. Our survival depends on implementing a social system that meets our actual needs, is sustainable and respects nature.[11]"

In a seminal paper "Capitalism and Ecology: The Nature of the Contradiction",[12] John Foster, an American sociologist, noted that capitalism's internal laws of motion extend out to phenomena that are usually conceived as external to the system, and he argued that we should turn to Karl Marx in discussing two crucial issues which are:

1. must ecological crisis lead to economic crisis under capitalism? and
2. to what extent is there an ecological contradiction at the heart of a capitalist society?

As one of the key elements in his ecological analysis, Marx employed the concept of a rift in the metabolic relation between human beings and the earth. Marx focused on the extreme separation of town and country under capitalism, which grew out of the separation of the mass of the population from the soil. Marx recognized that this metabolic rift represented a problem of sustainability and remarked that capitalism sapped the vitality of the everlasting sources of wealth—the soil and the worker. He developed an account of sustainability—the conservation and if need be "restoration" of the earth so that it could be passed on in an equal or "improved" state to the succeeding chain of human generations. Marx captured the essence of the contemporary notion of sustainable development, emphasizing the need to maintain the earth for "successive generations" and directly addressing such issues as soil nutrient recycling, pollution, sanitary conditions, deforestation, floods, desertification, climate change, recycling of industrial waste, diversity of species and other issues.

Is capitalism that currently governs both corporate and national interests capable of shifting its focus from short-term profit maximisation to an environmentally sustainable system? Radical action is called for by activists. But it would run the risk of remaining costly, often alienating large segments of the population along with corporate and national interest groups at a time when we are racing against the clock to avoid an environmental emergency.

Indeed, Johan Rockström, one of the world's most influential Earth scientists, recently argued that "activism is a necessary force for change, but it can be counterproductive if the indifferent majority thinks everything to do with the environment is about barricades, breaking down the world order and an alternative lifestyle – that doesn't attract the mainstream. We need all forces. Tree-huggers and frontier activists are very important, but they can't tip this whole thing over by themselves. We also need the bankers and executives. Why? Because we have only 10 years to cut emissions by half. We cannot change the economic model in 10 years. We can't forbid everyone to do things in 10 years. We can't re-educate whole populations in that time. We have to be very tactical.[13]"

In 2020, the OECD published a report "Beyond Growth: Towards a New Economic Approach" which was prepared by an Advisory Group composed of experts drawn from a diverse range of fields.[14] As regards the objectives of economic policy, it urges a move away from the traditional emphasis on GDP growth to a multi-dimensional conception of economic progress comprising environmental sustainability, rising human well-being, falling inequality and system resilience.

The prioritisation of efficiency objectives may have undermined the resilience of societies by overlooking equity and sustainability objectives. The emergence of the Covid-19 pandemic exacerbated previous trends, with clear asymmetric impacts among different income groups. Embracing a multi-dimensional set of objectives, as advocated by this report, and promoted by the OECD, would enable assessment of trade-offs, and complementarities, as well as identification of unintended consequences, to better guide policy choices and decision making.

Earlier this year, the OECD published a new report "The Inequalities-Environment Nexus: Towards a People-Centred Green Transition".[15] It suggests an integrated policy to be structured in four pillars, including measures designed to: (1) mitigate the possible regressive impact of pricing environmental externalities for vulnerable households; (2) achieve green growth with investment in human capital, through active labour market policies, well-targeted income support measures, and upgrading skills to facilitate labour reallocation; (3) address systemic inequalities with sectoral and place-based policies that facilitate social dialogue, social capital investments, social protection, skills and education investments to ease structural adjustment of local economies; and (4) ensure efficient and responsive governance to manage the green transition.

I strongly support these recommendations from the OECD, and at the same time want to stress that all of us must realise that we are in a race against the clock to avoid an environmental emergency. We must digest the transformation of economies and our own behaviour that is implied by the existential fight against climate change – even as a report published in August this year from the Intergovernmental Panel on Climate Change (IPCC) laid bare how little time we have left to accelerate the transition to a cleaner world.[16]"

*****

Notes

1. The communiqué of OECD Council meeting at Ministerial level:

   > Paragraph 16. Ministers discussed the challenges of ageing populations, a major priority for policy-makers, recognising that demographic and labour market trends in most OECD countries are likely to result in increasing numbers of people who are not working relative to working people, especially from 2010. They welcomed the report "Maintaining Prosperity in an Ageing Society" which proposes principles for interrelated reforms in many areas of social, economic and financial policy, in particular for health care and pensions systems. Societies must foster a climate conducive to "active ageing", providing support for people to lead active lives as they grow older. Ministers agreed to take into account these principles in developing national strategies and to monitor progress through the OECD, http://www.g8.utoronto.ca/oecd/oecd98.htm.

2. G20 – 2023 India, "G20 – Background Brief", https://www.g20.in/en/docs/2022/G20_Background_Brief.pdf.
3. The full text is available at: http://shigehara.online.fr/en/index.html.

   See also: https://www.dailymotion.com/video/xh5xan.
4. The full text is available at: http://shigehara.online.fr/en/index.html.
5. The full text is available at: http://shigehara.online.fr/en/index.html.
6. CIDOB's permission has been granted for the reproduction (with some abbreviations) of its conference report "Peace and Prosperity in East Asia" (January 2014) in this book. Its full text is available at: https://www.google.com/url?sa=t&rct=j&q=&esrc=s&source=web&cd=&ved=2ahUKEwj0v7efwceEAxUOiq8BHVjXDzQQFnoECBEQAQ&url=https%3A%2F%2Fwww.cidob.org%2Fcontent%2Fdownload%2F38151%2F594949%2Ffile%2FWAR%2526PEACE%2B2014_CONFERENCE%2BREPORT.pdf&usg=AOvVaw1RMcA8-1AFbwx3iOZw4pXC&opi=89978449.

7. Paul Samuelson, "For Japan, a message of optimism", The Daily Yomiuri, Tokyo, 2 June 1997.
8. OECD, "Going for Growth 2021: Shaping a Vibrant Recovery", 2021, https://www.oecd.org/economy/going-for-growth/.
9. In relation to the United States, the country traditionally used as reference in economic convergence discussions, living standards in most OECD countries generally continue to converge through 2060, although to varying degrees, see OECD, "The Long View: Scenarios for the World Economy to 2060", Fig. 5, OECD Economic Policy Paper, July 2018, https://www.oecd-ilibrary.org/docserver/b4f4e03e-en.pdf?expires=1632419011&id=id&accname=guest&checksum=B3C4F855F0657A5D895F05AC84ECEDC8.
10. According to the OECD baseline scenario presented in the above-mentioned paper (see page 8), China's share of world output is projected to peak during the 2030s at about 27 per cent and to decline slowly thereafter, while India's share keeps rising. Each accounts for a fifth to a quarter of the world economy in 2060.
11. David Klein, "Capitalism and Climate Change: The Science and Politics of Global Warming", January 2015, Gumroad Inc.
12. John Foster, "Marx's Theory of Metabolic Rift: Classical Foundations for Environmental Sociology", American Journal of Sociology, Volume 105, Number 2, September 1999.
13. Jonathan Watts, "We need bankers as well as activists… we have 10 years to cut emissions by half", The Guardian, 29 May 2021.
14. OECD, "Beyond Growth: Towards a New Economic Approach", 11 September 2020, https://www.oecd.org/governance/beyond-growth-33a25ba3-en.htm Intergovernmental Panel on Climate Change (IPCC).
15. OECD, "The Inequalities-Environment Nexus: Towards a People-Centred Green Transition", March 2021, https://www.oecd-ilibrary.org/environment/the-inequalities-environment-nexus_ca9d8479-en.
16. IPPC, The Working Group I contribution to the Sixth Assessment Report, "AR6 Climate Change 2021: The Physical Science Basis", August 2021, https://www.ipcc.ch/report/ar6/wg1/.

CHAPTER 22

Epilogue—Looking for Models in Pursuit of Economic Prosperity

In early 1998, Nout Wellink, then Governor of De Nederlansche Bank, asked me to deliver a keynote speech at the Emile van Lennep Memorial Conference on a "Global Order for Sustainable Economic Growth" to be held in Amsterdam in April that year. This invitation appeared to have reflected the fact that, in addition to my service as a central bank economist and practitioner for nearly 20 years, it happened that I virtually had a "career" as an OECD economist, having worked in different positions on four different occasions.

Emile van Lennep was OECD Secretary-General during my first two periods of service there.[1] Even after his departure from the OECD, I had the opportunities to communicate with him from time to time, both during my two subsequent periods of service at the OECD (1987–1989 and 1992–1999) and during my service at the Bank of Japan. He sent me his last personal letter in May 1996 to comment on my lecture at the Bundesbank's conference on monetary policy strategies, in which he recalled the debates between the Americans and Europeans on US monetary policy during the 1960s when he was Chairman of the OECD Working Party N°3. His letter demonstrated his continued strong interest in monetary and economic policy debates. He was scheduled to visit the OECD to meet Secretary-General Donald Johnston and myself as OECD Chief Economist on 8 October 1996 which, sadly, turned out to be the day of his funeral in his hometown of the Hague.

K. Shigehara, *The Bank of Japan, the OECD, and Beyond*,
https://doi.org/10.1007/978-981-97-5307-9_22

In my speech "Monetary and Economic Policy: Then and Now",[2] I reviewed developments in the OECD's multilateral surveillance in both macroeconomic and structural policy areas, and in its concluding section I said:

"It would be remiss of me not to conclude my talk today by recalling the contribution that Emile van Lennep made to ensuring that the world outside the OECD area was given proper attention. He was deeply committed to assisting development progress in poor countries both on moral grounds and because he saw that it would be a big mistake for the OECD and its Member countries to treat the developing world as just a marginal player in a world economy dominated by OECD countries. He strongly supported the 0.7 per cent aid target and the work of the OECD's Development Assistance Committee. But he brought to this work the perspectives of a banker concerned with sound financial structures and a firm belief in the basic correctness of the market economy principles on which the OECD's mission to foster world economic growth and welfare is founded. Emile van Lennep's constructive involvement with the issues of interdependence helped very much to lay the basis for the OECD's capacity to work today on policy issues in a global context."

Some four years after my speech at the Emile van Lennep Memorial Conference, I as a former OECD Chief Economist and Deputy Secretary-General was asked to contribute an article to the 40th anniversary issue of the OECD Observer (No. 235, December 2002). I entitled my article as "Looking for models in pursuit of economic prosperity",[3] in which I first wrote:

"Do not underestimate some of the economic and political achievements of the last few decades. And do not overestimate some of the present transformations either. In the search for stability and prosperity, there is much to learn and no country has all the answers".

Further on, I wrote:

"Looking at the economic difficulties of Europe and Japan these days, it is all too easy to forget some basic historical truths: in particular, that over the last forty years, western Europe and Japan have achieved unprecedented economic prosperity, and that their progress followed two devastating and debilitating world wars. Anyone that witnessed the flattened cities of Dresden or Hiroshima must never have imagined the recovery that was to follow. Within two short decades Japan and the former West Germany had established themselves as the second and the third industrial powers after the United States.

How did these so-called economic miracles come about? One reason was a sheer lack of choice. Deprived of military power to secure export markets and access to natural resources abroad after defeat, the onus fell on their well-educated workers, business managers, bankers and eager new state to achieve results. True, they were helped in these efforts by post-war international trade liberalisation and a generally favourable external climate, but it was by working together and targeting high value-added products, from automotive goods to science and technology, that high economic performance and social progress became possible. In effect, Japan and West Germany each forged their own market-based economic models whose efficiency and social equity were exemplary of how free market economies could succeed in the face of centrally commanded economies in the Cold War period."

(partially abbreviated)

"How and what basis can we bring large global economies together so that they might manage their affairs in "mutual self-interest"? Bilateral co-operation, unilateralism, independence: all these are possible, and not necessarily in mutually exclusive ways.

Take the European Union. It was born in large part from a desire to secure economic and monetary independence from the United States while fostering peace, co-operation and economic and social progress among Europe's main protagonists. It now has a single (albeit still evolving) market for goods, services, people and capital, while the euro has been introduced as the single legal currency in 12 EU countries. Moreover, despite widespread concern inside and outside the EU about the risk of increased European protectionism, the average level of its trade protection against non-EU countries has continued to decline. In terms of international institutional set-ups, the EU is the most complete model of regional integration and it marks one of the most significant achievements of the last four decades.

Another boon to Europe came from the unification of Germany in October 1990 and the shift of former Soviet bloc countries towards market economies. But this transition has had a less significant impact on world economic relationships than expected. A greater impact was to come from the emergence of high growth markets in Asia, notwithstanding their financial crisis of the late 1990s.

Nevertheless, the dissolution of the former Soviet bloc and the rapid economic development of China, which has started to open its market to foreign trade and investment, have changed the basic framework for international economic co-operation and reduced the risk of worldwide military confrontation.

China's opening up has given new promise to the burgeoning regional economic and monetary co-operation in Asia that also involves Japan, Korea and member countries of the Association of Southeast Asian Nations (ASEAN). This, and arrangements like the EU and the North American Free Trade Agreement (NAFTA), have raised the question of how to reconcile regionalism with the multilateral efforts towards liberalisation of international trade and investment that have been key to achieving prosperity in the post-war era.

Meanwhile, greater regional integration and globalisation present their own challenges. The latter, more often than the former, has been blamed by many as a cause of social and environmental distress, including job losses for unskilled workers, widening income disparity within and across countries, and deteriorating ecological and social standards, as well as increasing the instability of the international financial system. There is also a growing concern about ageing populations in most OECD countries and the economic, social and political strains that will arise in 2010–30 when the baby-boom generation reaches retirement. Policy response to these challenges should involve cutting across traditional boundaries of economic, financial and social disciplines.

No country has got all the answers. Even in the United States where spectacular overall economic growth in recent years has been accompanied by a soaring political and cultural influence around the world, the country's growing income inequality, its endemic violence and other deep social problems have raised serious doubts about the sense, let alone desirability, of the universal application of the so-called US model. At the same time, there has been delay in structural reforms that are needed to help Japan, Germany and several other European countries to remain efficient in the new age of globalisation and to meet the challenges of population ageing".

More than twenty years have passed since I published this article. Clearly, I was not right in all what I wrote there. First and foremost, I must say that I was wrong to write that "the dissolution of the former Soviet bloc and the rapid economic development of China, which has started to open its market to foreign trade and investment, have changed the basic framework for international economic co-operation and reduced the risk of worldwide military confrontation”.

In the summer of 2019, when relations between Japan and South Korea were extremely tense, I contributed an article entitled “Japan’s war crimes, colonialism and apologies” to the Japan Times.[4] I concluded this article by noting that “(B)oth Japan and Korea must aim for objectivity and impartiality in the grasp of their history. This is the only way to pave the way to our future together—there is much more that unites than divides us in an uncertain world”. A Jewish reader of my opt-ed sent the following comment to the editor of the Japan Times: “This is a very important article. It is said that those who truly love their country are those that criticize its bad actions, because they want to make it a better country”. It is suggested that readers of this book read this piece together with descriptions about the author’s experience during and after World War II in Chapter 2 “Prologue”.

This is not a place to review developments in world geopolitics since the end of World War II. All I would like to note here is that world economic prosperity and peaceful co-existence of human beings in the future depends on the wisdom of new generations to be obtained by learning from the mistakes made by previous generations.

* * *

On the Japanese edition of my memoirs published in December 2019, Kyoko Michishita, a Japanese writer,[5] sent me her comments:

> *It is clear that this book is of great importance to economic experts around the world, as noted by Donald Johnston, former OECD Secretary-General in his comment “your new book is very important for the OECD where there is so little institutional memory”.*
>
> *My interest, however, was in how this rare international figure of Japanese nationality, virtuous and genuinely cosmopolitan, was ‘created’.*
>
> *When the author was seven years old, his father was killed in action in the Battle of Okinawa at the age of 32. On the day of his funeral, in front of an urn filled with pebbles and sand of Okinawa, his mother wrote in her diary: “Kumiharu, 7 years old, Itaru 2 years old. From now on, I must work hard all alone until they both come of age”.*
>
> *It seems to me that this is the spiritual foundation of the author’s unwavering pacifism, democracy and humanism.*

Photo 22.1 Kumiharu Shigehara, recent photo (© Kumiharu Shigehara)

This book is not just a technical book on economics, but also a literary and philosophical book that shows how important it is to have not only knowledge and ability in one's own field of expertise, but also to always see problems from the perspective of the weak and to become a person of integrity in order to accomplish something in the world.

I sincerely hope that this book will be read by many young Japanese, especially those who have strong wills and dreams to make this world a better pace to live in.

While this English edition of my memoirs does not include as detailed descriptions about the history of my family as well as my childhood and education as in the Japanese edition, I nevertheless hope that young people around the world who "have strong wills and dreams and who will be responsible for the future of the world" will find something useful in the English edition as well (Photo 22.1).

Notes

1. OECD, "Fifteen Years of International Economic Co-operation: Selected Speeches of Emile van Lennep Secretary-General 1969-1984", Paris, 1984.
2. Kumiharu Shigehara, "Monetary and Economic Policy—Then and Now" in "A Global Order for Sustainable Economic Growth", edited by Age F. P. Bakker and Noud Gruijters, De Nederlandsche Bank and Nederlands Instituut voor het Bank-en Effectenbedrijf, Amsterdam, 1998.
3. Kumiharu Shigehara, "Looking for models in pursuit of economic prosperity", OECD Observer No. 235, Paris, December 2002, https://www.oecd-ilibrary.org/docserver/observer-v2002-6-en.pdf?expires=1708723301&id=id&accname=guest&checksum=7F4A62B167996275B9C4FCCF8CF92F1D

   Kumiharu Shigehara, "Japan at the OECD and the OECD in Japan", OECD Observer No. 298, Japan Special Edition, Paris, April 2014. https://www.oecd-ilibrary.org/economics/oecd-observer/volume-2014/issue-1_observer-v2014-1-en.
4. Kumiharu Shigehara,"Japan's war crimes, colonialism and apologies", The Japan Times, 28 August 2019, https://www.japantimes.co.jp/opinion/2019/08/28/commentary/japan-commentary/japans-war-crimes-colonialism-apologies/.
5. Kyoko Michishita's books include the autobiographical nonfiction written in Japanese "Dasubidānya, waga Karafuto (A Farewell to my Sakhalin)", Kawade Shobô Shinsha, Tokyo, 1996, for which she won the Rennyo-Shoô (a Japanese nonfiction literary award). Born in Kholmsk, Sakhalin in 1942, she and her family escaped from South Sakhalin to Hokkaido, Japan the year after the end of World War II. From 1905 to 1945, South Sakhalin was Japan's territory under the Treaty of Portsmouth that formally ended the 1904–1905 Russo-Japanese war. It was signed on 5 September 1905 at the Portsmouth Naval Shipyard in Kittery, Maine, United States (U.S. President Theodore Roosevelt was instrumental in the negotiations and won the Nobel Peace Prize for his efforts). In August 1945, after repudiating the Soviet-Japanese Neutrality Pact, the Soviet Union invaded southern Sakhalin.

Index

A
"Abenomics", 262
Abe, Shinzo, 242, 262, 263, 300, 420
active labour market policy, 385
Adamkus, Valdas, 400
Adenauer, Konrad, 44, 46, 197
ageing, 406–408
Aliber, Robert, 102
Amory, Dereck Heathcoat, 80
Andersson, Thomas, 199, 253, 388
André, C., 228
anti-inflationary monetary policy, 109
Aoki, Akira, 108, 172, 178, 185
Argentina, 329
Argy, Victor, 98, 104
Asbrink, Erik, 200
Asian crisis, 330
Asian Development Bank, 379
asset price, 182
Association of Southeast Asian Nations (ASEAN), 430
asymmetrical shock, 279, 280
Atkinson, Paul, 159, 307, 342, 346, 348, 350, 355, 358
Atlantic organisation, 81
Australia, 416
automatic stabilisers, 251
average tariff, 368
Axilrod, Stephen, 6, 66–69, 141, 143, 161, 167, 309, 316, 347, 348, 357

B
Baer, Gunter, 348
Baker, James, 170
Baker, Kenneth, 150, 161
balance of payments adjustment, 44
balance of payments constraints, 34
balance of payments imbalance, 44
balance of payments surplus country, 44, 46
balance sheet problem, 208, 211, 214, 247, 322, 323, 326
Baltic States, 377, 399, 401–403
Bank for International Settlements (BIS), 7, 58, 78, 142, 319, 321–323, 337, 342
  BIS capital adequacy rules, 220

K. Shigehara, *The Bank of Japan, the OECD, and Beyond*,
https://doi.org/10.1007/978-981-97-5307-9

BIS Committee on Banking Regulation and Supervision, 318, 322
BIS Committee on Bank Regulation and Supervisory Practices, 318, 319
see also Basel Committee on Bank Supervision
banking problem, 219
bank liquidity, 318
Bank of Canada, 142, 260, 261
Bank of England (BOE), 6, 10, 58–60, 142, 317
Bank of France (Banque de France), 27
Bank of Italy (Banca d'Italia), 9
Bank of Japan (BOJ), 1, 9, 15, 22, 23, 27, 35, 37, 38, 142, 170–172
Bank of Japan Institute for Monetary and Economic Studies (IMES), 188, 428
Banque de France, 26, 27
Barcelona Centre for International Affairs (CIDOB), 415
Baring, Rowland Stanley, 59
Barre, Raymond, 72
Barsony, André, 392
Basel Capital Accord, 322
Basel Committee on Bank Supervision, 322
Basle Accord on capital standards, 330
Basle Committee on Banking Supervision, 330
Bayoumi, Tamim, 238
beggar-thy-neighbour policy, 242, 252, 258, 415
Belgrade, 67, 69, 126, 127
Berger, Pierre, 91
Bergsten, Fred, 113, 146, 159, 161, 196, 199, 202
Bernanke, Ben, 300, 302, 307, 308
bilateralism, 365
Black Monday, 174, 180, 181, 222
Black, Stanley, 103
Black Wednesday, 273
Blessing, Karl, 46
Blinder, Alan, 279
Blumenthal, Michael, 113, 116, 123
Blundell-Wignall, Adrian, 348
Blunden, George, 318, 319
Bockelmann, Horst, 91, 96
Bô, Hideo, 114–116
Bonn, 121, 122
Boskin, Michael, 206
Branson, William H., 104
Bray, Nicholas, 356
Brazil, 321
Bretton Woods system, 13, 43, 46, 48, 51, 55, 57, 58, 61, 123, 226, 242, 336
Brexit, 351–353, 359
British Academy, 341
British pound, 29, 60, 63, 64
Brown, Gordon, 304
Brunner, Karl, 102, 103
bubble, 47, 175, 188, 227, 236
Budd, Alan, 14, 205, 304
built-in-stabiliser, 239, 245
Burgeat, Eric, 396
Burns, Arthur, 67, 68, 116, 166
Bush, George H.W., 241
Bush, George Walker, 241

C

Callaghan, James, 60, 61, 63, 68, 71–73, 81
Calvet, Pierre, 75
Camdessus, Michel, 140, 379
capital adequacy, 220, 322, 323
capital base, 323, 324
capital controls, 332–336
capital flows to developing countries, 166

capital standards, 323
Carli, Guido, 100
Carney, Mark, 292, 304
Carroll, Peter, 41, 80, 81, 83
carry trade, 226, 230
Carter bonds, 116, 123
Carter, Jimmy, 113, 123
Cecchini Report, 366
Center for Financial Stability (CFS), 302, 308
central bank independence, 304
Centre for Co-operation with European Economies in Transition, 391
Chalmers, Jim, 301
Chélini, Michel-Pierre, 68
Chernomyrdin, Viktor, 395, 396
Chiasso scandal, 319, 337
Chile, 327, 336, 399
China, 80, 370, 376, 377, 414, 416–418, 421, 422, 426, 430
Chouraqui, Jean-Claude, 357
Chubais, Anatoly, 396, 398
classical unemployment, 166
Clausen, Alden, 166
climate change, 406, 420
Clinton, William Jefferson, 226, 230, 411
cohesion, 382
Cold War, 73
Cole, Stephen J., 266
Common Currency Unit (ECU), 272
competition, 44
competitiveness, 110, 114
Concerted Action Programme, 120
Concordat, 319
Connolly, Bernard, 277, 292
consumption tax, 126
convertibility of US dollars, 40
convertibility to gold, 40
Cooke, Peter, 319
Coombs, Charles, 65
co-ordinated interest rate cuts, 172
core equity capital, 322
cost of inflation, 299
cost-push, 61
Cotis, Jean-Philippe, 249
Cousins, Kenneth, 147, 154
Covid-19 pandemic, 424
crawling-peg, 38
credibility of policy, 109
credit crunch, 324
credit rating agency, 330
credit risk assessment, 330
Credit Suisse, 319, 337
Crockett, Andrew, 7, 10, 14, 79, 83, 213, 243, 332
Crowe, John, 195, 198
Crown Prince Bertil, 199

D

Dai Xianglong, 393
Dale, Reginald, 176
Dale, William, 124
Dalsgaard, T., 228
Danilov-Danilyan, Viktor, 398
Dean, Andrew, 343, 357
Debré, Michel, 63, 72
de Espinosa, Lamo, 419
defence of the yen, 128
defense of the dollar, 64, 123
deflation, 41, 64, 248, 252, 253, 263
De Gaulle, Charles, 27, 60, 63, 72, 197
De Larosière, Jacques, 124–126, 196, 198
Delors, Jacques, 292
demand for money, 109
demand management, 34, 318
democratic values, 402
demonetarisation of gold, 65
De Nederlandsche Bank (DNB), 299
Denman, Roy, 145

deposit insurance scheme, 324
depreciation of the yen, 125, 126, 182
deregulation, 5
Deutsche Bundesbank (German Bundesbank), 44, 117, 142, 172
devaluation
  devaluation of the British pound (sterling), 29, 63, 64
  devaluation of the pound, 57, 59, 64, 73
  devaluations of the French franc, 63
Development Assistance Group (DAG), 80
Dicks-Mireaux, Leslie, 91
Dillon, C. Douglas, 83
dollar's "fee fall", 170
dollar convertibility, 67, 122
dollar excess, 73
dollar shortage, 73
domestic equilibrium, 51
domestic price stability, 38, 55, 123
dot-com bubble, 236
Dow, John Christopher Roderick, 62, 68, 205
Draghi, Mario, 104
dual pricing system for gold, 65
Dubinin, Sergei, 396
Dudler, Hermann, 96, 101, 104
Duisenberg, Willem Frederik, 82

E

East Asia, 326–328, 331, 416, 417
East Asian crisis, 228
East Asian economies, 327–329, 368
East Asian financial crisis, 222, 325, 379
"eclectic" approach, 307
economic growth, 43, 76, 107, 113, 117, 138, 387, 401, 407, 420
Economic Policy Committee (EPC), 7, 9, 44, 56, 72, 75, 76, 78, 86, 117, 141, 168, 249, 290
economic stagnation, 245
Economic Survey of Japan, 171
EC protectionist policy, 366
education, 376, 386, 409
EEC Monetary Committee, 74–76
effective degree of trade protection, 368
effective degree of trade restriction, 368
effective exchange rate, 110, 114, 118
effective rates, 110
Egebo, Thomas, 292, 293
Eisenhower, Dwight, 33, 66, 75, 81
elasticity pessimist, 61
Elmeskov, Jorgen, 357
emerging market economy, 329, 332
Emminger, Otmar, 44–47, 52, 55, 75, 77, 78, 114, 129, 316
employment, 373, 381
Englander, Steven, 292
environment, 12, 18, 19, 43, 175, 227, 257, 261, 281, 295, 296, 307, 309, 327, 329, 330, 336, 350, 354, 423
EPC. *See* Economic Policy Committee
Erhard, Ludwig, 44, 46, 52, 80
ERM bands, 274, 278, 285
ERM crisis, 273
ERM parities, 275, 284, 287, 288
escape clause, 297
ESD. *See* Department of Economics and Statistics
Estonia, 399, 403
euro-area crisis, 344
Eurodollar market, 315–317
"Europe 1992", 366
European Central Bank (ECB), 8, 9, 278, 300, 350

European Commission (EC), 366, 368, 373
European Community (EC), 365
European Currency Unit (ECU), 283, 284
European Economic Community (EEC), 74, 75
European Economic Recovery Aid Plan ("Marshall Plan"), 73
European Exchange Rate Mechanism (ERM), 272, 273, 276–278, 285–292, 296
European Monetary Institute (EMI), 278
European Monetary System (EMS), 272, 289, 299
European Monetary Union (EMU), 197, 276, 280, 288, 289
European Recovery Programme (ERP), 73
European Single Market, 278, 365, 366, 369
European Union, 300, 429
exchange control, 41
exchange rate policy management, 40
exchange rate stability, 166, 333
exorbitant privilege, 63
expenditure switching, 62
external equilibrium (external balance of payments equilibrium), 50
external reserves, 34
extra-EC trade, 366
exuberance, 328

F

Fay, John, 4
Fazio, Antonio, 9
Federal Open Market Committee (FOMC), 65, 66
Federal Reserve Bank of Cleveland, 143
Federal Reserve Bank of Kansas City, 187, 195
Federal Reserve Bank of New York (New York Fed), 128
Federal Reserve Bank of St Louis, 143
Federal Reserve Board (FRB), 6
Federal Reserve (Fed), 64, 117, 126, 142, 166, 170, 172
Federal Reserve Open Market Committee, 68
Fed-MIT-Penn Model, 104
Feldman, Robert, 253, 255, 263, 264
Feldstein, Martin, 169
final target, 92, 93
financial liberalisation, 173, 379
financial market liberalisation, 326, 331
First Republic Bank (FRB), 302
Fiscal Policy for a Balanced Economy, 89
fiscal policy management, 245
  expansionary fiscal policy, 119
Fisher, Gordon, 97
Fisher, Stanley, 103, 189, 238, 332, 337
fixed exchange rate, 13, 38, 329
fixed rate regimes, 329
Flandorfer, 147
floating, 47, 329, 414
floating exchange rate regime, 333
floating exchange rate system, 47, 51, 122
Ford, Gerald, 293
foreign direct investment (FDI), 334, 335, 384
foreign exchange control, 41
foreign exchange market intervention, 116, 123, 242
foreign exchange rate policy, 41
foreign exchange reserves, 49, 112
forward-looking policy management, 120

Foster, John, 423, 426
Fowler, Henry, 64
Francis, Darryl, 65–67
Fraser, Malcolm, 309
Freeman, Richard, 372, 376, 388
French, Doug, 69
Frenkel, Jacob, 103
Friedman, Milton, 67, 166
Fujii, Teruo, 236
Fujimoto, Genso, 114, 130
Fujioka, Masao, 112
Fukai, Michio, 108, 171
Fukuda, Takeo, 111, 113, 117, 121, 122, 124, 255, 308
Fukuda, Yasuo, 9
Fukui, Toshihiko, 9, 10, 108, 167, 178, 184, 185, 217, 243, 249, 253, 255, 256, 263
fundamental disequilibrium, 58

G

García, Enrique Martínez, 266
Gasòliba, Carles A., 416
GDP gap, 124
General Agreement on Tariffs and Trade (GATT), 43
General Agreement to Borrow (GAB), 58, 77, 78, 80
George, Edward (Eddie), 243, 244
Gerashchenko, Victor, 309, 396
German unification, 276
Gewirtz, Carl, 208
Giersch, Herbert, 45
Giscard d'Estaing, Valéry, 63, 140, 309
Gissing, George, 233, 237, 265
Gleske, Leon, 130, 140, 197
global economic and financial crisis, 411
global economic governance, 406, 411, 415
global economy, 402
global financial and economic crisis, 253, 341, 344
global imbalances, 339
globalisation, 333, 334, 365, 373, 375, 380, 386, 387, 430
globalised financial market, 308
globalization, 372, 373, 381
global market integration, 367
global monetarism, 102
global negotiations, 365
global order, 405, 427
gold dual price system, 65
Gold Pool, 64, 65, 68
gold rush, 64
gold standard, 370
gold window, 67
Goodfriend, Mervyn, 217, 218, 226, 229
Goodhart, Charles, 115, 348, 356
Gordon, Robert, 190
Great Depression, 181
Great Hanshin-Awaji Earthquake (Kobe Earthquake), 212
green growth, 420
greenhouse carbon (GHC) emission, 421, 422
Greenspan, Alan, 195, 240, 307, 411
Grew, Joseph, 19, 20, 24
Group of Five (G-5), 110, 171
Group of Seven (G-7), 110, 117
  G7 Summit in Bonn, 121
Group of Six (G-6), 110
Group of Ten (G10), 77
Group of Twenty (G-20), 411–415, 425
  G20 Mutual Assessment Process, 412
groupthink, 302, 303
growth target, 114, 119
Guffey, Roger, 195
Gurría, Angel, 359

Gyoten, Toyo, 46, 52, 82

H

Hacche, Graham, 357
Hagman, Bertil, 200, 202
Hamada, Koichi, 109, 133, 242
Hannoun, Hervé, 244
Hansen, Bent, 89
Hanwa Bank, 221
"hard currency" option, 150, 370
"hard" group, 284
Hardy, Jane Marie, 419
Harold, James, 45, 52
Harrod, Roy, 59
Hashimoto, Ryutaro, 230
Hata, Tadao, 53
Hawtrey, Ralph, 59
Hayami, Masuru, 4, 9, 49, 53, 120, 123–125, 128–130, 140, 147, 167, 241, 243, 244, 247, 249, 256, 263
Hayashi, Daizo, 48, 53
Hayashi, Fumio, 109, 133
health, 409
Heimann, John, 309
Heller, Walter, 75
Helsinki, 157
Henderson, Dale, 305
Henderson, David, 5, 205
herd instinct, 347
Herstatt (Bankhaus), 318, 337
Hewitt, Michael, 309
Hicks, John, 59
Higgins, Christopher, 149, 161, 167, 168
Hiltrop, Marius, 74
Himino, Ryozo, 186
Hiroshima, 16, 24–26, 428
Hirsch, Fred, 122
Hokkaido Takushoku Bank, 222
Holtrop, Marius, 82
Honda, Keikichi, 53
Hong Kong, 223, 329, 332
Honma, Tadayo, 227
Horie, Kunio, 22
Horie, Yasuhiro, 184
Horiuchi, Akiyoshi, 184
Hotel Plaza, 169
Howe, Geoffrey, 154, 155
Hozumi, Nobushige, 22
Hozumi, Shigetou, 22
Huisken, Ron, 418
Hu Jintao, 419
human rights, 402
human well-being, 421
Humphrey-Hawkins Act, 298
Hyman, John, 198
Hynes, William, 41, 80, 81, 83

I

Icard, André, 348, 357
Ikeda, Hayato, 38
imported inflation, 45
import-inducement coefficient, 115
import liberalisation, 39, 115
incomes policy, 60
income tax cut, 115
independence, 303, 304
independence of central bank, 190, 310
Independent Evaluation Office, 302
India, 416
Indonesia, 223, 327, 416
inequalities-environment nexus, 424
inflation forecasting, 301
inflation rate, 39, 109, 264, 299, 301, 383, 407. *See also* optimal inflation rate; two per cent inflation
inflation target, 190, 264, 296, 297, 301, 302, 304
inner core, 284

innovation, 380, 383–385
Inoguchi, Takashi, 418, 419
inscrutable Japanese, 115
InterAction Council, 308, 309
Intergovernmental Panel on Climate Change (IPCC), 425, 426
intermediate target, 92, 93, 297
internal equilibrium, 44
internal market integration, 367
internal vs external dilemma, 43
international balance of payments, 7
International Economic Association (IEA), 305
international economic diplomacy, 110
international mindedness, 1, 5
International Monetary Fund (IMF), 77, 78, 80, 117, 120, 121, 124, 320, 332, 335, 340, 412, 415
  IMF Articles of Agreement, Article VIII, 33
  IMF Articles of Agreement, Article XIV, 33
  IMF Executive Board surveillance, 346
  IMF Interim Committee, 116, 117, 332
  IMF World Economic Model, 119
  IMF World Economic Outlook (WEO), 237, 238, 346
international organisation, 1, 4
international trading system, 166
intervention currency, 116
Ireland, 57, 73, 284, 286, 344, 345
Ishida, Sadao, 91
Isohata, Kazuhiko, 61
Israel, 399
Issing, Otmar, 244, 305
Italy, 171, 421
Itoh, Masanao, 177
Ito, Takatoshi, 206, 228
Iwata, Kazumasa, 184
Izanagi boom, 193

J
Jackson Hole symposium, 187, 197
Jacobsson, Per, 45, 69
Japan, 80, 81, 115, 416, 420
Japan–US Structural Impediments Initiative Talks (SII), 175
Japan–US trade problem, 112
Japan bashing, 197, 205, 367, 369
Japan premium, 317
J-curve effect, 62
Jenkins, Paul, 224, 279
Jenkins, Roy, 61
Jiang Zemin, 419
Johnson, Harry, 102, 103
Johnson Jr., Manuel H., 172
Johnson, Lyndon, 64–66
Johnston, Donald, 7, 8, 11, 12, 14, 233, 249, 394–397, 399, 427, 431
Jordan, Jerry, 143, 144
Jurgensen, Philippe, 147, 228

K
Kansas City, 195, 199
Kashiwagi, Yusuke, 48, 51
Kato, Takatoshi, 128, 213, 220, 344
Katz, Abraham, 151
Kennedy, John Fitzgerald, 66, 75, 76, 81, 82, 346
Keynesian economics, 23, 103, 190
Keynesian unemployment, 166
Keynes, John Maynard, 24
Kigawada, Kazutaka, 49
Kimura, Takeyasu, 22
King, Mervyn, 6, 10, 95, 205, 243, 261, 299, 339, 353, 355
Kiriyenko, Sergei, 225
Kirkland, Richard, 161
Klein, David, 422, 426

Klein, Lawrence, 113, 149
Klock, David, 169
Kohn, Donald, 301
Koike, Ryoji, 177
Koivisto, Mauno Henrik, 103
Koizumi, Junichiro, 9, 10, 14, 234, 245–249
Komiya, Ryutaro, 49, 89, 176, 200–202
Kômoto, Toshio, 155
Korea (South Koea), 137, 222, 223, 259, 327, 328, 331, 392, 417, 430, 431
Koromzay, Val, 348, 393, 396
Kouri, Pentti, 103, 104
Kristensen, Thorkill, 46, 52
Krugman, Paul, 195–198, 202, 245, 248
Kudrin, Alexei, 398
Kuroda, Akio, 171, 178
Kuroda, Haruhiko, 11, 263–265
Kuznets, Simon, 371

L
labour market rigidities, 164, 340
labour mobility, 39
Lagarde, Christine, 359
Laidler, David, 102
Lamfalussy, Alexandre, 103, 144, 147, 278
Lamy, Pacal, 292
Languetin, Pierre, 130, 140
large-scale econometric model, 97, 98
Larre, René, 319
La Société Générale, 26
Latin American debt crisis, 322, 327
Latvia, 399, 400, 403
learning, 409
Lehman Brothers, 255–257
Leijonhufvud, Axel, 305, 306
Leland, Mark, 148, 321
Lemière, Jean, 279
lemming-type behaviour, 321
Lemoine, Françoise, 417, 419
Leutwiler, Fritz, 116, 129, 131, 133, 134
life-course, 409
lifelong learning, 376, 385
like-minded, 402
Li Keqiang, 395
Linder, Staffan Burenstam, 199
Li Peng, 392
Li Ranqing, 394
Lithuania, 399, 400, 403
Littler, Geoffrey, 179, 181
living standards, 35, 183, 296, 352, 353, 381, 407, 408, 420–422, 426
Llewellyn, John, 104, 134
locomotive theory, 113, 155
London School of Economics, 102, 341, 348
Long Yongzu, 394
Lou Jiwei, 394
Louvre Accord, 163, 169, 171, 180, 218
low-skilled labour, 374–377
low-skilled workers, 374
Lucas, Robert, 305

M
Maastricht agreement, 282
Maastricht Treaty, 273, 279, 283, 292
Macmillan, Harold, 45
macroeconomic-financial linkages, 343
macro-economic policy, 43, 148, 149, 190, 258, 286, 295, 315, 323, 329, 340, 369, 393, 394, 396, 398, 407, 413, 428
macro-prudential policy, 348
Maebashi, 15–17, 19
Maekawa, Haruo, 81

MAI negotiations, 377
Malaysia, 223
managed trade, 195
Marris, Margaret, 159
Marris, Stephen, 115, 118, 139, 143, 145, 146, 149, 151–153, 158, 159, 207, 316
Marshall, George, 73
Marsh, David, 14, 115, 133
Martin, John, 356, 361
Martin, William McChesney, 66, 67, 69
Marx, Karl, 423
Masera, Francesco, 100
Materov, Ivan Sergeyevich, 230, 395, 396
Matsukawa, Michiya, 111, 112, 114
Matsushima, Masayuki, 224
Matsushita, Shigeru, 186
Matsushita, Yasuo, 217
Mattes, Heinrich, 118
Mayekawa, Haruo, 1, 3, 4, 28, 116, 120, 128–133, 138, 157, 163, 166, 175, 177
"Mayekawa Report", 175, 176
McMahon, Christopher ("Kit"), 138, 139, 141, 142, 153, 154, 158, 319
medium-term economic growth scenario, 117–119, 121
Medvedev, Dmitry Anatolyevich, 398
Meltzer, Alan, 102, 189, 197, 198, 218, 225, 226, 231, 252, 367
Menashe, Isaac, 90, 91, 104
Meri, Lennart, 400
Mexico, Mexican debt crisis, Mexican peso crisis, 116, 123, 158, 321, 327, 331, 391
Michalski, Wolfgang, 350, 355
Michishita, Kyoko, 431, 433
micro- and macro-prudential policies, 379
micro-economic policy, 166
Middle East crisis, 59
Mieno, Yasushi, 108, 178, 184, 185, 187, 193
Miki, Takeo, 122
Miller, G. William, 116, 117, 123, 126, 316
minimum wages, 385
Mitterrand, François, 140, 141
Miyakawa, Shigeyoshi, 177
Miyake, Junichi, 184
Miyazawa, Kiichi, 171, 200
Mizoguchi, Zenbei, 241
Modigliani, Franco, 103, 104
Mondale, Walter, 113
monetarism, 147, 166. *See also* global monetarism
monetarist, 65, 67, 102, 103, 127, 140, 143, 147, 149, 154, 197, 225, 226, 246, 305
monetary/fiscal policy mix, 208
monetary adjustment scheme, monetary control scheme, 127, 139, 143, 144, 321
monetary aggregate, 109, 163, 271, 272, 281, 282, 297, 324
monetary and foreign exchange rate policies, 42
monetary base, 95, 96, 143, 246, 250
monetary policy management, 108
monetary policy studies (OECD)
  French monetary policy, 96
  German monetary policy, 96
  Italian monetary policy, 91, 95, 96
  Japanese monetary policy, 36, 91–95, 97, 99, 149, 151, 178, 185, 217, 241, 246, 249, 264, 306, 420
  UK monetary policy, 98, 303
  US monetary policy, 67, 97, 98, 123, 143, 158, 299, 307
monetary policy target, 108

monetary stability, 163, 176
monetary targeting, 109, 296
money (broad money, narrow money), 109
money demand, 108
money market management, 108
money supply, money supply targeting, 39, 46, 47, 67, 86, 93, 108, 127, 140, 142, 147, 154, 167, 171, 182, 210, 315, 321
money-supply, money supply targeting, 142
Monnet, Jean, 292
moral hazard, 220, 221, 347
Morinaga, Teiichiro, 3, 24, 67, 69, 110–112, 114, 116, 120, 123–128
Motoya, Sadaichi, 110
Mulford, David, 169
Multilateral Agreement on Investment (MAI), 353
multilateral currency adjustment, 86, 87
Multilateral Investment Agreement (MIA), 377
multilateral surveillance, 43, 55, 63, 258, 339, 341, 343, 346, 356, 366, 398, 412, 413, 415, 428
Mundell-Fleming model, 154
Mundell, Robert, 305
Mussa, Michael, 103, 214, 238

N

Nadal, Miquel, 419
Nagasaki, 159, 167–169, 173
Nagashima, Akira, 213, 220, 224
Nakamura, Susumu, 23
Nakaso, Hiroshi, 264, 267
Nakasone, Yasuhiro, 172, 175
Namikawa, Osamu, 4, 14
National Bank of Belgium, 344, 410
National Bank of Switzerland, 77
National Income Doubling Plan, 38
negative interest rates, 261
Nemtsov, Boris, 397
Neumann, Manfred, 102, 176
new technology, 365, 374, 381, 382, 407
new trade theory, 195
New York Fed, 128
New York Stock Exchange, 181
Nichigin, 38, 42, 123
Nixon, Richard, 40, 66, 67, 82, 293
Nixon shock, 40, 41, 49, 86, 107
Nobay, A.R., 102
Noda, Yoshihiko, 262
nominal income targeting, 273
non-performing assets, non-performing loans, 210, 213, 219–221, 227, 249
non-sterilised interventions, 215
non-tariff barriers, 366
North American Free Trade Agreement, 278, 391, 430
Noyer, Christian, 244
'N-th' country, 122
numerical inflation target, 108, 247, 264, 295, 296, 298, 299

O

Obasanjo, Olusegun, 309
Oba, Tomomitsu, 169, 172
OECD Centre for Co-operation with Economies in Transition, 395
OECD Centre for Co-operation with Non-Members, 391
OECD Chief Economist, 7, 110, 115, 248, 428
OECD-China co-operation programme, 392
OECD Committee for Monetary and Foreign Exchange Matters, 316
OECD Development Assistance Committee (DAC), 81

OECD Development Centre, 325, 379
OECD Economic and Development Review Committee (EDRC), 182
OECD Economic Outlook (EO), 121, 316, 346
OECD Economic Policy Committee (EPC), 80, 142, 316
OECD Economics and Statistics Department (ESD), 1, 14, 138
OECD Economics Department (ECO), 5, 14, 78, 79
OECD General Economics Branch, 3, 168, 184, 316
OECD high-level monetary experts, 316
OECD Jobs Study, 384
OECD Monetary Division, 9, 51, 69, 90, 95, 98, 99, 101, 102, 159
OECD Policy Studies Branch, 8, 322
OECD programmes for co-operation with other non-members, 399
OECD Secretariat, 9, 49, 76, 78, 79, 91, 98, 99, 111, 114, 115, 127, 132, 134, 138, 139, 143–145, 148, 150–152, 154, 155, 158, 159, 166, 179, 180, 207, 213, 214, 217, 220, 248, 249, 280, 304, 316, 372, 393, 399, 401, 402, 411
OECD Survey of Japan, 36, 37
OECD tax model, 402
OECD Working Party No. 3 (WP3), 5, 7, 9–11, 14, 44, 51, 56, 57, 59, 63, 71–73, 76–81, 86, 88, 89, 91, 94, 111, 114, 115, 118, 123, 127, 132, 133, 138–143, 146–149, 152–154, 157, 158, 228, 316, 318, 320, 321, 411, 413, 414, 427
official discount rate, 35, 171, 173
Ogata, Sadako, 9
Ogata, Shijuro, 4, 49, 53, 123, 170, 172, 177, 183
Ohira, Masayoshi, 111, 124, 127
Ohta, Takeshi, 178, 183
oil crisis, oil shock, oil price shock, 107, 125, 137, 317, 318
oil-producing countries, 111
oil-producing developing countries, 320
Oka, Akira, 27, 28
Okinawa, 16, 17, 431
Omori, Shozo, 22
Oort, Coen, 86
operating target, 127
operational independence, 307
optimal financial target, 271
optimal inflation rate, 299
Organisation for Economic Co-operation and Development (OECD), 1, 33, 75
Organisation for European Economic Co-operation (OEEC), 33, 73–75
Organisation of Petroleum Exporting Countries (OPEC), 126, 315, 316, 320
Osborne, George, 353
Ossola, Rinaldo, 315
Ostry, Silvia, 101, 138, 139, 143, 145, 146, 149, 158, 205
Ottawa Agreement, 57
output gap, 90, 118, 119, 239, 245, 256, 257, 260
output growth, 409

P

Pacific War, 17, 19, 125
Padoa-Schioppa, Tommaso, 8–10, 13, 388
Pagrotsky, Leif, 348, 350
Parkin, Michael, 102
pay drift, 60

Paye, Jean-Claude, 5–7, 179, 181, 187, 192, 233, 274, 292, 357, 392
peace, 197, 406, 415, 416, 429
Penn Square Bank, 321
pension, 407–409
Phelps, Edmund, 103
Philippines, 223, 416
Pierce, James, 98
Pinay, Antoine, 60, 63
Pinay plan, 63
Pintasilgo, Maria de Lourdes, 309
Pisani-Ferry, Jean, 358
Plaza Accord, 163, 169–172, 190
pluralistic democracy, 402
*Pöh*l (Poehl), *Karl Otto*, 129, 131, 197
policy co-ordination, 219, 262, 324, 325, 415
Pollack, Jacques, 81
Poole, William, 97, 169
Portsmouth Treaty, 433
Postuma, Suard, 57–59, 73, 74
potential growth, 118, 119, 124
Potter, Anne, 159
Potter, Stephen, 11, 104, 138, 159, 179
pound devaluation, 61
Pou, Pedro, 305
poverty, 385
price competitiveness, 38, 51, 57, 59, 61, 72, 87, 110, 114, 118, 247, 257, 259, 328
Price, Robert, 343, 348
price stability, 28, 34, 37, 38, 41, 46, 48, 50, 51, 55, 74, 123, 149, 166, 168, 173, 174, 180, 184, 185, 188, 190, 208, 209, 262, 264, 274, 283, 287, 289, 290, 296, 298, 300, 304, 308, 310, 370, 383, 414
Primakov, Yevgeny, 396
problem financial institution, 220, 221
pro-cyclical bias, 323
procyclical pressures, 323
productivity, 35, 37–39, 42, 51, 150, 152, 174, 213, 349, 350, 357, 370, 372, 373, 381, 407, 409
Programme for International Student Assessment (PISA), 361
prudential control, prudential standard, 175, 323, 339
prudential policy, 323, 343, 379
public funds, 213, 219–221, 227
public works investment, 115
Putin, Vladimir, 398

Q
Quaden, Guy, 344
quantitative credit control, 92, 99
quantitative easing, 237, 249, 258, 262
quantitative regulation, 90
Queen of England, 341
Quraishi, Al, 131

R
Rambouillet, 110
Rasminsky, Louis, 77
Raymond, Robert, 278, 279, 309, 343, 347, 350, 357, 358
Reaganomics, 151
Reagan, Ronald, 139–141, 145, 146, 172
real GDP per capita, 421, 422
real income and prices, 109
recession, 34, 107, 131, 139, 169, 218, 246, 251, 284, 306, 308, 351
recycling, 139, 318, 320, 337, 423
Regan, Donald Thomas, 151, 155, 156
regional integration, 373, 430

regionalisation, 367
regionalism, 365
regional surveillance, 346
regional trade arrangement, 369
regulatory reform, 375, 384
Reserve Bank of Australia, 161, 187, 298, 301
Reserve Bank of New Zealand, 260
reserve currency, 43, 52, 63, 65
reserve currency country, 50, 55, 57, 62, 63, 76, 99
reserve ratio, 90, 123
reserves (external), 34, 57
retirement, 409
revaluation, 39–41, 44–47, 49–51, 55, 112, 114, 242
Ricardian equivalence, 214
Richardson, P., 228
Rickett, Denis, 71, 77
Rieke, Wolfgang, 205, 277
Robbins, Lionel, 59
Robinson, Joan, 59
Rockström, Johan, 423
Roepke, Willhelm, 45
Rogoff, Kenneth, 252, 253, 307
Rome, 9, 213–217, 220, 221, 235
Ronji, Zhu, 392
Roosevelt, Theodore, 433
Rosa, Robert (Bob), 72, 73, 75, 77
Roulet, Caroline, 348
Rowan, David C., 97
Rubin, Robert, 229, 230, 411
Rueff, Jacque, 60, 63
rule of law, 396, 398, 401, 402
Russia, 377
Russian Federation, 391, 395, 396, 399, 402
Russo-Japanese war, 433
Ryecroft, Henry, 233, 237, 265

S

Saint-Simonian way, 292
Sakakibara, Eisuke, 224, 230
Sakhalin, 433
Sammons, Robert, 86, 90, 93, 104
Samuelson, Lee, 104, 134
Samuelson, Paul, 24, 420–422, 426
Sanger, Daniel, 230
sanitation, 347
"sanitised" surveillance reports, 347
San Juan, 110
Sapir, Andre, 358
Sasaki, Tadashi, 26, 49
Sato, Eisaku, 218
Sato, Setsuya, 243
saving-investment balance, 157, 158, 190, 191
Schlesinger, Helmut, 96, 172, 218
Schmidt, Helmut, 114, 122, 308
Schricke, Christian, 396
Schultze, Charles, 141
Schwartz, Charles, 119
Schwartz, Moises, 344
Schweitzer, Paul, 77, 78
Second World War, 15, 43, 57, 73, 197, 200
self-censorship, 347
service sector, 35
Shadow Open Market Committee, 102, 197
Shafer, Jeffrey, 8, 234, 348
Sheppard, David, 97
Shigehara, Akiko (née Akiko Yoshizawa), 25, 158, 159, 410
Shigehara, Fuyumi, 91
Shigehara, Hiroaki, 91, 234
Shigehara, Itaru, 17, 21
Shigehara, Iye (née Iye Inoue), 18, 21
Shigehara, Kiyosaku, 18
Shigehara, Kumiharu, 4–6, 17, 21, 25, 69, 133–135, 161, 201–203, 228, 234, 265–267, 277, 281, 283, 286, 287, 290, 293, 357,

358, 380, 386–389, 397, 403, 404, 416, 432, 433
Shigehara, Rutsu (née Rutsu Tanabe), 17, 21
Shigehara, Seizaburo, 15
Shiller, Robert, 103
Shimamoto, Reiichi, 111, 114–116, 120, 317
Shimomura, Osamu, 38
Shirakawa, Masaaki, 167, 255–257, 260, 262, 263, 266
Shizume, Masato, 177
short-sighted policy, 155, 325
Sierman, Mart, 401
Signature Bank (SBNY), 302
Silicon Valley Bank (SVB), 302, 303
Simonin, Paula, 100
Sims, Eric, 266
Singapore, 327
single currency, 280
Single Market, 350
Single Market project, 373
Sirou, Carol, 348
Slovenia, 399
Smith, Adam, 195
Smithsonian agreement, 47, 48, 87, 107, 122, 174
Smithsonian Institution (Smithsonian), 50, 51
social cohesion, 370, 382
social equity, 401
social market economy, 44, 52
social policy, 365, 385, 406
social security, 408
social services, 409
social welfare, 18, 44, 354, 380
social well-being, 409
Solana, Javier, 415, 416, 419
Solomon, Anthony, 132, 133
Solomon, Robert, 91
Sôôma, Kastumi, 36
South East Asia, 328
sovereign debt, 330, 344, 345, 349
Soviet-Japanese Neutrality Pact, 433
Soviet Union, 73, 80, 309, 391, 392, 395, 399, 400, 421
Spaak, Paul-Henri, 74
Special Drawing Rights (SDRs), 47, 65
Sprinkel, Beryl, 140, 143, 145, 147–149, 151, 154, 320, 321
stable currency value, 37
Stein, Herbert, 281, 293
sterilised intervention, 228, 329
sterling, sterling area, 57, 59, 61
Stigler, George, 24
St. Louis Model, 104
Stockholm School of Economics, 199, 369
strong yen problem, 262
structural policy, 115, 166, 190, 212, 227, 245, 323, 339, 340, 394, 396, 428
structural reform, 149, 175, 210, 217, 245, 248, 272, 282, 283, 291, 350, 370, 430
Sumita, Satoshi, 169–172, 185, 218
Summers, Lawrence (Larry), 198, 199, 213, 215, 225, 226, 279, 394, 398
Sunak, Rishi, 302
supervisory "capture", 347
supply-side, 115, 152, 245
supporting the US dollar, 116
surveillance, 325
sustainable development, 423
Suzuki, Yoshio, 154, 178, 185, 199
Svensson, Lars, 251, 253, 265
Swiss National Bank, 116, 129–131, 140, 142

T

Tachi, Ryuichiro, 22, 28
Takahashi, Korekiyo, 60, 125

Takenaka, Harukata, 186
Takenaka, Heizo, 245
Takeshita, Noboru, 169–171
Tanabe, Kumazo, 18
Tanabe, Makoto, 18
Tanabe, Sato (née Sato Yajima), 18
Tanaka, Kakuei, 218
Tanaka, Naoki, 186
Tanaka, Tsutomu, 154
Taniguchi, Makoto, 392
Tarafas, Irme, 309
Tase, Yasuhiro, 255
Taylor, Christopher, 103
Taylor, John, 158, 190–192, 202, 241, 251, 307
technological development, 374
technological progress, 381
technology, 375, 380, 381, 386
Thai baht, 223, 328
Thailand, 223, 327
Thatcherism, 154
Thatcher, Margaret, 147, 154
Thirlwall, A.P., 68
three-stage approach, 92, 93
Thygesen, Niels, 86, 93, 95, 98, 100, 102, 104, 343
Tietmeyer, Hans, 6, 169, 192, 205, 213, 272, 277
Till, Peter, 90, 91, 96, 104
Tobin, James, 77, 166, 214
Tosovsky, Josef, 309
trade conflicts, 370
trade diversion, 366
Treaty of Rome, 74
Trento conference, 305
Trias, Xavier, 416
Trichet, Jean-Claude, 6, 244, 273, 274
Trudeau, Pierre, 7, 138
Truman, Edwin, 66, 73, 143
Turner, Philip, 358
Tuveri, Jean-Pierre, 151
20thcentury, 405
21stcentury, 264, 380, 392, 405, 415
two per cent inflation target, 264
two-speed Europe, 284

U

Ueda, Kazuo, 184, 217, 218, 229, 264, 265
UK pound devaluation, 59
Ukraine, 397, 399, 403
UK referendum, 351, 353–355
Ulmanis, Guntis, 400
Ulmanis, Kārlis, 400
Ulmo, Yves, 138, 149
unemployment, 374, 381, 382, 385, 407
unit labour cost, 88, 174, 218, 340, 347
University of Chicago, 102
University of Liège, 410
University of Tokyo, 19–23, 28, 49, 167, 176, 184, 200, 217, 264, 418
University of Trento, 305
unrealised capital gain, 323, 330
US–Japan Summit, 113
Usami, Makoto, 36, 60
US-Canada Free Trade Agreement, 367
US dollar defence measures, 122, 124
US model, 430
Utsumi, Makoto, 20

V

van Agt, Andreas, 200–202
van der Bürger, Enst, 74
van der Mensbrugghe, Emmanuel, 343
van Lennep, Emile, 46, 52, 57, 68, 71–82, 87, 94, 98, 115, 120, 125, 145, 151, 152, 157, 159,

167, 168, 179, 207, 427, 428, 433
Vanston, Nicholas, 342, 348, 355
Vietnam, 416
Visco, Ignacio, 248, 249
Vocke, Wilhelm, 45, 52
Volcker, Mrs, 129
Volcker, Paul, 6, 46, 66, 79, 82, 122, 126, 128, 129, 131–133, 172, 195, 198, 226, 327

W
Wakatabe, Masazumi, 266
Wallich, Henry, 4, 129, 130, 133, 140, 143, 144, 147, 155, 157, 169, 190
Walter, Norbert, 309
Warner, 24, 25
Washington-based institutions, 325
Wass, Douglas, 154
Watanabe, Makoto, 81
Watanabe, Takatomo, 108
weak yen, 127
Weidenbaum, Murray, 141
Weisberg, Jacob, 230
well-being, 409
Wellink, Nout, 299, 427
Wessel, David, 267
West German Bundesbank, 129
West, John, 399
White, William, 183, 214, 348
Wicks, Nigel, 279
Wider bands, 277, 278, 291, 297
Wilson, Harold, 58, 60, 62
window guidance, 92, 180
Winters, L. Alan, 359, 360
Witherell, William, 392, 396
Witteveen, Johan, 82, 119, 124
Wolff, Guntram, 358
Wolf, Martin, 245
Wood, Adrian, 376
Woodley, John, 124, 125, 127, 128, 134
Working Party No 3 (WP3), 5, 7, 9–11, 14, 44, 51, 56, 57, 59, 76–80
World Trade Organisation (WTO), 292, 377
World War II, 11, 15, 44, 199, 400, 419, 431, 433
Wu Yi, 392–394

X
Xiang Huaicheng, 393
Xiang, Lanxin, 418, 419
Xi Jinping, 418, 419

Y
Yago, Kazuhiko, 11, 14
Yamagiwa, Masamichi, 24
Yamaguchi, Yutaka, 210
Yamaichi Securities, 223
Yeltsin, Boris, 395, 396, 398
yen depreciation, 147, 182, 216, 225, 230
yen revaluation, 41, 47, 49
yen's decline, 127
Yeo, Edwin, 111
Yoshino, Toshihiko, 38, 61
Yoshizawa, Takeshi, 25
Young, Ralph, 77

Z
zero, 217, 227, 239, 250, 300
zero bound on nominal interest rates, 238
zero inflation, 209, 214, 300, 309, 310
zero inflation target, 190
zero-interest-rate constraint, 242, 246
zero-interest-rate floor, 300
zero interest rate policy, 228, 236
Zhu Rongj, 394
Zijlstra, Jelle, 82

The manufacturer's authorised representative in the EU is Springer Nature Customer Service Centre GmbH, Europaplatz 3, 69115 Heidelberg, Germany. If you have any concerns regarding our products, please contact ProductSafety@springernature.com

Printed and bound by CPI Group (UK) Ltd, Croydon, CR0 4YY

01/10/2026

02225854-0016